ONE LESS CAR

In the series **Sporting**,
edited by **Amy Bass**

Also in this series:

ONE LESS CAR

BICYCLING AND THE POLITICS OF AUTOMOBILITY

ZACK FURNESS

TEMPLE UNIVERSITY PRESS
PHILADELPHIA

Zack Furness is Assistant Professor of Cultural Studies at Columbia College Chicago and a member of the Bad Subjects Collective.

TEMPLE UNIVERSITY PRESS
Philadelphia, Pennsylvania
www.temple.edu/tempress

Copyright © 2010 by Temple University
All rights reserved
Published 2010

Text design by Matthew Plourde

Library of Congress Cataloging-in-Publication Data

Furness, Zachary Mooradian
    One less car : bicycling and the politics of automobility / Zack Furness.
        p. cm. — (In the series Sporting)
    Includes bibliographical references and index.
    ISBN 978-1-59213-612-4 (hardcover : alk. paper)
    ISBN 978-1-59213-613-1 (pbk. : alk. paper)
    1. Cycling—Political aspects—United States. 2. Urban transportation policy—United States. 3. Transportation, Automotive—Social aspects. 4. Bicycle commuting—United States. 5. United States—Social life and customs. I. Title.
    HE308.F87 2010
    388.3'4720973—dc22

                                                                2009048506

♾ The paper used in this publication meets the requirements of the American National Standard for Information Sciences—Permanence of Paper for Printed Library Materials, ANSI Z39.48-1992

Printed in the United States of America

2 4 6 8 9 7 5 3 1

For Pea,
Who continues to tear up my maps

Those who have swallowed the cycle will not strain long at the Automobile; and after the first decent show of apprehension has been disposed of, the obvious exhilaration and novelty of the exercise begins to exert a charm. For there is joy in going quickly and in doing no work. . . . It is probable that in a year or two every one will be wanting to drive without horses, and to scour the open country at sweet will in a vehicle that can match the bicycle for lightness and for speed, while saving the superfluous element of labor. In other words, there is no reason why, within a decade at most, we should not see considerable changes in our present modes of traveling.

-Harry C. Marillier, "The Automobile," *The Eclectic Magazine of Foreign Literature*, 1895

I don't think it's unpatriotic to use so much gas. It's very patriotic. It's our way of life.

-Sue Smith, Chevy Tahoe owner, quoted in Neela Banerjee, "Made in America," *New York Times*, 2001

If a man feels that he can easily afford the expense of keeping a car and enjoys its use, there is no mode of recreation which, when properly indulged in, brings in more thorough enjoyment and benefit to the entire family. The speed maniac is passing, engine breakdowns on the road are practically a thing of the past, the era of hysteria has been replaced by an era of common sense, and more and more the automobile will become a delightful and useful adjunct to our social life. Here's to its golden future! Long life to the motor car and health and happiness to its swelling army of votaries!

-W. F. Dix, "Motoring for People of Moderate Means," *The Independent*, 1911

Get off the fucking road, asshole!

-Pittsburgh driver to the author, 2005

Contents

Acknowledgments

n many ways, this book is the end result of a series of interactions, questions, and concerns first set in motion when I started riding a bike to work and school in the 1990s. My interests in bicycling were then far more pragmatic than academic, and I never would have imagined devoting years to researching and writing about bicycles and car culture, whether in the form of a doctoral dissertation or as this much-improved/revised version that Temple University Press was gracious enough to publish. Consequently, many thanks are in order.

First and foremost, this project would not have been possible without the assistance and guidance of Jonathan Sterne, my graduate advisor, my friend, and a mentor in the fullest sense of the word. Carol Stabile runs a close second in this regard, as she is similarly responsible for my growth as a critical thinker, a writer, and a teacher. I am deeply indebted to them not only for their instruction on all matters pertaining to technology, media, cultural studies, feminism, social justice, and pedagogy but also for their immeasurable impact on my life.

A number of other people also deserve credit for their insights (any errors that remain in the book are my own): Gordon Mitchell and Andrew Weintraub, whose comments and suggestions made this an eminently better work; Jeff Ferrell and Stephen Duncombe, who gave me additional feedback on an earlier version of the manuscript; and Charles Komanoff, who shared not only his wisdom about bike activism and transportation politics but also valuable research materials and contacts. I am also grateful to the people who were kind enough to send me documents, photocopied articles, and other hard-to-find (print and digital) texts, including Ross Petty, Peter Norton, Jacquie Phelan, Aaron Wilcher, Michael Niman, Doug McCabe, and John Dowlin (the unsung godfather of bike zines). In addition, I thank all the folks who sat for interviews, took me for rides, shared their thoughts and stories, responded to e-mail messages, engaged me in conversation (and the occasional argument), granted permission for the use of their artwork or lyrics, and otherwise made invaluable contributions to both this book and my perspectives on bicycling and bike culture in North America (and abroad).

I owe sincere gratitude to my wonderful colleagues and former students in the Cultural Studies program at Columbia College Chicago, especially Carmelo Esterrich, Ann Gunkel, and Jaafar Aksikas. I also appreciate the generous support received from not only the entire faculty and staff in the Department of Humanities, History, and Social Sciences—including Krista Rogers, Oscar Valdez, Iris Parker, and my department chair, Lisa Brock— but also the following folks outside the department: Kevin Henry, Micki Leventhal, Ames Hawkins, and Doug Powell.

Prior to my years in Chicago, a significant portion of my dissertation-to-book revisions took place during my fortuitous stay in Seattle, Washington. Thanks go to my former students and colleagues at Shoreline Community College (Kathleen and Brooke) and especially to Karam and Sharon for making Seattle feel like home. I am also indebted to numerous friends and allies in my hometown—Pittsburgh—as well as to former residents who have since scattered as part of the great Iron City diaspora. These nobles include, but are certainly not limited to, Bay Woods, Antonis Coumoundouros, Maxwell Schnurer (and Elena), Mark Harrison, Rachel Courbis, Nate Doom, Mikey Seamans, Marissa Barr-Hartman, Leanne O'Connor, Jessica Ghilani and Chris Belasco (and Speck!), Mitchell Kulkin, Todd Ladner, Brian Garbark, Mike Rock, Jake Reinhardt, Jeff Kopanic, Steve McMillen, Dan Rock, Mary Tremonte, Reyghan Pierce, Genly Ai Pierce-Weaver, Five and Eric, everyone at Crazy Mocha with whom I spent the better part of my waking life for two years (Hilary, Angela, Shannon, Ken, Chaim, Dean, Andrew, Victor, and Al), and (more broadly) the punks. I owe additional thanks to Randy Nickerson, Steevo and Justin Cummings, Jim Robinson, Brad Quartuccio, Scott Bricker, and Eric "Erok" Boerer for sharing their perspectives on bicycling and to Gerry Kraynick for running the best bike shop on the planet. Extra thanks go to Doug Weaver and, especially, Kalie Pierce—one of my truest comrades.

I also hold the following people in great esteem: Aaron Jackson, Matt Lisowski, Adam Vrbanic, James Palazzolo, and Tim McGlynn, for their friendship and encouragement; Shirley Steinberg, Ammi Emergency, Ramsey Kanaan, and Joe Biel, for taking an interest in my work; Ryan M. Lewis and the Illinois Humanities Council; Chris Bull, for making me such a beautiful bike; my friends/bandmates in Everything Is Ruined (John Thompson, Eric Brose, and Sarah Jean McHugh); Maria denBoer, June Sawyers, Joan S. Vidal, and the entire staff at Temple University Press, particularly Micah Kleit—a man who has been more than generous with his patience and support throughout the entire publication process.

My sincerest thanks go to Debby Furness-Saletin (my wonderful and supportive mom), Zaban Furness (my brother/best friend), Steve Furness (my dad—may he rest in peace—who first took off my training wheels), Jeff Saletin and my newest brothers and sister (Erich, Jared, and Alex), my extended family in Rhode Island, and Joe and Linda Korey. Above all, and at the risk of downplaying the collective debt of gratitude that I owe the people listed above, my profoundest admiration, love, and respect are exclusively reserved for Laura Korey (and Lexi). The words "thank you" do not begin to convey the appreciation I have for her friendship, creativity, and kindness.

Portions of Chapter 2 were previously published in Zack Furness, "Biketivism and Technology: Historical Reflections and Appropriations," *Social Epistemology* 19, no. 4 (January 10, 2005): 401–417, reprinted by permission of the publisher (Taylor & Francis Ltd., http://www.tandf.co.uk/journals). Abridged and/or revised versions of Chapter 4 appear in Zack Furness, "Critical Mass, Urban Space, and Vélomobility," *Mobilities* 2, no. 2 (January 7, 2007): 299–319, reprinted by permission of the publisher (Taylor & Francis Ltd., http://www.tandf.co.uk/journals), and Zack Furness, "Critical Mass Rides against Car Culture," in *Cycling and Philosophy,* ed. Jesús Ilundáin and Mike Austin (Wiley-Blackwell, forthcoming 2010). A portion of Chapter 7 was previously published in Zack Furness, "Race, Class and Bicycling," *Bad Subjects,* no. 76 (2006), available online at http://bad.eserver.org /issues/2006/76.

I thank the following people, who were kind enough to give me permission for the use of their lyrics: Aaron Elliott (Pinhead Gunpowder, "West Side Highway"), Tony Croasdale (Rambo, "U-Lock Justice"), Geoff Hing (Defiance Ohio, "Bikes and Bridges"), Jeff Ott (Fifteen, "Petroleum Distillation"), Rob Miller (Amebix, "Largactyl"), Gee Vaucher (Crass, "Contaminational Power" and "Big Man, Big M.A.N.").

Note: All author royalties from the sale of this book will be donated to youth education programs coordinated by the following community bicycle organizations: Free Ride (Pittsburgh, Pennsylvania), West Town Bikes (Chicago, Illinois), and Blackstone Bicycle Works (Chicago, Illinois).

CHAPTER 1

Introductions
and Intersections

Two-Wheeled Conventions

In the week preceding the 2004 Republican National Convention (RNC) hundreds of thousands of activists from around the United States converged on New York City to demonstrate their collective dissatisfaction with the George W. Bush administration and the wars in Iraq and Afghanistan. Protesters arrived with handcrafted banners, makeshift signs, elaborate costumes, musical instruments, bullhorns, giant puppets, and droves of literature. Some people even brought their bicycles. For this latter contingent, the eight days surrounding the demonstration doubled as the Bike National Convention, a series of events hosted by New York City's direct action environmental group, Time's Up! Bicyclists both organized and participated in free bike maintenance workshops, direct action planning sessions, a bicycle carnival, and various group rides, including a scenic jaunt through the city's parks, a "dumpster diving" tour of Lower Manhattan, and radical history tours of community gardens, squats, and famous protest sites dotting the Lower East Side.[1] Before the start of the Republican convention, the visiting two-wheeled politicos joined bike riders from the five boroughs to take part in Critical Mass, a monthly bike ride/ritual held on the last Friday of every month in cities throughout the world. Originating in San Francisco in 1992, Critical Mass was conceived as a group bike ride and a leaderless celebration that ultimately grew in both size and popularity as a response to the continued marginalization of bicycling and non-motorized transportation in modern cities. Each month cyclists taking part in this "organized coincidence" try to fill the streets with riders to demonstrate their collective solidarity and send a message to the public: "We are not blocking traffic; we *are* traffic!"[2]

On Friday, August 27, more than five thousand cyclists swarmed the streets of Manhattan and brought auto traffic to a grinding halt on parts of the island. It was a tremendous display of pedal power and antiwar creativity, and by far one of the largest rides in the event's history. Equally historic was the staggering display of police force used to arrest 264 bicyclists, some of whom were not even on the ride. In addition to brutalizing a number of (unarmed) cyclists, the New York Police Department (NYPD) illegally seized 338 bicycles as part of their arrest evidence, going so far as to forcibly remove bicycles from nearby fences, bike racks, and signposts by cutting through locks with high-powered saws.[3] In the ten days surrounding the Republican convention, nearly four hundred bike riders were arrested, including Joshua Kinberg, the inventor of a bicycle that prints text messages sent from Web users directly onto the street in water-soluble chalk. Under the moniker "Bikes against Bush," he planned to use the device as an interactive performance art piece during the RNC and his arrest is notable because it took place live on national television while he was being interviewed (about his bicycle) on MSNBC's *Hardball*.[4] Without making a mark on the street or possessing any spray paint, Kinberg was charged with criminal mischief and his possessions were seized as evidence: his cell phone, chalk printer, and laptop computer were illegally held for more than a year and his bicycle was never returned.[5] Just two days prior to his arrest, Kinberg demonstrated the device in another televised interview, leaving an emphatic, if not ironic, message chalked on the sidewalk: "America is a free speech zone."[6]

Police continued to arrest and seize the property (bicycles) of hundreds of bike riders in the months following the convention, and in 2005 video evidence and written documents confirmed that the NYPD conducted prolonged surveillance on cyclists and Critical Mass organizers in the period leading up to the RNC protest, even infiltrating a small memorial ride staged in honor of a cyclist killed in traffic.[7] The city kept bicyclists and judges tied up in court for the better part of the next year, in part because they hoped to shut down Mass by requiring parade permits for roadway processions of twenty or more vehicles or bicycles, along with any processions of two or more people attempting to use the road "in a manner that does not comply with all applicable traffic laws, rules and regulations."[8] When the judge dismissed the city's claims, Sheryl Neufeld, of the New York City Law Department, responded with the unfounded assertion that Critical Mass "continues to be a danger to the public safety."[9] Charles Komanoff, an economist, veteran bike advocate, and former head of New York City's Transportation Alternatives, produced an economic report in 2006 that paints a sobering picture of the city's crackdown on bicyclists: it spent roughly $1.32 million harassing, arresting, and prosecuting people who took part in 24 bike rides between September 2004 and August 2006, the same 2-year period, incidentally, in which the city spent just $460,000 installing 15.3 miles of bike lanes in the 5 boroughs.[10]

The harsh response to Critical Mass in New York and a number of other U.S. cities clearly points to the perceived threat of leaderless public demonstrations just as it validates Dan Rather's prescient observation that "Americans will put up with anything provided it doesn't block traffic."[11] But what it fails to explain is why a bicycle ride, of all things, could ruffle so many feathers in cities with complex socioeconomic problems, school budget deficits, crumbling public infrastructures, and a slew of auto-related fatalities and injuries. Such dramatic and costly measures not only call into question the very function of public spaces and whether roads are indeed public; they also prompt a more basic set of questions about how and why bicycling can be simultaneously interpreted as a protest, a parade, a party, a threat to the status quo, and, even more bizarrely, a "terrorist-type behavior."[12]

Riding a bike is, of course, not always bound up with the tensions of police cruisers and undercover surveillance choppers. Millions of people in the United States love to ride bicycles and they do so for exercise and leisure, to visit friends and run the occasional errand, to attend college classes and compete in sporting events, to go camping in the country, and to explore city alleyways in the middle of the night. Bicycling is one of the most popular recreational activities in the United States and becoming a more attractive mode of urban transportation due in part to longer traffic delays, wildly fluctuating oil and gas prices, and the increasing costs of owning and operating a car. Indeed, the number of utilitarian, or utility, cyclists who use bicycles for some form of daily transportation or commuting is increasing sharply.[13] New York City and Chicago saw 77 percent and 80 percent increases in bicycle use between 2000 and 2006, while Portland, Oregon, a city boasting one of the highest rates of cyclists in the country as well as a vast cycling infrastructure and a vivid culture of bike devotees, witnessed a 144 percent increase in bicycle use between 2000 and 2008.[14] Amid surging gas prices and warm weather, cyclists came out in droves during the spring and summer of 2008, hitting the streets from Philadelphia to Los Angeles and in most cities in between.[15] New York City bike shops at one point had difficulty keeping new bikes in stock, while San Francisco bicyclists occasionally outnumbered automobile drivers on a few busy corridors.[16]

Despite these positive trends, the stark reality is that only 1 percent of the total U.S. population rides a bicycle for transportation and barely half as many use bikes to commute to work.[17] If these figures seem extraordinarily low, it is because they are. Less people ride bicycles in the United States than in almost every country throughout Asia and Europe, with the exception of England, with whom the United States is tied (along with Australia). In contrast, bicycling accounts for 27 percent of trips made in the Netherlands, 18 percent in Denmark, and roughly 10 percent in Germany, Finland, and Sweden.[18] China, despite its staggering pace of new automobile ownership, still has a strong reliance on bicycle transportation, and in Tokyo, Japan it is estimated that more people ride bicycles to local train and subway stations each day—as part of their work commute—than there are bike commuters in the entire United States.[19] John Pucher, a bicycle transportation expert and urban planning professor, best puts the U.S. figure into perspective by noting that Canadians living in the frosty Yukon (adjacent to Alaska) bike to work at more than twice the rate of California residents and more than three times that of commuters in Florida.[20] Even the Northwest Territories, just shy of the North Pole, boasts a higher percentage of bike commuters (1.6 percent) than three of the largest U.S. cities ranked among the best in the nation for bicycling, including Oakland, California (1.5 percent), Honolulu, Hawaii (1.4 percent), and Denver, Colorado (1.4 percent).[21]

Bicycling is not only a fringe mode of transportation in a country with more vehicles than licensed drivers; it is a form of mobility rendered virtually obsolete by the material infrastructure and dominant cultural norms in the United States. Navigating a U.S. city by bicycle is for the inexperienced cyclist or casual rider a seemingly daunting challenge if not a completely undesirable task. Of course, people can and do ride bikes in any urban environment, and the health benefits alone far outweigh the actual risks of doing so. But statistics are somewhat meaningless when one is faced with the actuality of sharing the road with an almost ever-increasing volume of automobiles, driven by a growing number of aggressive drivers, with shorter tempers, in bigger vehicles.[22] If and when one is capable of assuaging concerns over their safety (real or perceived), there are a slew of other issues for bike riders to contend with, the least of which is simply finding a safe place to park one's bike. For example, outdoor bike racks are generally scarce or inconveniently located, indoor parking facilities are almost nonexistent in U.S. cities, makeshift bike racks like parking meters are gradually disappearing from urban spaces (replaced by digital boxes), and most employers do not allow employees to bring their bicycles inside their place of work, much less provide facilities to shower and/or change clothes.[23] One can add to this any number of issues, including the prevalence of road hazards, a decreasing number of independent bike shops nationwide, and a relatively hostile street environment in which it is not uncommon for male drivers to sexually harass women on bikes and to intimidate, taunt (getting called "faggot" is all-too-typical), and occasionally kill male cyclists.[24] Even seven-time Tour de France champion Lance Armstrong is not immune from these general trends; he was threatened and almost run over by a vengeful driver following a verbal exchange on the road in the late 1990s.[25]

Whether one chooses to ride a bicycle or does so out of necessity, daily mobility quickly becomes an issue when some of the most mundane, routine experiences one has as a bicyclist are fraught with a degree of hassle that one rarely experiences as a driver. Sara Stout, a prominent bicycle advocate and car-free activist in Portland (Oregon), describes how this everyday sensibility begins to transform one's perspective about bicycle transportation and the need to effect some sort of change: "At first bicycling is utilitarian, it's just how you choose to get around . . . but it becomes political really quickly because it's hard to get around. There are difficulties at every turn, and there seem to be injustices at every turn. There's always a problem."[26] The problems Stout hints at, and indeed, the ones with which her activism is so comprehensively engaged, become political not simply because they adversely impact the mobility of bicyclists but because the burdens themselves are a set of restrictions preventing everyone—not just dedicated bike riders—from having the option to easily and safely utilize the cheapest, most efficient, and most practical form of personal transportation for short trips: the kind American drivers take more than 50 percent of the time they get behind the wheel of a car (three miles or less). These impediments, along with collectively poor access to adequate public transportation, high-speed transit, and even the most basic pedestrian infrastructure like sidewalks and crosswalks, also function, conversely, as a set of aids. They make it possible for people to see bicycle transportation as undesirable, dangerous, and/or childish; they make it easy for people in the United States to use cars for 69 percent of all daily trips of one mile or less, and they make it painfully comfortable for Americans to avoid taking collective responsibility for transportation-related pollution and oil dependency. Perhaps most significant, they make it seem natural for most adults to never consider the idea of riding a bicycle in the first place.

Automobility

The historical transformation of the United States into a full-blown car culture is commonly, though somewhat erroneously, attributed to choice or desire, as if the aggregation of individual consumer choices and yearnings necessarily built the roads, lobbied the government, zoned the real estate, silenced the critics, subsidized auto makers, underfunded public transit, and passed the necessary laws to oversee all facets of these projects since the 1890s. One of the primary stories used to bolster this broad-based claim is that of America's love affair with the automobile—a common trope in U.S. popular culture that colors our understanding of transportation history and also buttresses some of the most partisan arguments posed by the car's vigorous defenders.[27] It is unquestionable that many Americans do, in fact, love their cars and cling to the myth of "The Road" with the zeal of Madison Avenue and Jack Kerouac combined. However, the fidelity of the narrative is almost irrelevant when considering how it is put to use and for whom it is made to work. That is to say, while the love affair serves a variety of social and cultural functions in the United States, it is particularly compelling to a relatively small group of free-market ideologues and multinational corporations (particularly oil conglomerates) who largely govern and/or profit from the production, marketing, sales, and regulation of the automobile. Indeed, the love story satisfies two of the most cherished myths of free-market capitalism concurrently: it corroborates the idea that consumer choices equal authentic power (i.e., people vote with their wallets), and it normalizes the false notion that consumer desires ultimately determine the so-called evolution of technologies—a position that ignores the profound roles that material and cultural infrastructures play in the success of any technology, much less the development of technological norms. Such explanations not only are misleading; they also effectively downplay some of the most undemocratic and thoroughly racist decision-making processes at the heart of postwar urban development and transportation policy implementation in the United States, as well as the political influence historically wielded by what could easily be termed an *automobile-industrial complex*.[28] This is not to suggest that power is always exerted from the top down, nor to imply that the average person plays no role in the production or contestation of technological and cultural norms. Rather, it is simply a way of acknowledging that technological desires and choices, particularly those concerning transportation and mobility, are necessarily constrained by the profit imperatives of very specific and very powerful institutions and organizations.

These interconnections partly constitute what John Urry calls the "system of automobility": the assemblages of socioeconomic, material, technological, and ideological power that not only facilitate and accelerate automobile travel but also help to reproduce and ultimately normalize the cultural conditions in which the automobile is seen, and made to be seen, as a technological savior, a powerful status symbol, and a producer of both "modern" subjectivities and "civilized" peoples.[29] Even in its earliest uses, the term *automobility* refers less to a form of transportation than an ideologically and symbolically loaded cultural phenomenon. A *New York Times* contributor in 1922 writes, "As a rule, automobility implies higher individual power, better economic distribution and a potentially higher social state."[30] It is with good reason then that Steffen Böhm sees automobility as fundamentally political inasmuch as it "entails patterns of power relations and visions of a collective 'good life' which are at the same time highly contestable and contested."[31]

The "good life" that Americans learn to associate with automobility is partly due to the way in which driving is so tangibly employed in the construction of American-ness itself: it is a de facto expression of citizenship in the United States and a means by which one becomes part of the national "imagined community."[32] Benedict Anderson argues that one of the ways people participate in something as politically and geographically disparate as "the Nation" is through a shared, mediated ritual, and he points to the rise of print media—or what he calls print capitalism—as the basis for modern nationalism inasmuch as reading the newspaper is an "extraordinary mass ceremony" in which individuals engage in an activity that is simultaneously repeated by millions of other people, at the same time, every day, throughout the entire year.[33] Of this practice, Anderson asks, "What more vivid figure for the secular, historically clocked, imagined community can be envisioned?"[34] If one takes Anderson's question seriously, then with respect to the United States, the present-day answer to his rhetorical question is arguably quite simple: driving.

Driving, and more specifically the act of driving to and from work, is not only an integral part of American life, it is one of the most ritualized tasks performed by the largest number of U.S. citizens each day: roughly 120 million commute by car, including 105 million who drive alone.[35] This solitary/collective practice is a key practice in defining what it means to be American, or more accurately, what it means to *do* like an American. Thus, instead of imagining the nation through print capitalism, as Anderson argues, one might say that Americans imagine the nation through mobile capitalism or *auto capitalism:* a process wherein the United States is habitually reconstructed as a "republic of drivers."[36] Within this republic, the "gauge and emblem" of freedom is not the sovereign state, as Anderson suggests, but the gauge itself, which is to say the speedometer mounted on the dashboard of every one of the 250 million vehicles in the United States.[37]

The automobile resides at the core of the post–World War II American dream and it functions as both the literal and symbolic centerpiece of a narrative equating individual mobility with personal freedom. As William F. Buckley Jr. puts it, "The *right* to drive a car is the most cherished right in America, of special, sizzling importance to young people."[38] Thus, it is hardly surprising that Americans tend to shrug off the negative aspects of driving despite its obvious hazards (roughly 6 million crashes, 2 million injuries, and 42,000 deaths per year in the United States alone) or the multitude of environmental, social, health, and economic costs associated with automobility.[39] Nor is it surprising that critiques of the automobile are taken quite personally in the United States, often condemned as symptoms of a fringe ideology or manifestations of "cultural elitism."[40] Within this prevailing cultural context, driving a hybrid vehicle can just as easily signify smugness as the seemingly innocuous attempt to limit driving in a public park can imply support for an "anti-automobile jihad."[41] Putting one's critique into action can be even more problematic, as the ad hoc network of activists associated with Reclaim the Streets undoubtedly realized when the event—a traffic-blocking, guerilla-style street celebration—earned a spot on the nation's' draconian list of domestic terrorist threats: a designation giving the federal government and state police forces the unprecedented ability to prosecute potential dance party participants under the Patriot Act.[42] Because just as nationalism requires the creation of a certain set of "others" from which a citizenry can implicitly or explicitly define itself in contradistinction—such as foreigners, native peoples, and/or immigrants—the "republic of drivers" similarly requires a set of "others" from which its citizens can assert their ever-modern values of high speed, personal independence, and hyper-privatized mobility. Pedestrian rights advocates, environmentalists, and especially urban bicyclists all serve this role in various capacities. Consequently, not only do bicycle transportation advocates face the uphill battle of promoting non-motorized mobility to a car-driving, car-loving public; they are also charged with the onerous task of habitually defending bicycling and bike riders from disproportionate scrutiny, burgeoning hostility, and, on occasion, the coordinated efforts of major metropolitan police departments.

Pedal-Powered Critique

Against these odds, support for bicycle transportation is growing in the United States, and so are the ranks of those drawing critical attention to the intersecting problems of auto-supported sprawl, oil reliance, and "car addiction."[43] Indeed, there is a distinctly political impetus spurring many of today's bicycling advocates to challenge the institutions and practices of automobility as well as the spaces in which the automobile is materially and ideologically constructed as the king of the road. One can see this ethos at work in Critical Mass, but it is a disposition similarly embraced by a legion of bike enthusiasts, environmentalists, cultural workers, tinkerers, and a variety of "small-scale, autonomous groups" whose objectives are not part of the "dominant transport or leisure cultures."[44] The emergence of what Paul Rosen calls a *bicycle counterculture* began in the late 1960s and early 1970s, when pro-bicycle advocacy groups and anti-car environmental protests sprouted in the Netherlands, England, Sweden, France, and, most strikingly, the United States, where the ubiquity of the automobile has consistently thwarted both the viability of bicycle transportation and the development of cycling traditions common to Asia and Europe. Spurred by the urgency of the 1970s oil crisis and a passion for human-powered transportation, these bike activists, or *biketivists,* sought to address not only the everyday challenges and dangers facing cyclists on the streets but also the social, ecological, and spatial benefits of a radically efficient and otherwise sustainable technology: a "vehicle for a small planet," as Marcia Lowe puts it.[45]

In voicing their support for utilitarian cycling as an immediate and/or long-term alternative to the automobile, a growing number of Americans are beginning to see the bicycle as much more than just a utilitarian collection of metal tubes, wheels, chain links, pedals, and a saddle (seat). The bicycle is variously seen, and in many cases actively reconceptualized, as a source of self-empowerment and pleasure, a pedagogical machine, a vehicle for community building, a symbol of resistance against the automobile and oil industries, and a tool for technological, spatial, and cultural critique. Formal advocacy, independent media, and the creation of grassroots cultural practices are some of the tools with which people simultaneously convey their aspiration for human-powered mobility and their intense frustration with a car culture in which the rhetoric of the freedom of the road often replaces the actual right to freely use the road. Bicycling, in other words, is seen as a symbolically powerful gesture capable of signifying, for example, "support for alternative energies," or somewhat differently, a desire to not "spend life inside of a box."[46] Chris Bull, an independent bike maker and founder of Circle A Cycles in Providence, Rhode Island, indicates that biking is also part of a wider cultural shift that begins at an individual level, with people "pushing themselves in all areas of life to consume less, pollute less, live differently."[47] Indeed, many bicyclists are drawn to the idea of opting out—as much as possible in a petroleum-based economy—from contributing to the ever-increasing profits and power of oil and gas corporations. Sheldon Brown, the recently deceased guru of U.S. bike tinkerers, similarly alludes to oil-related wars as a reason why people cycle: he says he went from being an off-and-on bike commuter to a full-time devotee (with few exceptions) on the day Saddam Hussein invaded Kuwait.[48] Claire Stoscheck, a feminist bike advocate in Minneapolis, puts emphasis on the material simplicity of the bicycle and on the way riding fosters open-air connections with one's surroundings. More emphatically, she sees biking as a means of literally and metaphorically "subverting the dominant isolationist, individualistic, over-consumptive car culture."[49] Bicycling, as an antiviolence educator in California so eloquently puts it, is fundamentally political because "it bears witness to a commitment to change and the possibility of changing the way we think and act."[50]

The bicycle, like the automobile, is an object that becomes meaningful through its relationship to an entire field of cultural practices, discourses, and social forces. These linkages, or what cultural theorists call *articulations,* are not naturally occurring, nor are they due to the essence of the bicycle itself.[51] Rather, they are made: people construct, define, and modify these connections by writing about bicycles, displaying them in museums, documenting them in films, representing them on T-shirts and posters, singing about them, fixing them, and, of course, riding them. The intentionality of a specific rider, advocate, or documentarian can extend only so far, however, because the processes that collectively fix meaning around the bicycle, the act of cycling, or even the cyclist him- or herself are historically rooted, geographically and contextually specific, and shaped by dominant ideologies and everyday habits. Put simply, a bicycle means something much different when used by an RNC protester in 2004, versus a Chinese schoolgirl in 1968, a Swiss chemist in 1943, or a Pittsburgh (Pennsylvania) graduate student in 1999—all the more so if one accounts for the reasons they are riding, the directions they are going, the speeds at which they are traveling, and the types of bicycles they are pedaling. People can and do make bicycling meaningful, in other words, but not within a context of their own making.[52] Indeed, just as the physical movements of an urban cyclist are influenced by the presence of cars and framed by a road designed for cars, the processes with which we make sense of bike riders, bicycle technologies, and cycling are similarly framed by the norms and assumptions bundled up with automobility. The power of this regime, in other words, stems from its coercive spatial and temporal organization of bodies and machines, but also from its capacity to structure meaning: to mold the ways we think about, engage with, struggle over, and ultimately make sense of both transportation and mobility itself.[53]

By "renovating and making 'critical' an already existing activity," bike activists politicize bicycle transportation and in doing so reveal the extent to which bicycling—like all forms of mobility—is also made political in the context of "social and power relations that are systematically asymmetrical."[54] This dialectical tension is fundamental to the politics of bicycling with which this book is concerned: a set of issues that are in some ways "not about the bike."[55] Or should I say, they are not only about the bike. The politics of bicycling encompasses everything from the most pragmatic affairs of the urban bike commuter, to the rhetorical limits of bike advocacy, to the representation of bicycle transportation in mass media. More specifically, it encapsulates a set of complex questions about the role of technology in society, the importance of mobility in everyday life, and the broader struggles over how public spaces are used and disciplined, segmented and unified, celebrated and stolen. By focusing on the intersection of these issues and the myriad ways they play out through the contestation of automobility, this book not only pieces together a cultural and political map of the bicycle in the United States; it also uses the bicycle as an object with which to analyze and critique some of the dominant cultural and political formations in the so-called Western world.

Like all maps, this one is necessarily incomplete and shaped by the biases of its would-be cartographer. Consequently, cyclists solely interested in navigating through their respective interests in racing, fitness, or the fabled origins of bicycle technologies will likely find as little guidance and comfortable terrain here as social scientists seeking a neutral assessment of automobility, environmentalists yearning for a bike-centered treatise on carbon emissions, activists hoping for a bikes-as-freedom manifesto, or urban planners eager to find a concrete plan for the redistribution of concrete. Instead, the routes I highlight are meant to construct a more complex and explicitly politicized atlas that uses history, critical theory, media analysis, and ethnographic data to consider the prospects as well as the problems posed by bicycle transportation, cars, and the auto-mobile paradigm that connects them. In doing so, I hope to achieve a few modest and intertwined goals.

First, this book is meant to intervene in, and contribute to, a series of dialogues and debates about the socioeconomic, cultural, and political roles of transportation and personal mobility—most specifically, as they play out in the United States, where there is both widespread support for driving and a general "lack of research on the political contestation of automobility."[56] Second, by positioning the bicycle at the center of this conversation, I wish to draw attention to a legacy of bicycle transportation advocacy that is either ignored outside the relatively small circles of bicycle enthusiasts and historians or simply not documented. Finally, by critically engaging with the ideas, practices, and discourses of bike advocates I want to trouble some of their taken-for-granted assumptions to encourage a more progressive politics of bicycling that explicitly privileges the goals of social and environmental justice as part of a more robust vision of "transportation equity."[57] Consequently, this book is largely organized around a number of tensions that illustrate both how and why technology is never neutral, space is never empty, and mobility is never disconnected from power.[58] For example, Chapter 2 begins with a historical analysis that looks at the ways in which people both envisioned bicycling in the late nineteenth century and utilized a technology that Iain Boal rightly describes as an "ambiguous, contradictory thing."[59] The 1890s, in particular, was a period in which the bicycle was at once construed as both a liberator and a disciplinarian that ostensibly did the work of the moral reformer, the nationalist, and the industrialist by itself: it reorganized bodies away from sin, distraction, and sloth toward sobriety, rationality, and physical and moral fitness. Bicycling was a technological practice incorporated into a narrative of feminist emancipation, utopian socialism, and cultural resistance, and at the same time it was widely praised for its seemingly natural ability to affirm some of the most dominant norms of the era. Perhaps most significant, the set of ideas and practices that came to define the "bicycle era" ultimately, and ironically, laid the groundwork for the system of automobility against which today's bicycling advocates find themselves uncomfortably positioned.

The anxiety over the role of mobility as both an expression of technological liberation and a reification of the status quo is a contradiction that similarly frames Chapters 3 and 4, in which I turn attention, respectively, to the emergence of bike activism in the late 1960s and 1970s and the development of Critical Mass in the early 1990s. Like their bike riding counterparts in the 1890s, these later generations of bicyclists were/are necessarily preoccupied with the spatialities of mobility that define, and in some ways dictate, the function of the modern street and the basic ability of one to traverse it without requiring a car as a prerequisite possession. But whereas the bicycle era normalized bike touring, country rides, and practices otherwise used to escape the metropolis for greener pastures, the modus operandi of post-automobile bike advocacy emphasizes the importance of asserting, utilizing, and even contesting the urban space(s) in which the automobile reigns supreme. This lineage of activism, which extends from the Dutch Provo's free White Bicycle Plan in 1965 up until (and well beyond) the RNC protest outlined earlier in this chapter, positions bike advocacy as part of a pro-urban politics that emphasizes what Henri Lefebvre famously called the "right to the city."[60] It comes in the wake of years of auto-centric policies in the United States and Europe, and it stands in contrast to both the accepted paradigm of urban mobility and a mode of bike advocacy that sees politically motivated critiques of automobility as a hindrance to bicycle transportation, if not a contemptible project.

The prospects and limitations of both bike activism and a spatial politics of car culture are intricately connected to the process of communication, whether one looks at the actual discourses of bike advocates or considers the manner in which transportation technologies and bodies also become meaningful as sites where messages are produced and ideas translated. Chapters 5 and 6 address the relationships between transportation and communication in order to interrogate the often contradictory ways in which media work in conjunction with automobility. Chapter 5, for example, looks at how bicycling and bicyclists are represented in both entertainment and news media in the United States, in formats such as Hollywood films, television shows, print news, and broadcast journalism. Here one finds the development of specific narratives and stereotypes that do some important cultural work by legitimizing and ultimately reinforcing the dominant image of the automobile cultivated by/through the spectacle of auto advertising and the popular narrative of the infallible car. In contrast, I use Chapter 6 to explore some of the ways in bicyclists use independent or alternative media to articulate bicycling to an entirely different set of ideas and technological practices that constitute a DIY (Do It Yourself) bike culture in the United States. Through a variety creative outlets that range from punk music and zines to street art and blogs, bike enthusiasts contest a one-dimensional reading of bicycling and in doing so draw attention to the subcultures, technological practices, and political perspectives that animate their love for the bicycle as well as their critique of both car culture and the dominant paradigm of bicycle transportation.

Chapter 7 similarly engages with the ideas and practices implicit to DIY bike culture but I turn attention specifically to the network of community bicycle organizations and community bike shops that now dot the landscape in cities throughout the Americas, Europe, Australia, and parts of Africa. In addition to charting the development of bicycle education programs and the unique cultural/pedagogical spaces in which community bicycle organizations are housed, I discuss the social complexities of mobility that inform everyday bicycle mechanics as well as the coordination of local and international groups who facilitate bicycle aid programs as means to assist poor people in the so-called Third World or Global South. My aim in drawing attention to the latter objectives of community bicycle organizations is to explore some of the fundamental possibilities, as well as the contradictions, implicit in the desire to help change the world. That is to say, recycling and building bikes can function as an effective and empowering way to educate people and otherwise break down the barriers of race, class, and gender privilege that are interconnected to/with mobility. But when coupled with a paradigm of economic development in which the bicycle is positioned as a postcolonial tool for realizing the benefits of entrepreneurial capitalism, this set of practices raises important questions that demand further reflection and critique. Indeed, the final chapter also takes issue with the current socioeconomic trajectory of globalization as a way to reframe debates about the future of bicycle transportation, the limits of automobility, and the potential for realizing an American *vélorution* in the twenty-first century.

CHAPTER 2

Becoming Auto-Mobile

That the Automobile will follow on the bicycle may practically be regarded as certain. Everything has been leading up to it.

—Harry C. Marillier, "The Automobile," *The Eclectic Magazine of Foreign Literature*, 1895

Connecting Histories

Bicycles occupy a unique and somewhat awkward space in the intersecting histories of technology and mobility. Despite the wild popularity of the bicycle in the late nineteenth and twentieth centuries, its overall historical role is perpetually shadowed, in the United States, by the sweeping impact narratives told about the development of the steam ship, the railroad, and, of course, the automobile. Yet the history of the bicycle continues to garner widespread attention from bicycling enthusiasts and academics alike. In fact, written histories of the bicycle are almost as old as the modern device itself, with early accounts dating back to the midst of the bicycle craze of the 1890s.[1] Documentation of cycling technology, bicycle racing, and the initial bicycle era continued, albeit sporadically, throughout much of the period leading up to the present, and in recent decades bicycles are increasingly fashionable as an interdisciplinary object of study. Technology scholars, for example, have used the history of the bicycle as a way to document the influence of design on transportation habits and to make specific claims about the larger processes of technological production, development, and innovation.[2] Other academics situate the bicycle in the economic context of the late nineteenth century to explore some of the resonances between mass mobility, mass marketing, and mass production.[3] Geographers contribute to an additional dimension of the historical narrative by analyzing urban bicycle transportation through the lenses of public space, economics, and social norms.[4]

A persistent theme that emerges in scholarship and popular histories of bicycling is the influence of the bicycle in late nineteenth and early twentieth centuries. The bicycle is said to have exerted a revolutionary influence on everything from language and education, to women's clothing, to the gene pools of disparate rural communities.[5] Sydney Aronson's 1952 article "The Sociology of the Bicycle" typifies this approach in that he generally posits social change as a direct outgrowth, or consequence, of technological innovation. Yet despite Aronson's overly deterministic inklings, his conclusion is compelling: the "greatest significance of the bicycle was *the interference it ran for the automobile.*"[6] By interference, he specifically refers to the economic, technological, and legal developments that metaphorically and literally paved the way for the automobile; he counts innovations in mass production, repair shops, road building, traffic laws, and legal precedents as the key features that made the car possible. Cycling historian Ross Petty develops a number of these concepts in his careful research, including bicyclists' collective role in the development of U.S. traffic laws, the bicycle industry's development of mass marketing, and the use of bicycles by U.S. Postal Service and Western Union employees.[7] Glen Norcliffe similarly explicates the influence of Colonel Albert Pope's innovative model of mass production on the ensuing automobile industry, specifically crediting Pope with a number of the innovations typically attributed to famed automobile mogul, and failed colonialist Henry Ford, including the modernization of the labor process, the vertical integration of production, the creation of machines with interchangeable parts, and the construction of mass markets for transportation technologies.[8]

As much as this body of work helps to explain how the bicycle era "prepared the way for the automobile," there have been few attempts to critically interrogate the cultural formations linking the bicycle era and the automobile age.[9] Norcliffe provides a valuable point of entry for this task because he locates the meaning of bicycle technologies and the practice of cycling in the broader context of modernization, suggesting that the dominant paradigm of modernity—namely, scientific rationalism, a focus on individual autonomy, and a fascination with newness—prompted the technological innovations that gave rise to the bicycle and subsequently framed it as a symbol of modern life: a technological expression of progress.[10] Bicycles, according to his argument, gained meaning within this cultural context just as cycling—a performative and spectacular expression of the modern ethos—became one of the principal means by which modernity was "locally embedded" in North America.[11] Norcliffe helps to construct a more complex view of bicycles and cycling that ultimately draws attention to mobility as a crucial paradigm for thinking through the pitfalls and prospects of modernity, though he falls into the pattern of most cycling historians who either perpetuate a sharp division between the cultural assemblages of the bicycle and those of the automobile, or largely ignore the twentieth century altogether.[12]

Recent scholarship on automobility complements cycling history because it effectively maps the cultural trajectories that inform and are informed by mobile practices and mobile ontologies in the modern era. Collectively, this body of work explores how the system, or regime, of automobility functions, though it also fails to adequately account for the history of bicycle transportation or some of the various ways in which automobility intersects cycling practices.[13] If the automobile did not change society but simply provided a "new medium with which to express pre-existing cultural preferences," as David Nye argues, then why did these preferences find such convenient expression in the car?[14] Moreover, how were these preferences specifically shaped through bicycle riding? Unfortunately, histories of the automobile offer few answers. In the brief instances where the bicycle is mentioned in automotive history, it typically fulfills the role of the caveman in human history—a historical anecdote in an evolutionary narrative. There are, however, important exceptions. Clay McShane's illuminating transportation/road history, *Down the Asphalt Path,* constructs a fluid picture of technological mobility that accurately accounts for bicyclists' collective influence on the upsurge in urban street traffic in the 1890s.[15] Rudi Volti and James Flink also hint at the relationships between the bicycle and the automobile, though they do so in order to make contrasting points. Unlike Flink, Volti mischaracterizes the bicycle as a technology that simply exposed an a priori desire for automobiles, as opposed to organizing the very idea and practices of automobility itself. He suggests that the bicycle craze "revealed a hunger for personal transportation" that was apparently satiated through the automobile, whereas Flink gestures toward the constitutive role bicycling played in the development of the *automotive idea:* "It made the average person aware of the possibilities of individualized, long-distance highway transportation."[16] Hiram Percy Maxim makes a similar point when reflecting on the early production of automobiles: the reason his company did not build (electric) cars until 1895 was because the bicycle had not yet *"directed men's minds* to the possibilities of independent, long-distance travel."[17]

The convergences and discrepancies between these histories indicate layers of continuity between the bicycle era and the automobile age that I want to develop in order to reposition bicycling as less of an influence on the system of automobility than its initial point of origin and its most rudimentary form of expression. Bicycling, in other words, was the first mode of transportation to clearly articulate the idea of autonomy and personal mobility to technological practice. A critical analysis of this formative period thus not only reveals the extent to which cycling fostered the automotive idea; it also previews some of the major problems and prospects of automobility that would later become enshrined in American car culture.[18] By highlighting the tension between the emancipatory potential of the bicycle and its simultaneous use in the construction of a consumerist, individualist, and disciplinary paradigm of mobility, I want to complicate, rather than simply validate, the popular idea that the bicycle was and is a "freedom machine."[19]

Jonathan Sterne's work on sound reproduction, though unrelated to automobility, provides an instructive way to frame this relationship more concretely. In his discussion of radio listening as a cultural practice, Sterne points to a 1925 Brandes radio headset advertisement to suggest that the appeal of the device presumed a high level of intuitive knowledge about the act of listening itself. In short, one would not want to purchase a radio headset unless one already had a disposition toward radio listening that privileged domesticity, privacy, and the desire for technologically reproduced music— all of which were learned. Sterne's point is not only that radio listening is a learned technique but also that the headset ad "marks a convenient end point for a series of transformations in practical orientations toward listening" that began more than one hundred years earlier.[20] Thus, the headset—like the radio before it—crystallized a specific set of cultural dispositions and assumptions regarding the use and value of technologies, as well as the listener him- or herself. Following Sterne's formulation, I am suggesting that the emergence of the automobile actually marks an end point for a series of transformations in practical orientations toward mobility, technology, and space that were initially crystallized through the bicycle. These transformations were by no means natural or inevitable, nor were they simply the result of technological innovations in bicycle design. Rather, they were discursively and performatively produced by parties with heterogeneous and often conflicting agendas that were brought to bear on the production, consumption, uses, and meanings of the bicycle in the late nineteenth century. Consequently, it is crucial to look at how the discourses and practices associated with advertising, feminism, cycling clubs, and tourism organized ideas about the bicycle, as well as the people who rode them and the spaces in which they were ridden. In doing so, one can see how the key components of the system of automobility were put into place during the bicycle era. These include, but are certainly not limited to, the construction of a mobile subjectivity, the development of an entire meaning system around personal transportation, and the disciplining of bodies and the environment in service of autonomous mobility.

Manufacturing the Idea of the Bicycle

The bicycle, according to Ross Petty, was the first expensive, durable, luxury item marketed in the United States.[21] Bicycle advertising soared in the 1890s as manufacturers spent anywhere between $4 and $9 million per year on marketing, while retailers spent another $1 million annually.[22] Technological innovations, the falling price of bicycles, and the sheer popularity of cycling were all factors that increased bicycle sales over the course of the decade, but there was good reason for companies to believe that advertising directly impacted their sales. As a case in point, Petty cites the advertising expenditures and sales figures of Monarch Bicycles in the mid-1890s: "In its first year, 1893, Monarch spent a few thousand dollars and sold 1,200 bicycles. The next year, it spent $20,000 and sold 5,000 bicycles. In 1895, $75,000 worth of advertising sold 20,000 bicycles and in 1896, $125,000 was spent to sell 50,000 bikes."[23] The narratives and images found in early bicycle advertisements are particularly relevant because they gave explicit meaning to bicycles and the act of cycling. Indeed, the importance of creating an entire system of meaning around the bicycle was certainly not lost on Colonel Albert Pope, a pioneer in the production, promotion, and legalization of cycling. Pope not only created the largest, most innovative, and most profitable bicycle manufacturing company of the era—an achievement rivaled by his equally innovative practice of hoarding bicycle technology patents—he also helped to start the League of American Wheelmen (LAW) in 1880: an organization that became the largest and most influential bicycle advocacy group in the United States. Pope exerted force in a number of legal and political spheres and he was especially skilled at promoting his Columbia bicycles through racing competitions, endorsements, and advertising. Significantly, he recognized that the key to success was not simply the mass production or mass consumption of bicycles but mass consumption of the idea of bicycles.[24]

Unlike most of the advertising campaigns produced before the 1960s, bicycle ads in the 1890s were equally if not more focused on what bicycles meant than what they actually did, or rather, what their manufacturers claimed they would or could do. Bike businesses certainly produced their share of ads loaded with detailed product descriptions and semi-preposterous claims about the physical and social benefits of their goods, but for the most part, they embraced an entirely different aesthetic and rhetorical approach to advertising: one based on the aura of the bicycle. Images, rather than written messages, were the salient feature of these advertisements, and emotional appeals, as opposed to those based on reason, became the centerpiece of an emerging visual rhetoric of bicycle consumption.[25] Bicycle manufacturers throughout Europe and the United States experimented with a variety of artistic formats that lent themselves to elaborate imagery, most notably the poster. French cycle companies in particular embraced the poster format and enlisted a variety of skilled artists to construct entire visual narratives in their ads. Nadine Besse and André Vant document and categorize these publicity posters according to themes that include solar, zodiacal, and/or planetary symbols (meant to express supra-terrestrial elevation and performance); wings and flight (meant to express freedom); and sexualized images of women and goddesses (meant to express the ethereal, desirable qualities of the bicycle).[26]

By using advertising to imbue the bicycle with emotion and meaning, bicycle manufacturers also normalized cycling as a practice that included the act of consumption itself. That is to say, these rhetorics were used to produce not only desires for mass-produced goods and services but also an entirely new consumer subject: the cyclist.[27] By appealing to the cyclist as a specific type of consumer with unique tastes, bicycle companies could market a wider variety of products to enhance this burgeoning identity. As Norcliffe notes, these new consumer subjects were often men: "An enthusiastic male cyclist might have as many as three riding outfits: formal club uniforms were expected for parades, at least until the early 1890s; a more casual outfit with long socks, breeches, and jacket would be worn on regular rides; and light cotton outfits became popular for hot summer days. Racers would also have a racing outfit."[28] Many cyclists literally bought into this consumer identity by using bicycles and bicycle accessories to signify their participation in a modern popular culture, yet bicycle manufacturers in the early 1890s were still limited in their ability to transform women into cycling consumer subjects.[29]

Normalizing the Woman Cyclist

Elite women in Europe and the United States were the first to utilize cycling technologies, though most were excluded from riding the high-wheeler, or "ordinary," bicycle (the one with the big front wheel) as well as most models manufactured prior to the modern "safety" bicycle, which is essentially the bicycle as we know it today.[30] "Ordinaries" were incredibly difficult to operate and both clothing and behavioral restrictions made it nearly impossible for women to ride them. Early bicycles were specifically gendered for male use and those women who were the rare exceptions to this rule were mainly "an already suspect class of women: stage performers who used the high wheeler in an act."[31] Tricycle use, on the other hand, was passively supported in the 1880s and the design of the machines made them easier for women to ride: they were both physically easier to operate and many were built to allow for the accompaniment of a male chaperon.[32] Women could thus operate tricycles without dramatically challenging the dominant social norms of the period. Following the mass production of the safety bicycle in the 1890s, many women took up cycling and found in it a renewed sense of freedom and mobility. In the United States, the bicycle's role in the transformation of gender norms is buttressed by Susan B. Anthony's oft-quoted claim: "The bicycle did more to emancipate women than anything else in the world."[33] Women were certainly not freed by the bicycle, but one cannot overestimate the sense of liberation and empowerment experienced by the first women who transcended the domestic sphere on their own two wheels.

Female cycling was initially met with a considerable degree of resistance from men, the medical community, the church, and organizations like the Woman's Rescue League—a group that once claimed: "Bicycling by young women has helped more than any other media to swell the ranks of reckless girls, who finally drift into the standing army of outcast women of the United States."[34] Though bicycling was not explicitly forbidden to women, the social conventions governing etiquette, mobility, and desires all prolonged the acceptance of women cycling, just as they would eventually delay the acceptance of women driving in the twentieth century.[35] One of the well-documented debates of the 1890s focused specifically on women's clothing, particularly their use of bloomers, or "divided skirts," while cycling.[36] James McGurn recalls that the question of whether women should cycle was thus quickly transformed into question of "what they should wear while doing so."[37] Feminists seized the bloomer issue as an opportunity to mobilize against other forms of restrictive clothing, and by extension, restrictive social norms. Frances Willard, a prominent temperance activist and cyclist, famously used the corset as a rhetorical metaphor in her speech to the Women's National Council of the United States in 1891: "She is a creature born to the beauty and freedom of Diana, but she is swathed by her skirts, splintered by her stays, bandaged by her tight waist, and pinioned by her sleeves until—alas, that I should live to say it!—a trussed turkey or a spitted goose are her most appropriate emblems."[38] The burgeoning feminist movement rallied around cycling as a way to critique Victorian ideals of femininity and groups like the Rational Dress Society explicitly connected women's liberation to bicycling, via the issue of clothing. There was a significant and somewhat obvious overlap between the interests of clothing reformers, female cyclists, and feminists of the period since women were socially, economically, and quite literally constrained in their mobility.

Despite the near absence of women cyclists of color, who are incidentally never mentioned in cycling histories, the white women who rode bicycles did not articulate their practice to a singular vision of femininity. For some, cycling posed a challenge to the doctrine of separate spheres by "offering women a way to escape the physical confines of the home," which in turn, helped transform the gendered norms of public spaces by making them more inclusive to ("properly" behaved) women.[39] Frances Willard, on the other hand, consistently embraced a conservative position that specifically equated bicycling with moral refinement:

> That which made me succeed with the bicycle was precisely what had
> gained me a measure of success in life—it was the hardihood of spirit

that led me to begin, the persistence of will that held me to my task, and the patience that was willing to begin again when the last stroke had failed. And so I found high moral uses in the bicycle and can commend it as a teacher without pulpit or creed. He who succeeds, or, to be more exact in handing over my experience, she who succeeds in gaining the mastery of such an animal as Gladys [the name of the bicycle], will gain the mastery of life.[40]

Elizabeth Cady Stanton pioneered a rather different approach to cycling by connecting it to her explicitly politicized, though troublingly racist, narrative of feminist emancipation that included liberation from "conventions of fashion, from artificial gender distinctions, and from oppressive religion."[41] Unlike Willard, Stanton tied cycling to her critique of patriarchy, women's suffrage, clothing restrictions, birth control, physical mobility, and a transcendentalist-based, radical critique of organized religion.[42] Stanton embraced the bicycle as a vehicle with which one could literally and symbolically distance oneself from religion, arguing that cycling was a means to escape both the physical confines of the church and the moral tenets of self-denial and restraint.[43] Though she represents what was probably a small minority of women in the nineteenth century, Stanton's perspective on bicycling is notable both for its radical nature and because it prefigures analogous feminist support for cycling that emerges nearly a century later.[44]

In addition to feminist discourses, the popular press played a pivotal role in defining and framing bicycling for women in the 1890s, though it was often in tension with the stated goals of feminism. That is to say, while newspapers and magazines gave middle- and upper-class women some space in which to articulate their support for the practice, these outlets regularly published articles and images that clearly mocked women cycling. Advertising was a similarly ambiguous format in terms of establishing patterns of representation. Patricia Marks, for example, suggests that ads helped to normalize and popularize female bicycling by celebrating the freedom of the *new woman,* whereas Carla Willard takes a more critical position: she acknowledges that advertising may have dispelled negative perceptions of women bicyclists but it was not meant to empower women socially or politically. Rather, bicycle companies were far more concerned with using ads to create a female consumer subjectivity through a watered-down representation of feminism: "The anxious debates about female bicycling were implicit in many brand-product ads, where they were distilled in and quelled by the sales pitch."[45]

Advertisements, by their very nature, lack the capacity to explain or contextualize the social ramifications of consumer choices, and this, according to Ellen Garvey, was the vital work performed by fiction narratives in popular magazines.[46] These stories, she argues, worked in concert with bicycle advertising to create and amplify a larger discourse of consumption around female cycling. As part of an ongoing shift in the publishing industry, the commercial interests of advertising-supported magazines and the bicycle industry resonated to such a degree that seemingly noncommercial narratives either explicitly, or implicitly, promoted bike-riding women in the service of bicycle sales. Female cycling, in other words, had to be made "socially acceptable to sell safety bicycles to a larger market."[47] Bicycling, Garvey argues, was widely used as the centerpiece of magazine fiction that helped to diffuse the potentially disruptive political awareness of the new woman, namely by ensuring readers that bicycling would make women healthier, stronger, and otherwise more fit for motherhood. This type of appeal makes perfect sense in this period as arguments both in favor of and in opposition to women cycling were regularly justified in "medicalized" terms: "Antibicylers claimed that riding would ruin women's sexual health by promoting masturbation and would compromise gender definition as well, while probicylers asserted that bicycling would strengthen women's bodies."[48]

The profit imperatives of bicycle manufacturers, retailers, and advertising-supported magazines all contributed to both the legitimization and commodification of female cycling in the 1890s, but my point here is not simply that consumer discourses typically trump political/social discourses in popular culture or that heteronormative narratives can ostensibly sell any product (this much should be obvious). Rather, what seems more significant is the manner in which the entire debate over women cycling normalized the objectification of female mobility by making it a subject for public scrutiny: a practice that becomes commonplace in twentieth-century car culture.[49] That is to say, this period functioned as a "test drive" not only for the type of marketing techniques eventually used to sell women both automobiles and a consumption-based idea of liberation but also for men to utilize popular media as a tool for disciplining women's transportation habits and their mobility more broadly.[50] At the same time this process legitimized the corporate voice in debates about women's mobility, it also previewed the strategy of utilizing "abstract notions of freedom to encourage women to buy automobiles."[51] The normalization of female cycling—which is partly achieved through its commodification—thus produced an uneasy relationship between women, mobility, and the popular press that was similarly exploited once women got behind the wheel of the car.

In addition to manufacturing products, consumer subjectivities, and ideas about cycling, the bicycle industry of the 1890s created a distinct body of knowledge about mobility itself. Petty reminds us that the competitive marketing of bicycles was in reality a "continuous education regarding the benefits of this new method of locomotion."[52] The debate over women cycling clearly indicates that these benefits were not universally accepted, nor were they framed in a uniform manner: cycling was contested, discussed, and inter-preted because it was seen as a meaningful act, not just a leisure activity. The proliferation of discourses about bicycling are similarly consequential because they shaped a specific "image of the bicycle" that, according to Anne-Katrin Ebert, "had a great impact on politics and traffic legislation and shaped the conditions for cycling."[53] Indeed, Pope's $60,000 investment in the creation of *Wheelman* magazine—the first publication principally devoted to bicycle advocacy—speaks to these goals.[54] More important, these discourses created a new body of knowledge about autonomous mobility and personal transporta-tion that were not simply descriptive, but productive: they produced "norma-tive categories, prescriptions for proper conduct, and relations of power."[55] This power/knowledge was ultimately utilized to discipline mobile bodies, a process Jennifer Bonham describes as "fundamental in enabling the govern-ment of travel through self-regulation and the desire for freedom."[56] Self-governance was eventually coupled with an entire political, legal, and social apparatus (established largely by cycling clubs and the LAW) to promote a set of mobile norms and specific rules that could be externally governed through traffic law and safety discourses. Crucially, this process also normalizes the very idea that personal mobility should be self-regulated and internalized into the bodies of travelers. This dual process of discipline and subjectification, according to Bonham and Jeremy Packer, are fundamental to the paradigm of automobility and the eventual rise of car culture inasmuch as the success of automobility is dependent upon drivers being physically and mentally taught how to become drivers, that is, how to move, act, and think in very specific and calculated ways.[57] We often take these processes for granted because they are such familiar and mundane aspects of automotive transportation, but the following sections explore how they were, in fact, first articulated through the practice of cycling. Specifically, I look at how bicyclists were essentially pro-duced, or taught to physically act in accordance with a set of ideas about the bicycle and mobility itself. In other words, their bodies were not natural but rather "worked upon through relations of power and knowledge."[58]

Horse-Bodies, Bicycle-Bodies

Cycling's intimate composition of human and machine sparked a great deal of curiosity in the 1890s and a popular metaphor for the cyclist was the centaur—a half-man, half-horse creature from Greek mythology: "The wheel and the rider are one, as the centaur and his horse-body were one, and when the flight begins it is an intensely personal affair."[59] The centaur metaphor is fitting when one considers the frequent comparisons made between bicycles and horses in the period but it is also instructive inasmuch as it illustrates a changing set of values in the United States regarding animal and mechanical mobilities. Initially, the metaphor seemed to serve the dual purpose of contextualizing bicycling as a normal physical practice (like riding a horse) and placing bicycles on the same high pedestal as the horse, the "noblest of man's animal friends, his most loyal ally and co-worker among the speechless races."[60] Cross-referencing bicycles and horses was a way to "suggest elegance, social rank, and distinction," and this is evident in the way people lovingly referred to the bicycle as a "steel horse" or "magnificent steed."[61] But whereas the bicycle initially gleaned credibility from the horse, it quickly became the standard by which horses were measured:

> Its first cost paid, it requires no further expenditure except for occasional repairs. It does not have to be fed like a horse, and no one needs to be hired to take care of it. It extends greatly the region over which carpenters, masons, plumbers, or gardeners can make their work profitable, and to such it has become indispensable. [Bicycles] have all the advantages and none of the disadvantages involved in keeping a horse.[62]

Money was a determining factor in the shifting preference for bicycles because the price attached to the upkeep of horses was well outside the annual budget of an average worker—not to mention the obvious spatial limitations of keeping a horse in an urban residence.[63] Public health was also a serious concern; Clay McShane notes that by the 1880s, New York City was annually removing 15,000 horse carcasses and 150,000 tons of horse manure from city streets.[64] Bicycles offered a pragmatic alternative to this scenario as well as a technological solution that implicitly promoted the values of modernity over animal power. "The horse, it is thus apparent, has in a measure been superseded by science," as one writer put it in 1896.[65]

Comparisons and contrasts drawn between the horse and the bicycle in the 1890s suggest that people not only grew more comfortable with the idea of riding a personal vehicle instead of an animal but also embraced the new form of agency produced through their relationship to, and synthesis with, their bicycles. The cyclist, unlike the train rider, could go where he wanted, when he wanted to: he could express his autonomous mobility. In this sense, the bicycle was quite literally a machine for "becoming": a technology with which cyclists could actualize more of their own qualities that were presumably modern, such as efficiency and scientific rationality. The emerging preference for a bicycle-body instead of a centaurian horse-body was thus "deeply enmeshed with a cyborgian fascination of merging bodies and machines."[66] It was a way to literally fuse one's body with a technology heralded as an eraser of time and space, and a sign of a "superior civilization in development."[67] Indeed, Christopher Thompson recalls that nineteenth-century bicycle enthusiast Louis Baudry de Saunier unabashedly celebrated the cyclist as a new breed of human who was, in fact, a cyborg: a "man made of half of flesh and half of steel that only our century of science and iron could have spawned."[68] Surrealist writer Alfred Jarry echoed this sentiment some years later, describing the bicycle as an "external skeleton" that allowed humans to "outstrip the processes of biological evolution" that ostensibly kept man from realizing his true potential.[69]

If modern industry was responsible for the birth of the cyborgian cyclist it also played a distinct role in its evolution and guidance. As noted by Besse and Vant, cycle companies created advertisements that "deliberately pictured the new revolutionary hybrid creature."[70] Yet unlike Frankenstein's monster, who was carelessly abandoned by his maker, the cyclist was nurtured by a host of surrogate corporate fathers who hoped to profit from their creation. Jim Fitzpatrick illustrates this point in his critique of bicycle racing:

> When a champion pulls down a record the credit of his victory is claimed by the builder of his machine, the maker of his tires, the patentee of his saddle, and the manufacturer of his chain. Then the oil with which the chain was lubricated, the toe-clips which kept his feet on the pedals, the shoes he wore, the training oil used by him, the soap he patronized, and the pills which set his liver right, all have a share in the victory. The man himself is little else but a pedaling advertisement.[71]

Fitzpatrick's racer is not only a pedaling advertisement; he is also an assemblage of flesh, commodities, and technological research that would later evolve into the modern techno-cyclist Aaron Wilcher so poignantly describes as an expression of *velocipower*.[72] More important, the birth of this creature effectively previews the emergence of the *driver-car* or the *car-driver*, a "'hybrid' assemblage, not simply of autonomous humans but simultaneously of machines, roads, buildings, signs and entire cultures of mobility."[73]

Pseudo-psychology and Moral Cycling

Theorizing the cyclist as a modern human/machine hybrid indicates the need for bike riders in the late nineteenth century to construct an entire subjectivity around their distinct processes of both becoming and being technologically mobile. This project required a paradigm shift because whereas using horses for transportation represented a form of control that positions man over beast, the bicycle ultimately directs attention to a different form of control: that of man over himself. In other words, it is the human half of the new cyborg assemblage that had to be properly trained since one "cannot teach the bicycle anything, or accustom it to anything."[74] The cyclist of the late nineteenth century had to become more rational and capable of exercising the proper faculties to be autonomously mobile. Psychology is said to play an important role in this regard because although the cyclist cannot teach the bicycle anything, he must nevertheless learn to master it. This proves a difficult task because, according to one writer, "the wheel is inanimate, but it is an invention of mind, and is used by beings with minds, so that it has a true psychology."[75] If one follows this bizarre logic, the bicycle can never be voluntarily propelled, or presumably understood, by a person who lacks a complex psychological disposition or is, by default, uneducated. Indeed, mental discipline was thought to be a crucial part of cycling in this period because the ability to master the so-called psychology of the machine was a way to simultaneously demonstrate the superiority of the human intellect: "The power of the muscles do not depend on their size, but on their limberness and on the free and quick impulse imparted to them from the brain. As in fencing, the great power is the brain."[76] Psychological training similarly helped the cyclist to further distinguish him- or herself from the animal kingdom. A speaker in Chautauqua, New York, reinforces this point in a 1901 lecture: "I am well aware that there are monkeys exhibited that ride bicycles; but they are taught by minds. No monkey ever spontaneously mastered the bicycle. A human being explained it, as far as the monkey intellect could comprehend it, and when that failed patiently moved his arms and legs until the monkey availed himself of his hereditary power of balancing."[77] Statements about the psychology of cycling not only situate the practice as an activity reserved for rational people in the 1890s; they also effectively construct a discourse in which psychology is used to explain and interpret on-the-road behavior. The normalization of this discourse, as Jeremy Packer's work indicates, was eventually put to use in order to discipline automobile drivers by creating a "psycho-scientific grid of interpretation for the personal will to know the truth of thyself, thus positioning driving actions as signs of psychological maladjustment."[78] With respect to cycling (and eventually driving), the vague conceptualization of mobility-as-psychology is framed as a moral imperative: it is one's duty as a mobile citizen. Women cyclists were specifically targeted through this rhetoric because bicycling was initially thought to be an overly stimulating, if not erotic, practice that could easily cloud their better judgment. One writer even refers to the bicycle's subtle evil influence, a condition that can be overcome only through "moderation in the use of the wheel [and] a healthful habit of riding."[79]

In addition to psychological appeals, dozens of articles in the 1890s instruct readers about the physical aspects of riding a bicycle, and more emphatically, about how to properly use one's body.[80] An article from 1897 entitled "What We Gain in the Bicycle," illustrates this objective:

Free and deep breathing is interfered with when the leg-muscles are improperly strained, and in order to sit ramrod-straight in the saddle the bicycle rider must necessarily pedal almost altogether with the leg from the knee down, as his position gives him little control of the upper part of the legs. Most women have found this out at the sewing machine; by leaning the body forward at a certain angle the thigh muscles receive proper bracing at the hip-joints and so are enabled to do their work without undue strain.[81]

What is particularly interesting here is the author's reference to other forms of bodily training learned through technological practice: a sewing machine is described not as a tool for making clothes but as an instrument of bodily pedagogy.[82] Advice about proper cycling posture, while pragmatic in its orientation (as in good technique), was widespread in this period and often placed undue emphasis on the communicative function of cyclists' bodies. Garvey recalls that men who cycled in a hunched-over position (what one commonly sees among racers) risked being criticized and/or mocked for being a "scorcher," or reckless cyclist, while women were essentially banned from the posture because it was thought to be sexually stimulating and highly suggestive.[83] An upright riding posture, in other words, was a "measure of propriety and sexual innocence" for women, and it was also seen as an indicator of one's class position.[84] Christopher Thompson specifically discusses the latter connotation in early French cycle racing: "Erect posture distinguished bourgeois cyclists from working-class racers and the working-class youth who sped around town imitating their heroes, as well as from messenger boys and delivery men who now used the bicycle as a professional tool."[85] While people recognized that bodies could translate or communicate certain cultural messages through the act of cycling, many focused on the ways in which bodies were acted upon, inasmuch as bicycling offered a "means to experience with your own body the necessity of self-control and balanced conduct in life."[86] Moderation and temperance, in other words, were praised as the direct outcomes of bicycling because the practice allegedly made the need for sobriety self-evident:

> Cycling as a sport is still more interesting from a moral point of view. Quite a large number of our young men, who formerly were addicted to stupid habits, and the seeking of nonsensical distractions and vulgar pleasures are now vigorous, healthy, energetic, and *for the sake of this extraordinary machine* submit themselves to an ascetic rule of life and, induced by taste and passion, acquire habits of temperance, the imperative desire of quiet and regular living, and, most important of all, the steady exercise of self-control, by resisting

their appetites and doing, without hesitation, all that is required for effectual training.[87]

Unlike psychological discipline, which a bicyclist was meant to transfer from himself onto the machine, here one can see the bicycle becoming a prized instrument for its moralizing influence on the cyclist: it is a technology used to purify the sins of man.

Hygienic Cycling, White Folks, and the Nation

Conceptualizing bicycles as purification devices fits into a broader set of cultural narratives about cleanliness and physical exercise that were widespread in late nineteenth century, particularly the association between exercise and hygiene.[88] Numerous titles published in the United States make specific claims about the so-called hygienic function of bicycling, including "The Hygiene of the Bicycle," "The Psychological and Hygienic Influence of the Bicycle," and a book by H. C. Clark simply entitled *Hygienic Bicycling*.[89] These bodily directives were also promoted throughout Europe, where cycling's hygienic function was said to work on "flesh, as well as minds" in France, in addition to promoting "civil, moral and political idealism" among socialists in Italy.[90] The persistent emphasis on cycling's hygienic discipline runs parallel with, and often intersects, an intertwined religious orientation toward bodies and machines that was similarly expressed as muscular Christianity: a set of discourses and practices aimed at bodily purification and the enhancement of the soul through physical fitness.[91] The bicycle, in this sense, functions not only as a symbol of what humans might achieve through physical discipline—a body more efficient, clean, simple, and rational—but also as the literal instrument with which one can purify oneself in order to become more machine-like.[92] It is both significant and ironic that this religious disposition also jibed with the same capitalist ethos of efficiency that found its truest expression in, among other things, the development of manufacturing techniques that produced obedient man-machine laborers who toiled away in bicycle factories.[93]

Hygiene, as advocated by nineteenth-century cyclists, was not simply associated with religious purification of the mind or body; it was also a racially charged concept that one can still read into the present-day language we use to talk about ethnic cleansing, for example. As part of a wider discourse of eugenics, nationalism, and colonialism, hygiene implies the purification of race—the collective body—as well as the individual body.[94] Garvey argues that these prerogatives were linked to the promotion of women cycling, in particular, because there was a general anxiety over whether "white, nonimmigrant middle-class women were having too few babies."[95] That is to say, cycling was thought to create, among other things, healthier female bodies capable of perpetuating the white race. An article from *The Bicycle,* published in 1896, effectively frames this idea within the paradigm of hygiene itself: "Thousands of men and women are now devoting their bodies and minds [to cycling], and are not only reaping benefit themselves but are preparing the way for future generations which will be born of healthy parents; and in brief this epitomizes the hygienic side of the bicycle."[96] Women were clearly positioned at the center of debates over the physical reproduction of the race and the nation, but male cyclists were arguably the primary subjects of this discourse as well as its authors. Men actively linked bicycling with a racialized view of masculinity, not to mention a grossly inept view of history, which one can clearly see at work in the debut issue of *Outing, a Journal of Recreation* in 1882. It deserves to be quoted at length:

> Physical development necessarily entails mental and moral development also. The conquering races of the world have been races of individual heroes. Greece and Rome trained their youth to the highest state of physical perfection, and these became the conquerors of the world. When luxury and effeminacy undermined the Romans they were overrun by northern barbarians, who were men of marvelous vigor and endurance. The sturdy Goth swept the feebler Moor from the fair fields of Spain, and the Norman invader of England triumphed over the weaker Saxon.
>
> The Anglo-Saxon of today, the pioneer of the world, whose footsteps are found equally in the frozen regions of the pole and under the tropical sun of India—the same men in the cold of Maine and Minnesota, or under the heat of Arizona or Louisiana—is, first of all, strong and active in body, and his dauntless mind is the natural complement of the physical man.
>
> Animal force alone is not sufficient for the needs of our present civilization. The prize ring produces no heroes; but the bicycle makes men not only strong, but it leads them into such social intimacies as must develop their better natures.[97]

These sorts of appeals, or at the very least their racist assumptions, were most explicitly promulgated through local cycling clubs and formal cycling organizations like the League of American Wheelmen. Collectively, this male constituency framed bicycling in the late nineteenth century as a disciplinary practice used for the good of the nation, the race, and mankind.[98] Moreover, they positioned cyclists' bodies as the sites where racist, masculine visions of nationalism (as if there were any other kind!) are inscribed. Indeed, the author of "The Uses of the Bicycle" (quoted above) specifically asserts the function of cycling clubs in a manner that would have made Michel Foucault smile:

"Clubs are not a mere social union. They exercise restraint upon the individual in many ways, teaching him self-control and *submission to discipline.*"[99]

Cycling clubs certainly did not invent this approach to nationalism, nor were they the only organizations to link cycling and patriotism; Garvey and Norcliffe recall that bicycle manufacturers similarly positioned cycling as a nationalistic or patriotic practice, and the names bestowed on American-made bicycles were indicative of this trend (The Patriot, the Charter Oak, the Eagle, the Liberty).[100] Instead, cycling clubs did the work of localizing and reifying these concepts among their elite members by framing cycling as an expression of a nationalistic imagined community, a practice one can clearly see at work in the narratives and images cultivated by automobile corporations in the following century.[101] Many of the clubs throughout North America and Europe also organized themselves in a highly militaristic fashion, mirroring horse cavalries with their matching military-style uniforms and organizational structures.[102] This is perhaps unsurprising given the simultaneous use of bicycles in warfare, as well as the military background of cycling enthusiasts like Charles Pratt, the founder of both the first U.S. cycling club and the League of American Wheelmen. Norcliffe argues that the form of citizenship envisioned by Pratt "transferred the hierarchical arrangement of military power to a social setting, and kept it a male preserve."[103] In France, cycling clubs were even valued for their capacity to physically prepare soldiers, or potential soldiers, for battle deployment.[104]

Cycling organizations, in other words, effectively reproduced some of the worst aspects of nationalist ideology and male chauvinism in the training of men's bodies and minds in the 1880s and 1890s.[105] The privileged "insider-citizenship" of cycling clubs also set rigid parameters around the types of bodies and minds that were allowed to participate.[106] That is to say, they excluded those considered irrelevant to a white, masculine nationalist project, including Asian Americans, the poor, and most notably Native Americans—the perpetually absent "others" in North American cycling histories.[107] More specifically, cycling clubs notoriously barred African American bicyclists who were at the same time grotesquely mocked in droves of racist articles and images published in the popular press.[108] This was despite—or perhaps in spite of— the unprecedented success of bicycle racer "Major" Taylor (Marshall Walter Taylor), who is widely considered the first African American sports star. Black cyclists were explicitly banned from the LAW in 1894 and thoroughly marginalized in a period that defined bicycling, and by extension personal and public mobility, as an exclusive privilege reserved for middle- to upper-class whites. Andrew Ritchie, a renowned cycling historian and biographer of Major Taylor, contextualizes the ban on black mobility as part of a broader pattern of institutionalized racism and violence against African Americans; he recalls that the 1890s—the decade of the bicycle boom—saw more than 1,200 black men lynched by "hanging, burning, shooting and beating," and this is only the number of incidents that were officially recorded.[109] Throughout the twentieth century and up until the present day, the institutional constraints on black mobility—like racism itself—are and were inadequately interrogated, inexcusably permitted, and, indeed, rarely acknowledged as such. As a case in point, the League of American Bicyclists (LAB, the successor to the LAW) never bothered to officially revoke the ban on African American membership until former League president Earl F. Jones—an African American attorney and Louisville bicycling advocate—passed a resolution to overturn the rule (and posthumously grant Major Taylor official League membership) on June 5, 1999.[110] Jones's tenure as League president clearly suggests that the racist law was long abandoned as part of official League policy, but the fact that no LAB administrators, board members, or instructors ever formally raised the issue prior to 1999 is itself indicative of the manner in which white privilege enables individuals and organizations to avoid confronting the history and entrenchment of racism. Yet Jones's resolution, as well as a statement he made just prior to its passage, illustrates the very real need for bicyclists to grapple with this racist legacy, if for no other reason than to address the seemingly forgotten, or invisible, factors contributing to habitually low African American involvement in cycling organizations, cycle sports, and bicycle transportation more broadly. "Finally, I hope that the League, by taking this step, can lead cycling into more diverse and representative participation," Jones stated upon the resolution's passage.[111]

Shifting Gears

As noted in the previous few sections, cultural norms and discourses played a distinct role in framing the cyclist as a human/machine hybrid, a rational actor, a national figure, and a thoroughly modern individual who embodied all the characteristics of an emerging auto-mobile paradigm in the nineteenth-century United States. The cyclist was simultaneously a symbol, an icon, and a subject of intellectual speculation who precedes and prefigures the driver—the mobile citizen par excellence—as a central figure in popular discourses of the twentieth century. The construction of the cyclist was not just metaphorical: his or her body was made to act in accordance with a set of ideas and cultural discourses that ultimately defined the meaning of autonomous mobility as both a moral compass and a proper way of physically moving (sitting, pedaling, and steering) through space. "Discourses," as Tim Cresswell observes, "have their own geographies—their brute materialities that act on the bodies of those being constructed."[112] The production of racist, sexist, and xenophobic discourses by elite cycling clubs and organizations is a clear illustration of how this process works, inasmuch as it dictates not only which bodies are granted the status of cyclist but also, and more fundamentally, which people were even allowed to mount and operate bicycles in the first place.

At the same time cycling organizations effectively reproduced dominant ideologies and hegemonic cultural norms, the mass popularity of bicycling in the 1890s began to erode some of the social distinctions previously associated with bicycle ownership and use. Richard Harmond's study of this period indicates that the number of cyclists in the United States increased from approximately 150,000 in 1890 to 4 million in 1896.[113] As noted earlier, this transformation prompted Americans to hail the bicycle as a "social revolutionizer that never had an equal."[114] Europeans similarly contextualized the bicycle in epic terms, with French enthusiasts proclaiming the bicycle's influence as "more violent than any revolution."[115] Clearly this was no revolution in the ·political sense, but access to the bicycle was significant for many Americans and Europeans who were otherwise constrained in their mobility. More specifically, it marked the first time that women and non-elites had the ability to utilize personal transportation technologies in their daily lives and to operate them at their own discretion. Trains were certainly accessible throughout the nineteenth century, but in addition to being vehicles for mass mobility (rather than individual mobility), they also stigmatized and spatially segregated the working classes from their wealthier traveling companions. Railroad historian Wolfgang Schivelbusch notes that up until the 1840s English train travelers of the lower classes were "regarded not as recipients of passenger service but as freight goods," forced to ride in uncovered boxcars before the Gladstone Act of 1844 required third- and fourth-class carriages to be covered.[116] Rail transportation in the United States was similarly class segregated by the 1860s, though to a much lesser (or much less obvious) extent than the English system.[117] In the same way that bicycling allowed women to travel without male chaperons and transcend the ideological/spatial parameters of domesticity, it gave workers the possibility of traveling without both the connotation and physical experience of being a second-, third-, or fourth-class citizen.

The high cost of the bicycle deterred its use as a vehicle for the masses in the late 1890s, but as Dave Horton points out, this situation changed rapidly: "The late Victorian age saw the beginnings of the bicycle's gradual transition from a high status vehicle of the rich and leisured classes to one increasingly affordable to 'ordinary' people."[118] Nevertheless, class discrimination—like sexism—did not simply disappear with greater access to the bicycle, as so many popular accounts from this period would have us believe. Elite men took great pride in their ownership over cycling, and as pioneers of the hobby they sought to keep it purified from the metaphorical stench of the "great unwashed." Sylvester Baxter makes this point abundantly clear in an article published in *The Arena*, in 1892: "The fact that [the bicycle's] use began with gentlemen has set a standard which has been maintained. Although it has created a new branch of athletes . . . the wheelman's sport, like yachting, has never been *tainted with associations of low repute,* and it has remained clean and honorable."[119] Class tensions surrounded bicycling in the early 1890s—and this was not an entirely new phenomenon; elite English tricyclists arrogantly distinguished themselves from the lower class of bicyclists in the previous decade, particularly from "mechanics, day-laborers, chimney-sweeps [and] costers."[120] The Tricycle Union, formed by the wealthy members of the London Society in 1882, put pressure on British city governments to exclude bicycles from parks and made no bones about their disdain for the blossoming bicycle culture in England: "It is desired by most tricyclists to separate themselves entirely from the bicyclists, who are a disgrace to the pastime, while tricycling includes Princes, Princesses, Dukes [and] Earls. It is plain that the tricyclists are altogether a better class than the bicyclists, and require better accommodation on tours."[121] Fearing both the loss of their own material exceptionalism and the wider threat posed by working-class mobility, many bicyclists in the United States also reacted negatively to the popularization of the bicycle while simultaneously championing the machine as the great leveler of society. David Herlihy highlights this backlash in a magazine editorial from 1895: "Cycling will die out altogether with the fashionable element given the extent to which the sport has been taken up by the *hoi polloi.*"[122] Despite, or perhaps in spite of, elites' collective disdain for the poor, bicycling became a new way for people to travel, socialize, and in some cases, address the plight of the working class itself.

Cycling for a Redder Tomorrow

By the mid-1890s, cycling became "linked with new social movements in more concrete ways," most notably in socialist organizations throughout Europe.[123] German cyclists, for example, organized a socialist cycling club called the Worker's Cycling Federation: Solidarity (Arbeiter-Radfahrerbund Solidarität) in 1896, and by 1913 membership in Solidarität included more than 150,000 who declared themselves the "Enlightenment Patrols of Social Democracy" and the "Red Hussars of the Class Struggle."[124] The federation played an important role in politicizing German workers at a time when local and regional governments banned workers' organizations and unions, and while the exact political influence of the group is unclear, it is evident that they explicitly incorporated the bicycle into a narrative of class struggle.[125] For example, Anne-Katrin Ebert recalls a newspaper story from 1903 where Solidarität is praised for reporting the results of parliamentary elections independently of the bourgeois press: "In this portrayal, the sweaty, dusty cyclists who had traveled for hours tirelessly to report the results of their party to their people were a symbol of the efforts and the struggle of the working class and, at the same time, they represented the emancipation of the working class."[126] Solidarität facilitated recreational events and bike tours and organized a number of collectively owned and operated institutions, including a chain of bicycle shops, a bicycle factory, a biweekly newspaper called *The Worker-Cyclist,* and a network of restaurants and repair stations.[127] It was their flair for theatrics, however, that catches the attention of cycling historians: Solidarität evidently hosted parades on their own behalf where they blazed through the packed streets en masse, throwing political propaganda at the crowds.[128] The cyclists sped through the crowds in order to evade identification because German authorities enforced strict bicycling laws and had a general disdain for socialism. James McGurn writes, "The freedom, mobility and privacy of the bicycle were more than the authorities would tolerate. Significantly, Germany was one of the first nations to provide bicycles for its policemen and local militias—agents of social control."[129] In the years just prior to the first Nazi government it was estimated that Solidarität had more than 330,000 members, making it the (then) largest cycling organization in the world.[130]

While the mid-1890s witnessed emerging socialist support for cycling in Germany, the links between bicycling and socialism were arguably most pronounced in England's Clarion Cycling Club. Socialists in Birmingham founded the club in 1894, naming it after Robert Blatchford's popular newspaper, *The Clarion.*[131] Blatchford, who wrote under the name Nunquam, started the paper in 1891 as a way to articulate a non-dogmatic vision of socialism that David Prynn calls an "alternative way of life."[132] Englishmen and Englishwomen inspired by Blatchford's politics formed a variety of social clubs under the Clarion banner, using them to recruit socialists and bring like-minded people together. In 1895 the Clarion Cycling Club held their first national meeting, where it was decided that the main purpose of the association was to spread goodwill as a means to create a unified socialist front. Tom Groom, the driving impetus of the club, spoke to the marriage of cycling and socialism at this meeting:

> We are not neglectful of our Socialism. . . . To get healthy exercise is not necessarily to be selfish. To attend to the social side of our work is not necessarily to neglect the more serious part. To spread good fellowship is the most important work of Clarion Cycling Clubs. Then, perhaps, the "One Socialist Party" would be more possible and we should get less of those squabbles among Socialists which make me doubt whether they understand even the first part of their name.[133]

In addition to putting the social in socialism, Clarion Cycling Clubs pedaled their political message throughout England as cyclists sold, or gave away, thousands of *Clarion* newspapers and hundreds of thousands of copies of Blatchford's essay "Merrie England."[134] The Clarion organization even created a publication called *The Scout* to specifically instruct socialist workers and cycling propagandists (known as Clarion Scouts or "Clarionettes") as to how they could more effectively target and mobilize workers with their message. Dennis Pye, a historian of the club, writes:

> The importance of the bicycle in the work of the Scouts was emphasized by the paper's editor, who suggested the compiling of a list of speakers able to cycle twenty to fifty miles on Saturdays and Sundays to address public meetings in towns and villages which had, as yet, no Socialist organizations. Cyclist supporters could paste walls and fences with stickers bearing Socialist slogans, these being obtainable from the Clarion Office in London.[135]

Bicycling continued to play an important role in the mobilization of English socialists as the number of Clarion Cycling Club chapters grew to approximately seventy by the end of 1897. Cycling was further integrated with the activities of both the Clarion Socialist Choir and a traveling propaganda caravan started by Julia Dawson, who wrote under the pen name Mrs. D. J. Myddleton-Worrall.[136] Dawson, a feminist and socialist, coordinated a thirteen-week Clarion Women's Van Tour that featured feminist speakers who also distributed socialist literature; Clarion cyclists accompanied the rides to support to the feminist caravan and to supplement the propaganda effort.

Chapters of the Clarion Cycling Club continued to advocate the socialist cause during the first part of the twentieth century but gradually shifted their focus away from propaganda and agitation toward the promotion of socialism through the "international fraternity of sport."[137] Coincidentally, the club's de-emphasis on political activity happened at a time when the English working class actually started to take up bicycling in large numbers. Indeed, while the Clarion Clubs may have been ardent devotees to the socialist cause, their constituency and disposition was largely middle class: a situation that inevitably caused friction between cyclists and the actual laborers who viewed cycling as bourgeois activity. Dave Horton specifically notes that the Clarion's "anti-urban, romantic, back-to-nature outlook seems to have appealed more to middle-class socialists than working-class people."[138] And though it would appear that Clarion cyclists were out of sync with the day-to-day rhythms of working-class life, it is a mistake to simply dismiss them on such grounds. Indeed, the coupling of cycling and politics in other European countries speaks to a pervasive dissensus over what constituted authentic socialist endeavors, particularly when it came to sports. For example, Stefano Pivato recalls that Italian socialists initially expressed deep anxieties about cycling due to its association with leisure culture and bourgeois values; the younger wave of Italian socialists rejected sporting clubs as late as 1909, referring to sports—including cycling—as a "violent muscular reaction to the productive inactivity of the rich classes."[139] But other Italian socialists disagreed, arguing that the bicycle was, in fact, a class leveler and a beneficial tool for disciplining vigorous revolutionaries.[140] Following the 1912 National Congress of the Young Socialists, Pivato notes that more than seven hundred anti-nationalist, socialist cyclists paraded near Bologna, laying the foundations for what eventually became the Ciclisti Rossi, or "Red Cyclists."[141] Ciclisti Rossi officially formed in 1913 as part of an effort to link Italian socialism with sport, and like Clarion cyclists, they also coupled their activities with the dispersal of political literature: *Cicolo Avanti,* the club's newspaper, specifically promoted the bicycle as a vehicle "created for the benefit of the organized masses of workers."[142]

Following Horton, I believe the importance of the Clarion cyclists lies in not only their widespread promotion of socialist politics but also the way they expanded the "geographical and political horizons of both the middle class socialist cycling preachers and the working classes who would later embrace cycling."[143] In other words, Clarion cyclists increased the range of the socialist network in England and simultaneously innovated a new technique for the dissemination of socialist literature. And though Robert Blatchford's politics eventually grew increasingly conservative, racist, and militaristic during the 1890s, his essay "Merrie England" was nonetheless an inspirational, and thoroughly readable, socialist text that reached droves of new readers via the Clarion Scouts.[144] Eugene Debs, famed American socialist and co-founder of the International Workers of the World, wrote the following of Blatchford's seminal essay:

> His is one of the most simple, attractive and convincing writers on Socialism in all the world. Hundreds of thousands of copies of "Merrie England" have been sold and given away and the demand still continues. The work of Mr. Blatchford is specially adapted to beginners. He has the rare faculty of making himself interesting to the workingman and workingwoman, addressing himself to them in their own simple language and illustrating his argument in the same simple and convincing fashion. Robert Blatchford and his writings have contributed materially to the spread of Socialism in this country and are justly entitled to the grateful acknowledgment of the American movement.[145]

Rather than simply serving as a mouthpiece for Blatchford's paper, Clarion cyclists were part of a wider movement that sought to bridge the gap between radical politics and everyday life by putting a "*prefigurative* socialist politics" into practice: a way of "being the change they wanted to see in the world," to poach a well-worn phrase from Gandhi.[146] Prynn elaborates this point in his analysis of the Clarion movement:

> For all these organizations, a change in social values was seen as a necessary precondition for a more general improvement in the condition of society. To make a healthier and more just society, it was first necessary to make people "better," to alter human nature. In attempting to do this, it was believed that community living, fellowship and the expansion of the human personality would play a vital part, and it was thus towards these ends that their activities were directed.[147]

One can read a number of the cycling club's practices into this political/cultural project, including their advocacy for women's rights and their explicit coupling of gender and class politics—a notable achievement at a time when cycling clubs were dismissive of feminism and generally unfriendly, if not hostile, to female membership. The Clarions' advocacy for "fresh air and the countryside" was also progressive inasmuch as they promoted nature in slightly different terms than their middle- and upper-class counterparts: "Springtime is here and once again we turn our minds to wheels and sprockets and our backs on smoke town, let out on the open road, like true Bohemians casting off the shackles of conventionality."[148] Whereas most leisure cyclists in both England and the United States simply perpetuated anti-urban escapism through their countryside endeavors, the Clarion cyclists used the same experiences to frame, and ultimately support, their political agenda: "The frequent contrasts a cyclist gets between the beauties of nature and the dirty squalor of towns makes him more anxious than ever to *abolish the present system*."[149] In other words, the Clarion cyclists adopted a similar "fresh air" discourse promulgated by elites but they did so to argue for the radical transformation of the very conditions from which they sought refuge. Bicycling was not only privileged as a means to these ends; it was also seen as key component of an idealized socialist society.

Organizing Space, Escaping the City

Socialism and cycling may have found a convenient expression in both Solidarität and the Clarion Cycling Club, but the easy relationship between bicyclists and socialists was by no means universal. Unlike their comrades in Europe, the working class in the United States arguably had better access to cheap and/or used bicycles in the late 1890s but seemed to take little interest in using bikes to organize workers, recruit socialists, or create socialist sports clubs.[150] Robert Smith recalls that the Socialist Labor Party of America founded a Socialist Wheelmen's Club in 1898 with the expressed purpose of distributing political literature along routes from Boston to New York City, but there is little known about this "bicycle brigade," save the address of their headquarters and the look of their uniforms.[151] Cyclists in the United States certainly gave lip service to the idea of bicycles spreading equality, but the potential integration of bicycling and class struggle was not widely discussed in publications of the period. In fact, McShane writes that socialists in New York City actually led measures to fight bicycle traffic and opposed paving streets with asphalt to deter cyclists from using neighborhood streets as thoroughfares.[152] Preserving the traditional function of the street as a commons was a high priority for the predominantly immigrant populations who used these public spaces to socialize and play. In densely populated neighborhoods like the Lower East Side of Manhattan, defiant cyclists displayed little regard for such socio-cultural and spatial norms, thereby earning the scorn of the locals. Children, in particular, "showed their resentment of having their turf invaded by sprinkling glass on the street, or even stoning bicycle 'scorchers.'"[153] James McGurn makes an analogous point about class tensions that sprung from the intrusion of cyclists into German neighborhoods; he recalls the biting commentary of Wilhelm Wolf's cycling guide, published in 1890:

> Which cyclist does not have daily experience, especially when riding through city suburbs *breathed on by Social Democracy,* of unruly urchins dancing about in front of his wheel, throwing sticks and stones, being foul-mouthed and more besides. And often many of the adults in these districts, standing idly at their doors on Sundays and holidays, are not averse to such behavior.[154]

Cycling required an extensive ordering of spaces and geographies: it was a means of taming both the "unruly urchins" of city streets and the unruliness of the landscape itself, whether by default or design. Road building was one of the most crucial, if not the most visible, parts of this process in the United States and the League of American Wheelmen played a paramount role in the dual push for good roads and a federal highway program.[155] Traffic laws, which were greatly enhanced through the lobbying power of the LAW, further promoted bicycle transportation by rationalizing the street through communication; laws facilitated a discursive ordering of space that worked in concert with the material directives of road building. Collectively, these processes enabled cyclists to assert a new and seemingly natural order of personal mobility: "In the ultimate view of both the law and common-sense, man has the primary right upon the highway, and all animals of burden must yield, if there is occasion for yielding, to man. The pedestrian first, the man on any vehicle propelled by himself next, beasts afterward. This is the fundamental principle, which is as ancient as the body of the law."[156] Road building served important, pragmatic functions that should not be overlooked or dismissed in a historical assessment of U.S. transportation practices, but it was also deeply implicated in the logic of modernist evangelism: a cultural paradigm as consumed with the idea of civilizing native lands through technology and Christianity as it was concerned with the utilitarian trappings of getting from point A to point B.[157] James Carey argues that the moral meaning of transportation and communication—which one can clearly read into the good roads movement and the development of traffic law—were essentially one and the same: "the establishment and extension of God's kingdom on Earth."[158]

In addition to creating a would-be automobile infrastructure and bolstering the moral imperatives of Anglo expansionism, bicyclists' advocacy for road construction also contributed, albeit modestly, to an expanding "culture of suburbanization," despite Norcliffe's claim that there were no "bicycle suburbs."[159] Sylvester Baxter, for example, writes in 1892 that the bicycle was a leading factor in the development of "attractive suburbs," such as those outside of New York City: "Wherever there are good roads, there the wheelman will prefer to establish his home, and in New Jersey this consideration has been largely effective in giving to the Oranges a goodly proportion of their population."[160] Bicycling may have offered a convenient means of transportation for some suburbanites due to their close proximity to urban centers, but more important, it resonated with their desire to escape the perceived trappings of mass transit. Indeed, it effectively previews a cultural obsession with single-occupancy cars:

> For suburban commuters, the trolley ride contradicted all the values associated with the suburban dream. Trolleys were dirty, noisy, and overcrowded. It was impossible for middle-class riders to isolate themselves from fellow riders whom they perceived as social inferiors. Distancing themselves from blacks, immigrants, blue collar workers, and, in general those stereotyped as the "great unwashed," was often precisely why the middle classes had moved to the suburbs.[161]

The class-based desire to flee the city's "madding crowd," was a motivating factor in this period and part of a deeper escapist impulse that positions freedom as something explicitly attainable outside of the city limits.[162] Cycling was embraced in this capacity, in part, because it provided a way for urbanites to take refuge in the pleasures of the countryside: away from the dirty factories, crowded streets, and the general commotion of the poor urban populations who also called it home.[163]

Bicycling to the countryside was a way for people to enjoy the beauty and serenity of the natural world, though nature was typically revered in terms of what it did for the cyclist, namely, improving his or her mind, health, and morality. Indeed, cycling articles published throughout the 1880s and 1890s frequently argue that the best mental and physical qualities of man are brought about when he discovers the wonders of nature on a bicycle.[164] Access to the countryside was already commonplace following the development of the passenger train, but cyclists were particularly interested in the autonomy of traveling outside the fixed routes, rigid schedules, and physical confines of the train: "In contrast with this overwhelming experience of a technology that forced its rules upon the human being and imposed a distance between human being and environment, the bicycle was being portrayed as a type of technology that would allow humans to be in control again."[165] Bicyclists' interrelated desires for personal mobility, personal freedom, and a less mediated engagement with the aesthetics of nature ultimately, and quite ironically, helped to transform the natural geographies toward which they sought refuge from the city.[166] This combination began to cement the foundations of one of the key features of the auto-mobile paradigm: an instrumental view of both public and natural spaces. Nature, in other words, becomes valuable only insofar as it can be used, whether for group recreation or one's own leisure pursuits.

Landscaping

The countryside was obviously a real geographical space bicyclists traveled to in the 1890s, but this space was also produced by the act of cycling. Schivelbusch's assessment of train travel is an instructive point of comparison here because he is explicitly concerned with the effect of transportation technologies on the collective experience of space and time. According to his thesis, the high speed of train travel fundamentally distorted passengers' perception of the natural environment by inhibiting their ability to take in the details of their surroundings. At the same time, the train cultivated a new perspective that he calls the *panoramic view*: one that frames the landscape as an object to be aesthetically contemplated and appreciated, much like a painting.[167] This techno-aesthetic practice encouraged the objectification of the landscape and contributed to the development of a broader industrialized consciousness that frames space and time in the abstract.[168] Bicycling did not create the same subject/object split as the passenger train, but like train travel it facilitated a unique way of seeing that was both a literal vantage point as well as a conceptual framework that gave meaning to one's point of view, and by extension, one's form of mobility. An aptly titled 1895 magazine piece called "Some Thoughts on Landscape" hints at some of the ways in which bicycling constructs the landscape as both a subject of auto-mobile desire and an object of the bicyclist's gaze:

> Our high pressure, our covetous greed of the minute, have placed the bicycle upon the road in its thousands; and out of evil there has in this way come good, for it is to the green country that the fevered youth of the nation race, with rustling rubber and sharp-sounding bell. As they rush through the air and flash past the village and field, *there is borne in upon them the educational germ of a love for landscape;* they see, and they cannot help noting, the contrast between smoke-grimed cities and "fresh woods and pastures new."[169]

Here one can see bicycling contributing to a specifically aesthetic conceptualization of nature; one that resonated with a population that sought to preserve landscapes through photography. Indeed, several companies produced and marketed cameras explicitly for cyclists, including models that could be mounted directly to the bicycle itself. The Rudge-Whitworth Company even developed a rather cumbersome Photo-Tricycle that was pitched to *Scientific American* readers in terms of its ability to unite the goals of cycling and photography: "How many times has it not happened that the excursionist has regretted his inability to *fix the landscapes* and curious scenes that were unveiling themselves to his eyes?"[170]

The correlation between bicycling and photography is an interesting one because both practices framed and fixed the landscape in mutually reinforcing ways. Photography, for example, preserves an image of the landscape, but this representation arguably becomes powerful through its ability to reproduce a myth about the relationship between man and nature, not just the scenery. That is to say, by implicitly documenting the presence of photographers in the wild—as in the actual people responsible for snapping the pictures—landscape photography effectively mythologizes the photographer's tangible experience of the great outdoors: it is a way of using pictures to insert oneself, or more often ourselves, into an epic narrative of the frontier, God's kingdom, the wonders of nature, and so on. Bicycles not only facilitated access to some of the very spots that made scenic photography possible; they also allowed cyclists to experience the same vantage points and perspectives without the aid of the camera—hence an 1897 article that describes cycling itself as a way of composing an "outdoor picture."[171] Indeed, while the camera may preserve a representation of nature, the bicycle actually transforms the idea of nature into what Aaron Wilcher calls a "corporeal reality." Following Leo Marx, he argues that this bodily experience is culturally performative, in that cyclists actually "practice the spatial discourse of the 'middle landscape,' an urban cultural (con)text for the places 'outside' the metropolis, outside the

The bicyclist gaze? *(Courtesy of the Jim Langley Collection.)*

suburb."[172] Cyclists, if one follows the logic in the 1890s, create this experience with each and every turn of their cranks, thereby preserving the authenticity of the natural experience itself. In doing so, they transform the bicycle from a mere transportation device into a landscaping machine.

Tourism

Cyclists praised the scenic landscapes of the countryside and the "tonic influences" of fresh air and sunshine, but there was a palatable tension between their longing for nature and the grounding of the city.[173] Tobin's classic study of recreational cycling posits that bicyclists of the period were not actually anti-urban, but markedly pro-urban: they never wanted to be without the conveniences of the modern city. The areas just outside the city/suburb became an extension of the urban paradigm by way of the cyclists' roads, road maps, travel guides, and their collective desire for personal leisure and recreation. This disposition helped to cultivate modern tourism by juxtaposing the luxuries of modern Caucasian life with glimpses of the native world. Tobin suggests that the "touring apparatus" constructed by, and for, bicyclists provided them with the dual assurance that middle-/upper-class services would be available wherever they went, and that "undesirables" could be avoided by traveling designated routes with fellow bicycle tourists.[174] Bicycle tourism subsequently facilitated the development of hotels, inns, repair shops, and restaurants on popular travel routes, and the LAW exercised a great deal of muscle in forcing such institutions to cater to the tastes of their members. In an article published in 1896, a representative of the New York division of the LAW describes an arrangement whereby local establishments gave discounts to bicycle tourists in exchange for favorable coverage in the LAW's popular travel guides. The entire description reeks of exploitation, particularly because the author positions the fickle cyclist as the Darwinian judge and jury of family businesses: "Wheelmen are quick to discern and to appreciate the comfort of a well-kept inn, and are not slow to condemn the slovenly attempts of an incompetent host. And so it is that the fittest will survive, and badly kept hotels will inevitably lose the cyclists' patronage."[175]

Not all cyclists sought the comforts of traditional bicycle tourism, however. A spirit of adventurism simultaneously ran through this period and Thomas Stevens's "Around the World" bicycle odyssey captured the individualist ethos of cycling to a tee. Beginning on April 22, 1884, he published installments of his first-person travelogue until he arrived in Yokohama, Japan, in December 1886.[176] While Stevens offers a slightly nuanced, if not savagely racist view of "the other" from his position as a privileged bicycle tourist in the United States, his travels abroad go a step further by hinting at the ways in which bicycle tourism was largely informed by, and often explicitly articulated to, the ethics of expansionism, colonialism, and white supremacy.[177] For example, his meticulous visual interrogation and pseudo-biological analysis of an Afghani neighborhood reveal some of the key Orientalist themes that define not only his positionality as a privileged/entitled white tourist but also the role this subject position plays in the very construction of Western identity itself. It deserves to be quoted at length:

A small gathering of wild-looking men are collected at the landing-place, and my astonishment is awakened by the familiar figure of a Celestial among the crowd. He is a veritable John Chinaman—beardless face, queue, almond eyes, and everything complete. The superior thriftiness of the Chinaman over the Afghans needs no further demonstration than the ocular evidence that among them all he wears by far the best and the tidiest clothes. In this, not less than in the strong Mongolian type of face, is he a striking figure among the people. John Chinaman is a very familiar figure to me, and I regard this strange specimen with almost as great interest as if I had thus unexpectedly met a European. His grotesque figure and dress, representing, so it seems to me at the moment, a speck of civilization among the barbarousness of my surroundings, is quite a relief to the senses. A closer investigation, however, on the bank, while waiting for the guide's horse, reveals the fact that he is far from being the John

Chinaman of Chinatown, San Francisco. Instead of hailing from the rice-fields of Quangtung, this fellow is a native of Kashga-ria, a country almost as wild as Afghanistan. A moment's scrutiny of his face removes him as far from the civilized seaboard Celestials of our acquaintance as is the Zulu warrior from the plantation-darky of the South. Except for the above-mentioned comparative neatness of appearance, it is very evident that the Mongolian is every bit as wild as the Afghans about him.[178]

The colonizing impetus built into the "tourist gaze" of the cyclist was evident not only in Stevens's widely read travelogue but also in cycling guides, touring narratives, and other images published in popular magazines. Bicycle companies throughout the United States, Canada, and England proudly displayed advertisements featuring racist stereotypes of Native Americans as well as the interconnected themes of modernity and imperialism.[179] Historian Frederick Alderson also describes how the bicycle was explicitly written into adventure stories in the 1890s, no doubt to express the clash of modernity/civilization with the ancient/savage cultures of the world. He uncritically recalls a story published in *The Strand,* from 1899, in which a blonde heroine narrowly escapes death in Rhodesia by the grace of her "iron horse," a machine that apparently "played not a little on the *savages'* superstitious fears." In the throes of the getaway, her male companion manages to ride full speed up a hill, steering with only his left hand, since his right hand is used to fire "three shots from his revolver into the nearest of their *naked black pursuers.*"[180]

The desire to simultaneously admire and discipline natural environments—and by extension, their aboriginal populations—is one of the central tensions surrounding recreational cycling and bicycle tourism in the late nineteenth century. Each of these practices produced a distorted view of natural space, as they were both prompted by a culturally loaded desire for an authentic experience, whether escaping the confines of the city, creating a snapshot of the landscape, or preserving the feeling of being out there in nature. Gabrielle Barnett poignantly speaks to this tension in her analysis of the Redwood Highway, the 273-mile stretch between San Francisco and Eureka that, upon being built, gave motorists an opportunity to "experience premodern vision in select sites even as they enjoyed the benefits of ultramodern transportation on the landscape level."[181] By transcending the industrialized consciousness of the city and the railroad, automobile travel facilitated the sublime experience of the redwoods and perpetuated nostalgia for an "idealized preindustrial America."[182] She applies Walter Benjamin's concept of the *wish image* to claim that the slow pace of this specific highway created an aesthetic with which travelers could reconcile culture and nature by "envisioning emergent modernity through images of a lost past."[183] While Barnett reflects on early automobile tourism, she ironically summarizes the entire ethos of bicycle tourism as described by cyclists in the decades prior to the automobile or the Redwood Highway. This is less a critique of her work as much as it points to the fundamental role that bicycling played in organizing both this powerful visual disposition and a human-scaled experience of technological mobility that, for better or worse, ultimately became the basis of arguments made for driving. And while I would argue that the bicycle, not the automobile, combined "the best of nostalgic and modern ways of seeing," Barnett provides a way to conceptualize bicycle tourism as an attempt to resolve the cultural and spatial tensions of modernity and the pre-modern era.[184] More important, her analysis of automobility demonstrates how the leisure cultures of cycling and driving were barely distinguishable in their orientation toward the natural world: each positioned the singular driver as the visual/mobile surveyor of an objectified landscape; one in which the native populations are effectively erased so as not to detract from the wonders of modern mobility and an otherwise pristine view of the empty wilderness.

Conclusion

By materializing the promise of technological mobility and the desire for individual autonomy, bicyclists ushered in the automotive age at a more profound level than one can simply link through the good roads movement or the transition from bicycle manufacturing to automotive production. Indeed, the emergence of the car was not a matter of technological progress or evolution, just as it was not exclusively due to the development of adequate roads, traffic laws, or effective marketing. Rather, automobiles provided an almost logical solution to the culture of mobility forged by cyclists and the bicycle industry in the nineteenth century: a set of ideas, discourses, and practices that eventually displaced the bicycle as the premier automobile in the United States.

In addition, while the dominant paradigm of this early manifestation of automobility privileged cycling within the domain of the male Anglo-elite, bicycling was not simply a practice used to affirm the dominant social order.[185] The bicycle, in many cases, revealed the possibilities of individual mobility to such a profound extent that it became an apt metaphor for independence and iconic signifier of freedom itself. Feminists championed it as a source of empowerment and more literally as a means to escape both the stifling realm of forced domesticity and the watchful eyes of male chaperons. European socialists similarly embraced the bicycle as a symbol of liberation, a means for advocating radical social change, and a tool for articulating a cultural politics of the Left. So while bicycling fostered an auto-mobile disposition befitting an eventual car culture, it also created new opportunities for people to experience the pleasures of a radically efficient, non-polluting form of personal transportation that would not be duplicated in the car itself.

CHAPTER 3

Vélorutionaries and the Right to the (Bikeable) City

The common bicycle is emerging as an environmental weapon.

—Casey Burko, "Bicycle Riders to Parade for Ecological Reform," *Chicago Tribune*, 1970

There are several reasons why a bike saddle makes a fine soapbox, protesters say.

—Joshua Robin, "Bike National Convention," *New York Newsday*, 2004

If the bicycle magnified the inherently political tensions of mobility in the late nineteenth century, the automobile was instrumental in amplifying them to a previously unimaginable degree. The car became both a blessing and a curse in the early twentieth century as urban and rural populations in the United States either embraced the freedom of driving or were forced to adapt to the car's spatiotemporal trajectories. As automobility became exclusively redefined and repackaged around the car, the cyclists who played a crucial role in constructing this multifaceted system were either eager to get behind the wheel or eager to get out of its way. Small groups of bicyclists in Europe, Canada, and the United States eventually grew weary of this reductive binary in the 1960s and 1970s, choosing instead to position the bicycle as the centerpiece of an emerging critique of the automobile and car culture. This eclectic assortment of environmentalists, political activists, cycling enthusiasts, urban planners, and utilitarian commuters appropriated the bicycle as a symbol of resistance and a tool for thinking through the prospects of non-motorized transportation and pedal powered mobility. These vélorutionaries do not subscribe to a singular vision of the role bicycling can or should play in society, but what they share is a collective disposition that sees bicycle transportation as part of a substantive, even radical vision of cultural and political transformation. Activists involved with the Provo in Amsterdam, Transportation Alternatives in New York City, and Le Monde à Bicyclette in Montreal were among those who were not just riding bicycles but also theorizing them: thinking critically about the bicycle as a sociocultural and geopolitical technology. In doing so they brought cycling within the purview of environmentalism and urban reform, effectively highlighting the ideological, spatial, and environmental tensions of car culture by championing a competing vision of vélomobility whose core premises of pedal power, sustainability, and technology conviviality were as prescient then as they are instructive today. At once, these expressions of biketivism stirred people's imagination, prompted an intense backlash from politically conservative cyclists, revealed the prospects of alternative transportation advocacy, and ultimately laid the foundations for what is now an international movement of pro-bicycle activists. I draw attention to these efforts not to uncritically praise them, but to interrogate the complexities of an overarching technocultural project that is still unfolding.

The Automobile-Industrial Complex

Automobiles were relatively scarce in the United States until the 1920s, a decade in which the number of registered automobiles doubled from approximately 10 million to 20 million.[1] Henry Ford's innovative and arguably dehumanizing methods of mass production began to dislodge the automobile from its aristocratic roots, and his decision to lower the price of his vehicles in 1925 prompted many to make their first purchase. Approximately 1 in 4.5 Americans owned automobiles by 1929 and, as Catherine Gudis notes, the automobile became an "esteemed part of rural life as well as urban, helping to bring country folks the benefits of the city and helping city people escape to the country."[2] In addition, many city dwellers expressed frustration with monopolistic rail companies and crowded public transit systems (namely, streetcars) that left them eager for a modern alternative that the car seemed to fulfill. Yet despite the barrage of automobile and tourism discourses proclaiming the freedom of the road (or some variation thereof) in the 1920s and 1930s, the overwhelming majority of urbanites did not own cars and many people were resistant to the idea of transforming their entire way of life around them.

For the first few decades of the twentieth century, urban driving was often viewed as a nuisance and motorists were frequently seen as both a danger to public safety and a threat to the normal flows of everyday urban mobility.[3] Peter Norton offers a compelling history of the transition in urban driving from the 1900s to the 1930s, noting that both accidents and confrontations between pedestrians and motorists were common. And while courts tended to rule against city regulations impeding automobility, judges and juries took a favorable view of pedestrians' implicit right to the streets, almost always siding with them in cases stemming from car accidents in the 1910s and 1920s.[4] Indeed, Norton quotes a Chicago municipal judge from 1913 who ruled against a driver with the justification that "the streets of Chicago belong to the city, not to the automobilists."[5] Nevertheless, the economic opportunities seen in Ford's Model T and the burgeoning auto industry prompted financial/political elites to push for the inclusion of cars in major U.S. cities by the end of the 1910s—a clear indication that public opinion and public transportation were largely deemed irrelevant when weighed against their own desires for luxury goods and exhilarating hobbies (nearly 90 percent of urbanites did not own automobiles at the time). Mass media helped to grease the wheels of this transition by effectively shaping public opinion in favor of the auto industry, which in turn, reciprocated by purchasing large numbers of advertisements in their publications.[6] Major newspapers and magazines uncritically fawned over automobiles and unapologetically printed industry press releases and propaganda from motor clubs like the American Automobile Association (AAA).[7] Norton specifically highlights this cozy symbiosis to show how automotive interests and mass media contributed to the production of discourses that socially reconstructed the urban street for automobile traffic. For example, print media helped to introduce *jaywalker* into the public lexicon, a term that implied pedestrians acted like "hillbillies" wandering carelessly through the streets: "A *jay* was a country hayseed out of place in the city. By extension, a *jaywalker* was someone who did not know how to walk in the city."[8] The promulgation and eventual normalization of this term was one of the many ways in which urbanites were forced to comply with newly emerging rules, cultural norms, and discourses meant to discipline pedestrian mobility and redefine city streets as mere corridors for the automobile, as opposed to mixed-use environments for pedestrians, trolleys, and other vehicles.

Bicyclists played a central role in this rationalization of urban space, as noted in Chapter 2, but they were also among those forced to literally and figuratively concede the right-of-way to the car. Enthusiasm for cycling was still palpable at the dawn of the twentieth century, as evidenced by a traffic count—the only one of the period to include cyclists—taken in Minneapolis in 1906: bicycles accounted for "more than one-fifth of downtown traffic—four times as much as did cars."[9] Nevertheless, cyclists' became somewhat scarce in the wake of the bicycle industry's turn-of-the-century nosedive, a situation propelled by the collapse of Pope's American Bicycle Company in 1902.[10] In addition, many cyclists simply moved on to the new hobby of motoring, while most others lost interest in what was already being seen as a craze. Aside from the brief resurgence of cycling during the Depression, and to an extent during World War II, the telegraph messenger boys offer one of the few examples where bicycles were widely visible as utility vehicles in U.S. cities.[11] But even in this context bicycles were simply an efficient way for Western Union and their affiliates to maximize child labor in service of an emerging communications infrastructure: it did little to transform the public's perception of bicycle transportation, and if anything it further enhanced the association between the bicycle and boyhood (adult messengers rarely used bicycles for precisely this reason).[12] By 1941, 85 percent of bicycles produced in the United States were, in fact, children's "toys."

The 1920s and 1930s was a period when urban space was socially reconstructed for automobility, and also a pivotal moment in the nation's gradual though comprehensive shift away from bicycles and mass transit toward the full-blown car culture previewed in the Shell Oil *City of Tomorrow* campaign (1937) and the General Motors (GM) *Futurama* exhibit at the 1939 World's Fair, both designed by Norman Bel Geddes.[13] *Futurama*, which was part of the larger *Highways and Horizons* exhibit staged by GM, featured a massive highway infrastructure on par with those proposed by French architect/planner Le Corbusier in the 1920s and 1930s: an urban vision highlighted by concrete seas of high-speed motorized traffic. The World's Fair exhibit was the first introduction most Americans had to the idea of a vast highway system and it was clearly designed to inspire a collective sense of awe and an encounter with the "technological sublime."[14] If there was any doubt that the corporate-friendly U.S. government favored GM's model, this was put to rest when it published major reports outlining the prospects of analogous highway plans in 1939 and 1944.[15] Interestingly, representatives of Shell, GM, and the U.S. government all ignored Bel Geddes's suggestions—made in his book *Magic Motorways* and in meetings with project consultants—that it would actually be inefficient for people to utilize private cars within the city limits. His designs clearly composed the city within a network of highways, but he saw subway systems as the most practical and efficient solution for high-density urban transport.[16]

With the backing of major corporations and powerful public figures, the profit imperatives of auto-centric urban planning saw their truest expression not only in the fictitious realm of *Futurama* but also in the real-world actions of New York City planner Robert Moses, whose strategic architectural assault on New York City neighborhoods (particularly in the Bronx) functioned as the urban corollary for and a supplement to, the sort of ultramodern ethos ultimately enshrined in President Dwight Eisenhower's National Interstate and Defense Highways Act of 1956.[17] In the wake of smaller highway initiatives carried out since the turn of the century (most notably by urban planner Daniel Burnham), this act bolstered the status of the highway system as a pre-eminent national icon and secured unprecedented expenditures toward highway construction in the form of a permanent Highway Trust Fund—a multi-billion-dollar tax pool used to pay 90 percent of the costs for interstate highways and 50 percent for primary, state, and urban highways.[18] Eisenhower used the German highway system as a point of reference for what the U.S. infrastructure could/should become:

> After seeing the autobahns of modern Germany and knowing the asset those highways were to the Germans, I decided, as President, to put an emphasis on this kind of road building. . . . [T]he old convoy had started me thinking about good, two-lane highways, but Germany had made me see the wisdom of broader ribbons across the land.[19]

It is more than a little ironic that Dwight Eisenhower, Nazi fighter extraordinaire, was impressed by the efficiency of the autobahn and at once incapable of recognizing its deep implications in totalitarian logic.[20] While the autobahn project began prior to Adolf Hitler and was not solely reducible to the tenets of National Socialism, it was nonetheless ideological in its effects.[21] Historian Anne-Katrin Ebert recalls that Hitler's 1934 traffic law made the promotion of the car the highest goal of the Reich chancellor despite the fact that the estimated 16 million bicyclists outnumbered cars by roughly 8:1 in 1935. Thus, the priorities of Hitler's traffic edict asserted the rights of the wealthy minority at the expense of the rest of the people, who were later sold affordable cars built by slave workforces.[22] What Eisenhower called the "wisdom" of Germany's traffic plan was, in fact, a form of technological and spatial authoritarianism used to reposition the automobile as the exclusive focal point for urban mobility—a task largely achieved by coupling automobility with the promise of jobs (road building), economic prosperity, and the nationalist/expansionist mythos of *Lebensraum,* or "living space." Drawing comparisons between American automobility and Nazism—or Italian fascism, for that matter—might seem like a cheap way to build a case against the former, something akin to damning antiwar protesters for being un-American. However, this comparison is instructive inasmuch as it speaks to the similarly intertwined militarist/capitalist logic at work in the development of the U.S. highway system under Eisenhower:[23] that is to say, a comprehensive political project buttressed by the ideological articulation of mobility to nationalism, public defense, job creation, economic growth, and a technologically updated version of the frontier thesis—a uniquely American version of *Lebensraum* informed by the ethos of modernity, the mythos of the Wild West, and the corporate/religious philosophy embodied in Henry Ford's appeal for drivers to experience "God's great open spaces."[24]

Massive postwar expenditures on highway infrastructure cemented the automobile's centrality in U.S. mobility with over $55 billion in Highway Trust funds spent on the interstate system alone between 1956 and the end of 1972. Federal financing for mass transit was virtually nonexistent until money was set aside in the Housing Act of 1961, followed by the Urban Mass Transportation Act of 1964, a piece of legislation providing roughly $375 million over a three-year period—a figure paling in comparison to the billions devoted to highway construction.[25] It was not until 1973 that the Highway Trust fund was tapped for mass transit expenditures (minus funds for the actual operating costs, which were dropped under the threat of Nixon's veto), and the creation of an analogous Mass Transit Account was similarly postponed until 1983. Another eight years would pass before the federal government signed off on the Intermodal Surface Transportation Efficiency Act (ISTEA), one of the first pieces of comprehensive legislation to call for the inclusion of national pedestrian and cycling plans in state transportation planning. In other words, the first time walking and bicycling were seriously recognized as national/federal priorities, in terms of funding and the scope of the policy, was more than a century after the invention of the automobile. Yet according to the National Center for Bicycling and Walking, more than 40 percent of all state Departments of Transportation had not even complied with ISTEA's most basic requirement as of 2003: to develop a statewide, long-range plan for bicycles and pedestrians.[26]

The postwar redevelopment of the United States was problematic not only because it helped transform the metropolis into an *auto*polis but also because simultaneously it facilitated both mass suburbanization at home and the geopolitical policies necessary to ensure steady supplies of oil from abroad.[27] Tragically, these processes occurred almost immediately following a period when public transportation and walking were common, when more than half of U.S. car owners claimed they could do without their cars, and when there were more than 12 million bicycles in use by 1948, up from 9 million in 1940.[28] By contrast, cycling continued to find a place in everyday European life, particularly in England, where the cycling industry thrived and bicycles were widely used for both transportation and recreation prior to, and following, World War II.[29] Lewis Mumford was among those who spoke to the problem of U.S. automobility as early as the 1950s, seeing cars not as the end result of technological Darwinism but as a problem to be remedied. In addition to penning books on the subject, he used his "Sky Line" column in the *New Yorker* to wage a public battle against auto-centric planning and, more specifically, Robert Moses's catastrophically myopic vision of New York City as a driver's paradise.[30] In 1963, he stated:

The motorcar shapes and forms. Mutilates and deforms might be better words. We have the naive belief that we can satisfy the demands of the automobile by building more expressways, building bigger expressways, by widening existing streets, by trimming sidewalks. We are exchanging the meaningful and varied life of the cities for our increasingly monotonous life on wheels. The heart of the city should be served chiefly by rapid transit, buses, taxis and above all the human foot. The choice is clear and urgent: *Does the city exist for people, or for motorcars?*[31]

Jane Jacobs brought a similar set of questions to bear on the issue of transportation, but unlike Mumford, she did not see cars as the primary impediment to sound urban planning or a more orderly public sphere. Rather, she posed the problem in terms of the urban planning paradigm itself, specifically the assumption that cities could, or should, be designed in accordance with a grand plan or master narrative:

Automobiles are often conveniently tagged as the villains responsible for the ills of cities and the disappointments and futilities of city planning. But the destructive effects of automobiles are much less a cause than a symptom of our incompetence at city building. Of course planners, including the highwaymen with fabulous sums of money and enormous powers at their disposal, are at a loss to make automobiles and cities compatible with one another. They do not know what to do with automobiles in cities because they do not know how to plan for workable and vital cities anyhow—with or without automobiles.[32]

Jacobs viewed the chaotic rhythms and fluctuations of cities (especially neighborhoods) as implicit, vital parts of urban life that were either denied, or more tragically, conceived as obstacles to effective urban planning and development. She saw automobility in tension with the needs of diverse cities but she was clearly less interested in damning cars than in examining the possibilities for what cities could become: a project, according to her, that required the "attrition of automobiles" and more important, a renunciation of the paradigm facilitating car culture.

Mumford and Jacobs often disagreed and conceptualized automobility in rather different terms, but their mutual disdain for Robert Moses was clearly tied to his belief in its inevitability. Le Corbusier's auto-centric planning projects provoked equally impassioned critiques from Parisians in the 1950s, particularly from the group of artists/politicos associated with the Situationist International. The situationists, as they are widely known, abhorred the centrality of cars in urban design because, like Jacobs, they saw it as a symbol of a much larger problem: a spatio-cultural arrangement designed to suppress human spontaneity and willful participation in the city's construction. In the "Situationist Thesis on Traffic," Guy Debord writes:

> To want to redesign architecture to accord with the needs of the present massive and parasitical existence of private automobiles reflects the most unrealistic misapprehension of where the real problems lie. . . . It is not a matter of opposing the automobile as an evil in itself. It is its extreme concentration in the cities that has led to the negation of its function. Urbanism should certainly not ignore the automobile, but even less should it accept it as its central theme. It should reckon on gradually phasing it out.[33]

The parallels between Debord's ideas and those of Mumford and Jacobs are evident, but there are crucial political differences to consider. The situationists were not interested in creating more smoothly operating cities, safer environments for pedestrians, or garden cities designed to segment social life through utopian/dystopian plans. Rather, they saw urban planning, and especially Le Corbusier's modernist designs, as the materialization of capitalist ideology—a grotesque facade that masks, and ultimately reproduces, the alienation and passivity of consumer society, or what Debord famously termed *the spectacle*.[34] The situationists saw the "smooth circulation" of cars as the optimization of this ideological arrangement:

> A mistake made by all the city planners is to consider the private automobile (and its by-products, such as the motorcycle) as essentially a means of transportation. In reality, it is the most notable material symbol of the notion of happiness that developed capitalism tends to spread throughout the society. The automobile is at the center of this general propaganda, both as supreme good of an alienated life and as essential product of the capitalist market.[35]

From the situationist perspective, justifying the automobile and its infrastructure as practical was simply a way to mask the irrationality of a process that demolished thousands of homes and apartments, dissolved public spaces, and implicitly shattered the "dialectic of the human milieu."[36] But more important, accepting the logic of automobility was to accept the very ideology the situationists sought to destroy—a belief in both the "permanence of the present society" and the idea that revolutionary change was impossible.[37] This paradigm proved influential on dozens of artistic and political collectives in the following years, including a group of Dutch anarchists who, in the mid-

1960s, found a unique way of critiquing the "alienated life" the situationists associated with automobility and urban planning. But instead of taking up arms to start a revolution, the Provo took up the bicycle.

The Provo and the White Bicycle Plan

On May 25, 1965, several Dutch political activists formally declared their emergence as the "Provo," proclaiming themselves the "manifestation of a new, heterogeneous class: the Provotariat."[38] Roel Van Duyn, an anarchist and devotee of the Frankfurt School and philosophy, appropriated the term *provo* as a moniker that would be donned by a boisterous group of dissidents seeking to challenge the state and the tenets of capitalist culture.[39] With the help of Rob Stolk and Robert Jasper Grootveld—a performance artist known for leading weekly public "happenings"—Van Duyn and a handful of others sought to politicize the widely disillusioned youth of Amsterdam.[40] Richard Kempton recalls that the Provo saw the city's youth subculture (*nozems*) as a wellspring of revolutionary potential; they utilized both their journal and their public gatherings (street "happenings") to channel students' energy/ aggression in this direction, urging them to "*become* Provos, which is to say revolutionary nozems."[41] The Provo outlined its vision of creative anarchist resistance in a series of publications, beginning with a manifesto and a description of some of its main principles (here excerpted):

> Provo has something against capitalism, communism, fascism, bureaucracy, militarism, professionalism, dogmatism, and authoritarianism.
>
> Provo has to choose between desperate resistance and submissive extinction.
>
> Provo calls for resistance wherever possible.
>
> Provo realizes that it will lose in the end, but it cannot pass up the chance to make at least one more heartfelt attempt to provoke society.
>
> Provo regards anarchism as the inspirational source of resistance.
>
> Provo wants to revive anarchism and teach it to the young.
>
> Provo is an image.[42]

Van Duyn's theoretically inspired, revolutionary approach to social change and Grootveld's passion for public dissent, pranks, and performance art coalesced to create a short-lived movement that laid the foundations for a variety of long-lasting social changes in Amsterdam, including the first free "public use bicycle" program in the world.[43] Indeed, the first Provo action to spark widespread attention—and police retaliation—was its pronouncement of the White Bicycle Plan, an idea crafted by industrial designer and fellow Provo, Luud Schimmelpenninck. The White Bicycle Plan boldly called for a ban on all automobiles in the city of Amsterdam and proposed a free bicycle program to replace the "terrorism of the motorized minority."[44] In addition to other White Plans that advocated limited commercial development (White Housing Plan), free medical care for women (White Wife Plan), free daycare (White Kids Plan), and heavy taxation for polluters (White Chimney Plan), the White Bicycle Plan sought to politicize an important feature of everyday life: transportation.[45] Schimmelpenninck urged the municipality of Amsterdam to annually purchase twenty thousand white bicycles to supplement public transportation, all to be used freely by the city's inhabitants: "These White Bikes would belong to everyone and no one."[46] The bicycle plan was partly posed as a pragmatic response to traffic congestion in Amsterdam, but it was firmly grounded in a wider political critique linking cars to unjust capitalist infrastructures, environmental pollution, and consumer ideology:

> Amsterdammers!
>
> The asphalt terror of the motorized bourgeoisie has lasted long enough. Human sacrifices are made daily to this latest idol of the idiots: car power. Choking carbon monoxide is its incense, its image contaminates thousands of canals and streets.
>
> PROVO's bicycle plan will liberate us from the car monster. PROVO introduces the WHITE BICYCLE, a piece of public property.
>
> The first white bicycle will be presented to the Press and public on Wednesday July 28 at 3 P.M. near the statue of the Lieverdje, the addicted consumer, on the Spui.
>
> The white bicycle is never locked. The white bicycle is the first free communal transport. The white bicycle is a provocation against capitalist private property, for THE WHITE BICYCLE IS ANARCHISTIC.
>
> The white bicycle can be used by anyone who needs it and then must be left for someone else. There will more and more white bicycles until everyone can use white transport and the car peril is past. The white bicycle is a symbol of simplicity and cleanliness in contrast to the vanity and foulness of the authoritarian car. In other words:
>
> A BIKE IS SOMETHING, BUT ALMOST NOTHING![47]

Provos began the project by painting fifty bicycles with white paint, leaving them throughout the city for public use. Police quickly seized the bicycles, claiming they created an "invitation to theft," and Provos retaliated by stealing a few police vehicles. In conjunction with the bike plan, the Provo simultaneously advocated the White Corpse Plan as a way of confronting residents with the realities of automobile fatalities; the plan proposed that a driver who kills a pedestrian must use a chisel and hammer to "hack out the silhouette of his victim one inch deep in the asphalt," and then fill in the outline with white mortar to remind all "prospective murderers" of the need to drive more slowly.[48]

Bicycling has a rich history in the Netherlands and Ebert explains its popularity as a cultural phenomenon that was historically embraced as a point of national identification.[49] Bicycling achieved a prominent status in Dutch culture through the General Dutch Cyclists Union (ANWB), an organization dominated by influential political liberals from Holland's biggest cities.[50] In the late 1880s and 1890s, they promoted bicycling as a means to experience nature, to enhance national unity, and to assert "traditional Dutch virtues" in the face of industrialization and modernization.[51] The Provo was clearly a guttural reaction to the passive liberalism of Dutch society and can hardly be interpreted as an expression of traditional values, yet its appropriation of the bicycle was similarly meant to thwart the creeping influence of a new wave of modernization embedded in the automobile and symbolized by Western car culture. Indeed, the current popularity of cycling in the Netherlands makes it easy to assume that the Provo's stance against automobility was unnecessary or at least somewhat redundant in this cultural context. On the contrary, daily bicycling in the Netherlands reached a peak in 1960 and dropped by nearly 40 percent until 1977.[52] The increasing motorization of Dutch life in the 1960s and 1970s exerted a dramatically negative effect on bicycle transportation that ceased only in response to political pressure applied by cyclists. Miriam van Bree, a member of the Dutch Cyclists Union (Fietsersbond), underscores this point in an interview from 2005: "Everyone thinks the Netherlands is a cycling paradise, but if we didn't put bikes on the agenda they'd be forgotten. It's natural to cycle, but it's not natural to make policy."[53] The Provo sought to reverse this trend in the midst of its progression by politicizing both the automobile and the entire ideological framework it felt they symbolized.

Former situationist architect and Amsterdam native Constant Nieuwenhuys (known simply as Constant) greatly influenced the Provo's proto-situationist critique of urbanism; Henri Lefebvre even referred to him as one of the primary instigators of the youth movement.[54] In his essay "New Urbanism," published in *Provo* (no. 9), Constant argues that the use of urban space as a conduit for automobiles destroys the possibilities for authentic, non-consumer spaces:

Traffic's wholesale invasion of social space has led, almost imperceptibly, to violation of the most fundamental human rights. The traffic code has degraded the individual who proceeds by the only natural means of locomotion to the rank of "pedestrian," and has curtailed his freedom of movement to such an extent that it now amounts to less than that of a vehicle. So much public space is forbidden ground to the pedestrian that he is forced to seek his social contacts either in private areas (houses) or in commercially exploited ones (cafes or rented halls), where he is more or less imprisoned. In this way the city is losing its most important function: that of a meeting-place. It is highly significant that the police try to justify their measures against "happenings" on the public thoroughfares by arguing that such manifestations impede traffic. This is an implicit acknowledgement that high-speed traffic is king of the road.[55]

Constant's position is significant not only because he challenged the automobile as a usurper of social/material space but also because he revived and recontextualized the situationist critique in the struggle for sustainable transportation. The potentially practical applications of Schimmelpenninck's bicycle plan and Constant's "New Urbanism" paradigm were nonetheless ruthlessly attacked by the situationists, who saw the Provo as an ineffectual youth uprising lacking a revolutionary program: "There is a modern revolution, and one of its bases could be the Provos—but only without their leaders and ideology. If they want to change the world, *they must get rid of these who are content to paint it white.*"[56] Despite the situationists' scathing criticism—which they conveniently reserved for everyone except themselves—the Provo effectively politicized the bicycle as a symbol of resistance against car culture, situating the White Bicycle Plan within a radical critique of capitalism, public space, and environmental pollution. At a pragmatic level, the Provo simultaneously pioneered the first public-use bicycle program in Amsterdam, a model since replicated in European cities like Copenhagen (Denmark), Milan (Italy), Helsinki (Finland), and Rennes (France). In the United States, activists and bike enthusiasts similarly embraced the Provo philosophy by constructing yellow bikes, pink bikes, checkered bikes, and green bikes out of salvaged materials, leaving them on the streets for anyone to use.[57] While these programs have been largely unsuccessful due to bike theft and vandalism, their appearance in cities like Portland, Minneapolis–St. Paul (Minnesota), Boulder (Colorado), Olympia (Washington), Austin (Texas), and Princeton (New Jersey) inspired a new generation of cyclists and simultaneously introduced Americans to the very idea of public bike-sharing programs that have the potential to become a vibrant part of the urban transportation schema in the United States.[58]

Ecotactiques and Anti-automobile Shows

The Provo demonstrated how bicycles could be symbolically and pragmatically incorporated into public protests as well as a sustained critique of car culture. In doing so, it pointed to the bicycle as a utopian mode of transportation, one ideally suited for a more egalitarian and ecologically sustainable society. The Provos' anarcho-environmentalist successors, the Kabouters (meaning "gnomes" or "elves"), elaborated this aspect of the Provo agenda, surprisingly winning five council seats in Amsterdam and twelve others throughout the Netherlands in 1970.[59] Like their anarchist predecessors, the Kabouters were not interested in promoting athleticism or a specific cycling identity, but desirous of creating a political context where the bicycle could (ideally) become a practical, mundane, and universal feature of everyday urban life—a technological embodiment of environmentalism.[60] The effort to integrate bicycling into the fabric of radical politics and an ecological vision of post-capitalist urbanism resonates with a wider anti-automobile sentiment blossoming throughout Europe in the late 1960s and early 1970s. In particular, French intellectuals like Alain Touraine and Henri Lefebvre forged Marxist critiques of automobility, pointing to the car's central function in modern capitalism and its multiple roles as a pre-eminent consumer commodity, a bourgeois artifact, and a symbol of the subjugation of "lived space" for the sterility of "geometric space."[61] David Inglis offers a detailed account of the French theorists' critique of automobility and their collective disdain for car culture: "The French in general, and the intelligentsia in particular, were highly reflexively conscious of the roles played by the automobiles in society in part because, unlike in the USA, the rise of the car was not taken for granted or seen necessarily to be a harbinger of the benefits of scientific and technological modernity."[62]

Cars may not have garnered the same widespread cultural support in France, but, contrary to Inglis's claim, technological modernity was precisely the motivation for Le Corbusier's auto-centric vision of Paris in the first half of the twentieth century—a point duly noted by geographer David Pinder: "to be truly modern, so it was often claimed, Paris had to embrace the motor car."[63] Pinder recalls that the number of cars in the Paris region escalated dramatically in the wake of Le Corbusier's influence, from roughly half a million in 1939, to more than one million by 1960, to more than two million by 1965.[64] Parisian automobility correlated with, and undoubtedly perpetuated, the demolition and reconstruction of one-fourth of the city between 1954 and 1974, whereby more than half a million Parisians—mainly working-class and North African immigrants—were thrust to the city's outer realms while the professional and upper classes increased their urban presence by more than

50 percent.[65] André Gorz's 1973 critique of the "social ideology of the motor-car" makes a great deal of sense at a time when cars were the technological tools with which the newly transplanted Parisian bourgeoisie asserted their spatial and cultural authority:

> Mass motoring effects an absolute triumph of bourgeois ideology on the level of everyday life. It gives and supports in everyone the illusion that each individual can seek his or her own benefit at the expense of everyone else. Take the cruel and aggressive selfishness of the driver who at any moment is figuratively killing the "others," who appear merely as physical obstacles to his or her own speed. This aggressive and competitive selfishness marks the arrival of univer-sally bourgeois behaviour, and has come into being since driving has become commonplace.[66]

The French backlash against automobility in the 1970s was thus not only a repudiation of American cultural norms but also a renunciation of the entire hypermodern autopia previously articulated by Le Corbusier and subsequent-ly realized in Parisian redevelopment.

Environmentalism similarly began to play a distinct role in the critique of automobility as activists in Europe and the United States held pro-bicycle/anti-automobile protests on the grounds of ecological sustainability and clean air.[67] For example, a group of Chicago cyclists calling themselves Bicycle Ecology organized more than one thousand riders to participate in a Bicycle Ecology Day demonstration on October 3, 1970, and George McKay recalls an anti-road protest in November 1971 in which five hundred cyclists held a demonstration in Cambridge, England.[68] In April 1972, Parisian activists representing Friends of the Earth and the Committee for Ecological Liberation organized a much larger demonstration, in which as many as ten thousand cyclists took part in a bicycle *ecotactique* waged against "*la gangrene automobile.*"[69] In this celebration against the car, many partici-pants spoke to the need for limits on automobility while others symbolically donned gas masks and advocated a total ban on the car in Paris.[70] Cyclists gathered at the Arc de Triomphe before swarming the streets with enough people to effectively shut down traffic for the duration of the ride. While police attacked and arrested a number of cyclists at their post-ride picnic, the protest was covered nonetheless favorably in the press. The exceptions were newspapers published by the right wing, as well as the Communists, who condemned any "interference with the working man's right to drive his car where he pleases."[71] In June of the same year, the United Nations held its first Conference on the Human Environment in Stockholm and an activ-

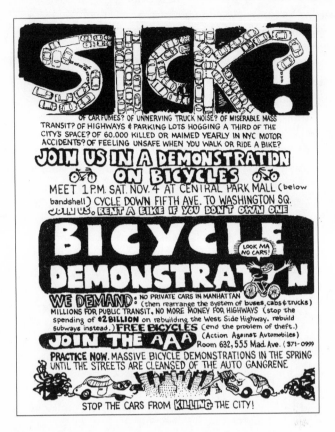

Action Against Automobiles protest in New York City, 1972.
(*Courtesy of Charles Komanoff.*)

ist group called Alternative Stad (Alternative City) simultaneously staged its own environmental conference in protest of the passive environmental objectives proposed by the United Nations.[72] David Gurin, a cyclist, urban planner, and then *Village Voice* contributor, attended the latter conference and describes how thousands of bikers took over a plaza in the center of Stockholm and proceeded to drive out the motorized traffic before parading through the city:

> Almost a thousand people moved down the street without adding a particle of pollution to the air and scarcely a decibel of sound—except for a man with a bullhorn who asked every few blocks, "What do we want?" "Fresh air!" the mass of cyclists responded. "And when do we

want it?" "Now!" A mother with a child on a back seat of her bike started a Swedish folk song about the perfumed air of spring and others joined in. The Stockholm equivalent of Broadway was momentarily quiet enough to hear un-amplified human voices in song.[73]

Gurin's documentation of the Parisian and Swedish demonstrations in the *Village Voice* functioned as part of a rallying cry for New York City activists to protest auto-centrism and environmental pollution, while calling specific attention to the benefits of bicycle transportation.[74]

Along with a number of bicycle enthusiasts, environmentalists, and a group of dissident city planners called the Urban Underground, Gurin organized a bicycle protest on Saturday November 4, 1972, marking the first action of a new group calling itself Action Against Automobiles.[75] The demonstration attempted to put the politics of the Dutch Provo and Alternative Stad to work in New York City, as cyclists called for the elimination of private automobiles in Manhattan, millions of dollars for public transit, and an end to highway spending. Bikers met in Central Park and proceeded to ride past the Greater New York Automobile Show, where they booed at the crowd and chanted, "Cars must go! Cars must go!" Following their "bike-by" protest of the auto show, cyclists rode together down Fifth Avenue toward Washington Square Park, slowing the pace of traffic in their wake and smiling at amused onlookers.[76] Gurin referenced the Provo and the European protests in a speech before the small crowd of cyclists (about 150) who gathered at the commencement of the event.

Activists planned an analogous rally about five months later to specifically agitate for bicycle lanes and bicycle parking facilities; it was clearly an environmentalist gesture but one also rooted in a basic set of survival instincts. That is to say, by 1970 New York City pedestrian deaths were at the highest since 1946 and this coincided with sharp increases in overall traffic deaths throughout the United States: fatalities numbered more than 50,000 per year from 1966 to 1973 (and again between 1978 and 1980).[77] Indeed, 1972 and 1973 were the two worst years on U.S. record for auto fatalities, with 54,589 and 54,052 killed, respectively. The "Ride and Rally for a New York Bicycle Lane Network" aimed to bring cyclists and environmentalists together in support for bicycle transportation, but it was also billed as a protest of the 1973 International Automobile Show taking place at the Coliseum.[78] A crowd of environmentalists turned out on April 7 to hear speeches and musical performances (including a concert by Pete Seeger) before a group of several hundred cyclists clogged traffic down the same stretch of asphalt from the Central Park Mall to Washington Square Park, via the auto show. The event doubled as the coming-out party for Transportation Alternatives (TA), an organization formed out of the short-lived Action Against Automobiles.

Rivvy Neshama (then Rivvy Berkman) wrote the initial grant to create TA and served as its first executive director, though she describes the group as being co-founded by "about fifty other people."[79] She recalls that the initial conversations regarding the direction of TA were somewhat divided between those who wanted to continue with anti-automobile advocacy and those who wanted TA to pursue a more positive direction that emphasized the benefits of cycling and a less contestatory anti-car rhetoric. Bicycle lanes and bicycle parking were the two main issues TA sought to address through a strategy that included public demonstrations, community outreach, and a persistent campaign to enlist support from New York City officials, politicians, and other public figures (beginning with those who were known bike riders). Neshama notes that she also worked with her mentor Marcy Benstock—one of the original Nader's Raiders—to include bicycle lanes in the Clean Air plans developed and/or revised at the time.[80] TA's first major success was a massive "Bike-in" demonstration/parade staged on Broadway Avenue on May 19, 1974. Participants estimate it drew roughly ten thousand people, including residents from all five boroughs and several prominent politicians like Senator Jacob Javits (an active cycling supporter) and Congressman Ed Koch.[81] News media outlets from the *New York Times* to *El Nuevo Mundo* featured extensive coverage of the Bike-in, highlighting the costumes, music, antique bicycles, and the thousands of pink and blue balloons attached to participants' bicycles, reading "Bike Lanes Now!"[82]

Le Monde à Bicyclette

Along with several other U.S. advocacy groups, including the San Francisco Bicycle Coalition, the East Bay Bicycle Coalition, the Bicycle Coalition of Greater Philadelphia, and the Washington Area Bicyclist Association, Transportation Alternatives effectively framed bicycling around environmental issues—both ecological and urban—and steadily mounted a series of demonstrations and campaigns throughout the mid- to late 1970s, including a persistent fight for bike lanes and bike parking that brought the Bring Back the Bicycle Committee together with American Youth Hostels.[83] Around this time, Robert "Bicycle Bob" Silverman and Claire Morissette founded a cycling advocacy group called Le Monde à Bicyclette that similarly embraced direct action and street theater to protest the land use, traffic congestion, and the environmental/health risks of automobility in Montreal. David Perry, a cycling expert and historian, recalls that Le Monde à Bicyclette members referred to themselves as "vélo-Quixotes," "vélo-holy rollers," and "vélorutionaries" committed to the goals of bicycle transportation and anti-automobile activism.[84] They utilized an array of techniques in their initial plans to make Montreal more bike-friendly, beginning in 1975. At that time, there were no bicycle facilities in the city and cyclists were even banned from using the bridges and tunnels crossing the St. Lawrence River. Prompted by such conditions, members wrote letters to officials, organized through legitimate government channels, and worked tirelessly to secure rights for cyclists in the city. They initially drafted their ideas into a "Cyclist's Manifesto" and presented it to Mayor Jean Drapeau along with a bicycle.[85] In addition, they argued before the Canadian Radio and Television Commission for restrictions on auto advertising, noting that cars were more harmful than cigarettes and alcohol, a gesture echoing the Provo's appeals to the city government in Amsterdam.[86]

These tactics contributed to modest gains for cyclists, but they were nowhere near as effective—or at least as widely publicized—as the creative strategies the organization brought to the streets (and the river). Le Monde à Bicyclette enacted a number of spectacular *cyclodramas,* or theatrical bike protests, staged to draw attention to the plight of cyclists and the dangers of car culture. Many of the cyclodramas focused on very specific issues, such as cyclists' collective inability to bicycle across the St. Lawrence River. Since they could not legally use the bridge, they satirized the situation by attempting to fly over it with winged bicycles, in addition to rowing canoes across the river with bicycles in tow. One Easter, the group performed a reenactment of the Red Sea crossing as a cyclist dressed as Moses attempted to part the St. Lawrence for the eager bicyclists lined up at the shore.[87] In addition to their river cyclodramas, Le Monde à Bicyclette also held various "space demonstrations" in Montreal. For example, cyclists constructed car-sized, wooden frames around their bicycles and rode them throughout the streets in order to protest the massive amount of urban space afforded to automobiles.[88] On another occasion, bikers filled parking meters and took over eleven parking spots on a main street for most of an afternoon. Journalist Nate Hendley notes that "Bicycle Bob" also spent two days in jail for painting illegal bike lanes on a city street, which was a tactic similarly used by Transportation Alternatives.[89] The most striking cyclodramas organized by Le Monde à Bicyclette were a series of mock accident scenes staged to protest automobile injuries and road fatalities. Ambulance Theatre, as it was known, featured "dead" cyclists sprawled out among fallen bicycles, stretchers, bandages, crutches, and fake blood. This technique was used to block the entrance of the Montreal Auto Show and it was also employed in their now infamous "Die-in" protest, which was scheduled on the first anniversary of the metro fare hike in 1976. Silverman recalls that about one hundred cyclists and pedestrians posed as car crash victims and blocked the intersection of Ste. Catherine and University with "corpses," bicycles, a coffin, and a four-year-old child carried on a stretcher.[90] The Montreal Die-in attempted to illustrate the carnage of automobility and dramatize the "car's most irrevocable consequence: death."[91] By combining grassroots advocacy with the dramatic flair of cyclodramas, Le Monde à

Bicyclette drew significant attention to the plight of cyclists in Montreal and its efforts propelled a cycling movement that has since made it one of the best cities for bicycle transportation in North America.

Framing the Bike

Activists involved with the early stages of contemporary (post–World War II) bicycle advocacy drew obvious attention to the friction between bicycling, driving, and the overall struggle for human-scale cities. Protest rides and mobile demonstrations served important symbolic functions that emphasized both the material and cultural processes of reclaiming small, yet precious, urban spaces from cars.[92] Cyclists effectively connected spatial issues to the environmental consequences of automobility, particularly the air pollution caused by driving and the ecological damage wrought by petroleum and oil use. The energy crisis of the mid-1970s—sparked by unsustainable transportation policies and the 1973 Organization of Petroleum Exporting Countries (OPEC) oil embargo against the United States—created a socioeconomic and political context where activists could speak to the importance of alternative, sustainable modes of transportation.[93] The embargo resulted in massive fuel shortages across the United States, the tripling of gasoline prices by 1974, and a ripple effect that destabilized international markets. It not only signaled the beginning of decade-long energy anxieties in the United States but also brought the intertwined politics of oil and war to the forefront of American life as drivers waited in long lines for gas, only to be turned away from empty fuel pumps. Coincidentally, 1973 also marked the first year since World War I that bicycles outsold automobiles in the United States.[94] Bicycle sales already doubled between 1970 and 1973 due to a renewed interest in cycling, but more than 43 million bicycles were sold between 1972 and 1974 alone. The oil embargo thus had a decisive impact on the number of bicycles sold in 1973 (close to 20 million) as well as the demographic shift in people using them: children's bicycles previously comprised the bulk of the market in the United States, but adult bicycles accounted for 50 percent of the sales in 1973.[95] Most people did not abandon their cars for bikes in the mid-1970s, but the prospects for bicycle transportation took on a whole meaning in this geopolitical context. That is to say, utilitarian, or utility, cycling became a more attractive option for many city dwellers and bike advocacy became an effective way to articulate those needs and desires.

Contributing to this paradigm shift were a number of interrelated, or at least intersecting, factors, including the growth of the appropriate technology (AT) movement and its popularization through E. F. Schumacher's *Small Is Beautiful*, published in 1973.[96] Schumacher, one of the primary theorists of AT, elaborated a holistic critique of industrialism and the logic of progress implicit to technological development. The book resonated with the technological anxieties many Americans experienced as a result of the Vietnam War, the energy crisis, and a growing awareness of the lethal hazards posed by environmental pollution. For better or worse, the AT movement directed attention to issues of scale, specifically the correlation between the size of technological systems and their effects on societies, which Schumacher describes as inversely proportional, hence smaller being beautiful. This line of inquiry is significant because it closely paralleled critiques of urban planning and transportation in the same general period. Jane Jacobs was among those who challenged not only the size and scale implicit to orthodox urban planning but also the spatial tensions between the needs of pedestrians and those required of automobiles. Ivan Illich similarly bemoaned modern transportation, though his critique dealt less with the size and scale of automobility than its high energy demands and its speed: "A true choice among practical policies and of desirable social relations is possible only where speed is restrained. Participatory democracy demands low-energy technology, and *free people must travel the road to productive social relations at the speed of a bicycle.*"[97] Schumacher, Jacobs, and Illich formed something of a holy trinity for bicycle advocates who used their theories to create a more philosophically informed analysis of cycling in the 1970s. Illich's ideas understandably took on a prominent role because he mapped an entire politics of technology around the bicycle itself, writing in *Energy and Equity:*

> Bicycles let people move with greater speed without taking up significant amounts of scarce space, energy, or time. They can spend fewer hours on each mile and still travel more miles in a year. They can get the benefit of technological breakthroughs without putting undue claims on the schedules, energy, or space of others. They become masters of their own movements without blocking those of their fellows. Their new tool creates only those demands which it can also satisfy. Every increase in motorized speed creates new demands on space and time. The use of the bicycle is self-limiting. It allows people to create a new relationship between their life-space and their life-time, between their territory and the pulse of their being, without destroying their inherited balance. The advantages of modern self-powered traffic are obvious, and ignored.[98]

If the bicycle became a prominent metaphor for the benefits of "small" and "slow" it was not simply because it made for a good argument on paper. Rather, bicycling played a distinct role in the everyday lives of its proponents, not only as a transportation device but also as an extension of the counterculture from which many bike advocates emerged.[99] As Arthur Asa Berger wrote of the newly popularized ten-speed bicycle of the early 1970s, it symbolized "the whole, counter-culture, self realization, nature syndrome."[100] Indeed, the counterculture in Europe and North America played a distinct role in the emergence of modern bike advocacy, perhaps more so than many of its current lycra-clad exercise advocates would care to admit. The eventual anxiety over cycling being too associated with the counterculture is nicely previewed in 1974 interview with former cycling champion John Allis: "Sponsors don't want some scruffy jeaned hippy going around waving their name in front of the public. They want somebody who represents them in a respectable way and I think bike riders are going to have to change their image that way."[101] This is not to say that all racers or utilitarian cyclists in this period were scruffy-jeaned hippie activists, or that environmentalism, anti-authoritarianism, and technological skepticism—three common dispositions of the counterculture—necessarily compelled every cyclist's desire to ride. But even the most cursory glance at the protest strategies and theatrics embraced by these bike advocates indicates their prior, or concurrent, relationships to the social movements and/or counterculture(s) of the period. This is clear enough with the Dutch Provo, Alternative Stad, and Le Monde à Bicyclette, but run-of-the-mill cycling enthusiasts also had somewhat of a fringe relationship with mainstream society. Charlie McCorkell, Transportation Alternative's second executive director and a thirty-year bike advocate/builder/educator, recalls that cyclists in the early 1970s were "much more outside the system then today," and Steven Faust, another longtime bike advocate and planner in New York City, says that cyclists were considered "sociologically marginal people."[102] Rivvy Neshama speaks clearly to the correlation between biking and the counterculture in describing the motivation for TA's 1974 Bike-in:

> I was thinking of what happened at that time to create a culture ripe for the idea. The environmental movement was new, idealistic, and hopeful, and that's the movement I came from. Urban planners were also idealistic and looking to create humane environments; Barry Benepe and Brian Ketcham were two of them, and two of our founders influenced by Jane Jacobs (David Gurin was also influenced by Jane). Health, being more at one with nature, and using our own resources were three ideals of the time, influenced by the *Whole Earth Catalog*. It was a time of be-ins, love-ins, smoke-ins . . . so it was natural to plan a huge Bike-in—one that would bring all groups together around a common dream.[103]

What is interesting about these early years of bike activism is that despite its cultural emphasis, there was also a firmly entrenched commitment to transforming bicycling and automobility through formal political channels, whether it be lobbying, hosting community events, meeting with politicians and urban planners, circulating petitions, and/or getting involved with local (and regional) governmental affairs. One of the prominent critiques of both the counterculture and appropriate technologists—who especially mingled in the pages of the *Whole Earth Catalog* as well as the back-to-the-land movement—is that they either advocated an individualist, escapist paradigm ("tune in, turn on, drop out") or tried to naïvely solve complex social/political problems by simply "living differently" or by using different tools.[104] Bike advocacy in the 1970s reveals the limitations and inaccuracy of this critique because cyclists were directly engaged with urban problems that are fundamentally social and political in their scope. Rather than arguing for cyclists to just do their own thing, groups like Transportation Alternatives, Le Monde à Bicyclette, the San Francisco Bicycle Coalition (founded in 1970), the East Bay Bicycle Coalition, the Bicycle Coalition of Greater Philadelphia, and the Washington Area Bicyclist Association (all founded in 1972), specifically worked to transform the urban milieu by addressing both the pragmatic needs of cyclists (and potential cyclists) as well as the overarching problems posed by poor urban planning and environmental pollution. Like Jane Jacobs, many saw unregulated automobility as a problem requiring a positive orientation and a realistic set of goals:

> Attrition [of automobiles], too, must operate in positive terms, as a means of supplying positive, easily understood and desired improvements, appealing to various specific and tangible city interests. This is desirable not because such an approach is a superior persuasive and political device (although it is), but because the objects should be tangible and positive objects of increasing, in specific places, city diversity, vitality and workability. To concentrate on riddance as the *primary* purpose, negatively to put taboos and penalties on automobiles as children might say, "Cars, cars, go away," would be a policy not only doomed to defeat but rightly doomed to defeat.[105]

It is clear that bike advocates did not always heed the last part of Jacobs's advice, but there was also a much stronger case to be made for taking a more pronounced stance against urban driving in the 1970s, particularly when one considers the roughly five hundred thousand people killed in traffic (in the United States alone) between the publication of Jacobs's first book and the beginning of the following decade. And while some bike activists were intent to pursue a more radical agenda or at the very least one sympathetic to Illich's systemic critiques of technology and capitalism, their general approach to politics was more in tune with the civic engagement of people like John Dewey or Ralph Nader than the dropout paradigm bemoaned by critics of the counterculture and the AT movement. These organizations formed through the collaboration of smaller activist groups and volunteers and solidified themselves through persistent organizing and the involvement of public officials. Charlie McCorkell notes the importance of this synthesis in creating momentum for bicycle advocacy:

> I always liked the big parades. We had a reported ten thousand on a ride demanding bike lanes, etc. This was long before recreational rides of twenty thousand had become fashionable. We did street theater—my personal favorite being bike lane painting. We swept the bridges, held demonstrations where cyclists were murdered by cars, rode around the Coliseum ringing our bells when the auto show was there trying to make the walls of "Jericho" collapse. The street action was aimed at getting press and getting a broader audience for our views. We'd block traffic and do it to make a point—usually a very specific point like our need for bridge access. But for every street action I estimate there were four or five meetings with government or civic officials. . . . I always believe that grassroots advocacy has to have a multi-front approach. Direct action, street theater, civil disobedience, leafleting, petitions, etc. are pretty much all useless expressions without formal advocacy to turn all the noise into direction and results. I have always believed that bike advocacy should be purposeful and if at all possible fun.[106]

The multi-front approach McCorkell describes here is certainly not unique to bicycle advocacy in this period, as one can find numerous social movements that seamlessly integrated street theater, direct action, and formal advocacy. But what it suggests is that bike activists recognized the need to create a political bike culture at the same time they cultivated a cultural bike politics. And while this wave of biketivism was not always successful, it illustrates some of the many ways that people made bicycle transportation a meaningful social issue, not simply an individual lifestyle choice.

Effective Cycling?

In the wake of the mid-1970s "bike boom," cycling advocates were able to mobilize support by effectively promoting the environmental benefits of non-motorized transportation at the same time they appealed to Americans' renewed interest in leisure cycling and the increasing popularity of physical fitness. Concerns over energy and the pressure exerted by bike advocates and environmentalists prompted governmental officials to respond by securing unprecedented funds for off-road bike paths (also called "cycleways" or "bikeways") and other cycling facilities. By 1974, approximately $117 million was spent on bike projects by all levels of government and off-street bike paths became one of the focal points for advocates seeking to address the problems constituted by an increasing number of cyclists on city streets and a higher number of bike-car accidents.[107] Former transportation planner and bicycle historian Bruce Epperson writes, "The belief was that since most people didn't like to bike in traffic and weren't very good at it, there was a need for separate facilities if large numbers were to be expected to ride."[108] Davis, California, was one of the models praised by advocates because of the city's elaborate bikeway infrastructure and the high number of users it attracted since its construction in 1967.[109] In addition to California's various bikeway projects (not limited to Davis), Chicago had thirty-six dedicated routes by 1969 and Milwaukee featured sixty-four miles of marked bikeways by 1970.[110] Cyclists in large cities also began to demand solutions to other tangible problems in the 1970s, such as the high rate of bicycle theft and a lack of available bike parking and racks—problems that unfortunately persist to this day. Government officials were surprisingly receptive to a number of proposals put forth by advocacy groups, even in car-friendly states like New Jersey, where the commissioner of transportation went on record in 1974 as saying, "we believe that bicycles can be important not only for recreation, but also as a means of transportation."[111] While utilitarian bicycling was never proposed as a substitute for automobility, the recognition of cycling as a legitimate (or potentially legitimate) mode of transportation indicates a then ongoing paradigm shift regarding the prospects of bicycle infrastructure, one that put cycling on the public agenda in a manner not seen since the turn of the century.

At the same time activists championed bicycles to address environmental problems and the energy crisis, a group of vocal critics began to emerge from what Epperson accurately describes as an "unexpected quarter—the cyclists already out there."[112] John Forester, an expert cycling instructor and advocate, came out as a fierce critic of the political trajectory of bike activism in the United States and the 1975 publication of his book *Effective Cycling* marked the beginning of a pro-cycling crusade against bicycle facilities, traditional bike safety programs, and environmentally focused bike advocacy. Forester's model of advocacy asserts that well-trained, knowledgeable cyclists do not require special facilities because they can ride safely in any traffic conditions. His Effective Cycling courses were designed to promote what he calls the *vehicular-cycling principle,* the belief that "cyclists fare best when they act and are treated as drivers of vehicles."[113] Forester fought the development of bicycle facilities, in both theory and practice, because he saw them as safety liability that actually caused more problems than they alleviated. In addition, he warned that the construction of bicycle facilities also gave government officials an alibi to banish cyclists from the streets, onto the paths. Andy

Clarke, the current director of the League of American Bicyclists, recalls that facilities built or designated in the 1970s were, in fact, poorly designed and cyclists were sometimes forced to use them by law. He specifically notes the importance of vehicular cycling (VC) advocacy in limiting the development of what he candidly refers to as "crappy" facilities.[114] At the same time, Clarke and most of today's prominent bike advocates recognize that while the VC paradigm had an important role to play in the 1970s, it largely over-exaggerated both the dangers of bicycle facilities and the threats posed to cyclists' vehicular rights.[115] Moreover, its popularity in the cycling club circuit eventually spawned a legion of persistent, uncompromising critics who effectively slowed the development of a bicycle infrastructure capable of accommodating the utilitarian needs, or recreational desires, of most Americans. While it is debatable whether the construction of an expansive cycling infrastructure would have necessarily encouraged more people in the United States to ride bikes (though studies point to this correlation), VC proponents helped to ensure the suppression of this possibility for more than two decades.[116]

Forester's hands-off approach to transportation planning and government intervention broke with the model of advocacy pioneered on the East and West coasts in the early 1970s, and the ensuing controversy over bicycle infrastructure largely divided advocates into two main camps: (1) those who conceptualized everyday cycling within the framework of environmentalism, urban planning, and the energy crisis—all of which required a revaluation of automobility and/or the establishment of a dedicated cycling infrastructure—and (2) those who supported John Forester's paradigm and saw proper training and education (rather than infrastructure, political activism, or impediments to automobility) as the sole ingredients for promoting bicycle transportation. Not surprisingly, Forester's ilk held sway throughout much of the late 1970s and 1980s because city officials found in VC advocates the cheapest and easiest course of action to pursue. Given the choice between spending money on urban planning projects or not spending it, an official's decision is somewhat easy to predict, particularly when infrastructure budgets began to decline in 1970, following a twenty-year growth trend. Epperson points to this economic factor, rather than Forester's ideology, as what largely determined the success of his anti-planning (i.e., anti-infrastructure) approach to bicycle transportation.[117] But while this helps to explain why Forester's ideas were well received by city officials and transportation decision makers, it does not account for why so many cyclists found, and continue to find, his philosophy appealing.

To his credit, many are simply attracted to Forester's instructional program because it does teach people how to ride safely and effectively, which is a central goal of virtually all bike advocacy groups. His program established a now longstanding tradition of bicycle education/training in the United States and also provided a theoretical correlative affirming cyclists' rights as legitimate users of the road. This was an important and somewhat radical stance at the time it first appeared because people faced a considerable amount of harassment while bicycling on city streets. Nearly all urban bike commuters of the 1970s and 1980s have stories about getting spit on, having cigarette/cigar butts or trash thrown at them, being verbally and/or physically threatened, and in some cases being intentionally hit by drivers. Ken Kifer, a prominent bike advocate who was killed by a drunk driver in 2003, wrote that he and other cyclists in Birmingham, Alabama, used to carry photocopies of the state's vehicular laws to show police officers after being repeatedly pulled over for illegally riding on the street.[118] Forester's longtime advocacy for cyclists' vehicular rights is an important reason why bicycle transportation has become more mainstream, or at least less dangerous than it was thirty years ago. But the problem, or should I say one of the many problems, with his paradigm is the extent to which it assumes that cyclists unwilling to cope with these specific factors, or the physical dangers of high-speed traffic (both real or perceived), are not only wrong but also irrational and ignorant.

Forester claims people suffer from a *cyclist-inferiority superstition*—an apparent "phobia" caused by the dual belief that cars are dangerous and that bicycle transportation ultimately benefits from the development of bicycle-specific facilities like off-street paths and "segregated" bike lanes (lanes with wide curbs separating cyclists from automobile traffic).[119] His pseudo-psychological justification for the irrationality of cyclists is their apparent inability to comprehend the facts about the safety of automobile traffic and the "real" dangers posed by bicycle facilities, though his figures are widely refuted by transportation researchers, bicycle advocates, and common sense.[120] Indeed, the publication of his thesis came in the wake of the worst years in U.S. history for automobile fatalities and the worst year on record for cycling deaths: 1,003 cyclists were killed on U.S. streets in 1975.[121] Yet this premise lies at the core of what most people, especially those outside the (small) world of bike advocacy, rightfully find to be an extraordinarily bizarre philosophy of bicycling.

It would be easy to dismiss Forester's cranky musings—like the assertion that charity bicycle rides are a "sham"—were they not so politically motivated or so widely read.[122] In his books and essays, bicycle advocates and environmentalists are consistently made out as the culprits who embody all the negative characteristics he sees as hindering effective bicycle transportation. For example, even the slightest recognition of the dangers of driving or the benefits of bicycle facilities earns one the title "anti-motorist," a term that VC proponents use to distinguish their supposedly benign agenda from those of "political cyclists" (i.e., irrational, uneducated environmentalists).[123] As political ideologues in their own right, VC proponents, or *vehicularists,* as they are sometimes dubbed, offer uncritical support for the politically conservative tenets at the heart of Forester's model of bicycle advocacy and transportation engineering:

> Unfortunately, those who are most likely to get in contact with transportation officials are the political bicyclists, because that is their mission. A transportation official has to decide whether he wants to work with their policy or not. The political side of this decision is in some respects a quandary. On the basis of self-interest, the roadway users—cyclists and motorists—should be in one corner and the anti-traffic forces—political bicyclists, residentialists, and environmentalists—in the other. . . . Assume, until you know otherwise, that those who have initiated contact with you are political bicyclists, and that *real cyclists have seen no useful reason to contact government.*[124]

Instead of praising cyclists for taking an active role in the political process or working toward a more egalitarian vision of mobility, Forester and his supporters frame government-funded bicycle facilities as restrictive, choosing to champion equality as a Reaganite ethos of every man for himself: "Same roads—Same rights—Same rules."[125] Equality, in this sense of sameness, is conceived not as the rectification of a national problem whereby one form of mobility (auto transportation) dominates public thoroughfares, receives a grossly disproportionate amount of government subsidies, and poses undue physical threats to pedestrians, cyclists, the elderly, children, and people of color. Rather, it functions as an ideological and political rationale for voluntary cyclists (those who ride out of choice as opposed to low income) to legitimize their participation in an already unequal matrix of public spaces.[126]

The idea that the street is somehow a space of equality, or neutrality, that one accesses by simply disciplining and ultimately demonstrating one's cycling skill is a premise that holds true only if one decontextualizes, if not totally ignores, all the relevant socioeconomic, physical, material, and cultural factors that influence—and in most cases dictate—everyday transportation choices. It virtually mirrors the claims of cyclists in the nineteenth century who, by virtue of their socioeconomic and/or racial status, could easily ignore the cultural restraints on public mobility because they were never subject to them in the first place. Not coincidentally, it is a group of mainly white, middle- to upper-class men who now reproduce this same ideology with recourse to similar vulgar psychological explanations. The main difference now is the brazen manner in which VC proponents use racially loaded terms like *segregationists* (bikeway advocates) and *ghettoization* (being forced into bike lanes) while they promote a paradigm that explicitly, and openly, condemns what they see as "affirmative action" policies.[127] One can peruse the archives of the *Chain Guard,* an online discussion list for VC advocates, to see just how pointedly the issue of bicycle transportation is framed in such terms. One person writes:

> I despair of responding at length to all the unending preferences for prioritizing the "special needs" of all the presumed incapable bike riders while we continue to ignore the development of informed, intelligent, safe, enjoyable, efficient transportation by driving a bicycle on normal roads with normal training and education easily achieved by almost all of us, while we promote equal rights.[128]

The lip service given to equal rights is nicely highlighted in later discussion about the formation of Bicycle Advisory Committees, which are groups that recommend localized policies for cycling. This is part of the prevailing wisdom on the issue of diversity: "Submit a list of names, balanced for all the 'politically correct' diversity, of people that you want the mayor or whoever to appoint to the BAC [Bicycle Advisory Committee]. Surely there are some black Basque lesbian quadriplegic pro-life vehicular cyclists you can have on the committee."[129]

Perhaps the most disingenuous aspect of vehicular cyclists mocking the issues of diversity and affirmative action is the total lack of reservation shown in formulating advocacy strategies that appropriate such terms to manipulate public opinion. A brief dialogue about advocacy strategies illustrates this point:

> Might it be possible to rally an adequate number of pedestrian advocates and bicyclist advocates behind the non-prejudicial "universal access" cause, and away from the anti-car affirmative-action campaigns that ensure prolonged friction between user groups, in order to speed the adoption of constructive public policy?
>
> My hope for "universal access" is to provide a paradigm and buzz-word for pedestrian and bicyclist advocates to say "yes" to without having to promote an anti-car cause. Shouldn't the audience that could be infected by such a meme be larger than the population that simply hates cars and the people who drive them?
>
> —Steven Goodridge

> Your Universal Access paradigm is excellent. The only problems are overcoming current inertia and getting its message out to a critical mass. Exponential numbers of people must be infected by the meme.
>
> Affirmative action for bicyclists has a huge following. Affirmative action in civil rights does too. It may be a better strategy to couch it as

segregationist vs. integrationist. It's harsher, which I think is necessary to convert/enlighten bike lane and path devotees.

—Wayne Pein[130]

Resorting to such convoluted measures to convert people away from simply having their own opinion, or preference, for travel shows how little credence most VC advocates actually give to those who either lack their cycling
instructor credentials or deviate from a hard-line stance that effectively shields
automobility from any and all forms of criticism. But to do so in a way that
consciously exploits such racially loaded concepts/terms is beyond distasteful,
particularly when it is done for the sole purpose of winning a self-constructed
debate. Vehicular cyclists' widespread use of affirmative action discourse, as
well as the segregationist/integrationist binary—which is by no means limited to this online community—demonstrates not only a fundamental lack of
sympathy and/or wisdom regarding the real issues of social justice but also an
astounding degree of unexamined privilege. For it is only a group of entitled
white people who can enjoy the privilege of utilizing such concepts and terms,
while simultaneously emptying them of their historical and political meaning,
with absolutely none of their own rights or liberties at stake.[131]

Buried deep within this arguably racist appropriation of equal rights
discourse lies perhaps the ultimate irony of the entire vehicular cycling
philosophy. That is to say, the inequality of mobility on U.S. streets is so
fundamental, so thoroughly built into the asphalt, that it creates the very
conditions making it necessary to persistently remind cyclists (or any other
non-motorists) of their rights. If U.S. roads were truly equally accessible to
both drivers and cyclists, there would no need for people to undergo specific
forms of physical and mental training to simply ride a bike, much less worry
about being maimed or killed for the slightest mistake while doing so. While
it is true that all forms of mobility require certain levels of training and practice to minimize danger, there are undue burdens placed on cyclists that are
physical, mental, and material. For example, biking in urban traffic not only
requires one to quickly survey and adapt to even the most minute variations
in traffic patterns and the street itself (i.e., potholes, cracks, litter); it also
demands a fairly high level of physical fitness, or at least more than is necessary to ride slowly on a bike path or to drive a car. These are just a few of the
many legitimate, rational reasons why people are scared, unwilling, or simply
disinterested in riding a bicycle through dense urban traffic, never mind taking the bigger step toward being an everyday cyclist or bike commuter. One
could argue that these are the terms to which one agrees if she or he wants
to ride a bike for transportation, but this is exactly the problem identified by
activists who see such terms for what they are: a set of unjust prerequisites
that are wholly antithetical to the goals of environmental sustainability and

transportation equity, not to mention the most pragmatic goal of simply getting from point A to point B safely, efficiently, and cheaply. Many of the politically minded bike activists of the 1970s, as well as those who now carry their banner, recognized that assuaging or addressing such fears was not just a matter of giving cycling lessons or promoting a self-help style appeal to assertiveness and confidence, but creating genuine alternatives that (ideally) give people recourse to material, tangible solutions for safe bicycle transportation. Lobbying for the construction of bicycle facilities and exerting public pressure for infrastructural changes were recognized as small, but necessary, steps in working toward this and other environmental goals.

Conclusion

In calling attention to the prospects of bicycle transportation in the late 1960s and 1970s, groups like the Dutch Provo, Transportation Alternatives, and Le Monde à Bicyclette (among others) actively imagined cities in which urban mobility would not have to be organized around the spaces, speeds, and trajectories of motorized traffic. Cycling was not seen as a cure all as much as a utilitarian goal that spoke to the larger and wholly inseparable problematics of pollution, oil reliance, public space, and public safety prompted by decades of unfettered support for auto transportation. This model of bike advocacy called for people to pragmatically intervene in the composition of the urban environment (through cycling, lobbying, and/or protest) and to ultimately question the dominant logic governing the materiality of "the urban" itself. It was a basic expression of what Henri Lefebvre famously called the *right to the city*: the right to "participate in urbanity, the right to appropriate the city not merely as an economic unit, but as a home and an expression of lived experience."[132] By the middle of the decade, the growing emphasis on vehicular cycling advocacy marked a clear shift away from conceptualizing bicycling as part of the larger project of progressive urban reform toward a paradigm that simply emphasized the right to bike. The resurgence of urban reform-minded bike advocacy in the 1990s began to gradually negate the impact of advocacy bent on preserving the dominant norms of car culture, but even with the growth of bike organizations and a wider awareness of numerous problems posed by cars, there is still a collective hesitancy for most cycling advocates to embrace stronger stances against automobility or the socioeconomic, cultural, and political conditions ultimately determining its shape.

Despite such tendencies, an emerging wave of bike advocates, urban planners, and activists are effectively reasserting the radical potential of vélomobility envisioned by the politicized bicycle advocates and die-hard cycling enthusiasts of the 1960s and 1970s. This trend is evident in the United States, where bike activists look to the past successes (and failures) of bicycle advocacy in an attempt to build a movement capable of transforming both public policy and public perceptions of bicycle transportation. Indeed, contemporary cycling advocacy groups articulate a diverse set of philosophical, political, and cultural strategies that are as equally indebted to the pro-bicycle, grassroots campaigns pioneered on the East and West coasts in the early 1970s as the anti-car theatrics of Amsterdam's anarchist Provos and Montreal's vélorutionary environmentalists. The active politicization, and publicity, of bicycle transportation in those decades may not have dealt a serious blow to the trajectory of car culture, but it set an important precedent for advocates and contributed a unique dimension to a then burgeoning bike culture of road racers, touring enthusiasts, urban commuters, and the first wave of mountain bikers and BMX riders. In doing so, they vocalized a joyous rallying cry for cyclists to take to the streets en masse, as both riders and protesters.

CHAPTER 4

Critical Mass and the Functions of Bicycle Protest

> Materializing freedom means beginning by appropriating a few patches of the surface of a domesticated planet.
>
> —Attila Kotányi and Raoul Vaneigem, "Elementary Program of the Bureau of Unitary Urbanism," in *Situationist International Anthology,* 1961

The White Bicycle Plan initiated by the Dutch Provo in 1965 marks an important and largely unrecognized moment for bicycle advocacy: it revealed how activists could politicize the bicycle as a direct response to the material and ideological problems posed by urban automobility. Theirs was an admittedly utopian vision, but one firmly grounded in the pragmatism of the bicycle, the ethics of egalitarianism, and a love of the city. Rather than seeing bicycles as nostalgic symbols of a bygone pre-automobile era, the Provo used them to reconceptualize the modern city and the prospects of a post-automobile urban future—one ideally organized around the geographies and flows of the bicycle. Activists scattered throughout Europe and North America similarly began to challenge the spatial domination of the automobile, seeking to "reclaim the streets" through public demonstrations and symbolic actions beginning in the early 1970s. By the end of that decade, London activists staged an event that largely prefigured the British anti-roads movement of the 1990s: roughly six thousand people gathered for the Friends of the Earth-sponsored National Bike Rally in Trafalgar Square on June 10, 1979.[1] Cyclists demonstrated their pedal power under the banner "Reclaim the Road," much to the chagrin of drivers in Westminster.[2] That same year, nearly fifty thousand Danish cyclists took park in a national campaign for more cycleways and half of the crowd staged a massive parade through Copenhagen's streets, effectively shutting down auto traffic in their wake.[3]

In 1992, bicycle commuters in San Francisco began to converge at rush hour on the last Friday of every month to similarly take over the street, demonstrate their collective strength, and send a message to the public: "We are not blocking traffic; we *are* traffic!" Conceived as a celebration of biking and an "antidote to the elimination of public space," Critical Mass has politicized thousands of cyclists, caused incredible controversy, and helped to transform public perceptions about bicycling.[4] This monthly event not only highlights the simple joy of bicycling with friends and strangers alike; it also gives bicyclists a chance to experiment with spontaneity, playfulness, and decentralized organization as a way to call attention to the dominant norms of bicycling and automobility. Critical Mass is a critical practice that, for better or worse, sparks a necessary dialogue about car culture and reframes the politics of public space around and through the bicycle. This chapter addresses the organizational, communicative, and performative aspects of Critical Mass to explore how its dialectic of theory and action positions mobility as a crucial terrain for cultural resistance and political struggle. Rather than offering an empirical account of event, I focus on both the intent of Critical Mass, as articulated by its participants, and how these sentiments fit into a wider set of practices meant to highlight, problematize, and at times celebrate the ways in which mobile practices and public spaces co-exist under capitalism. I specifically call attention to those aspects of Critical Mass that echo the spatio-cultural politics theorized and practiced by Situationist International in the late 1950s and early 1960s, which not only provide a useful lens to interpret Critical Mass but also illustrate the importance and timeliness of making space a primary category for political and artistic critique. Moreover, I want to think about the communicative and strategic functions of reclaiming public space through the bicycle and the impact Critical Mass has on larger debates about cycling, driving, and the process of bike advocacy itself.

Background and (Dis)Organization

Critical Mass emerged from the collaborative efforts of cyclists in the San Francisco Bay area who were involved with the San Francisco Bicycle Coalition, social movement activism, and the largely underground bike messenger culture that flourished throughout the 1980s and early 1990s.[5] The Commute Clot, as it was initially called, was first proposed as a monthly event to get bike commuters and other cyclists together for a group ride.[6] These monthly gatherings quickly began to draw more participants despite a lack of formal organization or an overarching dogma; initial rides drew around fifty or sixty people but within several years the numbers swelled into the hundreds and thousands.[7] Since early rides were designed to celebrate biking, it was, and still is, common for people to ride with costumes, decorated bicycles, signs, noise-makers, and, in some cases, with sound systems and live bands. Halloween rides, for example, consistently feature some of the most elaborate festivities and parade themes. Critical Mass has also been used to pay tribute to cyclists killed by automobiles, and occasionally integrated into political protests and Reclaim the Streets events: guerilla street parties thrown to celebrate both car-free space and the act of celebration itself.[8] Without a charter, a centralized network, or formal affiliation with any organization, the event spread to more than three hundred cities throughout the world with rides featuring as many as eighty thousand participants, or "Massers."[9]

Critical Mass is essentially a direct action, anarchic event in that rides are unsanctioned by city officials and riders are motivated by self-determination, self-rule, and non-hierarchical organization. Michael Klett observes, "within Critical Mass itself there are no leaders; organizers, yes, we are all organiz-ers—but we're not in charge. . . . [T]hat has been the key to its success."[10] His distinction between leader and organizer is a useful one because it points to the active role that participants must play in the event. Bike riders meet at designated spots on the last Friday of every month (in their respective cities and towns) to collectively decide on the route that will be taken; proposals are verbally solicited and/or circulated in the form of maps before being put to a vote. In some cases routes are decided in advance, but this practice is typi-cally discouraged in lieu of spontaneous and face-to-face decision making. Many of the techniques employed by Massers were developed in the early San Francisco rides, including the practice of "corking," which involves bikers positioning themselves at busy intersections to block, or "cork," traffic while the pack rides by. This tactic is intended to keep the group together while rid-ing through stoplights, and though technically illegal, it is designed to both maximize safety for cyclists (safety in numbers!) and minimize hassle for drivers (by keeping Mass moving at a reasonable speed). Still, this strategy—as well as the event as a whole—garners mixed responses from drivers, rang-ing from enthusiastic support to indifference to outright hostility. Motorists specifically express aggravation at the temporary seizure of "their" roads, as well as justifiable frustration with the antagonistic behavior of certain par-ticipants.[11]

Public officials and police forces are not universally opposed to the event, but the disruption of rides and the prosecution of cyclists have been com-monplace since it gained popularity in the mid-1990s. Police officers have harassed, arrested, intimidated, and even brutalized riders in San Francisco, Austin, Montreal, Portland, Seattle, New York, Minneapolis, Buffalo, and a number of other U.S. cities.[12] Indeed, police departments in Portland and New York City were respectively found guilty of keeping illegal files on Massers and conducting illegal surveillance on ride organizers.[13] Decentralized organization and open participation prove effective in minimizing such mechanisms of control, inasmuch as police typically try to arrest the leaders of a protest movement, or perceived protest movement, to exemplify their disciplinary power. Matthew Arnison, a Mass participant in Sydney, Australia, points to the irony of this situation in the opening lines of a 1995 essay:

> The cop says, "Who organized this? Who's in charge here?" The guy they're hassling says, "I don't know." He asks the guy next to him in a bike helmet, "Who's in charge?" The guy in the helmet doesn't know either. Picture a police paddy wagon parked across 3 lanes, surrounded by 100 people on bikes, all shouting "Who's in charge? Who's in charge?"[14]

Organizing autonomous events without clear leadership does not eliminate police intervention, as even this quote illustrates, but it promotes the longevity of Critical Mass by making both the identification of participants, as well as the co-optation of the event, that much more difficult.

Critical Mass has no leaders or rules per se, yet the faux-anarchist rhetoric of "no rules" tends to overstate the role that spontaneity actually plays in many rides. There are important elements of surprise and chance, to be sure, but people also go to great lengths to organize Mass and address logistical issues that take place before, during, and after events. Certain informal codes of conduct, or norms, have thus been established and debated in different cities. For example, Massers in San Francisco struggled to dissuade the aggressive, macho behavior of certain men who frequented rides in the 1990s. The "testosterone brigade," as they are often dubbed, were consistently reminded that their antics—such as taunting drivers and hitting cars—created problems for Mass and unnecessarily increased tensions between cyclists and the driving public.[15] Similarly, there have been lengthy debates on the Chicago Critical Mass e-mail list about Massers drinking alcohol on rides and whether participants have the right to make informal policies about such behavior.[16] These dialogues reveal how power is a central concern in the organization of Critical Mass and simultaneously show how the event is actively shaped by collaboration and discussion, not simply the ethereal whims of participants. I raise this point because Massers have the tendency to uncritically equate impromptu participation with genuine democracy when there are obvious limitations to the prospects for non-hierarchical participation in an unorganized, mobile event.[17] Steven Bodzin specifically raises this issue in an otherwise positive assessment of the ride: "At Mass, everyone is a leader, but some people are more leaders than others."[18] Questions surrounding the unofficial leadership of Mass are not uncommon but seem to arise most in places where rides consistently attract large crowds or where specific organizers are either seen as exerting too much force in the direction of the event or in its representation to the public. This is particularly true when Massers are interviewed by the news media and, by default, become spokespeople for a group with no singular viewpoint or ideology.[19]

Part of Critical Mass's notoriety arguably stems from the difficulty faced by those who attempt to label and define it; scholars Blickstein and Hanson note that it has been called "a protest, a form of street theater, a method of commuting, a party, and a social space."[20] This amorphous definition is both embraced and compounded by cyclists who also describe it as a "pro-bike, anti-car monthly action," a rebellion, a movement, a revolutionary act, and, conversely, "just a bike ride."[21] The inability of participants and observers to accurately pinpoint what Critical Mass is does not necessarily reflect confusion—although it does do that—as much as disagreement over the ride's meaning and purpose. Oddly enough, this is not coincidental; Critical Mass was/is specifically designed to be interpreted, shaped, and actively defined by participants, regardless of whether they agree. Veteran Masser and bike advocate Jym Dyer writes, "Participants are encouraged to implement their own ideas, and non-participants (including those who for various reasons are averse to the ride) are encouraged to join in with their ideas as well. . . . [B]e prepared to discuss your missives and defend your arguments!"[22] The decentralized framework of Critical Mass fosters a flexible rhetorical space where participants collectively give meaning to the event through face-to-face communication and the active production and dissemination of writing, art, maps, and other self-produced media. Xerocracy, or "rule through photocopying," is the dominant paradigm of Critical Mass and rests on the premise that anyone can print, photocopy, and solicit media that advocate and/or explain the ride. Bicyclists make flyers, stickers, posters, missives, and zines for distribution among riders and bystanders alike during events; many materials are also circulated online through a sprawling web of Mass Web sites. Artwork and images celebrating Critical Mass and bicycle transportation are common, particularly those connecting the bicycle to environmentalism, autonomy, and public space. Xerocracy is thus not only a means of shaping participant and public perceptions about bicycle transportation (through facts, statistics, images, and personal narratives); it is also part of a larger communicative shift, where cyclists take ownership of, and responsibility for, the meaning of the event. This process of defining, or naming, is a key feature of Critical Mass in that the production/solicitation of media mirrors the decentralized organization of the rides: both allow cyclists to "channel the energy and focus of the mass" through techniques that stand in direct contrast to those of the centralized, corporate institutions buttressing automobility.[23] Like Reclaim the Streets parties, the action is meant to be symbolic of its demands whereby cyclists critique the cultural, technological, and spatial dominance of the automobile by performatively asserting the power of both bicycles and bike riders.[24]

Performative Critique

Roads are technologies that play a fundamental role in the system of auto-mobility, both as material things that enable the circulation of auto traffic as well as ideological constructs that are consciously designed to encourage certain practices while inhibiting others. That is to say, in addition to facilitating travel, roads have enormous symbolic power and have historically been used to wield, and in some cases reorganize, socioeconomic and political power. The "fixing of spatiality through material building," as David Harvey argues, is not innocuous but rather a process of creating "solidly constructed spaces that instantiate negotiated or imposed social values."[25] In the road and highway systems, one can thus identify a matrix of motorized space that dominates cities and structurally limits the possibilities for alternative mobilities. For this reason (among many others), the construction and use of roads is often a source of contention as well as a focal point for a variety of social movements and direct action protests worldwide.[26] Critical Mass can be seen as part of this wider terrain of urban struggles waged against the process of spatial homogenization, for the twinned purpose of promoting bicycling and creating more participatory public spaces.

Unlike activist groups that attempt to physically transform roads through direct action or sabotage, Critical Mass riders take over the street to "assert a positive vision of how things should be in order to expose the current injustice of car dominated public space."[27] This mobile intervention points to the city as contested space of automobility—one mediated and dominated by auto infrastructure and the norms of driving.[28] In this sense, it shares a commonality with skateboarding, a practice Iain Borden describes as a method of appropriating and ultimately transforming the meaning and uses of urban space(s).[29] Borden specifically theorizes skateboarding as a critique of the dominant capitalist ideology governing the built environment inasmuch as skaters advocate use value over exchange value, pleasure rather than work, and activity instead of passivity.[30] Skateboarding's representational mode, Borden argues, is not that of writing, drawing, or theorizing, but performing—a way of articulating meaning through movement.[31] Despite the obvious and substantive differences between bicycling and skateboarding, a *performative critique* is an apt way of describing what bicyclists do when they take to the streets in Mass or en masse: not only do they use the environment in an unintended way (i.e., for a non-utilitarian purpose); they also simultaneously call attention to the cultural norms dictating both the prescribed function of the environment and the different ways it could potentially be utilized, traversed, or reterritorialized. Another important distinction between skateboarding and Critical Mass is that skating is an individual practice that, with notable exceptions, is not "consciously theorized," whereas Mass is typically used to amplify a critique:

> Bicycling is generally a very individual experience, especially on streets filled with stressed-out motorists who don't think cyclists have a right to be on the road. But when we ride together in Critical Mass, we transform our personal choices into a shared, collective repudiation of the prevailing social madness. The organic connections we've made (and continue to make anew, month after month) are the root of a movement radically opposed to the way things are now. As we continue to share public space free from the absurd domination of transactions and the economy, we are forging a new sense of shared identity, a new sense of our shared interests against those who profit from and perpetuate the status quo.[32]

To restate this, one of the implicit goals of Critical Mass is to initiate a break with dominant ideology through a direct intervention in the spaces where it is quite literally materialized. This tactic echoes the spatial politics of Situationist International (SI), or situationists, whose collective influence on the Provo I outlined in Chapter 3. To the extent that they theorized both a process of urban experimentation and the complexity of capitalist space(s), the situationists offer an insightful framework for interpreting Critical Mass and the tactical prospects of situationist mobility in the present day.

We Are Bored in the City . . .

Artists previously involved with the avant-garde groups COBRA, Lettrist International, and the International Movement for an Imaginist Bauhaus formed the SI in 1957 with the goal of creating a "revolutionary program in culture."[33] The situationists formulated a radical critique of the built environment called *unitary urbanism*—a premise at the heart of their opposition to the spectacle of capitalism.[34] They described the process of urbanism as the solidification of a passive, consumerist ideology that renders alienation tactile and material. Disrupting the physical and mental patterns nurtured by capitalism was fundamental to their belief in the revolutionary potential of everyday life, arguing that revolution would "originate in the appropriation and alteration of the material environment and its space."[35] Guy Debord, arguably the most well known SI theorist, claimed this revolutionary process could be initiated through the construction of "situations," or moments of everyday life transformed into "a superior passional quality."[36] Simon Sadler explains the theory of situationism advocated most fervently in the late 1950s and early 1960s:

> One only appreciated the desperate need to take action over the city, situationists felt, once one had seen through the veil of refinement draped over it by planning and capital. If one peeled away this official representation of modernity and urbanism—this "spectacle," as situationists termed the collapse of reality into the streams of images, products, and activities sanctioned by business and bureaucracy—one discovered the authentic life of the city teeming underneath.[37]

As part of their attempt to uncover the "beach under the pavement," situationists utilized the technique of the *dérive,* a method of exploration in which small groups of people "drift" through urban spaces to "notice the way things resonate with states of mind, inclinations, and desires."[38] Though the technique was influenced by surrealism and the Parisian *flâneur,* the *dérive* is not based on a willful submission to unconscious desires; rather, it is a means to creatively explore aspects of the city that have not been totally incorporated by the spectacle.[39] *Dérives* are typically conducted over a period of hours or days (even weeks), involving one or more people who drop their usual motives and routines—their work, leisure activities, and normal relations—to let themselves be "drawn by the attractions of the terrain and the encounters they might find there."[40] By studying the maps and notes taken from lengthy *dérives,* a practice called *psychogeography,* the situationists formulated different theories about how people could, or more precisely should, collectively disengage from the spectacle. Debord argues that spatial exploration and the "self-conscious construction of new subjective environments" are the keys to celebrating the "un-alienated areas of life."[41] The main idea of the *dérive* is thus threefold: it is a tool for analyzing and understanding the spatialities of capitalism, it is a tactic for imagining the possibilities of the city, and it is a playful technique intended to disrupt the commodification of leisure and desire.[42]

The *dérive* and psychogeography were developed in conjunction with the media-based tactic of *detournement*—an appropriative technique meant to transform "present or past artistic production into a superior construction of a milieu."[43] The hope was that the *detournement* could deny the implicit value of a cultural artifact (its authenticity) to reveal the artifice of the spectacle and the shallowness of capitalism; one can see this principle at work in the culture-jamming strategies employed by groups like The Billboard Liberation Front, Adbusters, and the Guerilla Girls, to name just a few.[44] Ultimately, the *dérive* and the practice of psychogeography were conceived as embodied versions of the *detournement;* in other words, one's everyday life could serve as a living critique of the spectacle through the creation of situations or experiments in behavior intended to transform participants' understand of, and engagement with, the city itself. Kotanyi and Veneigem explain, "The main achievement of contemporary city planning is to have made people blind to the possibility of what we call unitary urbanism, namely a living critique, fueled by all the tensions of daily life, of this manipulation of cities and their inhabitants."[45] The basic premise here is similar to Borden's conceptualization of the performative critique in that one's actions—which the situationists saw as the ideal expression of art—can invert the function of material spaces while simultaneously producing new, potentially radical spaces, even if the experience is only temporary. These "situations," Debord argues, create moments of participatory disruption—fissures intended to mobilize people for revolutionary struggle, or at least point to that possibility:

> The construction of situations begins on the ruins of the modern spectacle. It is easy to see what extent the very principle of the spectacle—nonintervention—is linked to the alienation of the old world. Conversely, the most pertinent revolutionary experiments in culture have sought to break the spectator's psychological identification with the hero so as to draw him into activity by provoking his capacities to revolutionize his own life.[46]

To put this another way, one might be able theoretically understand the possibility of life in a different political or cultural context, but it is impossible to collectively work toward revolutionary goals if one never experiences life outside the paradigms of capitalism and consumption. What Debord calls an "experiment in culture" is a means to initiate that break and (ideally) see beyond the confines of the society of the spectacle.

Overcoming Alienation, or the TAZ on Wheels

The situationists astutely recognized that one of the major obstacles impeding the transformation of cities, and by extension the transformation of a non-participatory culture, is the infrastructure and ideology of the automobile, and in particular, those parts of the environment where automobiles and capital have replaced the citizen as the focal point for design.[47] While they clearly blamed the urbanists and capitalists for the proliferation of this ideological arrangement, they also identified the deeper problem posed by the acceptance of auto-centric design: the inability for people to collectively see past the automobile in order to imagine something else. At the heart of Critical Mass lies a similar attempt to break the "topological chains" of spectacular consciousness, though it is not always framed in such heady terms.[48] Indeed, it is a relatively pragmatic way to intervene in what Mimi Sheller and John Urry call the "civil society of automobility," a markedly capitalist arrangement involving the "transformation of public space into flows of traffic, coercing, constraining and unfolding an awesome domination which analysts of the urban have barely begun to see."[49] The site where Critical Mass happens—the street—is a place where bicyclists can illustrate a viable, but admittedly partial, alternative:

> Critical Mass is an experience that goes beyond symbolic action, in spite of its enormous symbolic importance. It is a public demonstration of a better way of moving through cities. But during the time it is underway, it is more than a demonstration. It is a moment of a real alternative, already alive, animated by the bodies and minds of thousands of participants.[50]

The "real alternative" Chris Carlsson highlights here is the creation of a unique social space that Massers often contrast with the alienating impulses of car culture, or more specifically, the manner in which automobiles and the practice of driving engender clear technological and communicative barriers between drivers, their environments, and each other.[51] But while it is true that people who "dwell-within-the-car" frequently do so by themselves— particularly on the work commute—this isolation does not always produce alienation or loneliness, just as riding on a crowded elevated train does not automatically elicit a sense of community and conviviality.[52] As Michael Bull observes, many prefer the isolation of cars because they offer time for private contemplation and/or a sense of control over one's privatized acoustic space—a disposition also evident among the droves of iPoded mass transit riders found in big cities.[53] However, when the isolated practice of driving is analyzed as part of a broader pattern of privatizing and individualizing both public and work spaces, these norms are highly problematic. Joshua Switzky specifically notes the correlation between these trends: "In the age of private content-controlled, enclosed malls and sidewalk-less, single-use, subdivision pods, the only public space we know in common is that which we traverse by car. But in our cars we are usually alone, even if together on a 'crowded' road."[54] Alon Raab further reiterates this point, as he sees driving as the antithesis of an innate desire for exposure:

> From my bicycle seat, car drivers usually look miserable. Locked in their fiberglass and steel earth-polluting chariots, they move about in a stupor of noise, speed, and consumption, en route to the next gasoline fix. Their vehicles evoke in me, not the mass advertised images

of ease and freedom, but instead mobile coffins, brushing against endless other coffins, as they head towards those cemeteries called parking lots. Seeing bicyclists, the drivers become aware, if only for a second, of that time when they too were able to feel the world, not through a glass cage, but in a direct and particular way.[55]

While this is clearly a reductive view of driving, Raab expresses the sentiments of cyclists who see biking not simply as a transportation choice but as a means of overcoming the real and perceived alienation of automobility, or at the very least, the phenomenological and physical disconnection between mobile bodies and their environments. Indeed, the regular affirmation of this experience among thousands of individual bicyclists is part of what shapes both the context and desire for the collective, social experiment one finds in Critical Mass.

At the most basic level, cycling slows down the world in ways that tangibly affect interpersonal communication, most notably by promoting face-to-face encounters.[56] Scott Larkin, author of the zine *Go by Bicycle,* points this out in interview with the author: "The prospect of someone stopping to talk to someone when they're jamming by at thirty-five miles an hour is unlikely."[57] In addition, there is a sense among critics that habitual driving engenders an experience of cities that is not unlike tourism, inasmuch as urban spaces and landscapes are often abstracted into "pure, rapid, superficial spectacles."[58] Driving, according to this line of reasoning, physically distances people from both the materiality and the material realities of cities (i.e., the built environment as well as prevailing socioeconomic conditions) by facilitating a process that allows people to metaphorically and sometimes quite literally bypass the problems of cities altogether. The driver's gaze shaped through privatized mobility, Nigel Taylor argues, also objectifies and depersonalizes the world outside of the car in such as way that it transforms the environment, other vehicles, and even human beings into mere "things" that obstruct one's movement.[59] That is to say, while the car—like all transportation technologies—operates as a framing device, the "visuality of the windshield" becomes more than a casual or temporary looking glass when one considers both the ever-increasing amounts of time people individually spend "sealed off from the public and the street," as well as a broader cultural/legal context in which "the public" is increasingly being seen as a mere amalgamation of mobile private spheres—a condition Don Mitchell calls the "SUV model of citizenship."[60] The problem, in other words, is not necessarily what one sees or does not see each time one gets behind the wheel, but rather, the way driving shapes subjectivity and fosters a broader disposition toward urban space and urban life: an entire way of seeing.[61]

In contrast, the bicycle is construed as an "anti-spectacular device" inasmuch as it disarticulates autonomous mobility from the privatized experience of the automobile "capsule" and rearticulates it to a more tactile, direct experience of urbanity or "the urban."[62] Lee Williams highlights this sensation in an issue of *Cranked,* a zine devoted to bike culture in the Northwest:

> As urban cyclists we are intimately engaged with our city's neighborhoods in a way automobile commuters may never experience. We are incarnate, exposed to every element, rain-drenched and sun-warmed. Cyclists see the neighborhood for what it truly is: every pothole, piece of trash, and pile of shattered windshield glass along the road reveals to us the neighborhoods in the eyes of the city. On the other hand, we can smell the baking bread, gaze out from the vistas, and run our fingers through the tall grass alongside us as we ride. . . . For the cyclist, these myriad aspects of the city are immediate and tactile, not concealed behind steel and glass.[63]

Bicycling, in the simplest terms, transforms "out there" to "right here." But there is a much deeper sense in which this physical/technological shift becomes meaningful as a restorative act—a small way to subvert the fractioning of everyday life that André Gorz and Murray Bookchin, for example, see manifested in capitalism and reproduced/reified through the daily practice of driving.[64] It does not always foster a more authentic or real engagement with the city, as Williams and so many other bicyclists (and car critics) would have it, but it necessarily "forces a different kind of interaction with the world."[65] Louis Mendoza, who undertook a cross-country bicycle trip to research immigration and the "Latinoization" of the United States, suggests that this mode of interaction is "not always better . . . but that may well be the point."[66] Indeed, one of the reasons why bike riders are so passionate about bicycling, and by extension so excited about the idea of a bike culture in development, is because traveling outside of the *cage*—a term that motorcycle riders and some Massers use for the car—is seen as a point of entrée to a less mediated experience of the world that is precisely not predetermined or mundane.[67] Bicycling, in this sense, is quite literally a way of exposing oneself to "the social," and of embracing what Jen Petersen calls the "dialectical relationship with urbanity."[68] That is to say, riding a bike can cultivate a keen awareness of not only one's right to the city but also one's right to be produced by the city. Shelly Jackson speaks to this point in her zine *Chainbreaker:*

> I feel about this city [New Orleans] the way one dreams of feeling about the perfect love affair. I feel connected, forgiving, in full admi-

ration and acceptance for its beauty and its shortcomings. I never thought I could feel this way about a place. . . . [I]t struck me that the things I love about this city are things I may not have noticed or appreciated enough if it weren't for my mode of transportation, my lovely bicycle.[69]

Critical Mass may not provide this same experience for each of its participants, but in creating new permutations of social space through collective mobility, it opens up new possibilities that are both affective and political. Jeff Ferrell speaks to the latter aspect of this intervention:

Putting ourselves and our bicycles on the line, confronting automotive dominance through direct action, we invent the impossible: an island of safety, calm, and conversation in the middle of a busy street. And, in fine reflexive fashion, we inhabit this island with talk of Critical Mass rides in other cities, strategies for surviving encounters with motorists, sabotage in the workplace, anarchist history, and other subversions.[70]

At their best, such moments are likened to a temporary autonomous zone (TAZ), which Hakim Bey (aka Peter Lamborn Wilson) defines as "an uprising which does not engage directly with the State: a guerilla operation which liberates an area (of land, of time, of imagination) and then dissolves itself to re-form elsewhere/elsewhere, *before* the State can crush it."[71] Within this literal or metaphorical domain, the typical norms governing a material or social space are reworked for a brief moment in time, in the same way Mikhail Bakhtin envisioned the "free and familiar contact" of the carnival.[72]

One of the obvious problems posed by a political reading of the TAZ is that temporary moments of resistance do not do anything politically, as it were, much less provide a sustainable model for widespread mobilization. Murray Bookchin's scathing denunciation of "lifestyle anarchism," for example, takes issue with Hakim Bey's paradigm for precisely this reason:

Like an Andy Warhol "happening," a TAZ is a passing event, a momentary orgasm, a fleeting expression of the "will to power" that is, in fact, conspicuously powerless in its capacity to leave any imprint on the individual's personality, subjectivity, and even self-formation, still less on shaping events and reality. . . . The bourgeoisie has nothing whatever to fear from such lifestyle declamations. With its aversion for institutions, mass-based organizations, its largely subcultural orientation, its moral decadence, its celebration of transience, and its rejection of programs, this kind of narcissistic anarchism is socially innocuous, often merely a safety valve for discontent toward the prevailing social order.[73]

Bookchin's critique is insightful inasmuch as he recognizes the shortcomings of collective action not aimed directly at transforming the material, economic, and environmental realities of capitalism. But whereas Hakim Bey, among other anarchists, tends to overstate the prospects of the TAZ and other proto-situationist tactics, Bookchin similarly overstates their limitations. He wrongly assumes that activists who embrace creative forms of dissent necessarily do so at the expense of organized protest and movement building, which he sees as both politically efficacious and instrumental to the development of rational political actors. On the contrary, activists who employ such strategies often do so for precisely these reasons, as creative tactics are seen as complementary to—not mutually exclusive of—more traditional forms of political dissent aimed at transforming the material and cultural conditions of capitalism (i.e., coalition building; demonstrations; boycotts; civil disobedience; community organizing; and participation in local, regional, and/or state governments).[74]

The TAZ and other carnivalesque actions (in Bakhtin's sense of the word) can thus be seen as unique tools in a larger political toolbox, rather than a replacement for activism. Critical Mass, for example, is not a substitution for formal bike advocacy or the solution to the problems of car culture by any stretch of the imagination: many participants are admittedly apolitical and the event does virtually nothing to transform the structural conditions of automobility, the materiality of urban planning, or the basic parameters of everyday life in a capitalist society. What it succeeds at doing, however, is creating conditions in which people can actively imagine something different by physically doing it for a brief moment in time. It gives a bike rider a chance to "live the impossible," and to immerse oneself in what Charles Higgins describes as a *festive rolling adventure*:

> Though it raises the blood pressure of some rush-hour commuters, Critical Mass offers a change, if only for a few moments, in the domination of the streets. In place of tons of steel and glass is a rolling community of people who can talk to each other and experience safety in numbers. . . . Critical Mass provides an opportunity for average people to gather surrounded by other cyclists on the streets that otherwise threaten them.[75]

People who ride in Critical Mass frequently testify to the power of this experience because it obviously transcends the mere act of bicycling. Matthew Roth of New York City's Time's Up! states, "It is one of the few authentic experiences that I've had in a group setting," while Isral DeBruin, a college student at the University of Wisconsin–Madison, reflects on the perspective it lends to the city itself:

> I began to truly appreciate seeing the city of Milwaukee at street level, moving more quickly than walking, but without any glass or the sound of an engine between the buildings and me. I started noticing things I'd never seen before and felt the city in an entirely new way. I could feel the streets. I could feel the pavement.[76]

Radically transforming people's collective engagement with, and experience of, urban space (and mobility, for that matter) was for the situationists a radical gesture that manifests those aspects of humanity not totally suppressed by the logic of capitalism. Inasmuch as a single evening ride can profoundly alter one's "associations between city and transportation, politics and fun," Critical Mass is an "open work"—a gesture rooted in the positive refusal of constraints, the reconceptualization of urban space and the exploration of desires outside of, or apart from, the framework of consumption and utilitarian mobility.[77]

Semiotics of the Street

Critical Mass undoubtedly facilitates "meaningful connections with public space" but the physicality of this process, which I have discussed thus far as a performative critique, does not become meaningful through intentions alone.[78] While participants state their own ideas about what Mass is and is not, about what it does and does not do, the very nature of the experiment invites a level of interpretation that is completely unpredictable. The ride is contentious for precisely this reason: to its supporters, it symbolizes everything from pedal power to people power to the reclamation of public space, whereas its critics often see it as symbol of disorganization, lawlessness, and/ or a hatred of drivers. In the simplest terms, it provokes a response by way of its visibility. The anomaly of hundreds, sometimes thousands of cyclists taking over traffic is more than just a physical act; it is a profound visual spectacle that toys with the dominant semiotics of urban space.

City streets are spaces where cars, bicycles, people, and pavement both physically intersect and comprise a dynamic visual field made meaningful through interpretation. We are all readers of the street as much as we are its users, and the various assemblages of objects, practices, and rhythms constituting the ecology of the street function as signs whose referents always lay elsewhere. Moreover, there is no universal structure or singular formula that dictates the exact manner in which people connect visual signifiers or produce meaning. There are, however, dominant narratives and mythologies

Critical Mass in San Francisco, 2008. *(Photo by Eric Boerer.)*

influencing this process, and those pertaining to automobility—whether legal, vernacular, or entertainment-based—do a certain amount of cultural work by organizing and shaping the ways in which we collectively read and make sense of the street as the rightful domain of the car. Thus, when people stage parades, spontaneous street parties, or large protests that disrupt and/or temporarily repurpose the street, they also create visual events that stand in stark contrast to the normal, commonsense uses of urban space. The dominant signifier that typically organizes meaning in that space—the car—is suddenly vanquished, removed from its position of visual authority. In Critical Mass, the act of displacing cars with bicyclists—who themselves offer a noticeable contrast to the encapsulated driver—becomes symbolically consequential because of what the action connotes; it allows one to reread the street as space of transformation and/or possibility.[79] For example, Mass can render visible cyclists' critiques in a manner comparable to graffiti writing:

> Graffitists write their discord across perpendicular cement space, while Critical Mass cyclists ride their insurgence across horizontal cement space; and both employ a form used worldwide—a mode *du monde,* hanging their missive to the masses between the ocher-sky and slate-ground of urban public space.[80]

The comparison here is metaphorical but also suggestive of the ways in which the visibility of collective action is more symbolically powerful than textual appropriations of public space. That is to say, when one writes graffiti or participates in some type of street art or culture jamming, all that remains is the trace, be it a spray-painted tag, a new piece of art, or a smoothly doctored image. While such discretion is necessary for the act itself, it arguably leaves the impression that creative forms of rebellion are, in fact, only traces: visible referents of the absence of dissent. In contrast, Critical Mass offers an occasion for people to bring expressive dissent into the streets, making it palatable and putting it on display for everyone to see. This visibility is a constitutive part of the performative critique inasmuch as the act of reclaiming space is seen on the street, in real time, by participants and people passing by. Moreover, the act is also an "image event" that functions rhetorically within, and through, mass media representation.[81] Through the lens of the camera, bicyclists' bodies—and by extension their bicycles—can become the rhetorical vehicles with which the argument "we're not blocking traffic; we *are* traffic" is made. One can see this *body rhetoric,* as Kevin DeLuca calls it, at work in many images of Critical Mass, such as those depicting cyclists surrounded by a sea of cars—seemingly fighting for every inch of space—or in pictures where thousands of bike riders infuse entire city blocks in total opposition to the logic of traffic.[82] One of the strongest images, or genre of images, to capture the body rhetoric of Critical Mass are those in which cyclists have their bikes raised high above their heads, with their arms outstretched in a post-ride gesture of victory. This physical declaration, though initially popularized through Critical Mass in Chicago, is now an iconic symbol of bicycling, pedal power, and/or resistance to car culture: it is frequently used on event posters, flyers, zines, and other swag produced by and for cyclists. And whether Critical Mass participants realize it or not, the widespread proliferation of this iconography is itself an interesting appropriative act. That is to say, the image of a cyclist hoisting a bike above his or her head was not historically used to symbolize defiance or the reclamation of public space; it was instead an image utilized in a variety of advertisements for bicycles and bike accessories (in the United States and Europe).[83] Extracting this image from its branding roots and rearticulating it to an explicitly noncommercial, public event is an apt metaphor for the type of cultural shift from consumption to participation that so many Massers advocate on a wider scale.

As a significant visual phenomenon, Critical Mass fits into a wider set of communicative and/or symbolic practices aimed at critiquing the norms of automobility and otherwise debunking the myth of the "car without a single weakness."[84] A perfect example is the Green Hummer Project initiated by students and graduates from the Savannah College of Art and Design and Armstrong Atlantic State University, both located in Savannah, Georgia.

In 2004, Stephen Horcha and a number of friends built a pedal-powered vehicle—the Green Hummer—with a wood and metal frame designed to the exact specifications of a full-size Hummer SUV: the two front seat drivers powered the machine and up to three passengers could ride in the back. In addition to featuring the Green Hummer at a Savannah protest parade staged in opposition to the G-8 meeting held that year in Georgia (on an island roughly eighty miles from the city), the builders also took it on two dozen random excursions throughout Savannah in 2004 and 2005, commencing their vélomobile experiment with an Earth Day excursion into the suburbs where they flaunted the Green Hummer at the local shopping center (Oglethorpe Mall) and Wal-Mart. The crew also took trips to both Sonic and McDonalds in order to ironically indulge in the quintessential American ritual of getting fast food from a drive-through window.

Like other car-sized contraptions donned by protesting cyclists (Le Monde à Bicyclette) and pedestrians (Hermann Knoflacher's *Gehzeug*, or "walkmobile") in the 1970s, the Green Hummer makes its point by way of its sheer visibility: it is a mobile culture jam that highlights the bizarre reality of the spatial, material, and cultural practices that are thoroughly normalized within and through car culture:

This is the perfect SUV.

Our SUV is healthy, friendly, non-polluting, simple, inexpensive, fun, and socially responsible.

There are no black tinted windows to hide us from view. No air conditioning to further isolate us from the outside. No gas tank to fill and fill and fill. No greenhouse gasses pouring from the exhaust pipe. No frustration, no yelling, no honking, no road rage. No clocks to set, no alarm to annoy, no menus to scroll through. No video game system, DVD player, or GPS system. No "we own the road," "get out of our way," "don't slow us down" mentality.

When we ride the Green Hummer, we become part of our city. We have no illusions of flying through an empty city, devoid of traffic, parking problems, pedestrians, or street life like the drivers in television commercials. We expect people to talk to us. People ask questions, tourists ask for directions, traffic goes more slowly than we can pedal. We accept and expect little delays, and it's okay. We don't look for confrontations; we enjoy ourselves in our vehicle.

This bicycle is an attempt to make large numbers of people reconsider the ways that they move around their cites. Our SUV is the opposite of modern consumer culture, an anti-commercial. We want people to think independently of the corporations who program their televisions. We want people to see our pedal-powered, life-size Green Hummer cruise around a real city, and think about the contrast between advertising and the real world.

In advertising, cities are lifeless, cars are safe, drivers are happy, gas is clean, and you are not responsible whatsoever for traffic, pollution, your weight, the marring of our landscapes, or war.

Our SUV is for the real world.

The year after the debut of the Green Hummer in Georgia, a collective of bike-riding artists and activists known as Rebar initiated an event called PARK(ing) Day on November 16, 2005, with the purchase of two hours of time at a metered parking space in San Francisco. There, a small crew unpacked supplies from a bike trailer and proceeded to lay out sod, a tree, and a park bench, effectively transforming the parking space into a tiny park space for pedestrians. Favorable press coverage and the viral circulation of photos online cultivated a high level of interest and excitement for the event that materialized the following year when dozens of groups constructed forty-seven "parks" in thirteen cities on PARK(ing) Day, 2006. In 2007, the event featured the unprecedented production of two hundred "parks" in fifty cities, and it also marked the debut of the Rebar's PARKcycle: a sod-covered mobile instillation built in conjunction with artist Reuben Margolin. At twenty-two feet long with a solar-powered braking system, this pedal-driven "park" functions as both an artistic and technological triumph as well as an "open space distribution system designed for agile movement within the existing auto-centric urban infrastructure."[85] The designers rode the PARKcycle to San Francisco City Hall, where they proceeded to park in Mayor Gavin Newsom's personal parking spot in front of the building (he warmly greeted the builders and briefly inspected the device).

By "temporarily reframing the right-of-way as green space, not just a car space," Rebar troubles the slippery boundaries demarcating public spaces, as well of as those of the car itself (i.e., car versus not car). They, like the Green Hummer builders, encourage a more active and playful exploration of the processes bike advocates can use to remix the automobile and the automotive landscape, whether through guerilla theater, protest, or art installations. Urban Repair Squad, for example, is one of several ad hoc groups to similarly revive a technique that bike activists used to politicize automobility in the 1970s: the DIY bike lane. In 2007, Urban Repair Squad took the liberty of painting a few of their own bike lanes throughout Toronto (one in hot pink spray paint!) in response to city's faltering commitment to the implementation of official bike lanes; Toronto spent almost 50 percent less on bike lanes than its $73 million plan originally stipulated in 2001 and the city is also behind schedule on its construction of dedicated bicycle infrastructure.[86] Bike advocates in Los Angeles made similar appeals for bike infrastructure in recent years: one group used chalk stencils and homemade road signs to designate their own "4th Street Bicycle Boulevard," while a different group of Los Angeles riders outfitted one of the city's bridges with a professionally painted bike lane and an authentic-looking road sign that read, appropriately enough, "DIY Bike Lane."[87] In New York City, where bike lanes are increasingly prevalent but often ignored by drivers, cyclists initiated a lighthearted protest in which they traversed Manhattan in full clown suits and makeup in order to distribute faux parking tickets to vehicles parked in designated bike lanes—a gesture obviously meant to combine humor with concise message.[88]

Along with more playful forms of satire and culture-jamming tactics, bike activists also use art to engage with more serious matters, including the injury and death of bike riders. Ghost bikes, the stark visual landmarks revealing places where cyclists were hit or killed by cars, are a unique and emotionally charged example of this expression. Painted from top to bottom in white paint (hence "ghost"), ghost bikes are chained to posts or streets signs at the sites of accidents and typically feature a placard reading "Cyclist Struck Here" or "Killed by Car," though they range in format from anonymous inscriptions to the actual person's name and the date of the accident. While possibly influenced by the group Right of Way, which gained publicity for stenciling crime scene chalk outlines at sites where pedestrians and cyclists were killed by cars in New York City, the practice of constructing ghost bike memorials originated in St. Louis with Patrick Van Der Tuin and several volunteers who sought to bring attention to the dangers of auto transportation by documenting spots where bicyclists were hit, though not necessarily killed, by errant drivers.[89] Broken Bikes–Broken Lives, as the project was initially known, inspired cyclists in Pittsburgh to create their own ghost bikes, and they soon appeared in Seattle, Arizona, New York City, and, eventually, in more than two dozen cities in nine countries where they now primarily used as memorials for bicyclist fatalities.[90]

Ryan Nuckel, of the political art collective Visual Resistance—the group responsible for spearheading the ghost bike project in New York City—poignantly suggests that ghost bikes not only function as tributes to fallen cyclists and visible warning signs to drivers; they also inscribe cyclists into the collective memory of the neighborhoods in which they are placed.[91] In several cities, this process begins with the dedication of the ghost bike, which has become a ritual unto itself: bicyclists stage a memorial ride that commences at the site where the ghost bike is ceremonially locked into place, usually during a short service in which mourners pay tribute to the deceased. Though a sobering tradition, the creation and dedication of ghost bikes is a clear example of how bike activists use creative tactics to refocus critical attention on issues that are not only contentious and emotionally charged but also largely ignored and/or poorly contextualized in mass media. Moreover, they play a unique role in a process whereby bike riders interrogate the same problematics of urban transportation and public space with which Critical Mass participants are habitually engaged.

Influencing Arguments

The visibility and symbolism that make Critical Mass so exciting to its supporters are the same aspects that make its questionable legality and tenuous relationship with drivers frequent sources for scrutiny. In particular, there is an ongoing feud between cyclists as to whether the event is helpful or harmful to the larger project of bike advocacy; a debate exemplified by an archived 1999 e-mail "flame war" between Critical Mass supporters, participants, and critics (mainly "vehicular cycling" advocates) on the West Coast.[92] Like any online debate it features loads of ad hominem attacks, but as a document it reflects some of the major positions that cyclists have taken in defense of, and in opposition to, Critical Mass since its inception. To give some background, Sara Stout—a Critical Mass rider, veteran bike advocate, and co-host of the Bike Radio show on KBOO radio—wrote a piece for *Oregon Cycling* about the intimidating presence of police at Portland Critical Mass rides, namely, their tactic of "shadowing" (accompanying) rides and citing bikers for every possible traffic violation, including the most petty and arbitrary infractions. She rightfully argued that the police measures were unwarranted, costly, and otherwise discriminatory to bicyclists. Fred Nemo, a Portland artist/activist, and Jason Meggs, a Berkeley, California Mass participant and bike advocate, e-mailed Sara's article to several cycling listservs on the West Coast, in addition to the entire Berkeley city government. This touched off a massive argument about the legality and tactics of Critical Mass, especially the practices of corking red lights and occupying full lanes of traffic. The intensity of the debate—which is unfortunately repeated ad nauseum since the mid-1990s—revolves primarily around the ways in which bicycling is both presented and *re*presented to the public. For example, several supporters argue that Critical Mass is, or can be, construed as a collective act of civil disobedience that ultimately necessitates the violation of both traffic laws and cultural norms, particularly those seen as unjust or potentially hazardous to bicyclists.[93] Others denounce this view, maintaining that both the collective and individual actions of cyclists have ramifications for law-abiding bicyclists and bike advocates:

> If individual motorists aren't viewed as representatives of the entire motorized community, then bicyclists *shouldn't* be either. I AGREE! The problem is, we ARE representatives. We are a minority. A large group sees a single member of a minority behaving in a certain way, and the entire minority gets stereotyped. That is how things work![94]

In reading through these posts and the hundreds (if not thousands) of similar debates in online forums, one gets a clear sense that Critical Mass directly impacts the efforts of bike advocacy, but the exact nature of its influence is contested and often unknown.

Mass media representation complicates the issue and has significantly altered the stakes of Mass since its inception. The corporate press, in particular, habitually magnifies an image of participants as troublemakers, chaos-loving anarchists, criminals, and even potential terrorists worthy of undercover police surveillance.[95] Nevertheless, the pro/con binary typically used in debates over Critical Mass tactics is largely unproductive because it fundamentally ignores the rhetorical influence Mass can exert on bike advocacy even when it draws negative attention. For example, former San Francisco Mayor Willie Brown took a strong disliking to Critical Mass as its numbers swelled throughout his tenure as a city official. Following a three-thousand-person ride across the Golden Gate Bridge in June 1997, Brown began to ratchet up his public criticism, comparing participants to Hell's Angels and vowing to crack down on the ride. On July 25, 1997, more than five thousand people took part in the event and San Francisco police, under Brown's orders, intervened and proceeded to handcuff and arrest cyclists— many of whom were physically assaulted without provocation or resistance.[96] A number of suspects were carted off to jail, had their bicycles seized, and were each charged with failure to disperse, unlawful assembly, disobeying a peace officer, and blocking traffic.[97] Dave Snyder, the former executive director of the San Francisco Bicycle Coalition, describes how the ensuing media coverage reframed the coalition's agenda and ultimately influenced his approach to advocacy:

> The bicyclists' demand for safer streets for riding got more positive coverage in the media around the July 1997 meltdown than any other time in the past 100 years. Sure, it came with more negative coverage, too, but if you look at the coverage carefully, you'll notice that the negative coverage was about the ride. "Crack down on the unruly bicyclists!" When the media got to cover our agenda, it was overwhelmingly positive. All the opinion columnists felt they had to take sides, and even the most rabid car advocates had to admit, "sure, the bicyclists deserve more space on the roadway." When your enemies cede you that point, you know you have won![98]

Snyder asserts that Critical Mass is one of the best things to happen to bike advocacy because the media attention gave his organization—and others like it—a unique opportunity to publicize an issue typically ignored, or at best maligned, in the press. In other words, the perceived radicalism of

Critical Mass allowed him to exert a distinct amount of rhetorical leverage because the San Francisco Bicycle Coalition immediately became moderate in the eyes of the public, thereby securing a new public platform from which to express their views. The event functioned as both a pressure point for discourse and a possible incentive for transit/transportation agencies to increase their dialogue with cycling advocacy groups.[99] Martin Wachs, a professor of engineering and planning at the University of California–Berkeley, reiterates this point in his assessment of cycling infrastructure in San Francisco, noting that pressure applied by Critical Mass and other bike advocates in the late 1990s played a key role in the construction of a $147 million bike lane on the Oakland–San Francisco Bay Bridge: "It was included because a persistent, organized, and downright obnoxious group of advocates would not let go of the issue."[100] This type of political pressure is what social movement scholars call the *radical flank effect*: a scenario that sees more moderate elements of a movement directly benefiting from the pressure applied by radical activists.[101] Bike advocacy is a not social movement per se, but the same sort of communicative dynamics are clearly at work. Amy Stork, a co-founder of the Portland (Oregon) bike advocacy network *Shift*, speaks to this issue as both a cycling enthusiast and a specialist in strategic communication:

> I really appreciate Critical Mass because when you are going to change culture, it's good to have a radical wing, because that pushes folks toward the center. If people see Critical Mass and that appears radical to them, then putting a bike lane in seems reasonable. In places where they don't have Critical Mass, they think bike lanes are radical.[102]

It is impossible to accurately measure this rhetorical influence because bike advocates must actively make use of the flank effect, lest they run the risk of being labeled "radical," "anti-car," or simply a "Critical Mess."[103] Because just as it can legitimize formal advocacy groups, it can also undermine their efforts, or at the very least put them in the uncomfortable position of having to either distance themselves from Mass participants (who might be allies on other issues) or risk alienating drivers, politicians, and members of their own organizations. Noah Budnick, of Transportation Alternatives, articulates this anxiety when he suggests that the conflict and negative press surrounding Critical Mass ultimately discourages support for bicycling.[104]

Problems and Privilege

At the same time the contentiousness of Critical Mass can exert a powerful rhetorical influence on bike advocacy, it can also be persuasive in a more rudimentary and unfortunate way, namely, by encouraging people to stay home. Bike riders who would otherwise like to participate in the event often worry about potential conflicts with drivers or a possible confrontation with police. Chance plays an obvious role here, but the ebb and flow of conflict is more predictable in places where Mass attracts aggressive participants, or where the police express a fondness for hassling and/or arresting riders—the latter not necessarily due to the former, however. Regardless of the cause, this contentiousness can easily turn participants into ex-participants, even the most pro-bicycle, anarchist punk rockers like Rambo vocalist Tony Croasdale, aka Tony Pointless:

> I used to go to CM all the time. I stopped going because a lot of the people in Philly were being way too antagonistic to motorists. The way I see it is we ride together and if cars get pissed off, well that's on them. But when a car has a safe, clear way to move past the Mass and is respecting us as fellow vehicles and people purposely jump in front of them and block them in, that's different. And that was happening way too much.[105]

Choosing to avoid these situations is a decision Croasdale made because he disagrees with the tactics and general tone of the ride, and while it is certainly possible to pose the question of participation as an individual choice—which Massers tend to do—it largely ignores how participation in Critical Mass, or any facet of bike culture for that matter is necessarily structured by the same social privileges that influence all facets of public mobility and the use of public space. When the added element of police intervention is thrown into the mix, it becomes clear why Critical Mass can sometimes take on the appearance of an "Indiana University frat party," as Chicago resident Howard Kaplan said of his city's monthly ride in 2007.[106] Kaplan specifically refers to the visible party emphasis of Critical Mass Chicago, but his analogy incidentally hints at its homogeneous racial composition as well; this is assuming, of course, that Indiana University frat parties are not the bastions of ethnic diversity one might imagine them to be. Mass participants and frat boys are hardly one and the same, but it is nevertheless relevant to consider how white privilege, for example, enables certain people to take part in a quasi-legal public event that has, at best, a precarious relationship with police departments. Christopher Wallace, a longtime bike advocate, bike builder, and youth educator, speaks directly to this issue:

> Do people who have been historically profiled by the police want to place themselves with a group that is antagonistic to police? Most say NO and stay away. A black man once told me "if I join CCM [Critical

Mass Chicago] and you all piss of the police, WHO do you think they will arrest first, the black man or the white man? Now why would a black man want to join a group like that?" As long as there are self-centered young minds running bicycle anarchy, why would Arabs, African Americans, or up-standing citizens of any color want to join CCM?[107]

Wallace's rhetorical question, like the one put before him, is worth contemplating because the racial aspects of mobility challenge the scope and breadth of the bikes-as-freedom narrative at the heart of Critical Mass. More to the point, his inquiry is not without its precedents. For example, on May 30, 2003, police officers in Buffalo, New York, stopped the roughly eighty-person Critical Mass ride and began questioning cyclists before issuing a number of tickets. Heron Simmonds, a professor of ethics at Canisius College and the only African American rider, calmly intervened to question the officer about the situation and was promptly handcuffed and arrested. Bystanders verbally protested as Simmonds was taken to the squad car and Michael Niman, another college professor, took pictures until he was hit from behind and strangled down to the hood of a squad car. Eight other participants—none of whom raised a finger to the police—were hit with batons, choked, roughed up, and eventually arrested. The police charged Simmonds, who put up no resistance to the officer, with inciting a riot, fighting, blocking traffic, and a number of other charges carrying a maximum sentence of seven years in prison. Fortunately, the judge in the case agreed to examine dozens of photos that meticulously documented both the ride's progression and the baseless claims of the officers: he dropped Simmonds's charges, and most of the others, before the case went to trial.[108]

Critical Mass was not to blame for creating this particular situation—police clearly caused the conflict—but the incident highlights the point Wallace raises above: the first person singled out and arrested was the only African American on the ride. This could very well be a scenario in which it just so happened to be a black man who was arrested, but this explanation is itself the default thesis of white privilege—a pronouncement that simultaneously ignores both the historical and cultural constraints on black mobility as well as the structural racism of the entire criminal justice apparatus. Racial profiling not only targets African American motorists guilty of Driving While Black (DWB); it has also targeted cyclists for Biking While Black.[109] So-called confrontations with the police are rarely provoked by Mass participants, but at the end of the day the cause is irrelevant when considering its overall effect as a police magnet. As a case in point, the Pittsburgh police halted the Mass ride in March 2006, issued a number of citations to bicyclists, but ultimately arrested a young African American man who was not part of the ride, had no bicycle, and was merely trying to cross Penn Avenue (which was incidentally blocked by a police cruiser).[110]

Whether Critical Mass's contentious dialectic with the police does indeed have a discernable, measurable effect on its demographics is difficult to say, and my point here is somewhat broader. I emphasize the links between race privilege and public mobility in order to pose a simple question about participation in this public experiment: who is the *we* in "We Are Traffic"? This seems like a worthwhile question for riders to ponder, particularly because most large cities have more people of color who ride bicycles for daily transportation than there are white people doing the same.[111] Critical Mass may never be utilized as a platform for engaging with issues of race and mobility, or used to create a genuine movement against the racialized norms of car culture, but there are possibilities that present themselves if participants are willing to critically interrogate their positionality and attempt to build coalitions among people of different races, classes, ages, and genders who understandably have different stakes in improving urban mobility for bicyclists, pedestrians, and public transportation users. By its very nature, Critical Mass can do only so much to grapple with these issues, but the people brought together through the experience certainly can.

New Directions for the Bicycle

Despite the limited potential Critical Mass may have for addressing some of the overarching social issues framing public mobility, it has nevertheless broadened the political trajectories of bike advocacy and bicycle transportation. At the most basic level, the rides consistently spark interest in bicycle transportation and also nudge many people toward a more politicized engagement with transportation issues.[112] Monthly rides bring bicycling advocates together, inspire cyclists to get involved with local advocacy groups, and also provide an important network for activism that is at once tactical and social.[113] Dave Horton, for example, sees the event as an important tool for enhancing the "activist identities of individuals" and building a wider political community:

> Individuals share an alternative culture, but—for as long as they remain anonymous to each other—are unable to develop joint projects from their shared ways of life, values, and goals. Critical Mass made—and continues from time to time to make—visible and tangible the connections between them, transforming anonymous inhabitation of an imagined community into meaningful and possibility-laden participation in a realtime face-to-face community.[114]

The advocates/activists who emerge from these networks have indeed played crucial roles in putting cycling on the public agenda and pushing bike advocacy in new directions. Public space, for example, is a key feature of a pro-urban politics of cycling and an issue that Critical Mass positions as part of the terrain for cultural and political struggle.[115] By pushing the issue of public space to the forefront, cyclists highlight their own plight for spatial recognition and simultaneously bring necessary attention to the geographical dimensions of car culture. This is important because while the spatialities of automobility encapsulate vast networks of roads, highways, parking lots, and auto facilities, they are rarely subject to any serious criticism. That is to say, if and when the problems of car culture are brought forth into public dialogue, the parameters for critique are typically limited to the same recurring themes of traffic congestion, oil and gasoline prices, auto safety, road rage, hybrid cars, and, on occasion, the excesses of SUVs. These are all important topics for analysis, but interrogating these issues perpetually avoids any substantive dialogue about how the spaces of automobility impact and/or constrain the ways in which people think about, interact within, and ultimately utilize public spaces in their everyday lives. Critical Mass is a small but effective way to emphasize these connections as it points to a clear and demonstrative alternative in the bicycle itself.

The shape of the event—the actual mass—is another aspect of Critical Mass that expands the terrain for bike advocacy and the political uses of the bicycle. Carlsson says that in creating a moving, celebratory event, Critical Mass "opens up the field of transit to new political contestation, and pushes it to another level by pioneering swarming mobility as a new tactic."[116] Indeed, the model is apparently effective enough to be highlighted in the RAND Corporation's report for the National Defense Research Institute entitled "Networks and Netwars: The Future of Terror, Crime, and Militancy."[117] The authors of the study thankfully manage to distinguish bicyclists from international terrorists and drug cartels, but their respect for the tactical potential of "swarming mobility" is abundantly clear. And while bikes are not widely used in public protests, activists have experimented with this possibility at antiwar protests in Portland, Pittsburgh, Houston, Richmond, and San Francisco. The Republican National Convention (RNC) protests in New York City also featured the creation of *bike blocs*—groups of cyclists strategically incorporated into large street protests who have the advantage of being able to break up and re-form with a great deal of ease. According to Time's Up! which coordinated bike blocs at the event, they can give protesters a wider range of flexibility with their demonstrations and can provide logistical support to demonstrators on foot.[118] Moreover, the incorporation of bikes into street protests contributes to a festive atmosphere that not only "softens" the image of protesters but also "conveys an environmental message without a placard."[119] The most obvious impact that Critical Mass has as a strategic action is to create, or in some cases rejuvenate, people's interest in bicycles as vehicles for public expression. A new wave of creative bike demonstrations, protest rides, and celebrations ensued since Critical Mass gained popularity in the 1990s, including the somber memorial rides used to pay tribute to cyclists killed by automobiles, as well as the playful World Naked Bike Ride, started by activist/artist Conrad Schmidt as a protest against the indecency of oil.[120]

By presenting bicycling as something other than a competitive activity, an amalgamation of cliquey subcultures, or an Über-rational utilitarian mode of transportation, Critical Mass has at times successfully attracted new people to bicycling who are otherwise disinterested in the identity of being a bike rider. Charles Komanoff highlights the importance of this shift in a speech delivered to Bike Summer attendees in 2005:

> Critical Mass is generating new energy for cycling. Bringing in new riders. Providing training wheels, if you will, for cycling wannabes who find solo bike-riding too daunting. Creating a buzz for cycling. Providing a venue to dress up one's bike—a "pimp my ride" for cycling. Getting cycling out of its geek ghetto into someplace more appealing to the 99% of people who don't consider themselves "cyclists."[121]

Komanoff recognizes that Critical Mass appeals to a different crowd, or audience, than one can normally attract to bicycling through formal advocacy alone. His allusion to MTV's "Pimp My Ride" suggests that Critical Mass might even appeal to a younger crowd, or a demographic that values the aesthetic/stylistic dimensions of cool (i.e., non-geeky) transportation above utilitarian concerns: indeed, the sheer quantity of TV screens installed into cars during the half-hour program testifies to people's love of non-utilitarian transportation technologies. In this sense, Komanoff addresses some of the disparate reasons why potential cyclists might not be swayed by pragmatic appeals to environmental health, economics, or physical fitness that are commonplace in formal bike advocacy. This is not to discredit the validity or importance of such appeals, but to simply state the obvious: people are not going to start bicycling simply because it is efficient or good for the environment (as unfortunate as this might be). Komanoff's tacit point is that cultural norms play a profound role in one's decision to bike and Critical Mass gives people a chance to potentially rethink what it means to be a bike rider. This might ultimately be one of the reasons why people are "more prone to bicycle as a result of their experience" and why Critical Mass consistently attracts participants throughout the world.[122]

For people who are already interested in cycling or deeply invested in some facet of bike culture, the value of Critical Mass is not contingent on what it necessarily says to the public as much as it "benefits those who take part in it."[123] Sharing a collective experience with a group of fellow cyclists can be a profound moment for a biker, particularly one who is unaffiliated with, or uninterested in, formal cycling organizations, clubs, or traditional cycling events. It can serve as an introduction to a larger community of cyclists just as it can affirm, renew, or develop a person's commitment to bicycling or her or his identity as a cyclist. Ayleen Crotty, a veteran bike advocate and co-host of the Bike Show on KBOO radio in Portland, succinctly highlights this quality: "Some cities need CM to bring cyclists together. At its best, it is a forum for cyclists to meet, feel supported, and feel elated. To know they're not the only ones out there."[124] Charles Higgins also describes the value of Critical Mass in terms of its capacity to bring people together out of joy, frustration, and a general desire for both solidarity and community:

> Critical Mass provides an opportunity for average people to gather surrounded by other cyclists on the streets that otherwise threaten them. It is an expression of how many people think differently from mainstream society. Critical Mass originally intended to bring people together, at the same time and place, to ride home. It was and is an experiment with unpredictable consequences. That it grew and transplanted to cities all over the world says something about the collective frustration people feel about the streets. . . . In the end, the ride is likely to continue as long as people need a place to express frustration about invisibility and, conversely, to celebrate human-scale community.[125]

In creating a unique space where communities of cyclists can come together through their common love of the bicycle, Critical Mass serves an important ritual function that gives a tangible, human expression to the oft-used xerocratic slogan "Ride Daily, Celebrate Monthly." It is arguably the most cherished feature of the event and, incidentally, one of the characteristics its critics frequently overlook when they assess its value in instrumental terms. Judging Critical Mass based solely on a transmission view of communication, for example, subjugates the entire ritual experience by essentially measuring its utility as a communications technology—that is, how well it transmits a clear message to a passive audience. Interrogating the ways Critical Mass helps or hinders bike advocacy by sending the wrong message is not an unreasonable or irrelevant project, but it is only one way—not *the* way—to consider how meaning is produced and reproduced in this, or any other collective action.[126]

Conclusion

If Critical Mass is judged solely by its capacity to live up to the revolutionary rhetoric of its most vocal participants, then one can hardly call it a politically relevant action. The hegemony of automobile transportation cannot simply be unraveled through will power, even if the discourses of Mass participants adequately address the practices, social values, and mechanicals comprising the entire sociotechnological ensemble of the automobile.[127] Given these difficulties, there is a nagging temptation to dismiss Critical Mass as a mere novelty, or a token gesture akin to a "pie in the face."[128] On one hand, Critical Mass is simply a joyous prank on car culture, and an effective one at that. But Critical Mass is also much more than a prank. Like other forms of culture jamming, it can creatively highlight unequal power dynamics and problems with specific institutional arrangements. More specifically, the event thrusts the politics of automobility into public debate and simultaneously hints at a critical, utopian vision of mobility that is sorely absent from public discourse. For short durations, cyclists disrupt the automobile's domination of the city to demonstrate a fragmentary vision of two-wheeled mobility and human-scale community. When bike riders use this experience to interrogate the functionality, design, and ideology of urban space, they are actively questioning the parameters of urbanity itself, pushing others to consider what is possible, what could be.[129] In this sense, participants work as insurgent architects of mobility: a set of subversive agents who "desire, think and dream of difference."[130] Experimentation of this kind creates a literal and ontological space for people to imagine how resistance can be mobilized (pun intended) in new ways, and while it may not prompt a revolution or usher in the post-automobile era, it is fundamental to a strategic, radical reassessment of auto-mobility and the privatization and criminalization of public space(s). There is an important pedagogical value in this act alone that can point people beyond the bicycle toward more engaged, substantive forms of collective action.

At its best, Critical Mass is a raw expression of the utopian possibilities inherent in the city, and at the very least, it is a demonstration of creative dissent at a time when widespread cynicism, jaded apathy, and neoliberal ethics saturate the landscape with the same stench as that which emanates from the tailpipes of our cars. David Pinder rightfully argues that the ability to challenge dominant ideology in these circumstances is therefore "crucial for a politics of hope."[131] Consequently, even if these moments of dissent are fleeting, they give participants a chance to realize that they can use their voices, their bodies, and even their bicycles to make themselves heard. In this way, Critical Mass is a small reminder that "revolution is not 'showing' life to people, but making them live."[132]

CHAPTER 5

Two-Wheeled Terrors and Forty-Year-Old Virgins

Mass Media and the Representation of Bicycling

> Sadly, the bicycle came to be seen as a "low-status" symbol. The only grown man I ever saw riding a bike when I was a kid was Fred Benton, a fifty year old man who lived in a cardboard box in the lumber yard and rode around town drunk, cussing noisily at kids like me, carrying two buckets on the handlebars. He smelled like whiskey from a block away as he pedaled around searching for scraps of food or anything to trade for a bottle of cheap liquor.
>
> —Dink Bridgers, "Wheels of Fortune," *Dreamride*, 1997

> Bicycles are like masturbation—something you should grow out of.
>
> —Tony Parsons, "I Just Don't Lycra These Cycle Yobs," *Daily Mirror*, 2002

Kids were going crazy on their bikes back in 1979 and the television was partly to blame. Like suburban primates, the children of the disco era aped their television commercial peers and rode dangerously into the streets without looking. Or so goes the argument put forth by the U.S. Federal Trade Commission, the organizational body responsible for charging AMF Incorporated, one of the largest U.S. bike manufacturers of the period, with advertising its Evel Knievel brand bicycles and tricycles in an "unfair and deceptive way." Both of the commercials in question showed children riding carelessly onto streets, into alleys, and out of their driveways without slowing down to look for cars or other dangers; in one ad, two boys nearly collided with each other![1] As part of their settlement, AMF Inc. agreed to stop showing advertisements with children riding in an unsafe manner and complied with a request to produce public service announcements promoting safe riding.[2]

This case is just a footnote in the history of advertising law but it is interesting for how it frames the relationships between bicycling, mass media representation, and automobility. First of all, the fact that Americans actually cared about the way in which bicycling was represented to the public at some point in recent history is quite astonishing, let alone the idea of actually holding corporations accountable for what they show on television. Representations of utilitarian cycling are now all but absent from mass media in the United States, and it is particularly rare for television and film audiences to see an adult character using a bicycle as a normal, everyday mode of transportation. In the few cases where adult bicyclists are featured in U.S. entertainment media, they are generally portrayed as being far outside the mainstream; most are depicted as childish men, eccentrics, sexually odd characters, geeks, and/or financial failures. Negative perceptions of cycling are one of the many reasons why bicycles are widely considered a "forgotten mode" of transportation in the United States, but they serve an ideological function often ignored or overlooked.[3] The first half of this chapter deals specifically with how the representation of cyclists in films and television both produce and reproduce the cultural norms of automobility.

When analyzing media texts it is crucial to have a clear sense of both how and why mass media function in a given society. Thus, the additional reason I begin with the AMF case is because the cause-and-effect relationship it posits between media representation and human behavior is exactly the wrong way to analyze media power and its influence on transportation norms. Assuming that people simply mimic the images and narratives on television ignores the all-important cultural context in which television, films, books, or news become meaningful in the first place. That the kids watching these commercials knew anything about the real death-defying motorcycle theatrics of Evel Knievel was probably more detrimental to their behavior than anything they could possibly see reproduced by another ten-year-old on TV, particularly when the branding objective of the company was to specifically sell kids on the idea of being Evel Knievel through the use of their products. This is not to argue against restricting certain media content aimed directly at children or to dismiss the role of corporate oversight, but to point out some of the obvious limitations of criticizing media content based solely on what it does to people or what it makes people do (causality). For example, the entire AMF case revolves around a crucial question that is completely absent from the discussion: why would a bike-riding child potentially be in danger? As in most debates about the dangers of cycling—which I address at length in the second half of this chapter—the car is the lethal protagonist perpetually absent from analysis and free from critique. This scenario takes for granted that kids should necessarily avoid the street or that parents should naturally have to worry 24/7 about their child getting hit by a car. By never calling the system of automobility into question, the parameters of public debate about cyclists, pedestrians, and urban planning are perpetually skewed. My point in the latter half of this chapter is to take a step back to consider both how these debates are constructed through news media and why select narratives about bicycling and urban cyclists are habitually privileged over others.

The Bicyclist as the Lovable (Male) Loser

In a notorious and widely circulated essay entitled "A Cool and Logical Analysis of the Bicycle Menace: And An Examination of the Actions Necessary to License, Regulate, or Abolish Entirely This Dreadful Peril on our Roads" conservative satirist P. J. O'Rourke mocks bicycling as childish, undignified, unsafe, and downright un-American.[4] His musings, like those of all Libertarians (satirist or serious), should be taken with a grain of salt, particularly when one of his principal arguments against bicycling is its promotion of exercise.[5] Nevertheless, his essay still evokes laughter and smirks because bicycle transportation is thoroughly disregarded as a feasible option for most able-bodied Americans. In short, bicycling is considered a joke. This is hardly surprising when the most famous cyclist in the history of Hollywood film is arguably Pee-wee Herman, the bizarre and lovable character made famous by actor Paul Reubens in the 1980s. Reubens's collaboration with comic Phil Hartman and director Tim Burton resulted in 1985's *Pee-wee's Big Adventure,* a film about Pee-wee's quest to find his stolen customized bicycle—a plot clearly formulated as an homage to the Italian classic *The Bicycle Thief.*[6] For better or worse, this story about "a rebel and his bike" put cycling on the map of U.S. popular culture and has since attained the status of a cult classic. Within the exaggerated, campy world that Pee-wee inhabits, his bicycle obsession seems normal given the fact that he plays with toys, shops at magic stores, wears fuzzy bunny slippers, and lives in a house resembling a small carnival. Indeed, Pee-wee's eccentricities and goofy personality are all well suited for a mode of transportation typically associated with social misfits and pre-teens.

As Gary Snyder of the World Watch Institute notes, Americans view cycling for transport or work as either "uncool," a "children's activity," or "socially inappropriate for those who can afford a car."[7] Moreover, Pee-wee's boyish, effeminate persona is equal parts Peter Pan and what R. Anthony Slagle refers to as an extreme version of *the sissy:* a classic film stereotype used to negatively depict queer characters and "non-normative sexualities."[8] *Pee-wee's Big Adventure* is a hyper-fictionalized (i.e., over-the-top) film, but the narrative unmistakably ties bicycling to the lifestyle of a naïve and potentially queer eccentric whom mainstream Hollywood audiences may love to watch, but probably do not wish to emulate. Burton creatively gestures toward this exact theme in the final sequence of the film, a scene where Pee-wee and friends watch a dramatized version of his own story at a drive-in theater. In Pee-wee's Hollywood biopic, his character is played by a manly, bearded protagonist (James Brolin) and his red cruiser bicycle is replaced with a racing motorcycle.[9] With this brief meta-narrative Tim Burton alludes to Hollywood's practice of valorizing only hyper-macho, stridently heterosexual protagonists who are at least partially masculinized through their motorized transportation.

Bike-riding protagonists in entertainment media are few and far between, and like Pee-wee, they are often portrayed as boyish misfits and/or sexually "deviant." This image was popularized by the short-lived 1990s television show *Get a Life,* which starred Chris Peterson (Chris Elliott) as a thirty-year-old, irresponsible, idiotic paperboy living with his parents—a stereotypical sign of sexual immaturity, virginity, or queerness. Peterson's childish nature is clearly illustrated by his job and living conditions, but his low social status is also reflected by the fact that he uses a bicycle as his main source of transportation. Frank Oz's 1997 comedy *In and Out* similarly uses bicycling to accentuate a plot that revolves around the question of whether a bike-riding, neatly dressed, unmarried high school English teacher Howard Brackett is actually gay (he is "outed" early in the film by a former student during a televised awards show acceptance speech).[10] The caricature of the bicyclist-as-potentially-queer-loser was recently revamped and further popularized in *The 40 Year Old Virgin,* starring Steve Carell as Andy Stitzner—a naïve, geeky technician who works at a big box electronics store (à la Circuit City). Aside from his virginity, which dominates the thin plot of the film, Stitzner's weirdness is compounded by an obvious penchant for toys (à la Pee-wee Herman) and his bicycle—two character traits meant to connote childishness and social ineptitude. Bicycling, in this case, is either a symptom of social and sexual deviancy or its principal cause.[11] Thus, when Stitzner is juxtaposed with the other characters, his virginity and bicycle are consistently ridiculed: "I'm just . . . I'm trying to help you grow up, Andy. . . . I mean, *my God,* you ride a bicycle to work in a stockroom."[12] It is questionable whether audiences are supposed to instinctively equate the lack of a car with the lack of a libido, but it is difficult to deny the convenient relationship articulated between the two. Indeed, the only surprise of the film is that Stitzner does not ride off in a brand-new automobile after having sex for the first time—a move that would have secured his status as an authentic male in the eyes of American filmgoers. He remarkably manages to become a real man without having to give up his bike.

When bicycle riders in U.S. entertainment media are not explicitly endowed with childlike characteristics or sexual ambiguity they are still largely defined by their eccentricities, much like the neurotic, hyper-existentialist environmentalists in *I Heart Huckabees*.[13] But more often, cycling is used as a visual signifier of financial and social failure. A classic example is the 1986 film *Quicksilver*, which features Kevin Bacon as Jack Casey, an ex–stock broker who turns to a life of bike messengering after losing his fortune on Wall Street.[14] Casey is not a loser in the conventional Hollywood sense of the word; he is good looking, athletic, hard working, and the object of heterosexual desire (à la Jami Gertz's character Terri). But read within the context of the 1980s—a period when Wall Street and the yuppie lifestyle were mythologized in popular culture—it is significant that both cycling and bike messengering serve as their foils.[15] *Quicksilver* suggests that riding a bicycle—as a job, no less—is the very opposite of the American Dream; it is what people do when they hit rock bottom. The distance created between bicycling and yuppie materialism is probably one of the underlying reasons it remains a cult-favorite for many cyclists, but the overall bikes-are-for-losers theme is further reinforced by the film's other messengers who are involved in a drug-running scheme gone bad, including the ominously named Voodoo, played by Lawrence Fishburne.[16] The link between socioeconomic failure and bike messengering portrayed in *Quicksilver* has its comedic counterpart in the television show *Double Rush*, which aired on CBS for twelve episodes in 1995.[17] Robert Pastorelli starred as Johnny Verona, a guitar player who starts a relatively unsuccessful bike messenger company after his music career takes a dive. *Double Rush* is essentially a bike messenger version of the hit show *Taxi*, replete with a rag-tag group of lovable losers that includes a failed business school graduate, a couple of wise-cracking guys, and a danger-loving, zany bike messenger (David Arquette). It is perhaps not coincidental that this show came on the heels of the third season of MTV's *Real World*, in which a twenty-five-year-old San Francisco bike messenger named David "Puck" Rainey gained international notoriety/infamy—much to the chagrin of bike messengers—both for his self-congratulatory obnoxious behavior (e.g., nose picking, scab brandishing, not showering) and for getting kicked out of the group house after continually harassing roommate Pedro Zemora, an AIDS educator who died of the disease only months after shooting the series.[18]

The most recent additions to the bicyclist-as-loser cannon are the television comedy series *Arrested Development* and the film *You, Me and Dupree*.[19] *Arrested Development* stars Jason Bateman as Michael Bluth, a semi-neurotic businessman trying desperately to keep his dysfunctional family, and their business, from the brink of catastrophe. Bluth is shown riding his bicycle throughout the first season of the show and this is a clear allusion to both his frugal anal retentiveness and his family's financial problems. To reinforce the point of Michael being a struggling failure, he eventually (and hilariously) makes the transition from riding a bicycle to driving a stair truck—a vehicle used to exit passengers from small airplanes. The Hollywood comedy *You, Me and Dupree* stars Owen Wilson as the unemployed Dupree, an irresponsible dud who plays the role of unwanted houseguest to his newlywed friends. His loser status is made apparent by his couch-surfing lifestyle and is at least partly signified by the fact that he not only rides a bicycle but also wears a hockey helmet while doing so.

This list is by no means comprehensive, but in each of these examples bicycling is not portrayed as a normal activity as defined by mainstream Hollywood standards, much less a character trait contributing to the appeal of the protagonists' lifestyles. While audiences may root for these characters as the lovable—and always male—losers they are, these representations simply reinforce the idea that the everyday cyclist is either childish, eccentric, deviant, or in some way lacking the qualities necessary to either be, or become, a stereotypically successful and/or well-adjusted person (i.e., a responsible, straight white guy with a good job). It would easy to dismiss these fictional, comedic representations as insignificant, were these same attributes not consistently identified as qualitative factors dissuading Americans from wanting to either ride bicycles for transportation or identify as cyclists.[20] John Pucher, Charles Komanoff, and Paul Schimek specifically allude to this problem in their study of North American cycling trends: "The perceptions of cycling as lying outside the mainstream of American life discourage bicycle use."[21] Despite the overall positive image the authors find associated with sport and fitness, they astutely recognize that the "various images of cycling are so heavily determined in relation to automobiles that utilitarian cyclists are variously seen as too poor to own a car, 'anti-auto,' eccentric, or deviant."[22] Indeed, these stereotypes seem to function only inasmuch as they can frame bicycling in habitual contrast to the dominant representations of automobility. This contrast is quite specific, however. Bicycling is almost never shown as a unique mode of transportation with its own characteristics, rhythms, or nuances, let alone as a possible alternative to driving. It is portrayed, instead, as a debased form of driving—a mode of transport lacking both the technological advantages of automobiles and the essential cultural attributes that presumably make them so desirable (their aura). This same binary is mapped onto bicyclists, who are themselves presented as debased adults incapable of growing up or fitting in.

As much as these images and plot lines construct a skewed narrative about bicycling and cyclists, they also tell us something about the cultural role of automobility as a strikingly gendered phenomenon. The virtual absence of female cyclists in these and other films and TV programs illustrates the extent to which the anxiety over mobility is very much an anxiety about heterosexual masculinity itself. Without a car, it is presumed that men on bicycles are incapable of adequately performing their masculinity for other women, or each other, thereby running the risk of becoming toy-collecting eccentrics, thirty-year-old paperboys, or forty-year-old virgins. Because while the connections between driving and masculinity have a long history of representation in mass media, there is arguably much more emphasis today in openly glorifying the links between masculinity, male virility, and the automobile. Hummer's "Restore the Balance" advertising campaign (circa 2007) exemplifies this tactic: one of the company's television spots features a man whose male inadequacies—suggested by his tofu and vegetable purchases at the grocery store checkout line—force him to spontaneously purchase a sixty-four-hundred-pound vehicle to compensate for his lack of "meat." In addition to films and advertising campaigns (Hummer is one among many), the broader popular culture in the United States is similarly invested in pronouncing the stereotypical bonds between straight masculinity and driving. As a case in point, there are now tens of thousands of drivers attaching fake testicles, or "truck nutz," to the rear bumpers of their vehicles, symbolically transforming their SUVs and trucks into giant phalluses.[23] The message that one's vehicle "has balls" exhibits the subtlety of an "I'm with Stupid" T-shirt, but it is precisely their grotesque obviousness that makes them interesting, not as much for what they show (clearly), but for what they reveal. For in displaying one's goods to the public, so to speak, these men unquestionably validate every critic who decries the big vehicle craze in the United States as an insecurity contest over penis size. These dangling prosthetics—much like the three-ton machines to which they are attached—crudely illustrate the degree to which driving is culturally employed in the performance of heterosexual masculinity, just as they simultaneously reveal the extent to which masculinity is itself a performance—often a ridiculous one at that.[24]

Bicycling as Auto-Pedagogy

Mass media are obviously not responsible for inventing the dominant norms of mobility in the United States, but they play a collective role in renewing, amplifying, and extending the predispositions constituting dominant culture.[25] For example, bicycling can easily be made to symbolize the social failure and/or deviancy of adult characters because it is first and foremost an activity that is usually associated with youth culture. This stems not only from the actual popularity of bicycles among children in the United States—which is immeasurable—but also from the past reservoir of media images that effectively preserve bicycling in the domain of childhood. Before BMX-riding youth were popularized in 1980s films like *E.T.* (1982), *BMX Bandits* (1983), and *Rad* (1986), bicycle-riding children also dotted the landscape of 1970s family sitcoms, including *The Brady Bunch, Eight Is Enough,* and *The Partridge Family.*[26] Less obvious, however, is the common appearance of bicycle-riding children in television shows of the 1950s and 1960s, as well as bicycle advertisements of the same era. The images of freckle-faced, white boys and girls straddling new bicycles on Christmas morning, or pre-teens cycling to friends' houses in TV Land, were almost exclusively suburban depictions, ones that came to define, in part, an emerging image of suburbia as a space where bicycles and childhood went hand in hand. Like other aspects of early broadcast television, these images did a certain amount of cultural work by displaying a new set of social norms rooted in consumption and suburban domesticity. In particular, these programs and their advertising sponsors reinforced a narrative of the American dream as a technologically modern utopia replete with fully industrialized kitchens, the newest communications technologies, manicured lawns, and automobiles in every driveway. Ruth Schwartz Cowan and Lynn Spigel discuss the explicit gendering of this technological arrangement in their historical work, but one can also identify an important way in which technology—as mobility—is also hierarchized and stratified by age in the suburban fantasy.[27]

Whereas city living typically requires adults and children to share common experiences of riding busses, taxis, trains, and/or streetcars—not to mention walking—suburban mobility clearly delineates the lines between technological users. Put simply: bikes are for kids, cars are for grownups.[28] For one to become an adult in the techno-spatial context of suburbia means that one naturally has to become a driver, so bicycling essentially serves as a youthful preview of adult mobility—a set of training wheels for one's real experiences as a driver. This theme is rehearsed not only in bicycle advertisements and entertainment media of the 1950s and 1960s but also in the design of the bicycle itself. Manufacturers like Elgin, Shelby, and Mercury were among the companies to pioneer lavish art deco-style bicycles in the 1930s, largely mirroring the sleek lines, large frames, chrome highlights, and whitewall balloon tires found on automobiles of the same period.[29] Yet it was Schwinn and Murray who propelled auto-detailed bicycles to an iconic status in 1950s American culture as kids traversed the suburban landscape on their candy colored cruiser bicycles that for all intents and purposes served as mobile signifiers of the automobile itself—visual icons forecasting an eventual, and inevitable, transition to adult automobility.[30]

Media corporations clearly had a vested interest in promoting the products of their automobile-, oil-, gasoline-, and tire-producing sponsors, but there is nothing to suggest that television producers somehow conspired to keep cycling within the realm of children's play, particularly since most American bicycle companies were not even producing viable models of adult bicycles in the 1950s and early 1960s. Nevertheless, this does not change the overall effect of perpetually representing bicycling as a strictly youthful hobby or a practice useful only inasmuch as it fosters good driving sensibilities

Automotive pedagogy: the bicycle as pseudo-car.

(which is itself a dubious claim). Obtaining one's license, acquiring one's first car, and even getting in one's first accident are all seen as rites of passage in the United States, and these themes are repeated incessantly in mass media as both the central narrative—as in the slew of American road trip films—or as an ancillary component of the teen coming-of-age story (usually signified by one learning to drive).[31]

If the repetition and banality of the bicyclist-as-eventual-driver narrative was not made abundantly clear through advertising and the contexts of television and film, it was hammered home in the slew of instructional safety films shown to children and teens throughout the 1950s, 1960s, and 1970s. In the films that specifically feature bicyclists, there is a clear attempt to teach bicycle safety not as a set of skills for use into adulthood but rather as a set of skills ultimately beneficial for the burgeoning driver. In films such as *Drive Your Bicycle* (1955), *Bicycle Today—Automobile Tomorrow* (1969), and *I Like Bikes* (1978), bicycles are enrolled in a specific type of technological and cultural pedagogy about growing up in the United States—a process that requires one to accept automobility as an inevitable and universalized feature of everyday life.[32] The importance of this lesson was not lost on automobile companies like Chevrolet, whose 1954 film *Tomorrow's Drivers* does away with the bicycle entirely and shows a class of Phoenix public school kindergartners driving miniature pedal-powered cars through a rather comprehensive mock traffic grid that includes street signs, painted lanes, and concrete intersections.[33] We hear the narrator proudly remind us that "school children are learning about the automotive age before they learn their ABC's." General Motor's film *I Like Bikes* is a particularly effective and overt example of this growing-up narrative at work; it shows Lisa in her transition from five-year-old bicycle recipient (Christmas) to ten-year-old cyclist, to fifteen-year-old permit driver, all the while scrutinizing the bicycle's inherent deficiencies and the implicit danger of cyclists.[34] At five and ten years old, Lisa exclaims, "I like bikes!" But when Lisa turns fifteen, the jovial narrator says, "She likes bikes, but she *loves* cars. . . . When she gets her license, will she change her likes? Will she still like bikes? We'll see." Lisa's first attempts at driving are marred by negative encounters with bicycles: she accidentally crushes her own bike while backing out of the driveway and then barely misses an African American cyclist on the road. The following day she almost opens her door on yet another cyclist as the narrator responds in song:

> *I like bikes, but . . .*
> *they're so hard to see!*
> *Oh yeah, they're so hard to see.*
> *Look at me! [says a cartoon bike]*
> *I blend with fogs,*
> *I hide behind dogs,*
> *and when the thunder crashes*
> *I'm out there making splashes.*
> *I lurk in drives [said in a creepy voice].*
> *And when the sun gets in your eyes, surprise!*
> *I'm hard to see,*
> *so please, watch out for me.*

The next montage shows Lisa passing a cyclist who crashes on the street after riding through what appears to be a miniscule puddle—a scene that illustrates how bicycles, unlike the automobile, are totally unreliable:

A bike is easily upset.
You bet!
I like bikes, but . . .
little things upset 'em!
It's not only when I'm wet
that I'm easily upset [says a cartoon bicycle]
Just let me try to travel on gravel,
or tangle my chain.
Or run across a roadway drain,
or fall in leaves.
Jeesh! What a pain.
Little things upset us!

Subsequent scenes show school children carelessly darting into traffic on their bikes and another cyclist who almost gets hit after failing to pay attention to Lisa's turn signal. The film closes by reminding viewers that the fallibility of bicycles, as well as the inattention of their users, means that neither should be trusted. Indeed, this dual skepticism of bicycle and bicyclist is highlighted in several other instructional films designed to teach safe cycling habits, diligent attention to maintenance, and the perils facing children who disobey such techno-mobile norms.[35]

Media-as-Culture-as-Media

My point in analyzing these representations is not to suggest that we collectively lose our sense of humor about comedies, our sense of irony about campy educational filmstrips, or our love of Pee-wee Herman for that matter. Nor am I arguing for images of bicyclists that simply conform to the heteronormative, consumerist narratives dominating mass media, because with few exceptions, the bicycle industry and most cycling publications already succeed admirably at this goal.[36] Rather, I think it is important to recognize the ways that entertainment media either systematically erase bicycling from the landscape of popular culture or work in conjunction with other media texts to represent it in an ideologically loaded manner. Mass media—particularly entertainment media—do not simply reflect the dominant culture like so many mirrors to the world: they actively re-present reality and construct simulations of the real world through the use of the stock characters, predictable genres, standardized conventions and editing procedures, and politically conservative narratives. Indeed, the profit model of the corporate media industry rewards an adherence to these norms because they allow for the production of cost-effective media that minimize risk, both economic and ideological. The resulting products are far from benign and one can look to the historical use of racist, sexist, and xenophobic films and TV shows as clear examples of how mass media foster stereotypes, or what Walter Lippman famously called the "pictures in our heads."[37] Yet the meanings of images and narratives are not injected into audiences like serum through hypodermic syringes—a sentiment popularized by communication scholars in the first half of the twentieth century and later revamped through media effects research.[38] Indeed, audiences are diverse and often engage and interpret media texts (e.g., television shows, advertisements, and films) in ways unforeseen by their respective producers, advertisers, or distributors. Meaning is thus co-produced, or one might say co-authored, by viewers/listeners who negotiate media content within specific cultural contexts shaped by historical, socioeconomic, and political forces, as well as personal experiences, everyday practices, interpersonal communication, and other media texts.[39]

News plays a unique role in this process because it collectively frames and hierarchizes both social and political phenomena, as well as the images and narratives gleaned from entertainment. Like other forms of media, the news does not necessarily tell people what to think, but it does give audiences a limited set of ideas to think about.[40] This agenda-setting function contributes to the production of dominant cultural norms by telling people what is important, by defining the parameters of newsworthiness (i.e., which subjects/topics merit consideration), and by otherwise framing and legitimizing specific representations of the world. The ideological power of news, in other words, stems not only from what it says—or more often does not say—but also from the manner in which it presents itself as non-partisan, hence trustworthy. If news media are indeed important *cultural actors,* as Michael Schudson argues, then the meanings, symbols, and messages they produce about transportation and mobility weigh heavily on the everyday processes of driving and bike riding.[41] This cultural discourse, I argue in the following sections, exerts power inasmuch as it structures dominant narratives about bicycle transportation and bicyclists that promulgate automobility as either an ideal cultural arrangement, or at the very least, an uncontestable fact of life. Before explaining the unique problems this poses for urban cyclists, it is worthwhile to first recognize some of the positive trends in recent news coverage of recreational and utilitarian cycling.

The Good News (Sort Of)

News media in the United States rarely focus on bicycling in any substantial way, but if and when they do, the stories tend to highlight the benefits of recreational cycling and cycling-as-exercise. This is hardly surprising since millions of Americans, including children, families, corporate CEOs, seven-time Tour de France champion Lance Armstrong, ex-president George W.

Bush, and President Barack Obama, all ride bikes for fun, exercise, or sport.[42] Until recently, stories about utilitarian cycling and bicycle transportation were scant and unlikely to be featured in any national televised newscasts, though they occasionally appeared in national print publications like *USA Today* and *Time* magazine, as well as major newspapers like the *New York Times,* the *Washington Post,* and the *Los Angeles Times.* On the whole, news coverage of bicycle transportation has varied considerably throughout the last 130 years, depending on a number of socioeconomic, geographical, cultural, and political factors. For example, one will undoubtedly find more stories about bicycle transportation in cities like Portland, Minneapolis, and Seattle because they have vibrant bicycle cultures and some of the highest bike commuter rates in the country.[43] The same trend applies to Chicago, New York, and San Francisco because the sheer numbers of cyclists offer opportunities for human interest and/or lifestyle pieces about cycling, especially its health benefits—a process aided by the accessibility of local cycling experts and organizational representatives to whom journalists can source quotes and commentary.[44] The larger political context of the period can also impact the way news media cover, or choose to ignore, the bicycle. For example, the *New York Times*—a paper with one of the longest running Automobiles sections in the nation—ran a disproportionately high number of favorable stories on bicycle transportation in 1942, following the creation of the War Production Board, a federal organization charged with the task of rationing raw materials for military priority in World War II.[45] With automobile manufacturing at a standstill and both gasoline and rubber in short supply, mass transportation rates surged, as did the number of bicycle commuters and bicycle trips taken in the United States.

Like a number of advertisements circulated by bicycle companies in the early 1940s, newspapers helped to normalize adult cycling, if only for a brief period, by framing it as a pragmatic and patriotic endeavor meant to bolster the war effort.[46] Indeed, a number of major newspapers ran pieces in mid-January of that year about the sale of 750,000 Victory bicycles—minimalist machines made partly from recycled materials and produced by the two remaining bicycle manufacturers allowed to operate under the War Production Board's (WPB) mandate (on the contingency of U.S. military needs/demands).[47] Several of the articles were accompanied by pictures of Dr. Leon Henderson (then director of the Division of Civilian Supply of the Office of Production Management), who is seen riding a Victory bike while dressed in a full suit and fedora with a large cigar protruding from the side of his mouth. With him is stenographer Betty Barrett, who sits like a piece of pretty luggage inside the large front basket that came standard on one of the two Victory models produced for U.S. consumers.[48]

Bicycling as a patriotic response to wartime automobile and gas rationing. Leon Henderson and Betty Barrett riding a Victory bike in 1942.

News coverage of bicycle transportation increased both quantitatively and qualitatively in recent years for an additional set of interconnected reasons, including the sheer persistence and flak of vocal cycling advocates, the popularity of both urban cycling and physical fitness, and the mainstreaming of several U.S. bicycle advocacy groups in the early 1990s that tapped into the financial resources allotted to metropolitan planning and transportation networks through the Intermodal Surface Transportation Efficiency Act (ISTEA), thereby improving their capacity for activities like lobbying and public relations.[49] The last decade has thus seen large advocacy groups effectively publicize national campaigns like Bike-to-Work Week, Safe Routes to School, and Bicycle Friendly Communities, as well as more localized bicycle transportation initiatives.[50] Smaller, volunteer-based advocacy groups have also been relatively successful at securing news coverage for grassroots community events like Pittsburgh's Bike Fest, initiated in 2005. National broadcast news stories on bicycle transportation are still few and far between, but the trend toward more coverage—and more substantive coverage—is both palatable and likely to increase due to a faltering U.S. economy, instability in the

Middle East, and the prospects of oil and gasoline eventually returning to the highs achieved during the summer of 2008 (more than $144 per barrel and $4 per gallon, respectively). At the same time, news media have for the better part of the last three decades helped to produce a stereotype of urban cyclists as reckless, aggressive, and threatening to both pedestrians and motorists. In the following sections I examine these narratives to show how they problematize urban cycling and contribute to an overall climate of hostility against pro-bicycle and/or anti-car advocates in the United States. The corporate press contributes to this process in several key ways, such as representing cyclists as a threat to public safety, exacerbating and/or decontextualizing incidents involving bicyclists, and mainstreaming radical Libertarian policy initiatives into public debates over transportation.

The Bicycle Menace

Carnage and conflict are the favored tropes of U.S. news, so it comes as no shock that coverage of urban cycling frequently emphasizes accidents, fatalities, and confrontations, particularly those that can be easily spun into an ongoing war of bicyclists versus pedestrians, or more often a "wheel war" between bicyclists and motorists: "*The epic battle of bikes versus cars rages on.*"[51] Coverage of Critical Mass arguably presents the most definitive examples of the latter trend, as journalist Alex Storozynski illustrates in his assessment of New York City participants, whom he calls a "rogue group of aggressive cyclists playing a dangerous game of chicken."[52] Journalists habitually neglect hundreds of peaceful monthly rides in favor of reporting on those where the police intervene or a skirmish breaks out between Massers and motorists. In many cases reporters simply resort to punning with the phrases "Critical Mass" and "Critical Mess" while failing to accurately account for the nature of said incidents.[53] This is especially true in the coverage of rides where police show up and illegitimately harass participants. For example, the May 2003 ride in Buffalo, New York (mentioned in Chapter 4), elicited some of the following headlines and bylines: "Charges Fly as Bicyclists and Police Clash," "Riding at Their Own Risk," and "The Chain Gang: Bicyclists Face Off with Police, and the Ride Goes to Court."[54] One would naturally conclude that there was a fight or some direct physical confrontation involving more than cyclists' heads being slammed onto the hoods of police cruisers. The Minneapolis/St. Paul *Star Tribune* reports a Critical Mass incident on September 1, 2007, in a similar fashion; the headline and byline read, "19 Bicyclists Arrested after Rally Turns into Melee: Officers watching the event in downtown Minneapolis say they were attacked, escalating the confrontation."[55] The article exclusively quotes Deputy Police Chief Allen and provides no explanation for how a so-called scuffle between police and a cyclist was responsible for the swift deployment of a police helicopter and a small army of forty-eight officers from six different departments. In fact, the plethora of police officers were conducting what was most likely an illegal surveillance operation on political activists taking part in a weekend of protest planning for the 2008 Republican National Convention. The omission of such details is hardly atypical when it comes to routinely characterizing tens of thousands of cyclists, in cities throughout the world, as anarchists, radicals, and "anti-social freaks."[56]

Rather than contextualizing Critical Mass or exploring some of the actual political or cultural issues raised by participants, news media tend to cover the monthly ride in the same way they cover most controversial issues: "They stress polarization and provoke conflicts . . . showcasing the most belligerent drivers and cyclists."[57] Rides in San Francisco and Portland largely fell into this pattern of representation for much of the late 1990s as both local and national news media exacerbated the already palatable tensions between cyclists, drivers, and city officials. For example, when San Francisco riot police attacked and arrested a number of the five thousand (unarmed) participants in the July 1997 ride, the city's newspapers ran highly inflammatory pieces rivaled only by *Time* magazine's follow-up story entitled "The Scariest Biker Gang of All."[58] Ten years later, an uncommon and inexcusable incident of vehicle property damage still elicits a wave of incendiary reporting that makes it seem like a habitual occurrence. On the March 2007 ride in San Francisco, a minivan apparently ran into a Mass participant, and while accounts of the speed and strength of the collision vary, what is clear is that the driver tried to flee the scene and was stopped by a group of riders eager to castigate the driver and report her to the police. In retaliation to the attempted hit and run, an enraged biker threw his bike through the minivan's back window, clearly oblivious to the children seated behind the tinted glass (the kids were in the middle seats of the minivan and thankfully not hurt). The scenario was chaotic to say the least, but the antagonistic editorial duo Phillip Mattier and Andrew Ross quickly led off the attack against *Critical Smash* with B-movie caliber precision: "It was supposed to be a birthday night out for the kids in San Francisco, but instead turned into a Critical Mass horror show—complete with a pummeled car, a smashed rear window and little children screaming in terror."[59] Halfway through their hyperbole they finally inform readers that the incident actually began when the driver "tapped" one of the cyclists, as Mattier and Ross so gingerly define an encounter between a two-ton vehicle and a twenty-pound bicycle.

Critical Mass participants are in many situations partly to blame for their own negative press, as one can clearly see in this last example, but the bulk of stories published throughout the last fifteen years largely mischaracterize the worldwide event and its thousands of participants based on the actions of a few "massholes."[60] More significantly, the corporate press essentially rehashes the same critiques of urban cycling circulated in newspapers as far back as the nineteenth century: Massers are simply inserted into a preexisting narrative first constructed about "scorchers" in the 1890s and then modified to address the "recklessness" of urban bicyclists in the 1980s. The modern version of this narrative was largely developed and widely deployed in New York City following the deaths of three pedestrians who were struck and killed by cyclists (in separate incidents) within a six-week span during the summer of 1980.[61] These fatalities, though tragic and rare, were the proverbial tip of the iceberg for city residents already feeling swarmed by the surge of commuter cyclists following the transit strike only two months prior.[62] Tensions between pedestrians and cyclists were thoroughly enflamed by news coverage of the accidents and the *New York Times* was the most prominent paper to popularize an image of cyclists as both a public menace and a safety liability. By deemphasizing the hundreds of New York City pedestrians annually killed by automobiles—as well as the tens of thousands annually maimed—the press effectively began to normalize an emergent hostility against cycling in the early to mid-1980s.

Charles Komanoff, one of the activists responsible for re-founding Transportation Alternatives in this period, traces the backlash to the pedestrian deaths in 1980, but more broadly, to the cultural shift embodied by the Reagan zeitgeist: "If the symbol of the 1970s was the plucky bike commuter, it really got displaced by the mergers and acquisitions Wall Street guy sitting in a limo . . . being ecological didn't have the same currency as it did in the 1970s."[63] Komanoff's careful analysis of the relationships between transportation, socioeconomic conditions, and cultural norms does not position news media as the root cause of anger against New York City cyclists, but he acknowledges the tangible role the press played in fostering negative stereotypes and otherwise fanning the flames:

> By 1985 this whole idea had gotten loose and gained total cultural currency: *cyclists were a menace to society, a danger to pedestrians.* We heard about "kamikaze" cyclists and "kamikaze" messengers. It seemed like every newspaper had article after article like this, including the *Times,* who set the tone for the other papers. Some put more emphasis on cyclists, some said it was the messengers, and others talked about messengers *and* cyclists. So, cycling just became this pariah.[64]

Komanoff acknowledges how journalists and other news contributors (op-ed writers, letter writers) frequently blurred the distinctions between bike commuters, recreational cyclists, and messengers by framing cycling as a universally negative practice, one that ostensibly added a *"lethal volatility* to the urban scene" in 1986, a year in which errant bicyclists killed 3 pedestrians and caused 640 injuries.[65] In comparison with the 285 auto-related pedestrian deaths and 15,000 people injured by cars in that same year, the "lethal volatility" argument held little water when subject to scrutiny.[66] Nevertheless, bad press contributed to an already inflammatory public discourse and simultaneously set the stage for Mayor Ed Koch's eventual crackdown on city cyclists.[67]

Kill the Messenger

In 1987, Mayor Koch proposed a ban on bicycling in midtown Manhattan that would be in effect on weekdays between the hours of 10:00 A.M. and 4:00 P.M. His experimental plan was a thinly veiled attack on the city's bike messengers who were already subject to new regulations since 1984. A class action lawsuit officially halted the ban, but only after the city's messengers organized a slew of protest rides under the leadership of their newfound spokesperson, Steve "The Greek" Athineos: a messenger and founder of Mother's Messengers of NYC.[68] Athineos spoke poignantly and candidly about the importance of messenger labor and led nightly protests for more than a month leading up to the ban's implementation. Messengers effectively made their point through a mass display of solidarity and creative resistance. For instance, they sometimes rode the length of Midtown—slowly—in large packs that positioned cyclists ten or twelve deep across traffic lanes.[69] These protests, as well as the subsequent traffic jams caused by messengers stopping at every red light, were publicized on broadcast news and arguably brought positive attention to the plight of messengers. Athineos skewered Mayor Koch's policies when interviewed, but he was also subject to character assassination after city officials leaked his police file (including former drug charges) to news reporters, a move no doubt prompted by Athineos's public attacks on the mayor, namely, his insinuation that Koch had a penchant for "little boys."[70]

One of the underlying issues at stake with the bike ban—its racial implications—was unsurprisingly not part of the news narrative constructed around Koch's proposal, despite the fact that messengers, who were predominantly African American, Latino, and of black Caribbean descent, stood to lose the most from a workday bike ban. Charlie McCorkell, however, tackled the issue in the Transportation Alternatives newspaper *City Cyclist*:

> If a messenger were picked at random, the rider would most likely be male, black, and 22 years old. . . . [T]he ban may not be racist in intent but it seems to be in practice. Probably 70–80% of all bike messengers are minorities, while an estimated 90% of commuter cyclists are white. The ban says in effect: The 90% of cyclists who are white and likely to use the avenues before 10 am and after 4 pm are

allowed on the streets, but the 75% who are Black or Hispanic cannot use the streets when they are most likely to. The message is clear: if you are Black and ride a bike you are not welcome on the most afflu- ent streets of New York City.[71]

Incidentally, one of the only other publications to touch on the racial dynamics of the bike ban proposal was *Time* magazine, whose reporter (Frank Trippett) seemed interested only to the extent that he could delegiti- mize racial discrimination as both a pertinent issue and a topic for critical inquiry and debate. He claimed that New Yorkers' were just as frustrated with the antics of white "speed demons," therefore the ban could not be racist.[72] Bike messengers clearly bore the brunt of public hostility against urban cycling in the 1980s, particularly in New York City, Washington, D.C., and Boston, where newspaper reporters, columnists, and op-ed contributors openly castigated their aggressive riding style at the same time they ignored the rigorous physical, temporal, and economic demands placed on the mes- senger labor force. Moreover, they provided little context in which readers could potentially understand or evaluate messenger work in a more nuanced way.[73] Instead, writers attributed the collective "recklessness" of messengers to their "arrogant, scofflaw spirit" and, perhaps most disingenuously, to their greed: "recklessness so thoroughly motivated by greed ought to be easily deterred by meaningful enforcement."[74] One would assume from this and other accounts that messengers choose to navigate the city at top speeds to enhance their paychecks instead of seeing such tactics as the sole means by which one is able to earn a paycheck in the first place. For example, Frank Trippett writes, "Inspired by the fact that more deliveries mean more money, many messengers whiz around the city in pseudokamikaze style, heeding nei- ther red lights nor one-way signs, zagging on and off sidewalks, leaving behind a wake of screeching tires and cursing pedestrians."[75] Messenger companies almost universally hire messengers as independent contractors, meaning that workers receive no hourly wage, job security, health insurance, vacation pay, or sick pay despite working a very dangerous job and being subject to regular harassment from drivers, police officers, and building security guards. Yet employees in New York City—the proverbial lions' den of messenger controversy—made approximately $13,500 (average) per year in the mid- 1980s, according to McCorkell, and this figure assumes a ten-hour workday throughout the entire year.[76] Financial issues were then, as now, compounded by the delivery deadlines that messengers are by their very nature required to meet. Rebecca "Lambchop" Reilly, a bike messenger historian and former messenger, speaks directly to the dilemma this poses in terms of safety and lawful behavior: "There are times when deadlines can't be met, unless a mes- senger breaks the law. By merely dispatching jobs of that nature, there is the implied order to the courier to break the law."[77] Kevin Wehr reiterates Reilly's position and argues that messengers' aggressive riding style is a logical solution to the ever-increasing spatiotemporal demands of "fast capitalism." Their speed, in other words, is a necessary evil that ultimately reflects the broader demands imposed on labor forces via capitalism:

> To the casual observer, messengers may seem like lunatics on wheels. They are often represented in the media and the broader culture as the antiheros of the urban jungle: the dirty, smelly recurring figures in movies and commercials that symbolize the dark underside and accelerated pace of the city. If messengers ride like lunatics they do so largely because they have to: Ironically enough, the structure of the delivery industry marginalizes the messengers with low pay, slight job security, and almost never any health insurance or other benefits. . . . The fact that a guy on a bike can get something across the downtown core faster than any alternatives shows that some sectors of fast capitalism must still rely on decidedly "slow" technologies.[78]

By the end of the decade, the frequent repetition of stories about dangerous cyclists and kamikaze messengers produced an effective set of stereotypes, stock characters, and stock terms that would come to define news reporting on urban cycling. Anti-bike messenger columnists like the *Washington Post*'s Bob Levey, who once bragged, "in my gentler moments, I've called them law-flouting, obscenity-spewing, bath-needing, wild-riding, pedestrian-smashing madmen," helped to carry this trend into the 1990s by either inventing controversy where none existed or by exploiting specific messenger incidents/accidents for shock value as opposed to news value.[79] The consistency of these patterns is most evident in New York City, especially when one looks at reports on traffic fatalities. Komanoff, for example, notes that fifty sidewalk fatalities caused by automobiles in New York City between 1994 and 1997 collectively garnered less media attention than the death of one sixty-eight-year-old New Jersey man after he was hit and killed by a cyclist on the sidewalk in November 1997: "Following that incident, the *New York Times* churned out four articles, a column, and an editorial, 'Assault by Bicycle,' while a *New York Post* columnist thundered against 'an assassin on two wheels' and climaxed the media frenzy by insisting, '*The bicycle menace must be stopped . . . by any means necessary*.'"[80] Michael Smith, of the pedestrian/cycling advocacy group Right of Way, counterposes this incident with the death of another sixty-eight-year-old cyclist just two weeks later: he was also hit on the sidewalk but the vehicular homicide elicited only a one-paragraph story in *Newsday*.[81]

The cumulative effect of touting urban cycling as a threat to pedestrian safety was pernicious not only because it fostered periodic climates of resentment against commuters and messengers in the 1980s but also because it functioned pedagogically. That is to say, news media helped to teach people how to read bicycling as a problematic practice by encouraging public scrutiny of cyclists' behavior, by quoting the most reactionary respondents in articles written about cycling accidents, and by thoroughly decontextualizing the havoc automobility wreaks on pedestrians, cyclists, the environment, and drivers themselves. A formulaic story thus emerged by the end of the 1980s that, although factually erroneous, would be used to narrativize urban cycling in the following decades.[82]

The Car Driver as Victim

The corporate press may have utilized hyperbole in constructing the bicycle menace of the 1980s, but at the very least, the threat was rightly framed around the issue of pedestrian safety. Novice cyclists, inattentive riders, and careless bike messengers can, after all, pose real physical risks to city residents. But as the negative representation of urban cyclists wore on in the 1980s, one began to see more articles that explicitly included motorists in the ranks of those ostensibly threatened by bicyclists. Harold Gluck, a criminologist and police consultant, provides an early example of this tactic in a lengthy *New York Times* opinion piece published in the midst of the 1980s backlash. His exclusive concern with the safety of drivers was somewhat of an anomaly in 1983, but it serves as an instructive preview of the rationale now commonly used to condemn cyclists' risk-inducing behavior in the twenty-first century.[83] He begins by talking the reader through a detailed car accident scenario:

> You are driving your car along the main street of your home town. Your destination is the shopping center just outside the city limits. As a law-abiding citizen you keep within the speed limit. At every red traffic light you stop. You pride yourself upon two facts. First, that you are a very careful driver. And, second, that you are a courteous driver. There are cars parked along the street. In this day and age it is rare to find an empty parking spot vacant for more than five minutes along Main Street.
> The car in back of you wants to pass you, and the driver even blows his horn. You get your car a little closer to those cars parked along the street. This will permit that impatient driver to pass you on your left. And then it happens! Absolutely from nowhere at all comes the little child on his bicycle. [84]

After describing the child being crushed under the wheels of the car, Gluck callously argues, "The automobile is not a menace to the safety of the child or the adult on a bicycle. . . . [I]n fact, *it is exactly the other way around.*"[85] His assertions are striking not only because he inverts the logic of danger by literally positioning a small child as the aggressor against a twenty-five-hundred-pound vehicle but also because he presumes that readers will immediately identify with the driver, as if all people naturally see the world through the filter of the windshield. Readers are meant to see the automobile not as the technological usurper of this child's play space, but in humane terms that contrast sharply with the alleged juvenile delinquency of cycling: a point Gluck makes clear with an anecdote about a ten-year-old bicyclist allegedly causing a near fatality in a hit-and-run accident (the miniature driver fled the scene). The perils of such recklessness are reiterated in the accompanying newsprint llustrations of several long-haired cyclists—who coincidentally look more like hippies than children—swerving wildly through the streets as cars collide in their wake. Gluck concludes with a forceful call to action befitting the most hardened suburban commuter: "The drivers of these two-wheeled flimsy things are a menace to themselves as well to others. . . . [T]he time to protect the motorist from the bicyclist is now, and the sooner the better."[86] Here one finds a logical solution in regulating cyclists, arresting them, or more likely banning them from the street altogether.

The author's line of reasoning is perfect example of what Ben Fincham refers to as the "car driver as victim" sentiment, which he sees manifested in British public discourse about bike messengers, specifically, and urban cyclists more broadly.[87] Indeed, newspapers throughout England, especially London, played a central role in the production of this discourse over the last five years, effectively demonizing cyclists for threatening drivers' safety, freedom, mobility, and general way of life. At least this is what one would assume from reading the vitriolic commentary that routinely characterizes cyclists as fascists, Nazis, public menaces, road hogs, "scowling road hazards," and "two wheeled terrors."[88] More often than not, cyclists are simply dubbed *lycra louts,* a term batted around endlessly by U.K. journalists, pundits, and even Kate Hoey, the former British sports minister.[89] Journalist David Rowan offers a concise example of this prose in a mere two-sentence heading: "They blatantly flout the law, deliberately enrage drivers and stop at nothing in their war against the car. Now, as Brussels threatens to make motorists responsible for all accidents involving bicycles, the *Standard* takes to the road with the radical new breed of cycle guerrillas."[90] Fincham suggests that the emergent hostility against cyclists is a symptom of the frustrations posed by the current paradox of automobility in England, whereby the promise of freedom of movement is habitually curtailed by the actual temporal and economic costs of driving.[91] Traffic congestion in London, for example, reduces the average speed of automobiles to around thirteen miles per hour with rush hour speeds averaging eight miles per hour. This situation, combined with a surge in cycling rates since the year 2000, produced a context in which cyclists not only are more common but also travel faster than cars and are able to maneuver around them easily in the all-too-common traffic jam. Consequently, British drivers now tend to see themselves as victims of circumstance who need someone to blame, whether the Greens inhibiting road construction, or more often than not, the cyclist. This sentiment is effectively illustrated by the formation of the briefly lived Car Party—a pro-car political group that un-ironically solicited both support and empathy under the heading: *"For too long the British motorist has been suffering in silence."*[92] The eightfold increase in British drivers between 1952 and 2005—43 percent of which took place between 1980 and 1990 alone—suggests that silence must indeed be golden, but what it does not explain is why one can find analogous critiques of cyclists in countries where the aggrandized promises of automotive freedom are far less constrained than in central London.

Kate Hoey may use the *Mail on Sunday* to lovingly describes cyclists as "selfish, aggressive, law-breaking and infuriatingly smug," but one can find this same branding in Seattle, Washington, where the *Post-Intelligencer* alludes to the "sins of cyclists" that incense drivers the most, including "running red lights or stop signs, going the wrong way down one-way streets, splitting lanes by riding between two lanes, changing lanes or turning without signaling and a holier-than-thou attitude."[93] Journalist Anita Quigley offers a similar, though much more brutish, characterization of Critical Mass participants in Sydney, Australia:

> Critical Mass is actually selfish inner-city twats who have no regard for their fellow Sydneysiders: people who have worked hard all week and who just want to drive home. What Critical Mass fails to realise is that we don't want to spend our Friday night in gridlock while lycra-clad twits—with a police escort—whiz past to go have noodles and make the point that Sydney should be free of cars. These are probably also the same errant cyclists who ignore the road rules, jump red lights (thinking it's their privilege) and ride on the footpath.[94]

In each of these critiques, which I chose both for their vivacity as well as their representative qualities (there are hundreds just like them), one can identify a set of common themes and gripes used to construct a composite narratorial sketch of the urban cyclist in the modern city: he or she is dangerous, aggressive, law-breaking, and seemingly filled to the brim with self-righteousness, privilege, and/or indignity for the rights of others. Those who wield this bicyclist-as-menace story in the press typically do so in order to exact an agonizingly detailed level of criticism against cyclists' every maneuver, but in doing so they rarely say anything substantive about driving. Ironically, these silences still do some important work, which is to say that they reaffirm a shared common sense about transportation, morality, and public space: it is a narrative of automobility produced in absentia.[95]

Breakin' the Law, Breakin' the Law!

Normalizing the narrative of the aggressive, lawless cyclist is problematic for a number of reasons, the first being that drivers often attribute fault and/ or blame to cyclists in situations where they are either doing nothing wrong or acting in accordance with other road users. Indeed, qualitative and quantitative studies of British drivers conducted by the Transport Research Laboratory (TRL) reveal that drivers not only abide by an unwritten code of conduct based on a hierarchy, or "thugarchy," of vehicle size (bigger = better = more respect) but also admit to becoming annoyed with cyclists and driving aggressively as a tactical response.[96] These findings, based on a combination of interviews and drivers' responses to watching film clips of traffic scenes, also indicate that motorists systematically condemn cyclists' behavior with little provocation. Cyclists were criticized no matter how small the infraction and their maneuvers were similarly viewed as "inherent and dispositional" rather than as the result of context or the situation on a given street. In contrast, motorists' misdemeanors were typically "excused or justified in terms of the situational influences."[97] To put these findings in slightly different terms, the drivers in the TRL study—and I would argue throughout the Western world—use their own arbitrary interpretations of cyclists' nonverbal behavior to justify their criteria for courteousness and respect, on one hand, and the actions deemed worthy of scorn and condemnation on the other. More often than not, their critique of cyclists' behavior has little to do with the actual circumstances of a given traffic situation, seeing as how drivers partly interpret cyclists' level of skill and safety based on a visual assessment of their outfits (i.e., whether they dress like real cyclists).[98]

Publicly highlighting the so-called lawlessness and aggression of bike riders through news media serves an important function for the various norms of automobility. First, it reinforces the notion that drivers, unlike cyclists, are law abiding and above all else, rational. They are seen as high-speed manifestations of a new Cartesian dictum: *cogito ergo moveo* (I think therefore I move).[99] Bad driving is, by default, construed as an aberration, either the work of a few bad apples—namely, cyclists, motorcyclists, drunk drivers, or speed demons—or an unfortunate consequence of bad circumstances. This is hardly surprising because to admit that the system of automobility is inherently flawed or abhorrently dangerous is to thwart the logic buttressing a globalized advertising spectacle devoted to the maintenance and growth of the auto/oil industries, and the dual mythos of moral responsibility and civic duty historically articulated to good driving skills.[100] Nevertheless, this is the reality most evident in hospital records, national safety statistics, and anonymous driving surveys administered by insurance companies.[101] Indeed, nearly every relevant survey reveals that drivers routinely and systematically break traffic laws, and this is only what people admit to doing so while behind the wheel of a car. Yet when it comes to bicyclists' committing the same traffic violations—namely, running stop signs and lights or failing to signal before turning—it is construed as nothing less than the deterioration of the rule of law and the social contract of democracy: every blown stop sign reads like a slap in Thomas Hobbes's face, every Critical Mass a swift kick in Jean-Jacques Rousseau's groin. For example, Santa Monica council member Kevin McKeown, a cyclist himself, accused his city's Critical Mass participants of taking a "life-threatening risk," claiming they violated the "crucial social contract."[102] Walt Seifert, of Sacramento Area Bicycle Advocates, similarly warns of the slippery slope between traffic violations and anarchy: "Violating the law often is dangerous and it's always bad for the image of cycling. Like any other scofflaw behavior, it breeds disrespect for all laws."[103] Safety, in both a physical and a social sense, becomes the governing discourse in which the threat of the cyclist becomes a matter of fact. Yet this threat can be produced only within a discursive field, or set of narratives, where the dangers of automobility are dramatically distorted and the culpability in automobile-bicycle accidents is already assumed to be at least co-equal.

Distributing blame for auto accidents is taken for granted in most countries today, but this was not always the case.[104] Peter Norton recalls that up until the 1920s the blame for car accidents, particularly those resulting in casualties, was placed squarely on drivers and, significantly, on the general presence of cars in U.S. cities. Drivers who struck and killed pedestrians in this period faced public outrage and were sometimes beaten, and on rare occasions lynched, by witnesses.[105] The tone of public discourse began to shift in the mid-1920s, as auto interests initiated a comprehensive public relations campaign to distribute blame toward a combination of factors, including "reckless drivers, careless pedestrians and inadequate streets."[106] News media played a dual role in this process by embracing the emergent safety industry lingo—thus ending their references to causality-inducing drivers as "murderers" and "killers"—and by gradually emphasizing pedestrians' collective responsibility for their own safety.[107] So important was this discursive/ideological shift that Norton refers to it as "a foundation of the motor-age city."[108]

American cyclists have long been implicated in this same vision of traffic safety-as-collective responsibility, and news media similarly facilitate the process once used to regulate pedestrian mobility. Aside from the small wave of bicycle safety media produced in the 1950s and 1960s (public service announcements and instructional films), the press plays the dominant role in normalizing this same industry-friendly safety paradigm in its coverage of cyclists.[109] News stories on bicycle-automobile accidents resulting in injuries and/or fatalities bear witness to this trend; for example, rarely does one hear a story that fails to mention whether a cyclist was wearing a helmet at the time of his or her accident or death. At face value this is merely a descriptive detail designed to give a fuller picture of the incident, but the implication is that regardless of the circumstances, non-helmeted cyclists contribute to, if not directly cause, their own injuries or fatalities by not acting responsibly.[110] The disproportionate emphasis on bicycle accidents versus stories on bicycle transportation is just another way that urban cycling is portrayed as an inherently risky activity with distinct implications for the safety of drivers. This tendency is perpetuated by the repetition of dubious statistics regarding fault in automobile-bicycle accidents and thoroughly exacerbated by the bikes versus cars imagery played up in coverage of Critical Mass.[111] News readers are reminded, and in many cases taught, about the physical threats that cyclists pose to pedestrians, other cyclists, themselves, and drivers, as exaggerated as the latter claim might be.

Elitist, Arrogant Welfare Queens of the Road

Cyclists experience routine surveillance because of their inherent exposure on the road and this is evident in the way their clothing, postures, and physical features are casually referenced in articles dating back to the 1880s. In short, they are subject to the gaze of others, especially drivers. Scrutinizing cyclists' every traffic violation, no matter how mundane, allows drivers to utilize the news as a tool for cultural discipline: it has a panoptic function inasmuch as it encourages cyclists to self-regulate their behavior, and it also exerts a synoptic power that makes cyclists aware that everyone is watching. These disciplinary rhetorics are also used by cyclists to rein in their fellow cyclists' bad behavior, and by extension, to distance themselves from undisciplined mobility. Matt Seaton, author of the *Guardian* newspaper's "Two Wheels" column, succinctly articulates this position: "When a cyclist runs a red light, the rest of us might as well get out the old revolver and fire one off at our collective foot."[112] There is nothing terribly problematic about these sorts of claims when considering the backlash that both cycling advocates and everyday bikers endure as a consequence of the lawless reputation. But the underlying theme here is that cyclists must either choose to get their act together, so to speak, or simply resign themselves to dangerous conditions.

The problem, of course, is that despite the prevalence of localized bike cultures and a tangible sense of solidarity (or at least civility) among many urban cyclists, bicycling is at the end of the day a mode of transportation, not a club activity involving a group of people who necessarily know each other or even like one another. Put simply, there are no mass meetings at which the issue of blowing red lights or stop signs can be discussed, much less resolved. Nevertheless, there is an almost consensual agreement between bicyclists, pedestrians, and drivers to legitimize and perpetuate this pedantic and largely unproductive dialogue, including the borderline hysterical fanaticism with which British newspaper columnists condemn the act of jumping the red light. Consequently, bike riders either become seen as elitists who crave special treatment for their habitual lawlessness, or they emerge as hypocrites who have no basis from which to make complaints.[113] Charging bicyclists with some form of elitism is not a new phenomenon in the United States or the United Kingdom, and while it is often coupled with accusations of lawlessness (i.e., bikers thinking they are too good for the rules) the pejorative is largely directed at their attitudes, or more accurately, drivers' perception of their attitudes. The *New Yorker*'s antagonistically titled "Holy Rollers: The City's Bike Zealots," is one of many stories on urban cyclists that gives credence to the biker-as-elitist thesis by framing cycling as a form of "conspicuous presumption," or an expression of "urban piety."[114] As Philip Nolan of the *Daily Mail* illustrates, bikers can even signify elitism, "infuriating smugness," and a "holier-than-thou" attitude without saying a word:

> To the hardcore wing of their ungodly fraternity, all cars are bad. They are encouraged in this zealous fervor by Government ministers who proudly show up at the gates of Dail Eireann, slip off their trouser clips and empty their panniers of the days business, bathing Kildare Street in the rosy glow of their smugness.[115]

The irony is that while Nolan and his journalistic ilk take pains to emphasize the obviousness of cyclists' apparent self-righteousness, it is only through the production of such petty forms of semiotic analysis that most readers even have the faintest point of reference from which to decode something as inconspicuous and benign as a trouser clip or a set of saddlebags.

The elitist moniker, while applicable to some cyclists—though for an entirely different set of reasons—functions as an interesting rhetorical device because it subjects cyclists to the same sweeping critiques used against environmentalists and anti-car proponents for decades. By default, cyclists become part of the group that James A. Dunn, a Rutgers professor and automobile advocate, describes as the *elite vanguard*: "an elite group of anti-auto activists whose progressive ideas and individual agenda complement and reinforce one another."[116] Painting all anti-car activists and environmentalists with the elitist brush is an age-old conservative ploy to dismiss critiques of the status quo as radical, hence out of step with the values of the silent majority.

But it also does something quite specific, which is to define elitism as a moral or behavioral disposition rather than a set of economic, structural, legal, or spatial privileges. This is the primary way, indeed the only way, by which one of the cheapest forms of transportation on the planet is construed as elitist, whereas one of the most expensive and resource-intensive technologies is considered populist. If one frames the issue in terms of economics and systemic privileges, rather than attitude, it is clear that drivers collectively benefit from massive government subsidies spent on oil, gasoline, road construction/maintenance, and urban parking; not to mention the hidden costs associated with environmental pollution and traffic congestion (to give just two examples). Indeed, driving a car in the United States or the United Kingdom even gives one the personal privilege to accidentally, or perhaps even intentionally, kill another person with fewer worries about being arrested or imprisoned.[117] Given the breadth of privileges drivers enjoy, it is perhaps most ironic that the perpetuation of the elitism-as-attitude discourse gives recourse to an additional argument journalists play a key role in promulgating, which is that cyclists do not pay their share on the road. Bicyclists, if we believe the corporate press, are the welfare queens of the road, bent on taking advantage of an honest system. The *Seattle Post-Intelligencer*'s front-page feature article on December 25, 2007, illustrates the main thesis of this habitually recurring story: "Motorists help pay for roads with gas taxes, tolls and license tabs. Boaters subsidize maritime programs with vessel registration and boat launch fees. Maybe bicyclists, too, should pitch in for the costs of their trails and lanes."[118] As part of her quintessential anti-cyclist manifesto in the *Mail on Sunday*, Kate Hoey makes a similar appeal to the public: "Too often the cyclist acts as if he owns the road when in fact he has paid nothing to be there. They do not need a license and they pay no road tax. There should be room for everyone on our roads. But I think it is time that those who cycle have to face up to their responsibilities and pay something for its upkeep like the rest of us."[119] Demanding that cyclists take more responsibility for the road system by obtaining licenses or paying additional taxes is, first of all, an interesting phenomenon because of the dramatically low rates of bicycle use in the United States and the United Kingdom: roughly 1 percent and 2 percent of people in each country use bicycles for everyday transportation, respectively. In addition, even if we assume for a moment that most bicyclists do not own a car or have never previously owned a car—which is at best a ludicrous proposition—one is meant to see bicyclists as moochers who need to pay up like everyone else.[120] The fact that billions of collective tax dollars are currently spent on road construction projects each year is totally ignored, just like the billions spent before the current wave of victimized drivers took to the steering wheel.[121] Framing the issue in this way is at once ahistorical and absurd, but it is nonetheless interesting for the way it appeals to readers.

Normalizing the Driver/Consumer as Model Citizen

As with so many articles critical of cycling, news readers are meant to use their driving subjectivity as the basis from which to evaluate the merits of public policies and/or the disciplining of certain populations. That is to say, driving—not citizenship—becomes the de facto criteria by which one's rights and responsibilities are defined. And since ownership of the roads is implied by the various acts of consumption associated with being a driver—buying gasoline, insurance, and the automobile itself—this dual act of driving/consuming, translated as the right to drive, becomes the basis for demarcating authority over public space, public policies, and public funds. This privatized capitalist notion of citizenship produces, and is also reproduced by, the discursive split between "us" (drivers) and "them" (cyclists) one can see at work in most news stories, op-ed columns, and letters to the editor written about bicycling. As one woman writing to the *Orlando Sentinel* notes of bikers: "They use *our space* because they think they have the 'right' to do so."[122] David Hartgen, an emeritus professor at the University of North Carolina–Charlotte, makes a similar proclamation in a *USA Today* story about cities that are intentionally narrowing their roads to add more sidewalks and bike lanes for the community: "It's really just arrogance and selfishness on the part of usually very small groups of individuals. . . . [T]hey exert political power to 'take back the street,' but *the street is not theirs to take back.*"[123] The habitual reproduction of this non-driving "other" necessarily pits the interests of bicyclists—not to mention pedestrians and environmentalists—against those of the driver/consumer, whom we are meant to see as both anyone and everyone. Through this discursive transformation, bicyclists are turned into unwanted invaders of *our* space, self-righteous complainers telling *us* what to do with *our* money, and lawless freeloaders who refuse to follow *our* rules.

Framing the issue of bicycle transportation in this way is obviously problematic for cyclists and bike advocates, but the much bigger issue here is how the corporate press legitimizes and normalizes the consumer-based notion of citizenship at the heart of these debates. This problem is fueled by the news industry's institutional dependency on billions of advertising dollars from the automobile, gas, and oil industries, in addition to their uncritical reliance on both corporate public relations materials and the punditry of right-wing think tank associates whom *Reason* magazine editor Brian Doherty, accurately describes as "radicals for capitalism."[124] Indeed, the Reason Foundation is one of the many radical Libertarian nonprofit organizations whose experts not only serve as guest commentators on local and national broadcast news but also produce droves of articles, op-ed pieces, and reports regularly featured in local and national print news publications.[125] Their transportation policy agendas are generally devoid of any democratic oversights, governmental regulations, labor unions, environmental responsibilities, or mandated concerns for public health and safety. Readers and viewers are also never told that the Reason Foundation, the Competitive Enterprise Institute, the Heartland Institute, the American Enterprise Institute, the National Environmental Policy Institute, the Cato Institute, the Thoreau Institute, and the American Dream Coalition (to name just a few) are not only politically and ideologically connected but are also collectively funded by charitable foundations with direct and indirect ties to every major petrochemical, oil, and automobile corporation in the world. Specifically, these institutes are heavily funded by some of the richest, most politically powerful right-wing families and organizations in the Northern Hemisphere, including the John M. Olin Foundation (chemicals and munitions), the Scaife Foundations (Gulf Oil, banking and newspapers), and the Koch Family Foundations (oil and gas).[126]

Media scholars and watchdog groups have long criticized the institutional biases of the corporate news industry precisely because these sorts of organizations radically alter, if not dictate, the terms of debate on public issues like transportation. As trusted sources of information, corporate news fundamentally propagates the "ideology of the motorcar" by legitimizing the most radical supporters of automobility through a process that effectively repackages their agenda as centrist.[127] Critiques of automobility are subsequently framed as political and/or antagonistic to the status quo, regardless of whether the context justifies or even compels such criticism—a good example being the one thousand-plus New York City pedestrians annually struck by automobiles on the sidewalk or inside their homes.[128] Systemic and/or politically motivated critiques of automobility, like those espoused and/or performed by Reclaim the Streets and Critical Mass, are therefore subject to the same categorical skepticism bestowed on other forms of dissenting political speech.[129] These patterns ultimately reify, or make concrete, an ideology that is simultaneously at work in the relentless spectacle of auto advertising and embedded within the everyday realities of car culture. Moreover, this process thoroughly depoliticizes a highly political, and openly radical policy agenda designed to subject pro-transit and pro-bicycling perspectives to intense skepticism: a scenario every transportation activist knows all too well. In the name of objectivity, news organizations either pit these latter concerns against the publicity apparatus of corporate-funded Libertarian think tanks, or simply provide their analysts the forum in which to espouse support for unfettered automobility, highway construction, and the deregulation and privatization of public transportation services.

As a case in point, the *Los Angeles Times* featured a weeklong editorial debate about bicycling, bike advocacy, and transportation politics in 2008 (January 7–11), entitled "Bicycle Brawl." It is a significant news milestone because it is probably the first planned news editorial series about bicycling to be featured in a U.S. newspaper since the 1890s, and to my knowledge, the only debate to showcase dueling editorials from the same writers. In the interests of objectivity, the paper pitted two bike commuters for the debate, and the match-up is telling. On one side is Will Campbell, a Los Angeles blogger, and on the other side is Randal O'Toole, a Cato Institute Senior Fellow who also serves as the director of several pro-automobility, anti-environmentalist organizations, including the Thoreau Institute, the Independence Institute's Center for the American Dream, and the American Dream Coalition (also represented by cycling/driving advocate John Forester). With all due respect to Campbell, who is an experienced and well-spoken cyclist, he is not a representative of a major bicycling organization, nor is he a full-time advocate. O'Toole, on the other hand, is a nationally known mass transportation critic and the pioneer of free market solutions to environmental problems; he taught classes on the latter subject at Yale (1998), the University of California–Berkeley (1999, 2001), and Utah State (2000).[130] He also serves as a frequent news contributor and commenter, where he has suggested (among other things) that the horrific consequences of Hurricane Katrina were not due to endemic poverty, structural racism, or federal neglect, but rather, a direct consequence of people not owning enough cars: "What made New Orleans vulnerable was that a third of its households do not own an automobile."[131] That Campbell held his own in the debate is inconsequential when considering just how heavily the scales were tipped from the outset of this, or any other news piece that pits the proverbial weight of the car against the weight of the bicycle.

Conclusion

The habitual mischaracterization of utilitarian cycling, urban cyclists, and bicycle transportation in mass media is part of a larger process whereby the cultural supremacy of automobility is perpetually conferred through the norms of journalism and the pop culture narrative of the infallible car. By scapegoating a small minority of urban cyclists, an even smaller number of bike messengers, and a relative spattering of Critical Mass participants, corporate entertainment and news media avoid both the challenge and responsibility of either grappling with the prospects of alternative mobilities or questioning the systemic dangers of car culture. The cyclist, in the form of the "reckless" amateur, the "eco warrior," the "kamikaze" bike messenger, the "lycra lout," or the Critical "Masshole" simply becomes another minor character in an ongoing sitcom or news story that effectively diverts any substantial criticism away from the regime of automobility or its primary corporate beneficiaries. The construction of this paradigm may not be intentional, but this need not matter. With billions of dollars in advertising revenue at stake, news companies and their parent corporations have an implicit financial obligation to openly and/or tacitly reinforce an ideology that prevents reporters from ever referring to drivers as "assassins on four wheels," or loudly proclaiming "the automobile menace must be stopped . . . by any means necessary." Entertainment media do an additional amount of cultural work by simultaneously accounting for the presence of cyclists but only insofar as they become the butt of the joke. Any political reading of bicycling as environmentally sustainable, efficient, or cheap is totally erased. Because to show it any other way could potentially legitimize a critique of automobility, or at least raise questions that demand more explanation than television is capable of offering.

Whether they are making news or making us laugh, media corporations are institutionally organized to remind us that the problem of safety is not the daily, high-speed travel of millions of two-ton vehicles through dense urban centers, but reckless cyclists, careless children, clueless jaywalkers, bad weather, and alcohol. Similarly, the problem of transportation is not inadequate mass transit systems or nonexistent bicycle facilities, but auto unions, striking transit workers, environmental extremists, and taxes. And our big problem is certainly not a petroleum-based economy built upon the colonization of the Middle East and the perpetual suppression and slaughter of Arabs, but the lack of affordable parking downtown. Besides, the details just make for a bad story. It is much easier, and safer, to laugh at bicyclists for being forty-year-old virgins, social misfits, anti-car fanatics, and childish adults.

I know you are, but what am I?

CHAPTER 6

DIY Bike Culture

When someone becomes a daily bicyclist s/he makes an emphatic break with one of the basic assumptions and "truths" of the dominant society: that you must have a car to get around.

—Chris Carlsson, "Cycling under the Radar," in *Critical Mass*, 2002

Riding your bike is punk.

—Kim Nolan, "Debut Column," *Punk Planet*, 1994

On February 23, 2006, employees at each of the four Brooklyn Industries retail clothing stores in New York City arrived at work to find a message inscribed across their front display windows in etching fluid: BIKE CULTURE NOTE 4 SALE. The juxtaposition of the drippy phrase with the "tall bikes" featured in their display cases must have seemed quite odd, if not totally confusing, to people passing by. In the weeks before the *Village Voice* widely publicized the incident, bike enthusiasts and critics were already immersed in online forums debating how and why the store's display of handmade bicycles—particularly ones welded two frames high (hence "tall")—sparked such a strong reaction.[1] Suspicions were immediately cast on members of New York City's various bicycle gangs, groups known less for any traditional gang activity than for transforming junked bicycles into hand-welded mobile masterpieces known variously as "mutant bikes" or "freak bikes."[2] People familiar with the inner workings of bike gangs like Chunk 666, the offspring of Portland's original group of self styled "post-apocalyptic" bicycle geeks, or the Black Label Bicycle Club—the punk cousins of the even scrappier Minneapolis-based crew—brought some interesting perspectives to bear on the Brooklyn Industries debacle. In particular, a

handful of cyclists posting on two New York City blogs touched on the issues
of cultural commodification, highlighting the manner in which Brooklyn
Industries essentially co-opted an icon of anti-consumerism as a cheap marketing ploy. Others disagreed entirely and condemned the response as an act
of subcultural elitism, misplaced aggression, and stupidity: they questioned
how people could simultaneously promote bike riding and then penalize/
vandalize a business for infringing on "their" activity. Other people were
clearly just trying to get an answer to the question that non-bike riders were
undoubtedly asking themselves: just what the hell is bike culture and what
does it have to do with these big, weird-looking bikes?

The graffiti and the ensuing media squabbles may not provide any
definitive answer to the latter question, but they do hint at some of the ways
in which the representation of bicycling and the uses of bicycles themselves
are increasingly seen as issues worth debating and struggling over. Indeed,
the junk-welding architects spotlighted by the Brooklyn Industries incident
are just one part of a variegated network of bike enthusiasts who are actively
hacking, reworking, and modifying the meaning and function of the bicycle.
Chris Carlsson, for example, identifies the practices of an "outlaw bicycling
subculture" comprised of tinkerers, bike messengers, Critical Mass participants, and community activists who situate the bicycle within a political
critique of automobility, consumerism, and the norms of both formal bike
advocacy and the bicycle industry in the United States. Paul Rosen casts the
net a bit wider to address an additional group of cyclists, writers, bike designers, and engineers who form a cycling counterculture that pushes bicycling
in new directions by challenging the bike's conventional uses, by promoting
bicycle transportation as an alternative to car culture, and by appropriating
"the technology of the bicycle in ways that go beyond just its utilitarian role
in relation to transport, sport or leisure."[3] Whether part of an outlaw subculture, a cycling counterculture, or more broadly what I am calling "DIY [Do
It Yourself] bike culture," bicyclists are formulating new cultural practices
around bicycle transportation and incorporating the bicycle into a variety of
art forms and grassroots alternative media (i.e., media that are "produced by
the same people whose concerns they represent, from a position of engagement and direct participation").[4] Through the throaty vocals of punk songs,
the cheap ink of photocopied zines, the stylized editing of film documenta-
ries, and the formats of comics, performance art, radio, and blogs, bike riders
are actively forging passionate counternarratives of mobility that challenge
the automobile's hegemonic status as king of the road. The Do It Yourself
ethics fostered through the production and substance of such discourses are,
significantly, also a major part of a trend in which transportation technologies are themselves becoming more meaningful as "ideological terrains of
struggle."[5]

Using DIY as a moniker to describe an amorphous group of bike riders and practices first requires some clarification because the term obviously has multiple meanings. In particular, the designation alludes to both a spirit of self-reliance as well as a set of practices typically associated with the techno-logical tinkering of amateurs, enthusiast, and hobbyists. One can map much of bicycling's history within this interconnected framework as the DIY ethos informed the innovation and development of bicycles during the nineteenth century (via technological design and entrepreneurialism) and was similarly manifested in cyclists' ecstatic proclamations of autonomous mobility. This same dual meaning of DIY as both a process of fixing/building/altering bicycles and an expression of self-reliance was evident prior to the mass production of the bicycle and it persists well beyond the globalization of the industry.[6] Part of my interest in the 1960s and 1970s, for example, stems from the resurgence of these ideals among cyclists in the United States—the for-mer disposition expressed through the creation of the mountain bike, BMX, human-powered vehicles, and lowrider bicycles, and the latter sentiment conveyed through the discourses of bike advocacy and sectors of the environ-mental and appropriate technology movements.

DIY has a different connotation that is similarly relevant to this chapter, which Stephen Duncombe describes as an "an ethic born in reaction against a dominant society that considers culture primarily in terms of a profit-generating, commercial enterprise."[7] This disposition resonated, to varying degrees, within the counterculture of the 1960s and 1970s, but it was most vigorously—and loudly—championed by punks who embraced DIY as a guiding principle that translated into people starting their own bands, record labels, clubs, distribution networks, squats, and publications beginning in the late 1970s (in both the United States and Europe). Punk's collective contri-bution to both independent music as well its revival of the fanzine, or zine, format are well documented, but it is only within the last decade that most scholars and punk enthusiasts began to look past Johnny Rotten's sneer, the Ramones' speed, and punks' stylistic bricolage to pay proper attention to the politics of punk and its influence on cultural workers, activism, and the uses of technology. I bring up these different paradigms of DIY, one associated with bicyclists and the other linked to punk subculture, because I am specifi-cally interested in the ways they intersect and converge since the 1990s. While Rosen and Carlsson both allude to the role that DIY punk ethics and/or punks themselves play in the formation of the "cycling counterculture" and the "out-law bicycle subculture," respectively, I think there is a much stronger case to be made here, or at the very least an additional story to tell. That is to say, I want to more fully unpack the relationships between punk and bicycling not as a corrective to Rosen and Carlsson but rather, as a way to flesh out what I see as a potentially fruitful link between the their work.

As a set of texts, a network of alternative media producers/readers, a conglomeration of geographically localized scenes, and a critical ethos, DIY punk culture does some important work in terms of orienting people toward both a specific reading of automobility and a politically conscious engagement with bicycle. That is to say, just as biking prepped the way for the automobile in the twentieth century, I am arguing that the set of practices and dispositions fostered in DIY culture, such as the production of alternative media, advocacy for technological conviviality, and a critique of corporate power, have been influential on a variety of bicycling events and bike advocacy projects in the last two decades. To be clear, I am by no means suggesting that punk bands, zine writers, and scattered DIY punk communities are somehow the keystones holding bike culture together. Rather, my aim is much more modest, which is to use these subcultural linkages as case studies for understanding how and why bicycling becomes meaningful in specific cultural contexts or as a culture unto itself.

Biking Is Punk

"Riding your bike is punk," writes Kim Nolan in the debut issue of the zine *Punk Planet.*[8] Her 1994 proclamation now reads somewhat prophetically since bicycling seemed to become the punk mode of transportation de rigueur by the early 2000s, or at the very least the preferred form of mobility within the loose knit DIY punk community: the segment of punk subculture that could best be characterized by its scrappy aesthetics, anti-corporate politics, anarchist leanings, and passionate support for independent media production and participatory institutions.[9] Bikes are popular among this crowd in part because they are cheap, easy to fix, simple to ride, and allow for a great deal of autonomy: they are the DIY solution to everyday transportation. Yet bicycling also resonates with the ethics, feelings, lifestyle choices, and political dispositions that inform not only people's identities but also the music, writing, art, and indeed the entire set of practices that co-constitute punk as a cultural formation—and in some cases an entire way of life—as opposed to just a style of music or style writ large. People who ride bikes and identify with the punk label tend to see distinct analogies between alternative transportation, alternative media production, and modes of cultural resistance rooted in the rejection of dominant norms and consumerist values. The Dutch Provo, who aligned themselves with anarchists, antiwar activists, beatniks, freaks, and the like, actually articulated this punk disposition in the 1960s when describing their allies as a worldwide *provotariat* who dwell in "carbon-monoxide-poisoned asphalt jungles": they are the people who "don't want a career, who lead irregular lives, *who feel like cyclists on a motorway.*"[10] While an apt metaphor, this sentiment is also a truism for many dissidents who, like the Provo, do not simply feel like cyclists on the motorway, they are the cyclists on the motorway. Thus, it is hardly surprising that the DIY punk underground has spawned an array of politicized (if not politically disorganized) cyclists who are passionate about car-free living, technical skill sharing, and the idea of gaining independence from both the auto and oil industries.[11] Indeed, within certain scenes, custom built fixed-gear bikes, old beach cruisers, BMX bikes, converted single speeders, and thrift store "beaters" are as integral to punk culture as seven-inch records, zines, mohawks, and bad tattoos.

Bike riding and bicycles are prevalent in the lyrics and imagery of dozens of active and defunct punk bands such as Fifteen, Rambo, Dead Things, The Haggard, Latterman, Crucial Unit, Japanther, and This Bike Is a Pipe Bomb—a band whose stickers adorn bicycles throughout the United States and occasionally prompt irrational (and rather amusing) responses from police departments and bomb squads.[12] Self-styled "bike punx" are not the first to pay homage to bicycles in music, but their songs and lyrics have a tone that is markedly different from Queen's operatic "Bicycle Race" or Syd Barrett's psychedelic musings on Pink Floyd's "Bike."[13] For example, Divide and Conquer is one of the many hardcore (punk) bands to articulate a radical critique of automobility that, while slightly tongue-in-cheek, is a sincere response to the everyday frustrations of being a bike rider in a car culture, both literally and metaphorically:

> Trash the El Camino because the kids are ready to ride
> Go two-wheeled disaster! Shout it out: Bike Pride!
> Pissing every car off, we'll call them nasty names
> Extend the middle finger and ride in every lane.
> Bike Punx!
> With freedom on our minds and wrenches in our hands
> Fuck highway construction, let's go take the land
> We'll peddle through the cities, this war cry we will send
> When internal combustion meets the bitter end
> Bike Punx![14]

Through the production of punk music and other forms of alternative media, bike punx validate their personal experiences and opinions by "authorizing themselves to speak" and by "making public" their voices.[15] As Chris Atton notes, political dissidents frequently utilize alternative media to construct a "resistance identity" for themselves, but in most of the bike-specific media produced in the DIY punk underground the emphasis is placed more explicitly on how the practice of bicycling, rather than bicyclists' singular identities, is that which is "marginalized, devalued or stigmatized by dominant forces in society and culture."[16] Like Divide and Conquer, who show the same disdain for car culture as they do for the World Bank, the Christian Promise Keepers, multinational corporations, and animal vivisection, the defunct Philadelphia anarchist hardcore band, Rambo, articulates a resistance identity—a punk ethos—to urban cycling and bicycle transportation. One of their self-described odes to "bike militancy and self defense," is entitled "U-Lock Justice":

> For every time I hear them say
> "Get the fuck out of the way,"
> I will defend my right of way,
> That heap of steel I'm gonna slay
> I'll trash you, I'll bash you, I'll kick in your doors
> Break out your windows and scratch up your paint
> Apologize for oil wars
> Apologize for polluting my air
> In some cases, cars are ok
> But when I'm on the street you're all my enemies.[17]

Punk music can clearly serve as an outlet for venting pent-up aggression, as well as a forum for expressing radical perspectives on biking and automobility, albeit in brief stanzas and short bursts of energy. Yet not all bands do so with the same emphasis or for the same purpose. For example, punks also celebrate bikes in ways that highlight the unique and sometimes contradictory perspective that bicycling lends to the experience of the city:

> As I ride, I can feel the street
> Like a river, it flows rapidly
> Through the city, it propels
> Me towards a tragic, bloody crash, oh well
> An inch from death seems to be
> The only place to find some peace
> The only place to ride a bike and
> Feel alive and find a sense of pride
> And dignity.[18]

Bicycling, as Joshua Switzky argues, is an exercise in geography whereby cyclists "become intimately familiar with our networks of public spaces, and with a city's terrain and its inhabitants."[19] It is a form of mobility that renders cities imageable in ways that differ from and are at the same time connected to other ways of moving and dwelling: it is "one path to an alternative understanding of the urban," as Jen Petersen puts it.[20] The narratives produced about bicycling—whether in punk lyrics, zines, blogs, cartoons, or documentary films—contribute heavily to this process by (re)presenting and making meaningful both the totality of "the urban" and the nuances of living in a city. Indeed, the process of rethinking the city through the bicycle is as much discursive as it is physical: the various emotional and material (e.g., specific corners, potholes, and alleys) details in the everyday world of bike riders function as signposts and markers that construct "shadow maps" of cities that exist both within and outside of the purview of automobility.[21] In this sense, bicycles are actively enlisted in a distinctive process of "place making," as Erik Ruin, a printmaker and author of the *Trouble in Mind* zine, explains: "There's a way of knowing a city that's very particular to biking through it. The slowness allows you to really see things, even to stop and look. The speed gives you some safety and a distance that's really conducive to fluid thought."[22] For everyday riders, one's world becomes rearticulated around and through their bicycle as pragmatic cycling routes and favorite rides synthesize psychogeographical maps of spaces that are instinctively measured and charted in terms of their bikeability:

> Anywhere you want to go in Gainesville, you can probably get there from the intersection of university and main on bike in 20 minutes. From my house it's fifteen minutes to Ward's grocery, fifteen to No Idea [a punk record label], eight to Wayward Council Records, ten to school, twelve to my friends at the ranch.[23]

In the song "Bikes and Bridges," by Defiance, Ohio, one gets the sense that biking can even be a (partial) remedy to the confines and alienation of everyday urban life: "Even Columbus looks better on the back seat of a bike and / all my fears get washed away in a stream of blinking lights / and the concrete strip below seems less like a noose and more like a tie that binds or at least a tourniquet."[24] Alternative media prove fertile ground for mapping the emotional and cultural geographies of bicycling that are so important to people who ride, yet widely ignored. Indeed, one of the reasons I draw particular attention to punk music and zines is that they not only offer critical counterpoints to the media discussed in Chapter 5 but also fit into an entire paradigm and set of practices that are at once utopian and personal.

DIY punk, for example, has a long history of advocating alternatives to dominant norms of consumer culture—wage labor, rent, corporate institutions, war, consumerist ethics—whether in the form of protest and direct action, or more often, through practices that could be best described as politically motivated or politically aspirational. That is to say, while the object of radical transformation may ultimately be corporate power, patriarchy, or society writ large, punk politics are focused first and foremost on the transformation of oneself, in terms of both grappling with and responding to one's position as a political subject. In this sense, biking is a comfortable fit with a disposition that sees "the personal" and "the political" as a dialectic that begins at the most corporeal level. "The body," artist Jimmy Baker notes, "has always been central to punk culture," and he describes the pro-bicycle stance of his former band, the Awakening, as a way of "creating a resistant energy against the fog of subscribing to a petroleum answer."[25]

Biking, in this sense, is seen as an extension of the DIY ethos, or another way of "asserting self and autonomy," as bassist Mike Watt puts it.[26] Eric "Erok" Boerer, the membership and program director for Bike Pittsburgh, describes bicycling in similar terms, which is to say, a way of putting DIY ethics into action on an everyday basis: "My rediscovery of the bicycle was a way to make myself less dependent on others, especially bosses, mechanics, and oil companies."[27] While punk politics tend to stress the role of individual autonomy, here expressed as a form of self-reliance, it is a mistake to view this disposition as exclusively individualist. Rather, it is part of a paradigm that, despite its contradictions and limitations, is intricately tied up with both an "egalitarian impulse to share with one another" and a broader desire for social change.[28] As Chris Atton notes, the abbreviation DIO (Do It Ourselves)—originally suggested by *Squall* co-editor Jim Carey—is actually a more appropriate moniker for the "communal rather than individual response" to cultural and political norms cultivated in DIY culture.[29] Indeed, most punks who ride bikes tend to describe bicycling in terms of this individual-social dialectic, whether in their music, artwork, writing, or personal interviews, of which I conducted several dozen since 2003.[30] And while there are obvious reasons for people to see bicycling as a logical if not natural extension of DIY ethics, support for bicycle transportation is a fairly recent occurrence among punks and this phenomenon is still somewhat limited to a handful of U.S. cities. Joe Biel, a veteran zine writer, filmmaker, and founder of Microcosm Publishing, described the transformation to me in 2005: "Seven years ago, even people in the [Portland, Oregon,] punk scene didn't really get it. . . . [P]eople would throw eggs at me when I rode my bike! It wasn't how it is now, where it's becoming a lot more popular and accepted."[31]

Whether biking is now an authentically punk or subcultural activity is hardly Biel's concern, nor is it a question really worth debating given the arbitrary criteria people use to police the boundaries of their subcultural practices, identities, and allegiances. But what is interesting is the fact that an eco-friendly mode of transportation somehow became normalized within a van-propelled subculture once steeped in anti-hippie rhetoric and an alienated sense of no future. That is to say, if biking is a means for punks to partly opt out from corporate oil dependency, this stance is ironically hindered by the actual practice of being in a band inasmuch as punk musicians are perpetually, if not hopelessly, dependent on large, gas-guzzling vans for touring and playing shows, whether regionally or locally. Despite the enormous financial and mechanical hassles associated with buying and maintaining vans, they are an integral part of the cultural mythology of punk, and rock and roll more broadly. Punks romanticize the van as well as the entire spectrum of activities one can do inside of, or with, a van in hundreds of songs, dozens of zines, and thousands of tour stories.[32] "The van," Jason Trashville and Braxie Hicks astutely remind us, "has always been a symbol for underground music."[33] Consequently, when Dead Things, their former band, decided to tour their home state of North Carolina via bicycle in 2002, they engaged in what was both a creative experiment and statement against the auto-centric norms perpetuated by their own subculture:

> Oil: The biggest contradiction in DIY punk culture. We've always been dependent on it, and though there are alternatives, we haven't seemed to use them yet. In May, Dead Things, in an attempt to prove that DIY punks can do things more sustainably, communally and collectively, is leaving the van behind, giving a finger to Shell, Exxon, and all the other companies that have been destroying our planet and co-opting our lives for profit. We're getting on our bikes and pedaling our way around the south. This is not simply a tour of our little band. It is also an attempt to strengthen our small DIY punk culture that we've all been a part of for a good bit of our lives. This is everyone's tour because it can't happen without our community working together.[34]

Dead Things made a thirteen-hundred-mile loop through North Carolina, playing roughly a dozen punk shows and making various small-town appear-

Dead Things bike tour poster, 2002. *(Poster by Jason Trashville.)*

ances with members of the Asheville Recyclery community bicycle organization and the crew's "old timey" mountain music band, the Woodfin Outlaws.

Their bike tour might be an anomaly in DIY punk, if not a total aberration in the van-, bus-, and plane-propelled music industry, but it nicely illustrates the degree to which bicycling has become part of the paradigm of what it is means to be punk, or more accurately, what it means to do punk, inasmuch as punk is better understood as a set of practices than a prefabricated identity, a uniform aesthetic, or an adherence to a static notion of taste.

Desperate Bicycles, London Traffic, and Crass Technologies

The DIY ethics of punk, Paul Rosen argues, are not only rooted in widespread dissatisfaction with popular music, art, and the dominant norms of consumerism; they are also based on a collective desire for more participatory technologies and more democratic modes of technological production.[35] Self-published zines, independently owned and operated record labels, and grassroots distribution networks are examples of this technological disposition at work in the late 1970s and early 1980s. And while much of punk's critical energy took aim at democratizing communications technologies or their corporate ownership—albeit with varying degrees of lucidity—there are other instances where this disillusionment was aligned against an altogether different socio-technological arrangement: automobility. It is perhaps fitting, then, that the rallying cry for DIY punk—"it was easy, it was cheap, go and do it!"—comes directly from the chorus of a single released by Desperate Bicycles, an English band whose namesake proclaims an obvious affinity for human-powered transportation.[36] In addition to their moniker and a bicycling reference dropped on the B-side of their first seven-inch record (a song entitled "Handlebars"), they explicitly railed against the automobile in a 1978 carnivalesque tune called "Cars":

> *I hate cars. I hate cars.*
> *Using up my oxygen, giving us lead poisoning.*
> *I hate cars, noisy cars.*
> *Revving up beside my window when my heads up in the stars.*
> *I love bikes. I love bikes, beautiful bikes . . .* [37]

Desperate Bicycles' eclectic sound and cycling references contrast somewhat sharply with the overall aesthetic of early British punk, but their anti-automobile references were not unique in the United Kingdom. The Buzzcocks similarly professed their hatred of "Fast Cars" on their debut album, shortly after their mod/punk contemporaries, The Jam, released

"Bricks and Mortar" and "London Traffic," two songs linking the problems of modernist urban development with the encroachment of car culture.[38] With the advent of anarchist punk, or "anarcho-punk," in the late 1970s and early 1980s—a scene spearheaded (in more ways than one) by the band/collective, Crass—the interconnected problems of capitalism, culture, and everyday life were brought more explicitly within the purview of DIY punk.[39] Anarcho-punk hardly placed emphasis on transportation, much less bicycling, but it articulated a critique of technologies associated with, on one hand, the institutionalized violence embedded in nuclear power and military weaponry and, on the other hand, the perpetuation of a vacuous consumer culture symbolized by products like the American automobile: "I'm looking for something that I can call my own / Which ain't a Ford Cortina or a mortgage on a home."[40] Crass songs such as "Big Man, Big M.A.N" and "Systematic Death" place cars squarely within a dystopian world of social conformity, capitalist oppression, and violent misogyny in which one can achieve a "wonderful life" by toeing the line of "God, queen, country, colour telly, car and wife."[41] Amebix poses a similar critique of the car-as-social-conformity on its 1985 full-length debut, *Arise:* "A comfortable life? A car and a wife? / It's only a dream but it's fuckin' obscene. / You've learned to fit in, a vegetable!"[42] Symbolically bashing the car in the occasional punk song was clearly just another way for U.K. bands to make a statement about class privilege and dominant cultural norms in the 1980s, but it is nonetheless an interesting phenomenon that hints at a different common sense about mobility brewing in the U.K. underground—a sentiment that took on a significant role in the 1990s when anti-roads protests staged over the construction of the M11 link road in East London became the catalyst for the union of cultural politics and direct action that came to define DIY culture in the United Kingdom.[43] That is to say, while the anarcho-punk scene in the United Kingdom was by no means anti-car in any conventional sense, its fusion of DIY ethics, anarchist politics, technological critique, and eventually environmentalism was partly responsible for shaping a context in which anti-car/pro-bicycle perspectives make sense in punk culture. Thus, even if anarcho-punk was just a "straightforwardly cultural moment of resistance" as opposed to one that was actively "*doing something* in the social or political realm," as George McKay argues, it nevertheless did some important political work by both introducing radical ideas to large and geographically disparate audiences and by articulating a cultural politics that had, and continues to have, an important critical function, which is, to "ask what practices, habits, attitudes, comportments, images, symbols, and so on contribute to social domination and group oppression, and to call for collective transformation of such practices."[44]

The DIY punk scenes in the United States played an equally significant role in orienting people toward these positions, whether though live performances, the creation of participatory community spaces, or the production and circulation of music and zines. Political bands like the Dead Kennedys and MDC (Millions of Dead Cops) railed against corporate power and capitalist ideology, while punks affiliated with ABC No Rio in New York City and the Positive Force house in D.C.-connected punk politics and DIY activism in a variety of ways. As in the United Kingdom, environmental politics was also brought to the fore by a number of punk bands by the 1990s since the Earth First!' dedication to anti-corporate, "no compromise" strategies of environmental defense found natural allies in the political DIY punk and zine networks, first among anarchists and radical Leftists in the United Kingdom and eventually the United States. With the added influence of such environmentally oriented practices such veganism, punks began to produce more radicalized discourses equating environmental destruction with corporate capitalism, hierarchal governance, and technological growth.[45] Neo-Luddite theories of primitivism and "green anarchism" similarly took root among radical activists and cultural workers; this is reflected in zines like Green Anarchy and Fifth Estate and in the music/lyrics of dozens of punk bands, such as Oi Polloi, Nausea, and Antischism, to name just a few.[46] In addition, the first Gulf War served as a key connecting point between environmentalism, DIY culture, punk, and a radical critique of transportation in which cars became a target for critique and a suitable metaphor for ecological destruction and the perils of capitalism: "I've been having a hard time trying to justify / The clouds arising from the cars we drive / And a little too easy seems just a little too hard today / And I'm afraid my children are going to have to watch the world waste away."[47] Despite the anger vocalized against technology, the majority of radical activists and cultural workers were/are not active primitivists, as even some of the loudest critics of technology still support the use of sustainable technologies as well as machines used to either mass-produce media or amplify sound to deafening volumes. Indeed, much of the anti-technology rabble promulgated by/within DIY culture often confuses political and socioeconomic criticisms with arguments about the so-called nature or essence of technology. This is understandable given the interrelated and mutually reinforcing imperatives of technological growth, financial profit, and environmental negligence—a formation explicitly challenged, for example, in the anti-nuclear movement of the 1970s and 1980s—but within this paradigm technologies largely suffer for the sins of capitalism, as Mumford once put it.[48] In fact, much of the underground culture I am addressing here tend to advocate a form of neo-Marxist technoskepticism, a collective common sense that assumes technologies in and of themselves are not to blame for environmental and social problems, but rather, the dominant political, cultural, and socioeconomic structures in which technologies are put to use for profit and power at the expense of sustainability and freedom.[49] Creation is Crucifixion, a disbanded punk band affiliated with the anarchist/activist tactical media collective, the Carbon Defense League, articulates this disposition in a 2001 interview:

> We are attempting to find ways in which activists can infiltrate and subvert the socialization system to take away its power. Right now we live at a unique time in which some form of this can be done through communications and Internet technologies easier than more traditional physical means. *It is not the tool but the user of the tool that we despise.*[50]

Then as now, anti-car/anti-oil messages resonate with many punks and corresponded with a wider acceptance of bicycling as a politicized alternative to automobiles. Moreover, bicycles are cheap, and economic thrift is a serious factor within a subculture that actively promotes dumpster diving, squatting, and, in some cases theft, as an alternative to alienated labor.[51] In addition, there was as already a substantial crossover between bike messenger and punk subcultures on the West Coast in the 1990s, particularly in the San Francisco Bay Area, where bike messengering was one of the few professions that "allowed people with mohawks to earn a living."[52] Not all bike messengers were or are punks, but the crossover made bicycling more visible in the punk scene and punk ethics/practices more visible among bike messengers. For example, Lynnee Breedlove, who fronted the pioneering "dyke punk" band Tribe 8, started her own bike messenger company in 1991 called Lickety Split All-Girl Courier, while Markus "Fur" Cook—a well-known bike messenger and cycling advocate—published the influential bike zine *Mercury Rising* and played in L. Sid, one the city's many messenger bands who comprised their own underground scene. Greta Snider and America Meredith, authors of the zines *Mudflap* and *Voice of Da,* respectively, were two other Bay Area messengers who clearly linked bicycling, bike messengers, and punk culture in their zines—the latter in music reviews and the general aesthetic/attitude of her publication, and the former through a zine in which bicycling is explicitly brought within the framework of an entire punk lifestyle of train hopping, urban exploration, drinking and trouble-making, and lots of DIY fun with friends and allies. In addition to the bike zines that were initially published by messengers, the convergence between messengering and punk rock brought more underground attention to the politics of car culture in the late 1980s and early 1990s.[53] Critical Mass amplified these sentiments and simultaneously created a different type of public space where activists, messengers, punks, cycling enthusiasts, and bike commuters could come together to celebrate cycling each month. Moreover, the event's celebration of xerocracy encouraged cyclists to produce and distribute thousands of zines, essays, flyers, and images that actively politicized cycling and forged a radical, grassroots critique of car culture. Like a number of the early Critical Mass participants who were active in the punk and zine scenes, the ride became a point of cohesion for bike riders in the broader DIY culture and, in turn, this support has arguably been one of the driving forces in event's longevity and popularity. Put simply, the ethics of environmentalism, technoskepticism, and anarchism converged with the influences of bike messenger subculture and Critical Mass to create a context in which the practice of bicycling was appropriated, redefined, and articulated to DIY punk and the DIY underground more broadly.

Bike Culture as Technological Practice

Transportation technologies have long played a role in the construction of subcultural identity, though for quite different reasons. For example, the English "Mods" of the 1960s appropriated Italian scooters (Vespa, Lambretta) as an identity-marker of their continental affiliation, sophistication, and general European-ness, thereby distinguishing themselves from their "Rocker" rivals who coveted U.K.-made motorcycles as an expression of both British nationalism and an exaggeratedly masculine identity.[54] Yet despite their differences, these subcultures shared a similar interest in modifying and customizing their (respective) vehicles to enhance the techno-communicative functions of their machines, both on the street and as part of a broader style. With respect to the use of bicycles in DIY culture, certain forms of technological tinkering are similarly "linked to a dialogic cultural process," though it is one less rooted in style than practice.[55] A single-speed conversion, for example, is a common bike hack involving the removal of all gears, shifters, cables, transmission components (derailleurs), and extra parts on a standard road bike or mountain bike, save one gear in the front and one in the back. The end result is a one-speed, or single-speed, bike that functions much like a traditional beach cruiser or a BMX inasmuch there are no gears to shift and one's bike goes as fast as its rider can pedal; it is the technological equivalent of the three-chord song or the cut-and-pasted zine.

The single-speed conversion process not only eliminates a slew of parts that one must eventually replace or repair; it also makes the bicycle a more convivial machine by minimizing the tools and expertise required for most forms of maintenance, barring those that any cyclist can learn to do oneself (i.e., fixing a flat tire, repairing a chain, or adjusting brakes). The popularity of single-speed bicycles as well as their fixed-gear Spartan variants is clearly indicative of a growing dissatisfaction with the complexity and gadgetry of modern bicycles, and more specifically, the inability of people to repair and tweak their own bike parts.[56] As Paul Rosen notes, corporations like Shimano transformed the bicycle industry by promoting "built-in obsolescence and opaque product design," thereby forcing bicyclists to become "dependent on the expertise of professionals, and at the same time distant from those professionals."[57] The company's emphasis on creating less participatory, less convivial technologies is ultimately antithetical, Rosen argues, to the development of more "democratic technics" that both enable and empower people to become active participants in a technological process, as opposed to passive consumers.[58]

More cyclists are, in fact, rebelling against the technological norms of the bike industry by encouraging more convivial, hackable bicycle designs as well as the use of recycled and/or found parts. The "outlaw bike subculture" Carlsson sees coalescing around bike gangs, artists, community cycling project volunteers, and mutant bike welders is at the forefront of this trend: it is a subculture that "spontaneously reuses and recycles in ways environmental advocates of recycling can only dream about."[59] This shifting sensibility is not constrained to one specific subculture or geographical locale, however, nor is it limited to the production of bikes that are simply designed for fun. Indeed, there is a growing support for modes of tinkering and customization that are exclusively geared toward utilitarianism, whether in the form of stripped-down bicycles or more emphatically in the circulation of "open source" designs like Aaron Wieler's bike carts and bicycle ambulances or the cargo bike extensions that Ross Evans designed while volunteering in Central America and now sells through his company, Xtracycle.[60] These technologies have far-reaching possibilities as both individuals and organizations are beginning to utilize these and other DIY designs worldwide, whether in service of delivering AIDS medication to patients, carrying crops to markets and kids to school, or simply allowing people to use bikes in place of cars for everyday trips to the grocery store. Blogs, wikis, and Web sites like *Instructables* are additional outlets in which cyclists from all walks of life distribute accessible resources on how to engineer homemade bicycle components and accessories from found materials, salvaged parts, and random mechanicals that one can purchase at any local hardware store.

If the stripped-down, raw utilitarianism associated with modifying single-speed bikes is an expression of the DIY ethos, one can ironically find a more compelling example of DIY bike technics pursued in the exaggerated, non-utilitarian world of mutant, or "freak," bike clubs. Devotees of this eclectic form of bicycle production and customization spawned their own subculture in the 1990s that is as informed by punk ethics and urban scavenging as it is science fiction fantasy and an undying admiration for technological geekiness. The Hard Times Bike Club (HTBC), which later changed its name to the Black Label Bike Club, is widely credited with being the first of several bicycle clubs to emerge in the 1990s—including Chunk 666 (founded in 1993); the Subversive Choppers Urban Legion, or SCUL (Boston, 1995); Chopper Riding Urban Dwellers, or CRUD (Los Angeles, 1996); Dead Baby Bike Club

A member of Black Label Bicycle Club at Bike Kill in Brooklyn, New York, 2008. *(Photo by Gary Kavanagh.)*

(Seattle, 1996); and Rat Patrol (Chicago, 1999). Jacob Houle and Per Hanson founded the HTBC in 1992 and word quickly spread, as it is prone to do when a crew of tattooed punks and misfits start riding seven-foot-high tall bikes around the streets of Minneapolis, only to take their machines on the road as part of Circus Redickuless, a traveling punk carnival show founded by "Chicken" John Rinaldi, a tinkerer, musician (ex–Letch Patrol), and 2007 San Francisco mayoral candidate.[61] Karl Anderson, aka Megulon-5, started building his bikes in 1993 after reading about homemade choppers in Greta Snider's punk/bike zine, *Mudflap*.[62] Soon after, he and a group of friends started Chunk 666 and also began documenting their exploits in a self-titled zine that is widely credited with turning other people on to the idea of making choppers and mutant bikes.[63] According to Johnny Payphone, the erudite (though unofficial) spokesperson for Chicago's Rat Patrol, Black Label's tall bikes and Chunk's choppers are the two most iconic bike designs associated with their subculture, as well as the templates from which most people construct their own mutant or freak bikes.[64]

While punk musicians and fanzine writers frequently draw analogies between the DIY ethos and bicycling, mutant bike clubs quite literally apply the DIY ethic to bicycle technology itself. In doing so, they connect with a longstanding tradition of amateur bike tinkering that previously spawned new cultural practices and technological configurations in the wake of bicycles' mass production, which is to say when cheaper, hackable parts—and affordable tools—enter the marketplace in volumes large enough for amateur tinkering to become a sizeable social phenomenon. One can map this disparate technical culture in the United States, at least in hindsight, by the articles and photo essays published in popular magazines like *Popular Science, Mechanix Illustrated,* and *Modern Mechanix* in the 1930s and 1940s.[65] In the 1960s and 1970s, bike tinkerers played a more pronounced and pivotal role in the development of modern cycling trends and designs that one can see at work, for example, in the invention of Schwinn's Sting-Ray bicycle and its subsequent appropriation into two rather distinct techno-cultural formations: lowriding, which is a highly stylized set of practices and traditions rooted in the Chicano communities of Los Angeles, and BMX, which is a sport/activity pioneered by Anglo youth in the beach towns and suburban sprawl of Southern California.[66] Much farther north, in the woods of Marin Country, California, a slightly older group of "pot smoking peacenik misfits in flannel and denim" were similarly modifying and repurposing old Schwinn bicycles, though their designs were geared toward racing down mountains as opposed to slowly cruising city streets or jumping dirt mounds on outdoor tracks.[67] With each of these innovations, bike tinkerers were engaged in a participatory technological process that effectively blurs the lines between production and consumption—a scenario not unlike the one Gene Balsley documented in his classic study of the "Hot-Rod [Car] Culture."[68] Mutant bike builders toy with a similar set of technological binaries, but their interventions are actually far more radical inasmuch as they do not blur the lines between production and consumption as much as they actively erase consumption altogether: bikes are cobbled together from found, salvaged, gifted, traded, and/or scrounged (dumpstered) parts, and they are not sold when completed. This mode of mutant production reroutes the seemingly natural cycle whereby amateur bike tinkerers professionalize into business engineers who simply orchestrate the (outsourced) mass production of an entirely new wave of commodities and consumer goods; it also disrupts the way most of us are accustomed to thinking about technologies as having a definitive beginning (invention) and end point (the junkyard) in their lifecycle. That is to say, there is no closure in this particular process of technological development and innovation, just another series of entry points from which different groups of tinkerers and hackers can work.[69]

In addition to their noncommercial use and their deployment in a tongue-in-cheek, post-automobile/post-apocalyptic narrative (i.e., "the Carmageddon") the blatant excesses and non-utilitarian designs of mutant bikes speak to some of the crucial ways in which technologies become aesthetically, socially, and culturally meaningful.[70] That is to say, this mode of bike hacking is not designed to enhance one's speed or the functionality of the machine itself, at least not in any conventional sense of the word. Rather, it is a set of practices meant to be shared with and among friends: it is a communal activity and a way to have fun—literally and figuratively—with production, mobility, and the bicycle itself. On this point, Megulon-5 (Karl Anderson) of Chunk 666 writes:

> We do this to have fun, hasten the upcoming tribulation, and save the children. Some of us are fighting for the right to party, others are partying for the right to fight, and it doesn't matter which is which. We clear a space for ourselves on the street, and we like to think that we're an inspiration to some of those who want to see a cycling revival (and an enemy to those who don't want the revival to be fun). In the end, it doesn't matter. We only do what we do because we can't help it.
>
> It's ironic that the safest place to be on a bike in the city is in a pack of fucked up mutant tetanus machines. Isn't that backwards? Can there be any doubt that the slide into barbarism has already begun? Are you going to watch it on television and keep a straight face the whole time?[71]

The even bigger irony here is that while the people who make and ride these bikes have a playful if not Dadaist approach to their craft, their humor directs critical attention to the absurdities that are so thoroughly normalized through automobility and urban planning:

> People think that the post-apocalyptic world will be all rough and tough, hard living and scrabbling for survival, but that's not true at all. It'll be a glorious paradise! People will look back at today and talk about how crazy we were. They'll ask why we had to scamper across a street and take our lives in our hands just to pick up a six-pack. They'll wonder why we lived in cities made for cars, on streets made for cars with little access corridors on the side for peds [pedestrians], in houses with big central front doors for cars and little side doors for people. They'll laugh at pictures of people eating in outdoor restaurants with hideous views and smells of streets and parking lots.

They'll ponder the stupidity of neighborhoods full of parked cars that start blaring their sirens in the middle of the night for no reason. They'll wonder why manslaughter wasn't a crime when the killer was driving a car. They'll say, "no wonder civilization collapsed, everyone shut themselves up in big coffins when they wanted to go anywhere, nobody talked to each other—they could only say one thing, and that was HONK! HONK! FINGER!"[72]

Whether consciously articulated or put into practice, the intertwined production and use of mutant/freak bikes is a notable critique of the "rationalizing tendency of industrial and urban life" inasmuch as it transcends market-based social relationships, the sterility and uniformity of mass production, and the accepted wisdom of modernity that sees technological efficiency and the establishment of more orderly, disciplined, and otherwise productive forms of mobility (and leisure) as its highest priorities.[73] Moreover, the "freak bikers" responsible for constructing what SCUL calls a fleet of "experimental ships . . . an organized battalion of funk," recognize that desire and pleasure are so comprehensively structured by this rationalizing tendency that it is difficult for most people to think, feel, and socialize out of the logic of consumption and the everyday norms of capitalism.[74] Encouraging others to "heed the moronic dictum" or figuring out new ways of "injecting magic" into people's lives, as Rat Patrol's Johnny Payphone puts it, are thus part of a broader set of tactics aimed at revealing and demonstrating how it is possible to have anti-consumerist fun with a bicycle as well as the process of building new, participatory communities.[75]

Bike Culture Is (Not) for Sale?

Bike riding punks, zinesters, tinkerers, and mutant bike clubs are part of an "outlaw bike subculture" that contests the ideological and material norms of automobility as well as the prevailing wisdom, practices, and behaviors promoted by mainstream bike culture. They contextualize the bicycle as part of a radical critique of consumerism and embrace a DIY paradigm that is less escapist than it is a "life experiment, a form of resistance, and a WAY, a form of 'making do.'"[76] Bike riding and junk tinkering are in this sense just as informed by environmental ethics and a critique of auto and oil industries as they are a basic longing for community and/or a desire to live outside the trappings of suburban isolation, yuppie individualism, and a dead-end job that yields little more than the money needed to make monthly car payments—a cycle that illustrator Andy Singer poignantly lampoons in his cartoon "Drive to Work, Work to Drive."

While there is no ideology that binds this amorphous group of dissident cyclists together, their dispositions and practices are clearly at odds with the image and values promulgated by the affluent professionals who comprise both the core constituency of the League of American Bicyclists as well as the target demographic that *Bicycling Magazine* highlights in their promotional media kit (used to court prospective advertisers):

> These opinion leaders have become the most influential members of the cycling community and are driving the sport's growth: weekend club rides in major cities across the U.S. attract a crowd of investment bankers, lawyers and media executives; high-end brands that deliver unmatched performance and style in custom bikes costing $10,000+ are thriving; and bike tours in Italy, France and the Napa Valley are as popular for their world-class cuisine and wine tastings as they are for their epic rides.[77]

Bicycling is an increasingly popular activity among executives in the United States, where it is seen as both a leisure activity as a well as a "great business opportunity to make contacts, get face time with the boss or even sign off on deals."[78] Here, bicycling is oddly articulated to "competition and pain"—a practice seemingly designed to breed "top managers" and cut-throat corporate traders, as SugarCRM CEO John Roberts notes in a 2007 interview: "If you look at the type of human who is a Wall Streeter, you end up with a prototypical cyclist."[79] Randy Komisar, a Silicon Valley venture capitalist, captures the essence of this phenomenon in what could very well be the slogan for a demographic of cyclists who literally function as the antithesis of DIY bike culture: *"Bicycling is the new golf."*[80]

While bicycling may not be the "new golf" for everyone, it makes one wonder whether the graffiti spray-painted across Brooklyn Industries' display windows in 2006 (see the opening page of this chapter) would have been more appropriately punctuated with a question mark, because those aspects of bike culture that are truly not for sale seem to occupy a rather marginal position within the broader gamut of cycling practices. For example, bicycle industry analyst Jay Townley observes that the number of cyclists riding bicycles worth more than $4,000 increased from about 20,000 to 90,000 between 2000 and 2005, while the number of high-end road bikes sold in the United States—priced at roughly $1,100 a piece—increased fourfold in the same time frame (from 145,000 to 498,0000): these high-end bikes accounted for 15 percent of all sales and nearly 40 percent of the retail dollars spent on bicycles in 2005.[81] In addition to the emergence of a $10,000 bicycle market, guided winery tours, and leisure events with entry fees, even some of the most common cycling activities require specialized and somewhat expensive equipment (bikes, clothing, and/or accessories) as well as—ironically enough—an automobile for transporting bicycles to specific destinations, whether a road race, a Cyclocross course, a vélodrome, a BMX ramp, or a mountain bike trail in the woods.

My point in calling attention to these examples is that with so many cyclists staking a claim to the bicycle as a symbol of nonconformity, voluntary simplicity, and even liberation, it is important to recognize that the bicycle is still firmly embedded within a market economy that not only valorizes unsustainable consumption but also recuperates and depoliticizes some of the very ideas and practices that propel bike advocacy. To use New York City as an example, Brooklyn Industries was targeted for ostensibly using an anti-consumerist technology as a marketing tool in 2005, but it was hardly alone in exploiting the cultural cachet and green credentials of the bicycle. Several stores in Manhattan, including Camper, Stussy, J. Crew, and Paragon Sports—a sporting goods retailer that displayed bike-toting mannequins in a life-size storefront diorama, under the heading ONE LESS CAR—have showed their affinity with bike riding shoppers as of late.[82] During the 2008 Mercedes-Benz Fashion Week in New York City, DKNY took things a step further by strategically chaining roughly seventy-five bicycles to street signs and lampposts around New York City as part of a marketing campaign that was aesthetically designed to mimic the city's various ghost bike memorials. The DKNY bikes were spray-painted top-to-bottom in orange paint and lacked any distinguishable markings, save the company's Web address. Needless to say, bicyclists were not pleased with the gesture both for its crude co-optation of an extremely meaningful (and emotionally charged) symbol and for the level of ignorance DKNY showed in attempting to link bicycle transportation with both fashion modeling and an event sponsored by an elite automobile corporation. Many of the bikes were trashed before the city eventually hauled them away, much to the chagrin of corporation's representative who claimed the bikes were meant to "get people thinking and talking about bicycles as a healthy and fashionable way to get around the city."[83] That DKNY used the same orange bike gimmick to advertise men's underwear in London several months later clearly illustrates the hollowness of the company's appeal to the greater good, but one has to wonder whether the obviousness of the corporation's insincerity was the only thing that opened it up to such scrutiny in the first place.[84] That is to say, bike riders and advocates are seemingly so eager to see positive representations of bicycling (especially utility cyclists and bike commuters) in both the media and the public sphere that anything viewed as promoting said goals is almost implicitly shielded from critique, even when such tactics—such as the suit- and tie-wearing bike commuter prominently featured in Macy's 2008 Earth Day public relations campaign—are barely a "half a step above greenwashing."[85]

Puma's recent attention to urban bicycling is a case in point inasmuch as they are one of the most prominent companies (along with Pabst Blue Ribbon) that use traditional and/or guerilla marketing strategies to sell themselves as a pro-bicycling company and to solicit urban bike-riding consumers. Puma's efforts in New York City include sponsoring a bike messenger team (Team Puma), hosting the 2005 Cycle Messenger World Championship in New York, creating a traveling bicycle gallery tour (Re-bike) in 2007, branding a line of bicycles—some of which they donated to W Hotels Worldwide for their guests to use on Earth Day, 2008—and staging a two-week bicycle-themed art show at the Vice [Magazine] Gallery in Williamsburg, Brooklyn (September 2008).[86] Puma's previous bicycle-themed collaboration with *Vice Magazine* yielded a sleek "zine" about fixed-gear bikes (entitled *Puma Presents: Fixed Gear 101*) that was disseminated as a *Vice* insert. Though beautifully illustrated and informative, the publication's gratuitously urban focus—replete with images of tattooed and/or mohawk-clad bike messengers—was perhaps Puma's most obvious attempt to exploit the image of the "gritty bicycle messenger, and its abundant street credibility" in service of achieving brand recognition among a seemingly authentic and/or cohesive subculture of urban fixed-gear cyclists.[87] Tapping into a bona fide urban subculture (real or perceived) is undoubtedly a prized achievement in the realm of corporate cool hunting, and one the company nearly sabotaged in 2005 when it sent a representative to the Cycle Messenger World Championships in a Puma-branded Hummer SUV (which was later defaced with a Sharpie-scrawled note to the owner). Sadly, it was this faux pas rather than the corporation's abominable record of human rights abuses—Li Qiang, director of China Labor Watch, states that "Puma is the worst company in the industry" with respect to social responsibility—that seemed to cause the most consternation among participants, observers, and, eventually, online commentators.[88] Consequently, while Puma has backed events like the Bicycle Film Festival and lent financial support to messengers who, in turn, used the money for the benefit of the entire messenger community, it is one of a growing number of companies that are eager to cash in on the cultural cachet associated with urban bicycling. Yet unlike Patagonia's Critical Mass messenger bag, Pedro's Critical Mass Mini Tool, the Vans Fixed Gear Authentic shoe, or Iron Heart's $360 Cyclist Jeans (bicycle not included), the product Puma is most interested in producing and marketing is not a tangible commodity, but rather, bike culture itself: it wants nothing less than to infuse its own brand name and iconography into the media and cultural practices that co-constitute bike culture, thereby creating a bizarre feedback loop in which it can sponge the very authenticity it is attempting to manufacture.[89]

Fixed-Gear Bikes and Messenger Aesthetics, or "Give Hipsters a Brake"[90]

Of all the phenomena in American bike culture to prompt questions about cultural authenticity, media representation, and especially the uses of technology, the popularity of fixed-gear bikes has to be the most polarizing. As noted earlier, the recent visibility of single-speed bicycles is indicative of a growing interest in technological conviviality, utilitarian design, and a stripped-down aesthetic. Yet, the less-is-more impulse buttressing the single-speed trend hardly explains the current fascination with fixed-gear track bikes that, while beautifully refined, are designed in such a way that riding—and more important, stopping—is an unnecessarily complicated endeavor that requires a rider to apply resistance with his or her legs in lieu of handbrakes, since the pedals and rear wheel turn continuously in one fixed direction (like bicycles used in the 1890s).[91] Originally designed for high-speed track racing (hence "track" bike) and subsequently appropriated by urban bike messengers who praise them for their lightness, speed, and style, fixed-gear bikes—also called "fixies" or, in the United Kingdom, "fixed-wheel" bikes—are in some ways the antithesis of utilitarian transportation, save the minimal parts one must buy or replace on the machine itself.[92] What the bicycles lack in their ease-of-use is made up for with their mechanical elegance, their durability, and the way they reconfigure the act of cycling and the relationship between bicyclist and machine—an experience devotees habitually describe in quasi-spiritual language peppered by illusions to the "purity and simplicity" of the machine, the "almost mystical connection" between rider and bicycle, and the feeling that one's bicycle is an "extension of [one's] limbs," allowing one to achieve "Zen," or a "Zen-like state" comparable to "being in the 'The Zone' all the time."[93]

At the risk of minimizing the joy of riding fixed-gear bikes, let alone the corporeal and spiritual apexes their fans apparently reach through this practice, their desirability also seems tied to something much more basic, which is the cultural cachet one gleans by owning, riding, and/or displaying one: the fixed-gear bike has become a trendy icon of urban coolness, a "hipster gold card," as one magazine article puts it.[94] In this sense, riding fixed-gear bikes seem to offer a form of mediated or indirect utility to their users, inasmuch as the difficulty of riding them allows bicyclists to demonstrate their level of cycling skill, fitness, or mastery over their machine.[95] One can draw this inference from the slew of films, Web sites, and blogs devoted to fixed-gear bikes that focus much less on transportation and advocacy issues than on stunt riding, tricks, and aggressive maneuvering through dense urban spaces.[96] On the Internet, one also finds that showing off one's riding skill is seemingly of equal or lesser importance than simply showing off one's bike. For example,

Dennis Bean-Larson's *Fixed Gear Gallery* Web site is one of the many online showcases for bicyclists to demonstrate their participation in a specific taste culture cultivated by and for bike riders. Indeed, the bikes photographed on the site as well as their individual parts, and in many cases the very placement of such parts—as in the specific location of one's brake levers or the tilt of one's handlebars—function as visual footnotes that document cyclists' understanding of, or engagement with, highly specific aesthetic styles, and modes of consumption.[97] This indexical function is best highlighted in the satirical analysis of the "NYC Bike Snob," whose Web site features, among other things, brutally sarcastic critiques of the fixed-gear bicycle photos posted in online forums like *Fixed Gear Gallery, Velospace,* and the For Sale pages on New York City's *Craigslist.*[98] His ridicule highlights the rich semiotic intent behind the set-up of specific bikes, as well as the possible meanings embedded within each supposedly casual photo.

The whole practice of displaying bicycles online not only portends an obsession with style; it also illustrates the value many cyclists place on one's ability to synthesize new combinations of components within a visual terrain that is wholly unrelated to the actual production or use of bicycles. The Web sites, in other words, specifically underscore the role of the bicyclist as a savvy accessorizer who gains an identity, at least in part, by engaging in a "highly selective form of consumption."[99] Many of the more than nine thousand contributors to *Fixed Gear Gallery* and a handful of similar Web sites clarify this underlying meaning by including detailed lists of the components featured on the bicycles on display; these lists literally stand in for the owners of the bikes who are, incidentally, rarely photographed along with them. Indeed, there is an unspoken rule that human bodies must be entirely extracted from the pictures, as they presumably distract from a mode of commodity worship in which style is equated with the disembodied knowledge of consumer goods and elegant machinery. The result is something like a social networking site for commodities themselves: the bicycle's own version of *Facebook* in which humans simply function as administrators who are assigned the ancillary role of uploading photos and typing bios for the bikes. Humans are, however, the audience for these Web sites, and inasmuch as visitors are attracted not only to the aesthetics of the bikes on the screen but also to the idea of mounting, riding, and otherwise fondling them, it is hardly an exaggeration when people jokingly refer to such images as "bike porn": they simultaneously have everything and nothing to do with physicality of pleasure.[100]

The sheer prevalence of fixed-gear photo Web sites and other visual representations of the bikes (via film, artwork, clothing), suggests the prominent role that aesthetics and image play in their popularity. Consequently, it is one of the salient reasons why they are often denounced as a trendy, faddish, or indicative of a cooler-than-thou, urban chic—a material artifact on par with the now passé icons of "trucker hats and Pabst Blue Ribbon beer."[101] Bike messengers are some of the more jaded critics of the fixed-gear bicycle craze, seeing as how the trend is part of a broader co-optation of messenger culture in which track bikes (once ridden almost exclusively by bike couriers) as well as messenger bags, walkie-talkies, cycling caps, and even the most minute details of messenger garb (such as elastic key chains worn at the elbow joint) are donned by messenger look-alikes who are variously denounced as "missingers," "fakengers," "posengers," "dressengers," or, as one person bluntly puts it, "fake ass messengers."[102] Indeed, some of bike messengers' very own grassroots cultural practices, such as "alleycat" races—urban races organized by and for messengers since the 1980s—are also widely copied in recent years by cyclists with little or no connection to messenger work, save their look.[103] Corporations and designers similarly glean the "street creed" of messengers when it suits their financial interests:

> [In 2006] Lincoln wanted some well-known NYC messengers to appear in a print ad for their cars. The messengers turned them down and Lincoln used their street names in the ad anyway because they thought they sounded cool. . . . [T]he 1994 TV series *Double Rush* also used some names of well-known San Francisco messengers without permission or compensation.[104]

While this scenario is unquestionably irritating to messengers who do, incidentally, use certain commodities to "distinguish themselves from more orthodox cultural formations," the main issue here is not whether people are ripping off messengers' look or attempting to duplicate their cultural practices, but rather, how the popularization of this style and the proliferation of a caricature image of bike couriers serves to otherwise erase the labor of bike messenger work altogether.[105] That is to say, the elevation of messenger style reduces a working-class job, and by extension the labor issues associated with the profession, to a fashion trend for young, fixed-gear-donning urbanities or alternatively, a marketing tool for corporations—even ones that specialize in the production of enormous, gas-guzzling cars (Lincoln).[106] Thus, it is understandable why some veteran messengers take offense to both the commercialization of their so-called lifestyle and the emergence of rookie (new) messengers who take up the job as a way to validate or simply reproduce their own preconceived image of the messenger-as-subcultural-stylist.[107] Rebecca "Lambchop" Reilly, whose own work meticulously documents the nuances of bike messenger labor via oral histories, describes being shocked by her encounter with a new crop of messengers at a 2007 event:

They dressed and acted the part, but according to my old school com-
patriots a lot of them don't do standard messenger work like we did;
the job itself has changed immensely. Nowadays, instead of riding the
peninsula they're riding from office buildings to the courthouse and
doing a lot of legal work. They're strutting around with their fixies
and they don't know who the legends are, they don't know why they
are riding fixed. They think they invented the shit.[108]

One of the points to which Reilly refers is the actual history of messengers using fixed-gear bikes in the United States—a practice originating with
Caribbean immigrants who rode them in their countries of origin and subsequently used for them for courier work in New York City. There, messengers
embraced track bikes for their speed and agility though they also become a
point of distinction since it requires a substantial amount of control (and
style) to ride them properly on city streets. Consequently, when seen as part
of a wider trend that almost exclusively privileges the representation of bike
messengers as young, tattooed, carefree white rebels, the ahistorical attitude
that so irks Reilly is part of a process that, to varying degrees, not only de-his-
toricizes and de-labors the profession but also literally white washes—as in,
Anglicizes—messenger history by negating the crucial influence that people
of color had on the culture and aesthetics of bike messengering. Veteran bike
messenger and visual artist "Fast" Eddie Williams speaks to this tension:

There are people riding around with the messenger chain and the
bag who aren't even a messenger. To them it's mad cool, but to us it
was a job, you know? We had to dress like that. And there weren't
that many white kids as messengers back then. It was a lot of Puerto
Ricans and West Indians, and mostly blacks. And then as the years
went by there were a few whites that I know personally, and now it's
like the tables have turned. . . . Most of the messengers back then—
from '84 until the '90s—were from the islands. Cats from Jamaica,
Trinidad, and Guyana, they all flooded here in like '78. And that was
the messenger scene. It was the most beautiful thing I ever seen in my
life. After we finished work we would all get together in Washington
Square Park. And that's how you knew there were so many bikers. We
came from all over.[109]

Messengers do have their own cliques, styles, and ways of navigating both
the urban spaces and corporate culture to which they are oddly articulated,
but these attributes are all intricately tied up with, and necessarily secondary
to, the job itself. This prevailing labor consciousness, though unorthodox,
shapes the way they see themselves as workers and is one of the reasons why

they are so guarded about who speaks on their behalf and how they are represented to the public.

For example, Travis Culley's popular bike messenger memoir, *The Immortal Class,* received mixed reviews from messengers because of the liberties he took with a number of his personal anecdotes (several were allegedly stolen from other messengers) as well as his general lack of experience as a messenger (it takes years of experience for messengers to even be recognized—sometimes quite literally—by veterans).[110] That Culley's book is a poetic account of urban cycling or an eloquent treatise on the politics of transportation was never disputed; it was specifically his role as a representative of the messenger community that caused friction. Part of this tension stems from the way in which he dismissively handled messengers' criticism of his book: "Some of them want to believe it's noble to remain a messenger. They can criticize me, but to me messengering is a transient job for transient minds."[111] While messengering may indeed jibe with "transient minds," it is also a job that fosters an intense pride among its workers, many of whom do see it as a noble profession and are "fiercely proud of their work."[112] Moreover, it is not always an interim position from which one can decide to do something else, particularly when one accounts for the lack of job opportunities facing many of the people who have historically become bike messengers in the United States. To his credit, Culley does pay attention to the nuances of labor in his book, but the overall valorization of the messenger-as-struggling-artist-cum-urban-rebel narrative seems to unwittingly affirm, rather than challenge, the popular view of couriers as reckless thrill seekers who do not work a real job.

Style as Substance, Bike Culture as Production

While the popularity of fixed-gear bikes and a new wave of bicycling fashion serves as fodder for hundreds of articles published on the Internet and in the corporate press, much of this attention frequently translates into a reductive pro versus con debate about authenticity, fads, road safety, and/or the ambiguous relationship between bicycling and urban "hipsters" (who are, incidentally, rarely defined and/or critiqued with any degree of lucidity).[113] Consequently, it is easy to lose sight of the ways in which these facets of bike culture fit into a broader context. For example, most bicycling advocates tend to see the fixed-gear phenomenon as a mixed blessing where, on one hand, they are weary of biking becoming just another fad that results in people "hanging their bike next to the roller blades they don't use anymore," and at the same time, they recognize how it can work in precisely the opposite manner.[114] Eric Boerer, for instance, likens fixed-gear bikes to a "gateway drug" that turns many people onto other facets of bicycling and bike advocacy, just as fixed-gear rider Tony Fast concludes a rant against fixed-gear biking fashionistas with the assertion "If fashion gets people riding bikes then more power to it."[115] Indeed, the fact that bicycling is even remotely considered fashionable and hip in certain U.S. cities is hardly an insignificant achievement given the profound challenges facing those who simply attempt to alter, let alone transform, the dominant cultural norms and everyday habits associated with transportation. The popularity of fixed-gear bikes is not exclusively responsible for this development, but it has unquestionably focused more attention on urban cycling and is arguably instrumental in cultivating a different image and aesthetic that many now associate with bicycle transportation. Less obvious, perhaps, is the influence this once marginal and/or subcultural trend exerted on the bicycle industry in recent years.

As of the late 1990s, one would be hard pressed to find adults riding basic, one-speed bicycles for transportation in most U.S. cities and the prospects of finding a simple, utilitarian adult bicycle in a U.S. bike shop was also uncommon (let alone finding a fixed-gear bicycle or a sleek single-speed). As of 2009, nearly every bike company now features single-speed and fixed-gear bikes in their catalogue and this correlates with a renewed emphasis on manufacturing bicycles for everyday transportation (typically branded as "urban" or "city," models).[116] The revival of what most Americans readily call "granny" bikes is similarly widespread, as is the appearance of new lines of European-style bicycles designed exclusively for urban utilitarianism and low maintenance as opposed to speed or sport. No one can decisively point to a single trend or subculture as a cause for this shift in design sensibility, but the widespread visibility of fixed-gear and single-speed bikes on the road in the 1990s—first among messengers and hard-core cycling enthusiasts, followed by punks and the broader DIY culture—unquestionably piqued people's interest in durable, simple bicycles. Style, in this sense, is also "a function of politics" inasmuch as it plays a key role in the broader revaluation of the everyday uses of bicycles in the United States.[117] For example, the popularity of single-speed and fixed-gear bikes is encouraging a new wave of recycling and reuse: older, steel road bikes are now highly valued for their durability, performance, and aesthetics, just as older leisure bikes designed by companies like Schwinn and Murray are in vogue once again and part of a thriving secondhand bike industry facilitated by *Ebay, Craigslist,* and analogous resale/auction/barter Web sites. But more significant, the attention to aesthetics and bicycle design in recent years both correlates with, and is at least partly responsible for, a burgeoning interest in craftsmanship and the art of bicycle production. The North American Handmade Bicycle Show is one of the barometers for this trend: it began in 2005 with 23 exhibitors and now features as many as 150 custom bike builders who take part in the event and display their creations to thousands of visitors.[118] In Portland, Oregon, alone, one can find more than two-dozen independent bike builders, many of whom either apprenticed with other local builders or learned their craft at the United Bicycle Institute in Ashland, Oregon.[119]

Custom builders, who range from single individuals to family-run businesses, not only exert "an influence on trends and styles that is disproportionate to their market share"; they also constitute part of a broader movement of artisans, tinkerers, and skilled workers who are at once reconfiguring the role of independent, small-scale businesses in the North American bike industry and also demonstrating a sense of pride that famed messenger bag maker Eric Zo associates with DIY production: "I'm in the society of people who actually make their own shit."[120] This bloc includes messenger-owned bag manufacturers, utilitarian vehicle builders (namely, cargo bicycles and tricycles), specialized welders, artists who use scrap bike materials to make everything from jewelry to furniture, and bicyclists who are running successful bike shops and pedal-powered delivery services based on cooperative, worker-owned business models.[121] In addition to newer businesses, long-established independent companies are also getting a second look from cyclists who are (re)discovering the importance of durability, craftsmanship, and more localized modes of production embodied by companies like Wald, the Kentucky group responsible for producing most of the bicycle baskets seen in the United States since 1905.[122] Worksman Cycles, the oldest U.S. bike maker still in business, is another company that perseveres despite radical transformations in the bike industry since the company was founded in 1898. Over a century later they continue to turn out industrial-strength cargo vehicles, food service carts (including most hot dog and ice cream carts in service today), and several models of bicycle and tricycle from their factory in Queens, New York. In addition to setting a precedent for established U.S. cargo bike/trike makers like Human Powered Machines (Eugene, Oregon) as well as upstarts like Haley Tricycles (Philadelphia, Pennsylvania), Worksman illustrates some of the ways in which pedal-powered technologies can be used for work as well as leisure.[123] They also symbolize the possibilities for coupling domestic production with sustainable energy production in order to produce affordable vehicles: in 2007 Worksman became one of the first bike companies—and one of the few New York City manufacturers—to use solar panels in order to generate part of the energy necessary to run their factory (roughly 25 percent).[124]

Conclusion

Through the production of alternative bike media and the popularization of bicycling as a subcultural practice, bicycling gets brought into, and reconfigured within, an entire "network of empowerment" associated with DIY culture, or what Lawrence Grossberg calls an a *affective alliance:* an "organization of concrete material practices and events, cultural forms and social experience which both opens up and structures the space of our affective investments in the world."[125] Thus, while bicycles have become another scene-accredited lifestyle accessory for many urban punks and zinesters, the popularity and acceptance of bicycling is far more than a surface-level signifier of subcultural capital.[126] It is indicative of how people are redefining bicycle transportation and bicycle technologies on their own terms, in ways that both differ from and in many ways actively contest their dominant meaning and representation in the United States. More tangibly, these trends seems to play a substantive role in getting more people interested in biking overall, which is an achievement unto itself, and one that speaks to the profound role that culture plays in the (re)production of transportation norms. Of course, there is no way to empirically measure this in terms of cause and effect (the "punk factor"? the "zine effect"?), but there are numerous examples of how even media texts alone can prove influential on readers, never mind their reception in a cultural context that privileges bicycling as part of an alternative "whole way of life."[127]

The articulation of bicycle transportation to DIY ethics is significant not only for the way it frames bicycle transportation as a way of "Doing Mobility Yourself" but also for the way it brings a pragmatic feature of everyday life within the purview of subcultural practices. Because while underground culture can offer a "safe place in which to test out new ideas and to imagine a different way of ordering things," it tends to remain limited to a domain in which social problems are "magically" resolved, resistance is often reduced to style or representation, and anger that "might have been expressed in political action" is ultimately squandered.[128] The safe place, in other words, ends up functioning like the cultural equivalent of a nature preserve, whereby life flourishes inside the fences but the borders are, ironically, the only thing keeping the environment looking so vibrant. But by making automobility a relevant issue for scrutiny and by incorporating the bicycle into a participatory paradigm that also pays attention to technological practice and the importance of production and labor, DIY bike culture is instrumental in pointing people toward more substantive engagements with transportation issues (via advocacy, education, and urban planning) and more socially relevant applications of DIY ethics, whether for bike advocacy or, as I discuss in Chapter 7, the empowerment of communities.

CHAPTER 7

Handouts, Hand Ups, or Just Lending a Hand?

Community Bike Projects, Bicycle Aid, and Competing Visions of Development under Globalization

> The more people we can get on bikes and give them skills to fix them means less oil and money for the corporations. It means less environmental degradation. It means doing what we can in the belly of the beast to stop the war for oil. It means empowering people. It means community.
>
> —Mary Blue and Andrew Lynn, *Velorution: The Unofficial Documents of a Bicycle Underground*, 2004

nside renovated warehouses, old storefronts, and rickety garages scattered throughout the Americas, the seeds of a vélorution are being planted with wrenches and grease-stained hands. It is here, among piles of donated parts and bicycles once destined for landfills, that bicyclists utilize little more than volunteer labor and shoestring budgets to cultivate a variety of community bicycle projects aimed at educating youth, empowering volunteers, and providing people with affordable, sustainable transportation options. These spaces, as well as the community bicycle organizations they house, have become integral parts of the cycling infrastructure in an increasing number of cities, and perhaps more important, they give real substance to the notion of community that cyclists sometimes abstractly associate with, or attribute to, bike culture. The various organizations, subcultures, and cliques of cyclists mentioned in the preceding chapters do contribute to a broader vision of bike culture that is represented through media, experienced through public events, articulated through advocacy, and ultimately defined through everyday practice. Yet one of the challenges they face is how to create lasting alternatives that transcend the whims of cycling fads, the small-scale proliferation of grassroots media, or the excitement of a monthly bike ride. In the United States, where I continue to focus attention in this chapter, community bicycle organizations achieve these ends by putting DIY ethics to work in service of creating independent institutions, recycled bike initiatives, youth curricula, and various programs that pay attention to some of the distinct ways in which mobility is intricately connected with race, class, and gender privilege. Significantly, their engagement with these issues is not limited to the cities they call home: a number of community bicycle organizations also play a key role in supplying regional, national, and international bicycle aid programs with shipments of reclaimed bicycles and parts, and when possible, volunteer support. These programs, which span several continents and dozens of cities worldwide, not only help people gain access to affordable transportation in places where money and resources are scarce; they also facilitate connections between local and global mobilities, reminding us at once of the utopian prospects of solidarity and the myriad pitfalls of economic globalization.

Community Cycling Programs

The exact origin of community cycling programs in the United States is difficult to pinpoint, but the Youth Bicycle Education Network traces the roots of contemporary programs to two models of education and activism, the first of which was developed in 1974 by organizers of the Union City Teen Employment Program in Union City, California.[1] As part of their mission to provide work, employment referrals, and income for teens, the program taught bike mechanics to teenagers who operated a bicycle repair shop and hosted Build-a-Bicycle workshops for people in the community.[2] The program's dual emphasis on experiential hands-on pedagogy and youth empowerment was not immediately replicated in other communities, but it found a similar expression in the Bicycle Action Project, which Charles Hammond started in 1988 as a storefront classroom and experimental education program for unemployed adults and at-risk youth in Indianapolis.[3] Its endeavors included partnerships with work incentive programs and the development of a curriculum that taught bicycle repair and bicycling awareness to aspiring mechanics and commuters.[4] The Bicycle Action Project focused acutely on the needs of youth by employing people over the age of sixteen as educational instructors or supervisors, and it also pioneered an Earn a Bike (EAB) program in which kids learned how to repair and/or rebuild bicycles by trading their labor for a free bicycle that they worked on themselves. Bike mechanics/educators at St. Louis Bicycle Works further developed the EAB model in the following years and it eventually became a standard feature of community cycling projects in the United States and Canada during the 1990s.[5]

A different model of community bicycle organization began in 1983, when a Boston bicycle mechanic named Carl Kurz founded Bikes Not Bombs (BNB) as a way to reclaim bikes from the waste stream and simultaneously protest the violence inflicted by the U.S.-backed Contra forces in Nicaragua. Like Food Not Bombs, the goal of the group was to create a solidarity movement that called attention to U.S. militarism and to do something practical for people in need. Instead of gathering dumpster-bound food to cook meals for the homeless, BNB reclaimed dumpster-bound bicycles for distribution among teachers and health workers in the war-torn country. With the assistance of sympathetic bicyclists, activists, and bike donors, Kurz and co-founder Michael Replogle (a transportation planner in Maryland) began to refurbish used bicycles for their first shipment in 1984.[6] Other chapters of BNB sprouted in U.S. cities and college campuses throughout the 1980s despite the U.S. embargo against Nicaragua; by the end of the decade there were more than twenty U.S. chapters coordinating the collection and delivery of thousands of bicycles to Nicaragua, Haiti, and Mozambique (to name just a few of their many recipients).

The Bikes Not Bombs strategy of combining bike recycling and education set an important precedent for cyclists in the United States to develop similar programs in their own communities. Indeed, by the time BNB began to focus more explicit attention on disadvantaged youth living near their Jamaica Plain headquarters in Boston, the Indianapolis Bicycle Action Project was already in full swing and students at Oberlin College (Ohio) were also busy operating the Oberlin Bike Co-op as a resource for students to gain free access to tools, recycled parts, and mechanic training. Throughout the early 1990s a number of nonprofit community bicycle organizations sprouted nationwide, including ReCycle Ithaca's Bicycles, or RIBS, which began in 1990 under the name Operation Free Bike, as well as New York City's Recycle-a-Bicycle, which started as a project of Transportation Alternatives before becoming its own independent entity and one of the international leaders in bicycle-oriented youth education. Similar community bicycle organizations offering youth programs, EAB initiatives, and/or bike mechanic training now exist in more than two dozen U.S. states, four Canadian provinces, and a number of cities throughout Europe, Australia, Africa, and both Central and South America.[7]

Operations

Community bicycle organizations vary in their size and purpose but the majority are small operations staffed by volunteers who collect used and/ or donated bikes, facilitate access to tools, and/or feature some type of EAB

Bikes Not Bombs: peace activists outside the U.S. embassy in Managua, Nicaragua, 1987. *(Photo by Robert Croma.)*

program. As with other nonprofit organizations, adequate funding and space are always in short supply, limiting the ability for most organizations to work beyond the scope of their recycling and EAB efforts. However, certain groups have been successful at securing steadier sources of funding through grants or through their affiliation with other established nonprofits, especially those that work on transportation and/or environmental issues. For example, Recycle-a-Bicycle, the Community Cycling Center (Portland), and Bike Again! (Halifax, Nova Scotia) offer a wide range of educational, safety and training programs, and have lent additional support to Public Use Bicycle programs, community art initiatives, and/or local activist projects. On the whole, organizations like Free Ride (Pittsburgh), Plan B (New Orleans), the Asheville Recyclery (Asheville, North Carolina), Le Club de vélo Freewheels (Montreal), Bike Woks (Seattle), and the Bike Kitchen (San Francisco) have literally recycled tons of bicycles destined for landfills and simultaneously created spaces where people can have free access to tools, equipment, volunteer assistance, and mechanical training. More important, they create empowering programs that facilitate the development of local communities around the bicycle.

The majority of community bicycle organizations are organized by environmentalists, activists, teachers, and/or other critically minded cyclists who see biking as either an alternative to, or a stance against, automobile transportation and car culture. Some groups are more overtly political, framing their programs in ways that address the environmental, economic, and social costs of automobility. Bikes Not Bombs is a clear example of this philosophy at work, as noted by their former executive director Rick Jarvis:

> Addressing political issues is an integral part of BNB. . . . All of our work is intended to support people's ability to choose safe, clean and sustainable forms of transportation, and to do so by cooperating across the boundaries of nationality, gender, race and class. By shipping bikes overseas to self-help groups in the coming year, while engaging the hearts and minds of young people in our own community, we will continue to oppose the dominance of militarism and energy monopolies over people's lives, no matter where they live.[8]

Volunteers from a number of community bicycle projects throughout North America largely echo Jarvis's sentiments and articulate a message of solidarity with poor and oppressed peoples. The criteria for a community bicycle organization put forth at the 2005 BikeBike! conference—an event organized to promote communication, skill sharing, and knowledge between like-minded community groups—reveal these ethics at work:

- Nonprofit bicycle organizations
- Bike shops that are accessible to people without money
- Shops that have an educational focus, teaching others how to fix bikes
- Shops that are volunteer-run
- Organizations that ship bikes to communities suffering from First World colonialism and its effects
- Shops that provide free or low-cost services to the community
- Organizations that recycle bicycles and parts[9]

A politicized, social justice-oriented approach to bicycling is certainly not a requirement for starting a community bicycle organization, but it is a comfortable fit with a set of programs that (1) implicitly critique the wastefulness of capitalism through recycling, (2) promote an environmentally sustainable mode of transportation, and (3) advocate self-empowerment and participation as direct alternatives to consumption and alienation.[10] Indeed, the creation of educational and mentoring programs aimed at people of color and the poor—those most under-represented or ignored by the predominantly white, middle-class network of U.S. bike advocates—are crucial ways in which cyclists affirm the role of community within the larger project of political and/or social change. These collaborations certainly do not guarantee a collective struggle for unity and social justice, but the attention many community bicycle organizations pay to the dynamics of race, class, and gender is a necessary step in the right direction.

Race, Class, and Bicycling

Transportation and access to transportation resources are both intricately connected to race and class.[11] African Americans and the urban working poor, for example, suffer from a lack of transportation options not unlike their disproportionately poor access to affordable housing and other basic daily goods and services, such as neighborhood grocery stores.[12] Consequently, community bicycle organizations that intentionally facilitate programs to assist the poor and communities of color not only provide a rare service in a profit-based economy—access to free services, learned volunteers, and the use of tools and resources that would otherwise be unavailable or prohibitively expensive—but also are engaged (whether explicitly or implicitly) with intersecting issues of race, class, and transportation. The Dead or (A)live bicycle collective in Indianapolis is one of many groups that see themselves functioning in this capacity: "Any action involving bikes as transportation almost inherently involves addressing class issues, since transportation is harder to achieve if you are not of a more financially stable class. Our bike giveaway program will be directly servicing the economically disadvantaged classes."[13] In the attempt to create programs that genuinely involve people in the community, volunteers use whatever means at their disposal to make bicycling part of the solution to adults' everyday transportation needs, as well as the needs of their children. For example, The BikeShare program in Toronto partners with several community centers to have bike-sharing hubs accessible in low-income areas; BikeAgain! provides services for the local immigrant population in Nova Scotia; and the Working Bikes Cooperative in Chicago distributes bicycles to people in need and sells low-cost bicycles out of its storefront in the Near West Side.[14] Robert Galdins, of the Re-cycles Bicycle Co-op in Ottawa, explains his organization's sliding scale for services and used bikes/parts:

If it seems like someone is low income and can't afford something, we will either sell it to them at a reduced price or give it to them for free. We always trade volunteer time for use of the shop for personal projects, allowing people of low income the opportunity to use our shop free of charge. We've also given away dozens of bikes to organizations that help the homeless, developing countries, and families in women's shelters.[15]

The Community Cycling Center in Portland is one of many organizations that similarly values participation as a form of currency when payment is not an option. In fact, it took a cue from its successful youth programs and developed the first adult EAB program in the nation called "Create a Commuter," which provides low-income adults with fully outfitted commuter bicycles, lights, a lock, a helmet, a pump, as well as training in bike maintenance, safe riding, and route planning.[16] Among other notable endeavors, the organization also provided free bicycles and services to residents of Dignity Village, an intentional homeless community that began as a tent village under the city's Fremont Bridge.

Community bicycle organizations are principally organized to foster participation, skill building, and a sense of accomplishment through one's own labor—goals that are an especially important feature of recycled bike and EAB programs catered to youth. Teenagers, especially those considered "at-risk," seem to benefit substantially from their participation in these programs, as they are model examples of service learning that utilize experiential pedagogy.[17] In some cases, bicycle education programs are integrated into other community initiatives aimed at preventing youth violence, such as Cycles of Change in Oakland (California) and Neighborhood Bike Works in Philadelphia. It is significant that these efforts provide young people access to spaces based not on discipline or surveillance, but cooperation and mentorship. Hands-on atmospheres, like the ones facilitated in community bike shops, help to teach kids of all ages self-discipline, patience, respect, and cooperation, values that are sometimes "hard to grasp in the traditional classroom."[18] For example, the processes of bicycle assembly and repair require a working knowledge of mathematics, engineering, and reasoning skills that are frequently neglected in educational settings where these principles are by necessity, or pedagogical choice, taught without tangible materials or real-world applications most young people consider valuable.[19]

Cyclists who work with children or teenagers recognize that bicycle programs are successful when they encourage students to cultivate their own interests and/or aesthetics. As a result, certain groups actively incorporate artistic and creative practices into their programs, far beyond the basics of bicycle construction, maintenance, or bike safety. For example, the Third

Ward Community Bike Center in Houston, Texas, created an ArtBike program for fifth and sixth graders in the Project Row Houses in which kids fixed up a fleet of bicycles and designed papier-mâché "art helmets" for use in a Martin Luther King Jr. Day parade. Third Ward's "chopper club," which is now part of a wider set of programs aimed at local teens, teaches bike repair and welding skills through the creation of homemade, motorcycle-esque choppers and lowrider bicycles; San Francisco's Bike Kitchen has also experimented with a welding-intensive chopper class for teens. Programs like these not only foster peer education and skill sharing but also provide opportunities for teens who are uninvolved, or lack interest in traditional after-school activities, or simply have few creative outlets available to them. Put simply, kids take pride in their creations and often feel a sense of community in spaces where people of different races, classes, and ages come together through a common love of bicycles, tinkering, and art.[20]

Youth programs create learning environments where participation is valued as highly as money and where education has a literal currency. This is an important goal in and of itself, but it can also be a way for older participants to learn skills that are both highly marketable (bike mechanics) and rewarding. In the wake of long-established programs in Union City, St. Louis, and Indianapolis, cyclists affiliated with groups like Pedal Revolution (San Francisco) operate comprehensive employment and job-training programs for youth between the ages of fourteen and twenty-one, just as Bikes Not Bombs operates a Bicycle Recycling and Youth Training Center in Roxbury, Massachusetts, that offers a hundred-hour mechanic apprenticeship course for people age fifteen and up. Perhaps most important, bicycle education programs can teach youth to make some of the larger connections between transportation and other socio-environmental issues impacting the neighborhoods or cities in which they live. Karen Overton, the co-founder of Recycle-a-Bicycle and a tireless promoter of environmental education, states that the skills young people acquire are not just technical; they encourage youth to actively participate in the betterment of their communities.[21]

Community Bike Spaces

Iris Marion Young claims that one of the salient features of new social movements is their advocacy for participatory institutions that "provide services or promote political goals marginal to, or outside the authority of the state."[22] While bicycle advocacy is not a social movement unto itself, the creation of participatory institutions is a vital way in which cyclists empower themselves, establish relationships across race/class boundaries, and foster an alternative cycling culture based upon DIY ethics. By and large, these institutions operate "outside of economic logic" and in marked contrast to the norms of capitalism: cooperation is emphasized over hierarchy, participation takes the place of consumption, and "garbage" is turned into useful goods through productive, rather than alienated, labor.[23] The actual material spaces created and utilized by community bicycle organizations are paramount to these objectives, as they constitute part of a non-profit, and in some cases anti-capitalist community bicycling infrastructure. In this respect, one can find organizational and ideological similarities between community bike spaces and a number of radical bookstores, infoshops, and community art venues scattered throughout North America and Europe. Thus, it is hardly surprising that some of the same people involved in the development and organization of community bike spaces are, or have been, involved with similar political and artistic participatory institutions. For example, in my hometown of Pittsburgh (Pennsylvania) the community bicycle organization Free Ride initially began in a storefront adjacent to the collectively run show space called the Mr. Roboto project—an all-ages, DIY punk music venue that operates through membership dues and volunteer labor.[24] Free Ride shared this space, dubbed the "Multitool," with The Big Idea infoshop and both projects were, at one time, at least partly staffed by the same group of punks and activists who attend (or play) shows next door. In addition, Free Ride's rent costs were kept to a minimum through supplementary income made from bands that rented practice space in the basement of the Multitool. Both the Big Idea and Free Ride eventually moved into their own spaces, and Free Ride now utilizes part of a warehouse owned and operated by Construction Junction, a retailer of surplus and used construction materials. Like the Mr. Roboto Project and The Big Idea, Free Ride is an institution that provides services to the immediate neighborhood as well as an interconnected activist and arts community; it is also an important social and cultural space for bike riders to congregate, learn from their peers, and share their experiences and perspectives on cycling.

Community bike spaces often function as hubs for the same counter-cultural ethics fostered by radical bookstores, activist projects, and independent music venues. Nick Colombo, a volunteer with the Working Bikes Cooperative and West Town Cycles (both in Chicago), suggests that community bike projects are a good introduction to the "subversive yet innocuous rebel subculture of people who like bikes."[25] Indeed, they often look different, feel different, and fundamentally are different from most commercial cycling institutions. At the surface level, this might entail the presence of homemade bike stands and wall decorations made from oddly configured bike parts, or more visibly, the co-mingling of random volunteers with busy teenagers, tattooed punks, and people who look more like poster boys (or girls) for professional cycling. But more important than the convergence of aesthetics or subcultural styles are the ways in which community bike spaces casually integrate the pragmatics of bicycling with the utopian impulses of collective/cooperative projects. Like the infoshop, which grew out of London's anarchist squats in the 1980s, community bike spaces function as part of a different public sphere that provides forums for "alternative cultural, economic, political and social activities."[26] They function as sites where vernacular folk knowledge about bicycle commuting, transportation, maintenance, and tinkering is at the same time shared and co-produced. This plays an integral role in the development of localized knowledges about bicycling just as it has a critical pedagogical function for people enculturated to see bicycles as toys for children and fitness buffs, rather than transportation vehicles or hackable machines used for pedal-powered technologies. This type of dialogue and example setting can positively influence the ways in which volunteers and visitors evaluate bicycling as a mode of everyday, urban transportation. Rick Jarvis specifically notes the impact it can have on kids: "Many of the members of Bikes Not Bombs are carfree, and this gives our youth the ability to see that there are adults who are not dependent on fossil fuels and car payments."[27]

While I am highlighting the participatory, anti-consumerist orientation of community bike spaces, and see them playing an integral role in an emerging U.S. bike culture, this is not to say that commerce is implicitly antithetical to the process of community building or the production of vernacular bicycling knowledge. In fact, neighborhood bike shops in U.S. cities have historically fulfilled these same social, educational, and community functions for bike riders and cycling enthusiasts. Charlie McCorkell sees local bike shops like Bicycle Habitat, which he co-founded thirty years ago, as some of the vital places where bike culture is spread, "whether it is through the owner's commitment [to cycling] or one cyclist talking to another."[28] Bicycle Habitat, like many U.S. bike shops founded in the 1970s, serves as a retail/repair business, a hub for experienced cyclists, and a support system for local bike advocacy.[29] For example, the store not only helped to organize support for the bike messengers who protested Koch's proposed bike ban in 1987 but also raised the funds used to mount the legal challenge responsible for halting the ban. Since that time, the shop has supported a wide range of local cycling initiatives and events in New York City, from repair classes and community service to co-hosting the "Why I Ride" bicycle art exhibition in 2007.

Kraynick's Bike Shop in Pittsburgh, Pennsylvania, offers another quintessential example of how a bike shop can function as a hybrid business/community space/archive/workshop for local cyclists. Indeed, the owner and proprietor Gerry Kraynick stopped selling bicycles a number of years ago to focus exclusively on bicycle repair, maintenance, and the sale of new, used, and hard-to-find parts (which he has stockpiled into a spectacle unto itself). More often than not, Kraynick forgoes the opportunity to profit on a repair job and, instead, encourages people to fix their own bicycles. He offers anyone free access to tools and workstands in the back of the store, never requiring patrons to submit identification or adhere to any other rules than the honor system and common sense. Consequently, the shop is a frequent meeting space and point of intersection for a diverse range of city cyclists. Brad Quartuccio, a Pittsburgh resident and co-publisher of the *Urban Velo* zine, describes it as a space that even flattens the distinctions between race and class, albeit temporarily:

> Everyone is an equal inside the store because everyone there has some connection with bicycles. It tends to bring people across the vast social spectrum of life together in one place. On my latest visit to the shop I met up with a middle-aged tinkering soul attempting to attach an electric motor to his recumbent. Sharing the stand next to me was a man in his mid twenties building up a nice looking road bike straight from parts in the shop. Standing outside was a group of urban youths debating on the best way to fix a flat tire.[30]

Kraynick's store, like his vast knowledge of cycling, is extremely unique and functions as an invaluable (and revered) resource for the immediate neighborhood, local cyclists, and several generations of bike tinkerers and hobbyists. In addition to a smattering of cooperatively owned bike shops like The Missing Link Bicycle Coop (a Berkeley, California, institution since 1971) and The Hub Co-op (founded in Minneapolis in 2002), Kraynick's Bike Shop and Bicycle Habitat illustrate some of the different ways in which retail stores can also function as cultural and educational corollaries to nonprofit community spaces.

Gendered Mechanics

At the same time community bike spaces are actively involved in the production of bike culture and the promotion of participatory ethics, they are obviously not without their faults. The development and smooth operation of any alternative institution necessarily involves a great deal of attention to everyday behavioral issues that can and do arise, particularly with kids. But more challenging is the process of addressing problems posed by larger issues, such as the dominant cultural norms associated with mobility and gender.[31] For example, women in the United States share a large burden of the responsibilities involved with the use and maintenance of motor vehicles, yet the institutions of automobility are historically dominated by, catered to, and almost exclusively owned by men. With very rare exceptions, men own all of the automobile and auto parts companies, they comprise the majority of the automotive workforce (production, engineering, sales, and mechanics), and they are more prone to learn automobile maintenance from a friend or family member at some point in their lives.[32] In addition, their aggressive tendencies behind the wheel (broadly speaking) perpetually create dangerous climates for other drivers, cyclists, and pedestrians on the street.[33] With so many cyclists professing their resistance against the norms of car culture, one might naturally assume that critics would cultivate an analogous critique of gender. Yet some of the most predominant masculine norms of automobility are widely evident in bike culture, whether the competitiveness and male camaraderie associated with racing and bike messengering, the promulgation of sexist images and discourses within the bike industry, the exclusivity associated with technological tinkering and maintenance, or the mere discrepancy between the numbers of male and female cyclists in the United States.[34]

Put simply, men exert a dominant presence in bike culture and machismo is not uncommon. Alex McFarland, a mechanic at North Portland Bike Works, jokingly (and disparagingly) refers to this scenario as the "dude factor."[35] It is often associated with one's proclaimed toughness as a daily rider (i.e., how far, how fast, and how hard one rides), one's mechanical expertise, and/or one's preoccupation with cultural capital (i.e., who has "the coolest bike, or the coolest track bike").[36] But regardless of the cause or its many symptoms, there is a palatable boys' club mentality associated with cycling that marginalizes many women and particularly dissuades them from becoming bike mechanics or messengers, or working in some facet of the bicycle industry. "Biking *is* different for us women," as Shelly Jackson, a bike mechanic and writer in New Orleans, reminds the readers of her *Chainbreaker* zine, "from trying to get respect as a mechanic or even as a customer in a bike shop, to being taken seriously when we apply for jobs as messengers, deliverers, or in shops as mechanics, and even (surprisingly in this day and age) how we dress on bikes."[37] There are a number of social and cultural factors contributing to the prevailing gender divide among cyclists, but the gendered practices associated with maintenance and mechanics are unquestionably factors that affect women who ride bikes. Tori Bortman has observed these problems during her years of experience as a messenger, bike mechanic, and bike educator in Oregon:

I continually meet women that don't know how to fix their bikes, and it's not because they don't have an interest but because of the intimidation factor. I don't think that a lot of men understand what it's like to be intimidated because a lot of men have been privileged, whether it's because they had an older brother who taught them about bikes, or they rode their BMX and had to learn to fix it when they were 14. But at 14, girls are encouraged to be pretty and look good for the boys. That's what our concentration is at that point, but it's usually not sports or biking, unless your dad is into biking or your older brother is into biking. There's more guys doing it [fixing bikes], there's more of a culture, and there's not this intimidation factor. Women are scared to ask questions, scared of looking stupid, and I want that to end.[38]

The process of bicycle maintenance is often intimidating for women and girls not only because of a lack of opportunities or a ready mechanical knowledge about bikes—which Bortman partly ascribes to male privilege—but also because of the negative attitudes from male cycling friends, bicycle mechanics, and employees at bike shops. In many cases, women receive the same condescending treatment from male bicycle mechanics as they typically do from male auto mechanics: women are thus put in the frustrating and sometimes humiliating position of being forced to rely upon men for even the most basic forms of routine maintenance. While the inability to fix one's bicycle may seem insignificant to the casual rider, it can potentially raise safety issues for women who use bikes for daily transportation, as Elicia Cardenas, another bicycle mechanic/educator/advocate in Portland, explains: "I was afraid to ride my bike because what happens if I get a flat and I'm stuck somewhere and I don't know how to change it. That puts me in a potentially dangerous situation, whereas if I know how to deal with it, then I'm golden."[39] For Cardenas and other women who get interested in daily bicycling, learning how to diagnose and fix problems instills an important degree of autonomy and independence, and it is also empowering.

This sentiment is one of the reasons women have played such key roles in founding, organizing, and/or facilitating the growth of community bike projects throughout the United States. Because of the involvement of feminist women (and men) in community spaces, there is also a widespread effort to address gender issues within the context of bicycle maintenance and bicycle education. This is a matter of not only providing female visitors with equal access to tools, workshops, and learned volunteers, but also developing classes that appeal to women and girls and creating space where women can work, teach, or learn without the judgment or scrutiny of male counterparts—an experience that Andalusia Knoll, a co-founder of Free Ride, describes from her years as a mechanic. She writes:

I would absolutely hate it when men would hang out waiting for their repairs. In fact, it was totally incapacitating for me and I would be physically incapable of fixing the bike. It was kinda embarrassing because I felt like the men would watch over me cause they didn't actually think that a girl could fix the bike, and then I would get so nervous that I wouldn't be able to do it. They could have been watching just to learn how to do the repair, but I just couldn't deal with it.[40]

This scenario is not uncommon and a number of stories in Andalusia's feminist bike zine, *Clitical Mass,* similarly illustrate the problems facing female mechanics who are routinely scrutinized and surveilled by their male counterparts. Adrian, one of the zine's contributors, recalls a particularly aggravating experience while trying to simply repair a set of wheels at a community bike shop:

"Are you re-spoking that wheel?"

"Yeah," I reply.

"You know, you won't be able to do that." I stare blankly, not understanding, and he continues. "Where did you get those spokes?" he asks.

"Up front." It had taken forever to sort through the unorganized boxes of spokes to find the right size for my wheel.

"Well, spokes are different lengths for different wheels," J. explains, "and you have different sizes there. It won't work," he concludes in the patient voice of an adult speaking to a small child. . . . J. continues, "Re-spoking wheels is *very* hard. Only a couple of people I know (both males, I realize as we talk) have been able to do it . . ."

I finally ditched him, and both wheels have all new spokes. But I definitely felt shitty about the whole encounter. . . . I guess it's just part of being a girl in bikeland (although bike girlfriends of bike dudes don't seem to have the same problems I've had), but I'm sick of it. Hey bike boys, do me a favor. Just lemme do my bike girl thing. 'Cause even though I don't have a penis, that doesn't mean I can't use a wrench.[41]

As a way to circumvent these issues, a host of community bike spaces designate specific days during the week or month that are exclusively reserved for women and/or LGBTQ (lesbian, gay, bisexual, transgender, queer/questioning) persons who wish to learn bicycle maintenance or have an experience of bike culture unmediated by the hetero/male norms of technological tinkering. These policies help to cultivate an alternative to the masculinized environment of most retail bicycle shops, where women are often assumed to be either unknowledgeable about the workings of a bicycle or incapable of fixing their own machines. But they also head off some of the same gender tensions that continue to arise in alternative settings, whether through the day-to-day operations of a space or the relationships between volunteers and visitors. Greg Rothman, for example, admits that even an intentionally anti-sexist space like RIBS in Ithaca, New York, can quickly turn into a "dude shop," and John Gerken alludes to the same problem at Plan B, the community bike space where he works in New Orleans:

> It can be an intimidating space—messy, dusty, not well-lit, in a big funky warehouse. Lots of guys in various states of dude-ness. Issues of gender have been raised and addressed in a variety of ways; right now we have a women-only day twice a month and it's great that we have a good mix of people involved in general, all the time. Still, there is no denying that it can be intimidating to walk into a place like that, for anyone, especially if you don't know anyone else there and/ or don't know much about bikes.[42]

As noted, community bicycle organizations are not without their problems, but their collective attention to gender privilege is one of their distinguishing and most progressive characteristics, not to mention one of the primary reasons why community bike projects continue to attract so many women and girls. As Jacquie Phelan notes, "The sign of a really progressive shop is when it's got a filthy-fingered female fixing funky frames."[43] The egalitarian structure of these spaces not only encourages women to participate but also nourishes an emerging consciousness about the relationships between biking, feminism, gender, and mechanics. In Portland, Oregon, women bike mechanics are prevalent in a number of local institutions, including the Community Cycling Center and City Bikes, a worker-owned retail/repair co-op. At North Portland Bike Works, the entire collective has at one point been owned and operated by women. Kim Fey (aka Kim Fern), the co-founder of the shop, as well as a zine writer and originator of the Portland Radical History Bike Tour, describes the visibility and presence of women in Portland's bike culture as somewhat remarkable, and she specifically notes the unique gender dynamics at her shop:

> Our entire staff are women, except for Alex, and that's unheard of in this country, let alone the world. I've talked to people in other countries, and they can't believe it. They say, "You *really* have six women and one guy?" Our entire board of directors was all queer women at one point; two were transgendered. We're this very different, amazing conglomeration of people.[44]

Though Portland is somewhat of an exception to the rule, women bike mechanics are now more prevalent throughout the United States and community bike spaces have both contributed to and complemented this trend. In particular, the presence of women mechanics and strong female role models

Cat, from Neighborhood Bike Works in Philadelphia, Pennsylvania. *(Photo by Carina Romano.)*

prompts more women and girls to become bicycle mechanics, everyday bike riders, and dedicated bike commuters. Gender is also being acknowledged as prerequisite issue for community cycling organizations to address, and female-only mechanic nights, women's bicycling workshops, and programs like Girls in Action—a series of classes Bikes Not Bombs designed to teach ten- to thirteen-year-old girls bike mechanics and riding skills—are an important part of this process. Moreover, they are integral to the broader reassertion of feminism in bike culture that can be credited to pioneers like Jacquie Phelan, the professional mountain bike champion, writer, and founder of WOMBATS (the Women's Mountain Bike and Tea Society); to the consistent advocacy work of Chicago's Cycling Sisters; and more recently, to women like Claire Stoschek, a Minneapolis/St. Paul bike advocate who co-founded a class-conscious women's bike advocacy group and also created the first academic course devoted to the study of bicycling and gender, entitled "Bike Feminism: Theory, Community and Mechanical Exploration."[45]

Feminist cyclists, including an increasing number of men, collectively carve out intellectual and tangible spaces for women to articulate and validate their own vision of the bicycle in society. Still, there is still a long way to go before sexism ceases to be a dominant factor in U.S. bike culture, as well as a global problem that keeps many women from riding bicycles at all.

Bridging the Local and the Global

The socioeconomic complexities of racism and sexism shaping transportation norms in North America are unquestionably more pronounced in the so-called Global South, where poverty and the legacies of colonialism and corporate imperialism exert a powerful influence on the daily movement of billions of people. Tragically, the relative immobility of the world's largest and poorest populations is one the direct consequences of the very policies that historically yielded the high-speed, energy-intensive, and thoroughly mobile ways of life enjoyed by most North Americans and Europeans. When Bikes Not Bombs began coordinating the collection and delivery of secondhand bicycles to Nicaragua, this seemingly small gesture initiated what has become an international movement of community bicycle organizations aimed at addressing these very issues. Their initial projects, beginning at the Instituto Juan XXIII social justice institute at the University of Central America, focused on training Nicaraguan teenagers to help assemble, repair, and maintain the bicycles shipped from BNB chapters in the United States. Kurz also worked with the Sandinista Labor Federation to train mechanics who assisted in bike distribution efforts aimed at the teachers union and health care workers union, and by the end of 1985, BNB started a full-scale bicycle shop in Managua (in the Montoya neighborhood) under the supervision of the Organization of Disabled Revolutionaries.[46] There they trained local mechanics who eventually operated the store independently and used a small portion of its revenue to assist in the future delivery of bicycle shipments from BNB chapters.[47] Their organizational model, which emphasized partnerships with local and/or indigenous organizations, as well as mechanic training and transportation assistance for sustainable development projects, was intended to help recipient groups eventually develop independent bicycle programs and repair businesses to meet the needs of their own communities.

Until the late 1980s, Bikes Not Bombs operated under the umbrella of the Institute for Transportation and Development Policy (ITDP), the organization BNB co-founder Michael Replogle started in 1985 to promote non-motorized transportation and to influence transportation policy developed by multilateral organizations such as the World Bank, the International

Monetary Fund (IMF), and the Inter-American Development Bank (IDB). While BNB volunteers agreed, in theory, with the overall aims of the ITDP in the 1980s, Kurz recalls that collectives in Boston and the Bay Area were among a number of BNB volunteers who differed with Replogle regarding the efficacy of working with multinational lending and trade organizations. Consequently, BNB opted to become an independent entity in order to focus more exclusively on the grassroots implementation of their own programs: "BNB collectives wanted to continue the direct people-to-people aid as our primary focus, workshop by workshop, expressing solidarity and anti-interventionist politics."[48] The distinct, though complementary, approaches to foreign aid and bicycle advocacy embodied by BNB and the ITDP are predominantly the same ones at work today, whereby organizations largely focus on either (1) the collection and distribution of used bicycles, or (2) the promotion of sustainable transportation policy research and the implementation of programs designed to reduce pollution and oil reliance. More often than not, organizations involved with either set of objectives work in concert. For example, nonprofit bicycle aid groups such as the New Jersey-based Pedals for Progress (PfP) or the Bikes for the World (in Washington, D.C.) are primarily responsible for collecting, packing, and shipping bikes, in addition to making all the proper arrangements for their delivery (to countries in Africa and Central and South America). However, the acutal distribution of bikes, as well as the facilitation of educational programs, is largely carried out by a variety of recipient groups ranging from small charitible organizations to the ITDP, to the larger network of non-governmental organizations (NGOs) that have direct or indirect ties to multilateral economic organizations and/ or U.S.-funded government initiatives like the Peace Corps, the U.S. Agency for International Development (USAID), and the President's Emergency Plan for AIDS Relief (PEPFAR).

The Village Bicycle Project (VBP), an organization founded in 1999 to create transportation options for Ghana's rural residents and farmers, is a one of the groups that facilitates the actual on-the-ground distribution and sale of bikes donated by North American and British organizations like Bike Works (Seattle), Recycle-a-Bicycle (New York City), Bikes Not Bombs, Working Bikes (Chicago), and Re~Cycle (Essex, England). The VBP primarily uses donated bikes to conduct mechanic training workshops in rural communities: up to twenty participants who are selected by a village committee each pay a small fee for the workshop and receive a bicycle at the end of the session.[49] In 2006, the VBP trained nearly one thousand people in bicycle maintenance for the second in a row, hosting forty-three one-day workshops in nineteen villages.[50] Like the VBP in Ghana, a number of bicycle aid organizations rely extensively on partnerships with donor groups in the Northern Hemisphere that provide shipments of used bikes as well as volunteers. Maya

Pedal, located in San Andrés Itzapa, Chimaltenango (Guatemala), began in 1997 as a collaborative project with the Vancouver-based PEDAL, a group specializing in the design and construction of pedal-powered technologies. Independent since 2001, Maya Pedal manufactures and distributes pedal-powered machines, or *bicimáquinas,* to indigenous peoples operating small businesses or sustainable environmental projects in the region. *Bicimáquinas* are constructed from recycled bicycles and perform various functions, including shelling and grinding grain, pumping well water, de-pulping coffee, hulling macadamia nuts, extracting corn, washing clothes, and making roof tiles. These machines are vital resources in a region where an estimated 90 percent of the indigenous population lives below the poverty line.[51] Maya Pedal, like most organizations receiving bicycle shipments from community cycling projects, trains local bicycle mechanics and facilitates the sale of donated bikes to defray the shipping costs of future containers. Pedals for Progress (PfP), founded by ex–Peace Corps volunteer David Schweidenback in 1991, is one of the groups responsible for perfecting this distribution model and has since become the largest international recycled bicycle distributor in the world, sending more than 117,000 bicycles and tons of parts to recipient groups on several continents. In addition to the pioneering work of Bikes Not Bombs and the border-blurring efforts of smaller groups, such as Bikes for Chiapas and Bikes Across Borders, PfP's success has not only drawn significant attention to the prospects of local-global community cycling partnerships but has also inspired a recent wave of donor organizations in the United States (Village Bicycle Project, founded in 1999; Bikes for the World, founded in 2005), the United Kingdom (Re~Cycle, founded in 1998), and Canada (Cyclo Nord-Sud, founded in 1999; Bicycles for Humanity, founded in 2005).[52]

This network of bike recyclers, community groups, and program facilitators is necessarily limited in its capacity to confront the staggering intersections of poverty and mobility in so-called developing counties—a task irreducible to transportation solutions alone—but is nonetheless successful at utilizing community partnerships to provide hundreds of thousands of people with affordable, sustainable transportation. Perhaps most important, these efforts draw much needed attention to both the material and human relationships between local and global mobilities.

Addressing the Gaps in Development Programs

The proliferation of grassroots bicycle aid programs and the growth of international organizations like the ITDP are part of critical, transportation-based analysis of globalization that engages with what Arjun Appadurai calls "problems of the global everyday."[53] Collectively, they address some of the major gaps in economic development programs, including autocentric lending policies, proper attention to gender issues, and the technological problematics of development itself. For example, the ITDP's goal of redirecting transportation development funds away from automobile infrastructure, and toward non-motorized and public transportation projects, stands in marked contrast to the dominant paradigm of transportation development projects carried out in most countries, inasmuch as the reproduction of American-style automobility was, and still is, championed as the key to economic prosperity and social stability. Constructing highways and automobile infrastructure in developing countries is, of course, tragically myopic when one considers that bicycle transportation is cheaper, safer, efficient, and highly accessible to both urban and rural populations. So why, one might ask, have the mobility needs of the world's poor been so widely ignored by the dominant trends of Western transportation development projects?

A 1996 study on the benefits of bicycle transportation in Uganda points to one possible explanation: it is an unfortunate oversight caused by a lack of adequate information. That is to say, the author suggests the World Bank, IMF, and BMZ (Germany's development ministry) "may have been" reluctant to promote bicycle transportation because decision makers either underestimated the potential of non-motorized transportation in the region, or simply lacked the factual knowledge and studies to properly steer their attention to the problem.[54] On the contrary, I would argue that producing such a charitable reading of World Bank and IMF's transportation policies, either in this study or elsewhere, is a remarkable achievement in and of itself, particularly since these institutions have systematically and haphazardly poured money into automobile infrastructures since the early 1970s. These lending practices, as Replogle argues, not only disregard the mobility needs of 90 to 95 percent of Africans (to give one example) who are unable to own or maintain automobiles but also contradict the recommendations of studies published by both the World Bank and other multilateral organizations.[55] For example, a pilot study published in 1985 by the United Nations Conference on Trade and Development (UNCTAD) and the Global Agreement on Tariffs and Trade (GATT)—hardly enemies of the automobile and oil industries—blatantly acknowledges how "motorization benefits only a small segment of the populations in developing countries."[56] In sharp contrast to these findings, the World Bank's "China Transport Sector Study," published in the same year, did not even mention the word *bicycle* in the text: this was a period when bicycles accounted for roughly 30 to 60 percent of all daily trips made in Chinese cities and the annual bicycle production rate in China was more than 30 million.[57] The World Bank's 2007 report, "A Decade of Action in Transport," indicates a firm commitment to the same ill-founded policies today: roads still account for nearly 80 percent of the World Bank's global "transport commitments" and its study makes virtually no concrete recommendations for improving non-motorized transportation infrastructure or policies worldwide.[58] The report does manage to mention the word *bicycle*. Once.[59]

As a direct consequence of both autocentric lending policies and the unwillingness of corporate-focused lenders to hold road-building projects to the same standards of accountability and compliance required of public transit and non-motorized transportation projects, the infrastructure for an export-friendly, though largely inaccessible system of automobility, is widespread in cities throughout the so-called Global South.[60] That the development of modern transportation systems focuses almost exclusively on economic productivity in the form of trade, as opposed to accessibility and safety, is hardly surprising since this same imperative was embedded in colonial transportation development projects of a previous era. The railroad system constructed throughout Africa and Southeast Asia, for example, was specifically designed to reorganize workers into urban centers and to facilitate the extraction of both raw materials and goods.[61] Consequently, today's urban systems, Akin L. Mabogunje writes, "owe much to the colonial transportation policies."[62] Automobile corporations and their oil-producing partners unquestionably profit through the current arrangement by reaching the untapped markets of the developing world they eyed up for three decades, but the vast majority of Africans still lack access to affordable, efficient transportation.[63]

Bicycles not only offer a logical and pragmatic solution to this problem of the "global everyday"; they are also beneficial to those groups traditionally ignored within the dominant paradigm of economic development theory—rural women and girls. Bicycles are, in fact, tremendous assets to women in developing countries inasmuch as women "shoulder the biggest burdens of transportation in terms of the time spent traveling."[64] Women are the family members most often responsible for obtaining water for rural households, and they typically function as the primary caregivers for children as well as the sick. Rural women with access to a bicycle are thus able to relieve themselves of roughly half of their transport loads, while saving themselves hours each day in overall transport time, which is hardly insignificant.[65] Girls similarly benefit from having a bicycle in the home: a study carried out in rural Mozambique, for example, found that girls are more than 30 percent more likely to be enrolled in primary school when their family owns and uses a bicycle on a regular basis.[66] Despite these benefits, there are very real constraints preventing women from gaining wider access to bicycles, whether because of religious views, traditional gender roles, or the same patriarchal and economically structured norms that adversely affect the mobility of women worldwide.[67] Attempting to understand and potentially transgress these gendered boundaries—or at the very least, to recognize the ways in which they impact non-motorized transportation norms—is a crucial step toward creating successful bike transportation programs that not only appeal to women and girls but also give them the tools and knowledge necessary to continue making use of bicycles for daily transportation. Transportation researchers like Julia Philpott and Karen Overton have been instrumental in bringing the relationships between gender, economics, and non-motorized transportation to the attention of international NGOs, and there are a number of organizations that actively engage with these issues in their daily work.[68] The Village Bicycle Project, for example, stipulates that a certain number of seats in each of their training sessions (20 percent) be reserved for women, and in 2006 it went a step further by hiring women mechanics to teach bicycle maintenance workshops for other women and girls in Ghana: forty people participated in 2006 and forty more signed up for the program in the first month of 2007 alone.[69] Working Bikes, a Chicago nonprofit founded by veteran activist Lee Ravenscroft in 2001, is one of the many community bicycle organizations that specifically contribute shipments of bicycles to NGOs that actively support gender-conscious development programs and directly assist women's organizations in Africa and Latin America.

In further contrast to the status quo development paradigm championed by multilateral lending and trade organizations, community groups like PEDAL, Maya Pedal, Bikes Not Bombs, and especially the Salvadoran Center for Appropriate Technology (CESTA) advocate a model of sustainable development that emphasizes conservation, ecological preservation, and the use of appropriate technologies: those that are "compatible with local, cultural and economic conditions (i.e. the human, material and cultural resources of the economy)" and utilize "locally available materials and energy resources, with tools and processes maintained and operationally controlled by the local population."[70] Whereas the appropriate technology (AT) movement in the United States collapsed beneath the weight of the first Reagan administration, its core premises continued to animate the work of numerous development aid organizations and transportation-minded NGOs in the 1980s and beyond.[71] CESTA's Ricardo Navarro is among those who saw the potential of AT as a means to pragmatically address a range of intersecting environmental, socioeconomic, and health problems in El Salvador, all of which, incidentally, multiplied during the country's civil war and worsened with the development of fifteen free-trade zones and an exploitative *maquila* industry in the 1990s. An ardent supporter of sustainable technologies, he rightly argues that ecological problems in El Salvador are inherently social and political.[72] Consequently, CESTA's vision of sustainability is wide-ranging: it emphasizes both a critical revaluation of production and consumption, and the need for a passionate, scientifically grounded environmental movement. It operates educational programs in more than fifty municipalities and has four main divisions (Ecobici, Ecojute, Ecobosque, Ecomarino) that engage with mechanical, agricultural, environmental, and marine issues in El Salvador, and Central America more broadly. Ecobici, a set of programs designed to teach people how to locally manufacture and utilize pedal-powered machines, is not only the precursor to Maya Pedal but also the outgrowth of CESTA's longstanding commitment to non-motorized transportation and community empowerment. Indeed, Navarro's 1985 book *La Bicicleta y los Triciclos: Alternativas de Transporte para America Latina* articulates a substantive plan for non-motorized transportation, domestic bicycle production, and bike advocacy in Latin America: it offers one of the clearest and most comprehensive assessments of the role that appropriate transportation technologies can potentially play in any country.[73]

Transportation organizations that emphasize the role of AT, whether tacitly or as prominent part of their objectives, are not neglectful of the realities faced by poor people who need to make do in a capitalist economy. At the same time, the goal of utilizing appropriate technologies is to foster a level of ecological sustainability and democratic control over the means of production that is otherwise absent. Jordan Kleiman, a historian of the AT movement, explains that early theorists of AT did not reject industry itself, but rather the ideology of industrialism: "The relentless push for economies of scale and labor-saving technologies even when the result is to aggravate poverty and degrade work, overpower nature to the point of threatening the biological systems necessary for human survival, and undermine economic and political democracy."[74] Kleiman's analysis reveals the extent to which the condemnation of AT as politically visionless or naively consumed with the goal of improving society through the production of "a better mousetrap," as AT critic Langdon Winner puts it, is actually a gross misrepresentation of a paradigm that poses unique possibilities for interrogating the prospects and limitations of technological productivity itself.[75] Similarly problematic is Ivan Illich's critique of the "intermediate technologist" as one who operates as a "superior tactician paving the road to totally manipulated consumption."[76] Indeed, to see groups like Maya Pedal, CESTA, or BNB as economic tacticians is to assume that the promotion of appropriate or intermediate technologies necessarily causes, rather than critically responds to, the realities of poverty and ecological crisis prompted by capitalism and free market ideology. In this respect, Illich's otherwise prescient critique of so-called Third World development work is flawed not because it lacks nuance but because it fails to account for what people can or should do when industrial capitalism is already in full swing, whether altering the cultural landscape, destroying ecologies, or funding right-wing militias in service of year-round banana supplies in Midwestern grocery stores.[77] Populations are certainly capable of organizing resistance movements to radically transform structural inequalities, but such movements take time and are entirely dependent on a host of circumstances beyond any one group's capacity to address. This is particularly true for indigenous peoples who, by the very nature of their statelessness and/or political disenfranchisement, cannot exercise power over multinational corporations or redress grievances to the nation-states that occupy their lands and horde their resources (legally or illegally). To varying degrees, the entire planet's population has been made to comply with the mandates of global capitalism and should not be starved, malnourished, or polluted to death until the primary causes of such maladies—namely, those associated with global capitalism itself—are rooted out. Thus, advocating for the use of appropriate and/or sustainable technologies as means to tackle the seemingly insurmountable problems of poverty, ecological destruction, and a lack of affordable transportation may not be the perfect solutions for less (economically) developed countries, but contrary to critics, it is arguably the best way for people to address short term needs in hopes of thwarting the colonialism → poverty → capitalism → poverty → structural adjust-ment → poverty cycle that has come to define modern globalization.[78]

The Problem of Development Discourse

Bicycles play a profound role in providing mobility, pleasure, economic opportunity, and sustainable transportation to people throughout the world, and their potential benefits in less industrialized countries are irrefutable. Indeed, the importance of localized bicycle aid programs, transnational partnerships between community bicycle organizations, and the range of advocacy/policy work carried out by the ITDP cannot be overstated. With this in mind, I want to focus attention away from the actual material prac-tices of these organizations for a moment to consider a different way in which they function at the level of representation. That is to say, part of the work that these organizations do is to contribute to the production of a dis-course about development that speaks directly to the relationships between mobility and poverty, economics and labor, modernization and transporta-tion. Consequently, I want to problematize this aspect of bicycle aid and sustainable transportation advocacy not to dismiss it, but to consider how this discourse has tangible effects on the ways people come to understand both the role of non-motorized transportation in the Third World and the paradigm of development itself. In short, the ways in which bike advocates, policy wonks, and participating community bicycle organizations frame their agenda to American audiences matters. Because just as this discourse can inform people about the problems in developing countries and garner sup-port for worthwhile causes, it can also "reproduce the political conditions for globalization itself."[79]

Criticism of Western development projects is wide ranging. Its detractors often point to the problematic assumptions built into specific aid programs as well as the general failure of many well-intentioned volunteers to critically engage with—or even understand—both the historical and cultural contexts of their work, or the depth of the problems they may be unwillingly perpetuating.[80] Technological development, for example, can play a key role in fostering sustainable agriculture, basic mobility, and employment opportunities in postcolonial economies, but it is also the cornerstone of a set of political, economic, and cultural practices that ultimately reinscribe the power dynamics of colonialism and imperialism, albeit in different forms. Honor Ford-Smith highlights the central problematic of the development paradigm, particularly the way it is poses "primarily as a process of economic growth through which poor countries are modernized and become absorbed into the market while becoming increasingly reliant on Western science and technology."[81] Since many people in the Third World are too poor even to buy a used bicycle, organizations aimed at fostering economic development through bicycle transportation necessarily employ a set of theories that are normalized through practice and perpetuated through discourse (as in what people literally say about the goals, tactics and achievements of their programs). For example, one can see the influence of development theory in the organization of the Village Bicycle Project when David Peckham describes the relationships between technological development, mobility, and the target audience for VBP's programs—a group he terms the *productive poor,* or those "clever, hard working people who are stuck in poverty at least in part because of lack of access to transport."[82] The benefits gained from the purchase of a new bicycle, Peckham argues, create a ripple effect or what could best be described as a small-scale model of trickle down bikenomics: "For example, a farmer gets a bike, and is able to transport more produce to more diverse markets, raising the food supply, and her/his income, which is spent mostly in the community close to home."[83] Peckham points to economist William Easterly as providing the kind of methodology the VBP employs, namely, utilizing bottom-up solutions to poverty, as well as pricing incentives to help ensure that people value the goods distributed by his organization.[84] He writes:

> Village Bicycle Project strives to work within the market system. The legacy of giving everything away fosters inefficiency and a free lunch mentality as well as disrupting markets. *When things are given away it is difficult to know if the recipient understands or values the gift.* If tools are randomly given away we learn nothing about what mechanics would be willing to pay on the open market for these tools. VBP learned in 1999 that tools would be readily bought at 10% of cost. When tools are valued enough to be paid for, it is far more likely that they will be used regularly and productively.[85]

David Schweidenback, of Pedals for Progress, also believes that "people don't take care of things they're given for free," and he describes the objectives of his organization in similar terms: "We are an organization seeking economic growth. One cannot spur a capitalistic economy by giving things away. Giving things away actually damages an economy."[86] As a firm believer in the inherent benefits of entrepreneurial capitalism, Schweidenback habitually affirms the importance of giving people a "hand up" instead of a "hand out."[87]

The question of whether people do, in fact, place more value on goods they are required to purchase—an idea behind so-called incentive pricing—is the subject of an ongoing and heated debate among economists and NGOs: the debate concerns a variety of case studies pertaining to the Third World distribution of items like malaria-thwarting mosquito nets, condoms, and water purification chemicals.[88] Recent studies cast doubt on the accepted wisdom of pricing incentives, but my point is not to dispute the "hand up" approach to aid by legitimizing the obscenely narrow and wholly ideological parameters of development theory these concepts encompass.[89] Indeed, the bigger issue at stake here is how the entire discourse of economic development, as well as the practices of many NGOs, are fundamentally opposed to the values of social justice or a radical reworking of the few progressive possibilities that globalization does, in fact, present. Using pregnant women, AIDS patients, and other poverty-stricken people as methodological test groups for measuring the success/failure ratios of incentive pricing and social marketing schemes are indicative of this miserable regime at work: one wonders how many women contracted malaria as a result of pricing experiments with insecticide treated nets, or how many children died of cholera from similar policies enacted to measure the dispersal of Clorin, a chemical used to purify water. The notion that handouts make people either incapable of appreciating or understanding the goods they receive is by no means unique to development theorists and NGO workers, but it is nevertheless a highly ideological and ahistorical proposition that legitimizes some of the most fundamentally dubious claims of capitalism, namely, that objects become useful or valuable only when they enter the realm of financial exchange.[90] Indeed, the implicit failure of this theory is evident when one considers that the sole reason bicycle aid programs exist is because Americans, Canadians, and Europeans annually throw away millions of perfectly good bicycles and parts that should ostensibly be valued, if not cherished, by their purchasers (according to "hand up" proponents).

The logic of the "hand up" paradigm presumes that people universally gain a sense of self-worth through the act of consumption or through the processes by which one becomes a consumer in the first place, namely, one's (forced) participation in a market economy. And while proclaiming the moral and ontological benefits of earning one's keep may be a commonly held premise in so-called Western societies, it is highly problematic when one considers, for example, the manner in which it was historically exported onto, or more accurately invaded, the African continent. That is to say, the project of European colonialism was instrumental in teaching these socioeconomic lessons through a combination of brutal forced labor practices, genocidal campaigns, and propaganda efforts aimed at emphasizing both the material and spiritual rewards of market-based labor. One of the commodities enlisted in this dual process of cultural pedagogy and capitalist evangelism was, ironically enough, the bicycle. Historian Nancy Rose Hunt alludes to the use of bicycles among nurses working with missionary and colonial medical professionals in the Belgian Congo during the 1920s. She recalls that the medical establishment adopted the bicycle as a practical means of expanding services but it also became a highly coveted "marker of the middle class," a technology used to cultivate a "native colonial 'high'—or évolué—style."[91] Along with its utilitarian applications, the bicycle had an enormous signifying power: it was an object that tacitly reaffirmed not only the material rewards of capitalism but also the intertwined cultural, economic, religious, and medical project of colonialist modernization.[92] That the bicycle was employed in production of a native style or was even remotely connected to the mythology of progress in the Congo is most bizarre when one considers the specific, if not emotionally detached, role the Euro-American bicycle craze had on catalyzing the genocidal enslavement of the Congolese people: their forced labor in rainforests yielded, in part, the rubber necessary to mass produce John Dunlop's wildly ·successful pneumatic (inflatable) bicycle tire.[93]

Osumaka Likaka's historical work on Zaire/Congo similarly alludes to the manner in which bicycles were used to signify the economic and moral benefits of European colonization, in this case much more overtly and emphatically. He notes the importance of the bicycle as a status symbol that colonizers donned on only a few highly productive cotton-growing households—a practice clearly meant to signify the rewards of complying with the new capitalist agricultural system.[94] Agricultural exhibitions held in colonial Zaire were part of this elaborate propaganda effort aimed at selling the population on both the benefits of cotton production and the values of modern development. Likaka recalls a one-act play performed (by locals) at an exhibition on November 4, 1939, wherein bicycles are specifically used to demonstrate these purported benefits, and it is worth quoting at length:

A CYCLIST: Hey! Friends! How do you not know that today is the great
    feast? How come you are poorly dressed and isolated natives in
    the past?
A PERSON: Hey! (*indicating his group*). Friend, do not make fun of us.

Are we not sad and poor people? You, you are rich men, you are the white man's men.

A CYCLIST: Well, how come you are saying that!

A PERSON: Yes, you are not a clerk as compared to us?

ALL THE CYCLISTS LOOK AT EACH OTHER: We, clerks! (*guffawing*). We are clerks!

A PERSON: I am not lying while saying this, you are rich men, you have nice clothes for the feast and nice machines!

ALL CYCLISTS (*laughing*): Hey! Friends, these are not machines, they are bicycles!

A PERSON: Its name is a bike, is it not?

ALL CYCLISTS: Surely, you are an "uncivilized native," you do not know what a bicycle is!

ALL PEOPLE: Are not we vulgar taxpayers? Is not a taxpayer's lot to bewail?

A CYCLIST: Hey! Hey! Why is a taxpayer to be bewailed? Look, friends (*showing the handsome group of cyclists*). Do we all not pay taxes?

ALL CYCLISTS: Yes, but we also cultivate cotton, we prepare large fields and if God helps us, we have large harvest. So we earn big sums; some have 700 francs (*here, all cyclists speak at once*). I have 800 francs, another 1,000 francs, [and so on].

THE PEOPLE (*stunned*): Well, do not tell us jokes, you are making fun of us!

THE GUY: Why do you not cultivate cotton? Anybody who desires to have a lot of francs cultivates cotton and this is the reason why we of Uele, we have a lot of money. (*everybody agrees*) Well, today is the big feast in Buta, the feast of cotton!

A PERSON: Tell me friends what is this feast for?

A CYCLIST: Why do we have this feast? Because the white man wants at the same time to show us all the benefits of cultivating cotton and showcase a farm where cotton is best cultivated.

A PERSON (*turning toward his friends*): Friends, let us go. . . . We will also cultivate cotton. We will no longer be idiots. We will also have nice dresses and bicycles.

[At this moment the brassy music arrives at the side of the stage, playing a military parade.]

A CYCLIST: Well, friends, let us go! Let us march behind the music, now the big feast has begun.[95]

My point in calling attention to the colonial legacy of the bicycle through these admittedly partial snapshots of African history is not to equate violent colonization with the distribution of bicycles by U.S. or transnational NGOs, but rather, to make a simple point: the bicycle, like other technological artifacts and modes of transportation, has a loaded history that cannot be extracted from a wider set of economic practices and power relations in which the bicycle was and is deployed. Consequently, there is something terribly unsettling about promoting African bicycle transportation as part of a wider economic development plan that, once again, utilizes the bicycle's signifying properties as a status symbol or marker of social taste: "At the risk of sounding a bit Darwinian, if we gave bikes away to society's losers, what would that do for the general impression of bikes? Instead, by making bikes more affordable, they become more associated with success, and psychologically more attractive."[96] The present-day promotion of the bicycle as a pragmatic technological means to an end vision of cultural and economic development all but demonstrates the moral bankruptcy and ultimate failures of an economic system that once promised, ironically enough, the means by which one could obtain a luxury commodity such as a bicycle. Work, in other words, is now promoted as its own luxury reward in the twenty-first century: the bicycle is simply there to facilitate the process.

Like widespread poverty or the lack of access to schools, jobs, and clean water, the need to introduce or reintroduce bicycles to many African nations reveals the extent to which modernity and capitalism were never meant to benefit Africans in the first place, though the dominant narrative produced by Western economists, politicians, and most NGOs suggests otherwise. All too often, the root cause of Africa's maladies is instead attributed to Africans themselves; they are seen, Manji and O'Coill argue, for what they are not: "They are chaotic not ordered, traditional not modern, corrupt not honest, underdeveloped not developed, irrational not rational, lacking in all of those things the West presumes itself to be."[97] In addition to these characteristics, development theory also stresses the importance of combating the "culture of dependence" ostensibly cultivated by lazy and/or entitled populations who collectively expect a "free ride from a passing NGO or rich uncle," as David Peckham puts it.[98] Consequently, the multifaceted project of development demands the retraining of its subjects in order to instill the right attitude and moral fitness, lest they plummet down the path blazed by Americans. People's faith in the merits of modernity and free market capitalism also requires restoration: one has to "*believe* in social mobility," as Thomas Friedman preposterously asserts while defining social class as "a state of mind, not a state of income."[99] However, affirming the implicit infallibility of free market economics to countries presently suffering from free market policies is no small feat, particularly when the same modes of domestic agricultural and industrial production that buttressed the entire Western success story are perpetually eschewed in order to promote structurally adjusted economies based on the exportation of a few specific commodities and luxury goods (à la colonialism), as well as the development of a retail and service sector in which workers become entirely dependent on the importation of all goods they must sell (or service) in order to survive. Tourism is another option, though it similarly requires the importation of tourists as well as the creation of an industry in which workers must cater to tourists' fluctuating travel budgets, their fickle desires for Third World authenticity, or their collective nostalgia for an exoticized past in which the "other" comes to life in a diorama of his or her natural habitat.[100]

The remedy for poverty prescribed by the newest wave of Western doctors (of economics) necessitates micro-lending schemes aimed at providing small loans to so-called barefoot bankers and others who lack access to credit, as well as the revitalization of the social mobility narrative—most commonly framed in terms of entrepreneurialism. Pedals for Progress, for example, aims to provide the people of less economically developed countries with bicycles in order to "unleash their entrepreneurial spirit," just as World Bicycle Relief positions the bicycle as a technological catalyst capable of fueling an individual's "entrepreneurial drive."[101] One of the main reasons why an "entrepreneurial spirit," as well as "cleverness," "creativity," "ingenuity," and "innovation," are so highly valued within this framework is because these characteristics are seen as the tools with which individuals can purportedly pursue individual solutions to a set of historically shaped, economically rooted, culturally entrenched, and otherwise social problems; it is the classic Horatio Alger story modified for the postindustrial, buzz-word-chirping "creative class" in the United States.[102] In conjunction with the Great Man interpretation of history, this mythos of bootstrap capitalism enables someone like Schweidenbach to seriously and uncritically proclaim: "The elimination of poverty is never a governmental affair; the elimination of poverty is a personal issue."[103] The overarching theme promulgated by most, but certainly not all, microenterprise advocates differs little from the core philosophy of market fundamentalism, save their emphasis on the inherent goodness of social entrepreneurialism and the value of helping people in poverty. Conveniently, the latter position shields such antidemocratic impulses from judgment inasmuch as a critique of their free market ideology is easily and mistakenly construed as a critique of aid itself. When in fact, social entrepreneurialism—regardless of its success stories—is simply a privatized business paradigm in which the good intentions of businesspersons or, alternatively, the good vibes of former-hippie CEOs like Whole Foods' John Mackey, are meant to replace social movement activism and the mechanisms of democratic accountability required to genuinely empower populations. For example, Muhammad Yunus—the entrepreneurial guru, Nobel Peace Prize winner, and co-founder of Grameen Bank—concedes that free market capitalism has not remedied the problems of the Third World, yet his utopian/dystopian vision of society is free from the presumably inefficient trappings of popular representation, regulatory agencies, social services, and accountability implicit to a functioning democracy:

> I believe that government, as we now know it, should pull out of most things except for the law enforcement, the justice system, national defense, and foreign policy, and let the private sector, a "Grameenized private sector," a social-consciousness-driven private sector, take over its other functions. . . . *The private sector, unlike the government, is open to everyone.*[104]

Michael Strong, another microfinance and entrepreneurial champion best known for his ahistorical and thoroughly cultish conceptualization of *flow*—"A World of Healthy, Happy People Doing Good and Having Fun"— goes a step further by lamenting the very processes of dissent and unrest at the heart of democratic, civic participation: "For most of a century, idealistic people have been encouraged to use anger, protest, lobbying, and legal action in order to make the world a better place. While most certainly some of these behaviors and activities were necessary, *we have reached the point at which the social benefit of such behaviors is decreasing.*"[105] Micro-enterprise programs and micro-lending practices are not implicitly antithetical to progressive political goals, nor does their implementation require an uncritical faith in market economics. Bikes Not Bombs, CESTA, Maya Pedal, and Working Bikes are just a few of the organizations that either operate or contribute to effective development-focused micro-businesses that see appropriate technology, ecological sustainability, and social justice—rather than bootstrap capitalism—as the end goals of their work. They recognize that even within the constraints of capitalism, bicycle transportation and pedal-powered technologies can be part of a larger shift in the way people potentially organize their communities, care for their environment, and exercise more democratic control over their means of production. Sadly, their collective critiques of corporatism and free trade policies compromise the minority position within a network of aid organizations hoping to cultivate the budding entrepreneur ostensibly trapped inside every postcolonial subject.

The prospects of creating a sustainable or viable business in virtually any postcolonial country are dependent on a multitude of tenuous factors, the least of which are the whims of international markets, the lending and trade policies of transnational bodies like the World Bank, IMF, and WTO, the price of oil, and the general economic stranglehold that multinational corporations have on both global resources and trade. Within this globalized economic context it is still possible for bicycles to make a dramatic and indeed critical difference in people's quality of life, whether improving access to clean water and marketplaces in rural Ghana, enabling better home care for AIDS patients in Namibia, encouraging rural girls to attend school in Mozambique, or facilitating coffee production for co-operative farmers in Rwanda. For these and many other reasons, international bicycle donation programs as well as their supplementary educational initiatives, are invaluable. What needs to be questioned, then, is certainly not the merit of distributing bikes to people in need or the value of promoting affordable and environmentally sustainable transportation, but rather, the uncritical assumption that people can literally pedal themselves out of poverty, given the opportunity to do so. Bicycle aid programs and international organizations like the ITDP are obviously incapable of effecting the type of change necessary to transform socioeconomic conditions on a global scale, and they should not be judged by such unrealistic standards. What they can do, however, is to help cultivate policies, practices, and discourses that challenge, rather than normalize, the prevailing wisdom of development theory and the myth of apolitical development.[106] Indeed, if the ultimate goals of bicycle aid programs are not simply to deliver bicycles to developing countries but to increase Americans' collective awareness of the global interconnections between mobility, economics, and environmental sustainability, then it is crucial to engage U.S. bike donors, cyclists, and bicycling organizations with the overarching problems posed by economic and cultural globalization. Every media interview, brochure, and collaboration with participating cycling organizations offers a unique pedagogical opportunity for international bike donors to bring these issues to the table, much like Bikes Not Bombs brought the U.S.-backed Contra war within the purview of promoting bicycles as a form of social justice. Drawing cyclists' collective attention to such problems is merely one way in which to emphasize a deeper understanding of the complexities of mobility and immobility, poverty and privilege. Part of the work, it seems, is making people aware that these relationships even exist.

Conclusion

Critiquing the ideology of the economic development paradigm may seem like a dramatic detour from initially discussing the merits of grassroots Earn-a-Bike programs, but in many ways it is the most logical place one could end up. That is to say, the most important lessons one can learn from people reclaiming, remaking, and redistributing bicycles at a local level are precisely those upon which the foundations of a more equitable society must begin: mutual aid, skill sharing, reusing resources, teaching, learning from one another, and realizing that there is plenty of everything to go around. By fostering environments where people can actually put these ethics to work through participation, community bicycle organizations strive to create genuine community spaces that address a pragmatic material need in urban neighborhoods at the same time they enable people, in various capacities, to empower themselves and engage with some of the deeper socioeconomic, racial, and gender issues that are always and already implicated in the uses of technologies and the production of mobilities. One can only hope that these objectives, as opposed to those championed by free market economists, become part of the basis for a more humane and more sustainable vision of development in the twenty-first century. Indeed, these bicycle projects effectively remind us that organizing responses to the everyday problems posed by larger social and economic injustices should not be a matter of simply giving people a "hand up," but of creating the conditions in which people can collectively transcend the logic of capitalism altogether.

CHAPTER 8

Conclusion, or "We Have Nothing to Lose but Our (Bike) Chains"

Let us not permit either self-seeking special interests, or well-intentioned long-haired enthusiasts, to hamstring the march of motor transport progress, much less drive us back to the horse and buggy days.

–Thomas P. Henry, "Address to the Annual Meeting of the Councillors of the American Automobile Association," 1936

Ladies and gentlemen, I bring you the Democrats, promoting 19th century solutions to 21st century problems. If you don't like it, ride a bike. If you don't like the price at the pumps, ride a bike. Stay tuned for the next big idea for the Democrats: Improving energy efficiency by the horse and buggy.

–North Carolina Congressman Patrick McHenry, addressing the U.S. House of Representatives, 2007

The Nineteenth-Century Solution to Twenty-First-Century Problems

Congressman Patrick McHenry, the Republican representative for the 10th District in North Carolina, briefly addressed the House on August 4, 2007, in an attempt to sway votes against a renewable energy bill (HR 2776) that ultimately passed.[1] The provisions of the bill included, among other things, a measly tax break of $20 a month for workers who commute by bicycle—a total figure translating to roughly $1 million per year, or what the United States spends on the wars in Iraq and Afghanistan every four to five minutes.

"Your Bicycle Misses You." *(Photo by Max Estes.)*

The irony of the modern combustion engine being developed prior to the bicycle boom of the 1890s was noticeably lost on McHenry (see quotation above), who grandstanded before the House by feigning shock over the supposed bicycle solution being proposed for the country's transportation system and its reliance on foreign oil (the bill made no such allusions). That every "one less car" on the road literally does translate to less oil used on any given day was similarly overlooked in the congressman's sermon—a virtual rerun of the same liberal-baiting speech delivered by American Automobile Association (AAA) President Thomas P. Henry to his association's annual meeting in 1936. Indeed, the Henry–McHenry homily has been effectively touted by political and economic elites since the inception of the automobile and will undoubtedly play a role in future attempts to paint all non–automobile cheerleaders (even random participants in the wholesome National Bike to Work Day) as neo-Luddites bent on forcing Americans down the collective path of the Amish.[2]

Consequently, the most profound and tragic irony of the scenario to which the congressman alludes is not only that the same smog-producing nineteenth-century technologies are still used to address twenty-first-century transportation problems but also that the dominant paradigm of automobility is similarly trapped in a supposedly bygone era. That is to say, the presumed currency of the automobile as a timely and perpetually modern solution to everyday transportation is necessarily contingent on our continual faith in, and reproduction of, the same nineteenth-century mythos of unfettered technological progress as well as the same colonialist, militaristic practices and ethics at the root of this techno-cultural project. Indeed, widespread resistance to the very thought of seriously utilizing non-motorized vehicles for urban transportation is a luxury that takes for granted the logical consequences of an illogical paradigm of mobility: environmental pollution, the persistent erosion of public spaces, innumerable car wrecks, oil wars in the Middle East, road rage, ever-increasing traffic jams, and one of the leading causes of death for people between the ages of five to twenty-four worldwide.[3] Suffice it to say, we can clearly do much better for ourselves. And more important, we have to.

Decelerating City Traffic 100 Percent

One of the points I emphasized in this book is that bicycles are not the solution to transportation problems just as any technological fix is incapable of solving problems that are hardly reducible to technology in the first place. Nevertheless, the shifting geopolitical, ecological, and economic landscapes require us to think more concretely and indeed more pragmatically about the vast potential of bicycles and pedal-powered technologies in the twenty-first century. One of the major obstacles preventing a more rigorous analysis of the future of transportation is the virtual invisibility of non-motorized technologies as a real alternative among even the most critical thinkers who write on the politics of oil, environmentalism, and/or climate change. Of the plethora of books devoted to these subjects in recent years, one is still hard pressed to find more than a cursory discussion or token reference to non-motorized transportation despite the obvious prospects that bicycles and other pedal-powered technologies—such as pedal cars, recumbent bicycles, tricycles, and pedicabs—pose for the United States and for much of the world's population who dwell in dense urban centers, small towns, or villages where an automobile infrastructure is either economically unfeasible, culturally undesirable, or geographically impossible.

On the rare occasion when bicycle transportation is broached outside activist circles or the field-specific discourses of urban planning, public policy, and economic development, one finds a spectrum of debate—at least in the United States—book-ended by the cynicism of faux-anarchist primitivists and the neocolonial rhetoric of faux-democratic free marketeers. In anticipation of the global techno-apocalypse, John Zerzan surmises the jaded ethos of would-be hunters and gatherers who offer little more than the redundant prognosis:

"It is not enough to buy bicycles instead of cars."[4] An equally hopeless view is espoused by right-wingers like ex–Republican congressman turned Heritage Foundation Distinguished Fellow Ernest J. Istook Jr., a man who blamed the tragic 2007 Minneapolis bridge collapse, in part, on federal monies allocated to mass transit and bicycle paths by implying that vast amounts of tax dollars spent annually on automobile transportation somehow ensure the safety of a public infrastructure that he and his ilk systematically de-funded and de-prioritized since the New Deal era.[5] The fact that Mr. Istook, a staunch opponent of public transportation and of Amtrak in particular, once chaired the U.S. House Appropriations Transportation Subcommittee is indicative of why the federal government is only now considering the idea of actually funding and improving, rather than dismantling and maligning, the only nationwide passenger rail system in the United States.

Somewhere between these poles, a market-friendly environmental centrism is taking root through the advocacy of politicians like Al Gore and scientists like Kenneth S. Deffeyes, the geologist most credited with drawing public attention to Hubbert's "peak oil" hypothesis.[6] On matters of transportation, Gore benignly calls for "higher mileage cars" while Deffeyes speaks for the bulk of Americans who ironically see human-powered transportation— not the one hundred-year anomaly of the automobile—as part of an unrealistic, even radical, set of objectives:

> One possible stance, which I am not taking, says that we are despoiling the Earth, raping the resources, fouling the air, and that we should eat only organic food and ride bicycles. Guilt feelings will not prevent the chaos that threatens us. I ride a bicycle and walk a lot, but I confess that part of my motivation is the miserable parking situation in Princeton. . . . A better civilization is not likely to arise spontaneously out of a pile of guilty consciences. We need to face the problems *cheerfully* and try to cope with it in a way that minimizes problems in the future.[7]

Even if one disregards the violent, ongoing struggles over oil resources or, for example, the lesser known horrors of the Bridgestone/Firestone rubber plantations in Liberia, the most basic spirit of pragmatism dictates that the implications of global climate change require a set of environmental and transportation solutions more rigorous and impassioned than those capable of being measured by a "cheerful" yardstick.[8] Pleasure does, of course, play a crucial role for environmentally progressive practices and this point is certainly not lost on bicycling advocates who celebrate the joys of bicycle transportation in their formal and informal advocacy: a common pro-bicycle slogan printed on T-shirts, stickers, and other swag reads, "Put the Fun

Between Your Legs!" Bicycling, in other words, may offer opportunities for "being environmentally good" without requiring one to abide by puritanical codes of conduct, but this differs quite dramatically from the idea that fun should be a mandatory prerequisite for activism or that environmentalism should always be cheery and non-confrontational.[9]

Indeed, there is something profoundly unsettling and self-congratulatory about any form of environmental advocacy content with sacrificing rational critique and tangible political results in lieu of making people feel good, particularly when a nation's collective emotional coziness stems from radically unsustainable socioeconomic and ecological practices. Widespread appeasement of this disposition in the United States finds its clearest expression in the handful of topics that are still considered taboo for mainstream environmental debate: environmental racism, meat and dairy production, and driving. The latter activity is defended with a Charlton Heston-esque vigor that positions the steering wheel as the device from which Americans will ultimately have their cold, dead hands pried loose—a scenario that has, unfortunately, been the grim reality for millions of U.S. drivers since the beginning of the twentieth century. Instead of assertively grappling with one of the major ecological problems of the day, we are settling instead for a charade of a debate about transportation and environmentalism in which fuel efficiency and hybrid power are buzzwords in a new "green" lexicon: an obfuscating discourse that (once again) directs attention to a set of individualized solutions for a complex of cultural, political, and otherwise globally embedded problems. We speak of one's carbon footprint, for example, as the indelible mark of environmental impact when it would be more accurate to talk about a city's tire track, a nation's skid mark, or a culture's road rash. Within these narrow parameters, corporations and other "green" capitalists prove themselves adept at reframing and repackaging environmentalism not as a radical political movement or a struggle for social justice, but rather, a feel-good lifestyle for a new demographic of consumers who are supposed to be satiated by the eco-friendliness of new automotive interior fabrics, or somehow impressed by the "green" features of new hybrid SUVs—vehicles capable of achieving the futuristic efficiency of Ford's 1908 Model-T (up to twenty-one miles per gallon).[10]

In the United States, where the longevity of automobility is firmly secured by the country's populist support for passive environmental goals and free market capitalism, it is likely that an affordable electric car will make the illusion of never-ending automobility that much more tenable, just as critiques of driving will seem all the more grouchy and unfounded if oil ceases to become *the* issue. Yet buried within the burgeoning love affair with the electric car— or at least the idea of the electric car—is a much dirtier love affair with the invisible protagonist of the impending electric car drama: coal. Coal energy might produce the bulk of U.S. carbon emissions and particulate matter (pollution), but it also provides most of the country's power and is currently the subject of a massive re-branding campaign led by Republicans and Democrats eager to tout the wholly fictitious process of burning "clean coal" with minimal environmental impact.[11] Burning coal is, of course, simply the final task in a comprehensively energy-intensive and ecologically destructive process that includes blowing up mountains in Appalachia and otherwise poisoning entire ecosystems and groundwater tables in and around coalmines, coal-fired power plants, and underground coal ash repositories.[12] Even if we were able to blindly disregard these factors and somehow minimize the potentially catastrophic ecological damage implicit in a coal-fueled transportation system (i.e., electric cars), there is still the none too small matter of the country's already strained electrical grid, which Americans saw falter quite dramatically during massive blackouts in the summer of 2003.[13] One does not require a degree in engineering to safely assume that this very infrastructure is totally incapable of supporting an additional 100 to 200 million electric cars' worth of power on a daily basis. Though it is worth noting that people who do have such credentials, namely, the American Society of Civil Engineers, gave the U.S. energy infrastructure a "D" on its 2005 "National Report Card," downgrading it from its 2001 "D+."[14]

My point here is quite simple: the automobile has no long-term future in the city. This is not to say that people are going to stop driving anytime soon, but even if the United States is capable of either (1) maintaining cheap oil prices indefinitely, (2) replacing and/or retrofitting more than 200 million U.S. vehicles with electric engines or biofuel modifications, or (3) revamping the entire energy grid in service of single-occupancy vehicles, there is simply no way to avoid the inevitable spatial limits of urban automobility since the U.S. population is expected to increase from roughly 300 million to 430 million by 2050 (the total urban population worldwide is expected to double from 3.3 billion to 6.4 billion in the same period).[15] As Norman Bel Geddes astutely pointed out in 1940: "The plain fact is that there is simply not enough room in cities, under present conditions, to accommodate the traffic."[16] Barring the complete evisceration of urban centers for new swaths of traffic-clogged roads, there will necessarily come a time when it will be totally unfeasible, if not impossible, for drivers to avoid hours of daily gridlock in every U.S. city: a virtual *Auto Mass.*

At present, Americans already spend between 38 and 46 hours a year sitting in traffic at a cost of $78 billion to the U.S. economy. According to the Texas Transportation Institute, this enormous figure comes in the form of 4.2 billion lost (work) hours and 2.9 billion gallons of wasted fuel (58 supertankers' worth of oil).[17] In addition, the American Society of Civil Engineers estimates that the federal government would have to start spending $9.4 billion per year on bridges (27 percent of all U.S. bridges are currently "structurally deficient") and between $94 billion and $120 billion per year in order to actually improve—not just maintain—the national road system, to which it also gave a "D" grade on its 2005 infrastructure report card. The U.S. Department of Transportation anticipates a demand for ground transportation in 2050 that is roughly 250 percent larger than today, though the number of roads are expected to increase by only 10 percent in the same period.[18] Studies conducted at MIT in 2001 similarly warn of unsustainable levels of gridlock, just as John Fisher, of the Los Angeles Department of Transportation, anticipates "nearly all day long" congestion in Los Angeles by 2025—a figure likely to increase dramatically by 2050.[19] The World Bank's 2007 transportation report adds much to the anxiety over U.S. gridlock; it projects unprecedented growth in the worldwide use of automobiles over the next two decades, noting that "more cars may be built than in the 110-year history of the industry."[20] Still, the problem of gridlock is perhaps best illuminated in the work published by the pro-automobile lobby and their right-wing think tank allies. Their case against gridlock is unsurprisingly couched in a comprehensive appeal for more cars and roads, but in highlighting the contemporary problems of automobility, they ironically forecast the impending transportation crises that will undoubtedly ensue barring a wholesale shift away from their own policy recommendations.[21] For example, the Reason Foundation estimates it will require $837.8 billion to reduce severe and moderate traffic congestion by 2030, including the addition of 228,073 "lane-miles," which is enough pavement to cover an area the size of Chicago, Philadelphia, Seattle, and Miami combined.[22] These figures, however, speculate on only the price tag for a congestion-reduction plan by 2030, not on a plan designed to tackle the long-term congestion problems brought on by population growth. At present, the amount of total land specifically devoted to the automobile in the United States (namely, roads and parking spaces) could already fill up the entire state of Iowa and nearly all of Connecticut.[23]

So the question is, just how many more resources are necessary to fix congestion for drivers in 2040? 2050? 2070? How much more farmland will be paved over? Pollution emitted? Money squandered? And more specific to the claims of Libertarians, how is it conceivable to perpetually construct highways and roads without either relying on the government's powers of eminent domain—which right-wingers abhor—or the forceful seizure of private property from citizens who choose not to comply with the privatized highway schemes promulgated by Reason scholars? Hashing out these core hypocrisies or speculating fifty to seventy-five years into the future is, of course, not the business of the Reason Foundation or any other capitalist think tank, because any pragmatic assessment of the long-term trends associated with our current socioeconomic regime necessarily engenders a sense of panic that rightfully calls into question the tenets of a system designed to myopically yield short-term rewards at the expense of long-term sustainability. At the very least, the dire ecological, financial, political, and spatial problems posed by another century of automobility throw a considerable wrench into the preposterous Libertarian notion that there is no such thing as society.

The very real prospects of natural resource scarcity, Auto Mass, and/or Oil Mass (prohibitively expensive oil and gas) suggest that imagining a long-term future for urban automobility is nothing short of a faith-based initiative that requires the gross denial of basic facts, an unrequited trust in the market, continual hope for a technological savior, and an unwavering belief in "the notion of progress in a single line without goal or limit"—a sentiment Lewis Mumford rightly describes as "the most parochial notion of a very parochial [twentieth] century."[24] Consequently, the appropriate question when contemplating the not-so-distant future of urban transportation is not if automobility will become obsolete, but when.[25] Ironically, even William Clay Ford Jr., the current president of Ford Motor Company, recognizes the value of this disposition: in November 2000 he stated, "The day will come when the notion of car ownership becomes antiquated. If you live in a city, you don't need to own a car."[26] Reframing the issue in this manner is both reasonable and entirely responsible when one considers the gravity of not planning for a post-automobile period. "Such a planning posture," Maurie Cohen argues, is "actually vital due to the extended timeframe required to commission and construct new transport infrastructure and its exceedingly long lifespan once it becomes operational."[27] Regretfully, the core questions of *if* or *when* are virtually absent from mainstream political discourse in the United States and this perpetual shortsightedness not only prevents a substantive discussion about the need for unprecedented federal and state commitments to high-speed transit, light rail systems, and pedestrian infrastructure but also precludes the possibility of seeing bicycles and pedal-powered transportation as effective alternatives to the automobile for more than half of the daily U.S. car trips that amount to up to three miles.

A Shift toward the Bike?

The bicycle, Andrew Ritchie writes, is "an ideal solution for certain kinds of people in certain situations."[28] Based on the short distances Americans repeatedly drive every day, one might assume that the bicycle is already an ideal solution; we just have to get people on bikes, right? There are plenty of advocates who take up this position and strive to achieve their goals by educating the public, training cyclists, and attempting to transform the overall image of bicycle transportation. Encouraging people to change their transportation habits in order to become the certain kinds of people who ride bikes is, of course, an admirable and necessary goal. But if bicycle transportation is to play any significant role as a viable form of urban mobility, then this approach must be entirely turned on its head. That is to say, the object of transformation should be the certain situations that make bicycle transportation onerous, dangerous, and generally unappealing. Making American cities bicycle friendly is obviously a good start, but it is not enough to achieve what should be an extremely modest long-term transportation goal in the United States: using bicycles and other pedal-powered technologies as part of a strategy to eliminate all of the very short trips (one mile or less), most of the short trips (75 percent reduction of trips between one and two miles), and half of the longer ones (two to five miles) currently made by car. Indeed, emphasis must be placed on a combination of strategies for promoting cycling, including the development of comprehensive urban bicycle infrastructures that allow anyone, not just experienced cyclists or athletes, to ride comfortably and without the anxiety of either pacing auto traffic or slinking between moving and parked cars on the street. Bicycling, in John Pucher's terms, must be made "irresistible."[29] In conjunction with traffic-calming measures in residential areas, the development of car-free urban spaces, and the implementation of strategies to reduce overall levels of driving, off-road bikeways and separated bike lanes are the best long-term investments for promoting cycling and for making it easier, and more enjoyable, not to drive.

Yet, at the risk of minimizing the profound need for a comprehensive overhaul of transportation priorities and infrastructure in the United States, it should be clear by now that one can "never make transportation an issue unto itself."[30] As former Bogotá mayor Enrique Peñalosa notes, "It is not for traffic engineers to decide how we are going to solve transportation problems, it is a political decision."[31] Peñalosa, who is credited with revitalizing both public transportation and public spaces in Colombia's capital city, urges us to ask a more poignant and profound set of questions when framing the issue of mobility: "How do we want our city to be? How do we want to live?"[32] By posing the questions in this way, as a matter of our collective right to the city, Peñalosa rightfully focuses attention on the philosophical, social, and cultural issues with which citizens must be engaged, as well as the political solutions necessary to address the problems connected to and through transportation. In short, he reminds us that we are still setting the bar too low. Because in order to genuinely transform the certain situations that make vélomobility and a prosperous bike culture a seemingly utopian fantasy in the United States—as opposed to a pragmatic, sustainable, and fundamentally cheaper way of getting around—it is indeed necessary for Americans to grapple with some of the big questions pertaining to the environments in which they live and would like to live. And as Jen Petersen puts it, one must also be willing to ask oneself a more self-reflexive, dialectical question: "What sort of city do I want to shape me?"[33]

Imagining a collective shift toward the bicycle necessarily involves a broader rethinking of the spaces we inhabit and the ways we go about meeting our daily needs. This is perhaps the real threat posed by critiques of automobility, and by extension, the prospects of working toward a society in which the automobile is intentionally phased out: both projects force us to confront a much broader set of issues than transportation alone. Because, as Bruce Epperson points out, "It's almost like Einstein's unified field theory, there really is no such thing as transportation, there is only this one big thing called *housingjobstransit.*"[34] To this, one could also add *foodschoolshospitalsretail* (among other things).[35] Consequently, the idea of minimizing automobile transportation in any U.S. city—even hypothetically—raises a number of admittedly crucial questions that are frequently put to pro-bicycling and anti-car activists. They include, but are not limited to, the following:

- How will I get to work?
- How will we get people to the hospital?
- How will my kids get to school?
- How will our food be brought into the city?
- How will our mail/packages get delivered?

There are, of course, innumerable solutions to these problems and dozens of activists and scholars who tackle these nuances with precision clarity. But my point here is somewhat broader: by relying on the automobile to solve each of these problems, we perpetually avoid asking an entirely different, and ultimately more productive, set of questions:

- Why are there no safe cycling routes or efficient forms of mass transit where I live?
- Why are there no doctors, schools, or grocery stores in my neighborhood?
- Why should my kids not be able to walk to school?
- Why is there no affordable housing or locally grown food in the place where I live?
- Why is my employer subsidized to move out of my city, my county, or the country?
- Why are there no pedal-powered delivery services in most cities or pedal-powered vehicles designed for comfortable winter riding?

The thorough normalization of automobility inhibits our capacity to ask the latter set of questions (or ones like them) because it dominates our day-to-day rhythms and serves as the crooked yardstick by which we measure both the viability of more sustainable, human-scaled cities, or the prospects of more equitable forms of mobility. Moreover, it normalizes the process of thinking like an individual driver, instead of a social citizen with basic needs, requirements, and democratic rights. As a result, any of the big questions pertaining to long-term mobility, urban planning and transportation in U.S. cities are perpetually deferred in favor of the same repetitive and easily solvable debates over *how* instead of *why*.[36]

A collective shift toward the bicycle could and should entail an analogous shift toward public transit, affordable urban housing, more localized modes of food and energy production, and, crucially, more attention paid to the importance of the spaces and places in which we live: Dave Horton even suggests that in the struggle for environmental sustainability, "it might well be the spatial impacts of car free life which ultimately prove more important than the direct ecological impacts of 'one less car.'"[37] But perhaps more fundamentally, a collective shift toward the bike in the United States requires a rigorous and radical reassessment of bicycle production and trade policy, since roughly 99 percent of the bicycles sold in the United States are imported. This is not an appeal to racist nationalism or jingoism as much as it is a matter of common sense and a pragmatic way to envision a broader movement for bicycle transportation that can include, and should rightfully praise, the labor of bicycle factory workers, welders, independent bike builders, tinkerers, artisans, and a multitude of small businesses and communities that stand to gain from an American vélorution.

Building a "Better Mousetrap" Industry

One of the major problems facing bicycle transportation activists in the twenty-first century is that the totalizing logic of globalization and the realities of free market capitalism frame the prospects of a successful bicycle culture around the importation of bicycles and the enhancement of retail and repair industries, as opposed to encouraging more centralized, more localized, or at the very least, more geographically regionalized modes of production. Because as Paul Rosen argues, "a globally equitable bicycle industry would need to be centered around small companies using local resources to supply local needs."[38] Ricardo Navarro postulated as much in the 1980s in that he saw local control of the means of bicycle production as an end goal in Latin America, and also part of a wider effort to both democratize technology and normalize the use of sustainable transportation in everyday life.[39] But whereas Navarro spoke to the unique problems posed by the virtual absence of bicycle production in Latin America—more specifically in El Salvador and Nicaragua—the situation in the United States and in Rosen's native England is quite the opposite: once-thriving bicycle manufacturing sectors were systematically eliminated in the last two decades.

For example, nearly 70 percent of the 29 million bicycles sold in the United States between 1973 and 1974 were manufactured by U.S. companies, and 20 years later domestic production still accounted for more than 60 percent of the total number of bikes sold (8 million out of 13 million).[40] However, in the years following the implementation of the North American Free Trade Agreement (NAFTA), this scenario changed quite dramatically: U.S. bicycle corporations dismantled U.S. manufacturing facilities to the degree that only seven hundred thousand of the 20 million bicycles sold in 2000 (3.5 percent) were made domestically.[41] By 2007, the National Bicycle Dealers Association estimated that 99.65 percent of the bicycles sold in the United States were imported from China, Taiwan, and Hong Kong.[42] There are a number of mitigating circumstances leading to the demise of U.S. bicycle manufacturing aside from international competition, including mismanagement, corporate greed, and the failure of certain bicycle companies to adapt to popular trends. For example, Schwinn not only supported the same companies that eventually became its primary competition (notably Giant) and missed out on the opportunity to become a major player in both BMX and mountain bike production—its management apparently referred to the mountain bike as a fad—it also made a number of shrewd moves to avoid reinvesting in either its Chicago production plant or its experienced workforce.[43] When Chicago Schwinn workers unionized under the UAW and went on strike in 1980, the company responded frostily and went on to close the plant in 1983, moving its equipment and engineers to the Giant Bicycle Company factory in Taichung, Taiwan.[44] Schwinn proceeded to open a new manufacturing plant in Greenville, Mississippi, where it hired inexperienced bike makers for lower pay, in a facility located seventy-five miles from the nearest interstate highway.[45] The plant lost more than $30 million and was closed in 1991, just one year prior to the company's bankruptcy declaration.[46]

While Schwinn is now widely seen as a textbook case for how not to run a company in the so-called postindustrial era, its story is rarely used to highlight the negative impacts of globalization on the environment, on the U.S. workers who lose their jobs and trade unions, and on the multitudes of Mexican and Asian workers who are subsequently and systematically exploited. Rather, we are meant to see the company's missed opportunities, lack of innovation, and brand deterioration as the hallmarks of its failure, as opposed to seeing the entire bicycle industry as a symbol of everything wrong with globalization and the corporate race to the bottom. Indeed, one of the most symbolic events to highlight the negative effects of globalization on American workers took place at another bike factory in July 1998, when Huffy Bicycle Corporation, then largest in the United States, closed down its Celina, Ohio factory and fired the entire staff of nearly a thousand workers despite high overall sales that year (previous years were financially tumultuous). The workers' union, which voted to voluntarily accept a 20 percent pay cut in 1995 to keep the plant running in Celena, met with Huffy officials in April 1998 to recoup the 20 percent restoration in their salaries, in addition to reimbursement for lost wages between 1995 and 1998.[47] Rather than attempting to find an equitable solution to the situation, Huffy fired everyone two months later and shut the plant down. On their last day of employment, Celina bicycle workers bore the humiliation of meticulously replacing Made in the USA stickers with Huffy's new globe logo: Huffy's final semiotic transformation into a new, global enterprise. Workers made their own symbolic gesture that day when each person left a pair of empty shoes in his or her parking space outside the factory, as if to remind Huffy of both the human cost of the company's decisions and the inability for anyone else to fill their shoes.[48]

Huffy went on to close plants in Mississippi and Missouri in 1999, firing 1,800 workers who were already paid $2.50 less per hour than Celina's $10.50 wage. The company moved a number of these jobs to Nuevo Laredo, Mexico, where workers earned less than $4 per hour, before closing operations in 2001 in order to centralize manufacturing operations in a Chinese factory where workers earned between 25 and 41 cents per hour while logging sixty-six to seventy hours per week (up to nineteen hours per shift).[49] Charles Kernaghan, of the National Labor Committee, notes that Huffy's new employees were also forced to work compulsory overtime while living in cramped, company-owned dormitories with as many as twelve workers housed in each room.[50] Yet, just two months prior to the closure of the Celina plant, Huffy's board apparently voted itself an "18.4% increase in their annual retainer fee" while CEO Don Graber subsequently made an additional 9 percent in the wake of the factory closure, raising his salary to $1.1 million (not including $1.7 million in stock options).[51] According to the National Labor Committee, Huffy posted sales of $584 million in 1998 with a gross profit of $97.5 million.[52]

Including Huffy, five corporations (Dorel, Dynacraft, Huffy, Rand, and Kent) and their subsidiaries now comprise roughly 80 percent of the U.S. bike market, while the other 20 percent of bicycles are largely produced by three additional corporations (Giant, Merida, and Ideal) that similarly operate via a network of supply chains and outsourced labor that is difficult to accurately map out. Consequently, it is incredibly hard to find out where most bikes are even made, never mind gaining access to clear information about the actual labor conditions and environmental practices connected to specific bicycle factories.[53] Even so, one has to wonder whether this information would sway the opinions of most cyclists one way or the other. I say this because even the most banal event like the U.S. bike industry's annual Interbike trade show reveals the extent to which neglecting labor issues is thoroughly embedded in the norms of a seemingly progressive industry. For example, in his speech delivered at the 2007 Bicycle Leadership Conference, Interbike show director

Lance Camisasca outlined specific criteria for attendees to consider when planning future Interbike events, including adequate space, good weather, accessible airports and lodging, bike-specific demonstration facilities, and, most revealingly, *"relaxed labor union regulations."*[54] Perhaps it is unfair to judge the bicycle industry based on an annual event that is both owned (Interbike is also a brand) and staged by the Nielsen Company—a multinational media conglomerate dedicated exclusively to the perpetuation of consumer capitalism—but in many ways Interbike *is* the U.S. bike industry, not simply its public face. The event could not succeed without the enthusiastic participation of bike industry leaders and companies who are as seemingly eager to trot out their newest models of bicycle as they are the scantily clad, large-breasted models hired to accompany them.[55] Indeed, the emphasis on image cultivated at Interbike is fitting for an industry in which workers' rights are rarely questioned, much less problematized, by both bicycle businesses and their consumers.

Chris King, the owner and proprietor of one of the most respected and environmentally responsible bicycle component manufacturers in the United States, is one of the few insiders to actually offer a public critique of the labor practices and policies supported by the bike industry.[56] And if bike shop conversations, interviews, and online forums are at all indicative of U.S. cyclists' general thoughts about the industry, their reservations about production tend to stem less from actual labor issues or environmental concerns than from the poor quality of the bikes that the U.S. imports from China (to use a common example).[57] Indeed, the habitual recourse to arguments about quality is usually tied to a defense of companies that, instead, import high-quality bicycles from Taiwan. Cyclists cite the prevalence of labor laws and environmental regulations at Taiwanese factories as the justification for such claims, despite the fact that the lines between the bicycle industries in Taiwan and China are far from discrete. Tony Lo, the president of Giant Bicycles—the largest bicycle manufacturer in the world—is actually quite clear about this relationship: he claims there are actually two "Taiwan" bicycle industries: "one in Taiwan and one in China."[58] He specifically notes that 80 percent of China's bicycle exports are actually controlled by Taiwanese companies like Giant, and he makes reference to three hundred additional Taiwanese companies that own and operate manufacturing facilities in China.[59] Giant, for example, invested $12 million in its fourth Chinese factory in 2007 (in Tianjin), around the same time that Merida—another major bicycle corporation in Taiwan—built its second plant in Dezhou.[60] Taiwanese corporations not only control Chinese bicycle exports and produce their own bicycles in Chinese factories; they are also China's primary bicycle customers, purchasing 65 percent of the 56 million bicycles the country churned out in 2006.[61] Moreover, bicycle corporations in Taiwan are by no means averse to outsourcing further production to countries like India, Vietnam, Thailand, and the Philippines, where manufacturing costs are minimized through the exploitation of workers and corporate-friendly trade policies.[62]

The problems posed by a globalized bicycle industry are, of course, not reducible to Taiwan or China any more than they are the attributable to India, the United States, Canada, England, or any number of Western countries that collectively support the policies, as well as the entire socioeconomic regime, enabling multinational corporations to exploit workers and the environment for the sole purposes of ensuring higher profit margins, growth potential, and/or shareholder revenue. Within this context, the difficulties posed by simultaneously recentralizing the means of bicycle production and decentralizing (and democratizing) its ownership, are manifold. As noted previously, the bicycle is already a fully globalized technology and has been for more than a century: it is virtually impossible for any company or country to manufacture a bicycle from scratch without importing parts, let alone the raw materials and technologies necessary to produce such basics as sturdy steel frames and tires.[63] Even Raleigh, whose massive production plant in Nottingham, England, was once an icon of vertical integration, still relied on other companies to produce its ball bearings and tires at a time when every other part on its bicycles was manufactured in-house.[64] Despite this conundrum, there are very real possibilities for working toward a more egalitarian vision of production that could simultaneously minimize the bicycle's environmental impact. In order to think through these options, bicycle advocates and professional cycling organizations that profess an honest interest in creating a healthier, more sustainable world through bicycle transportation must begin to offer more substantive explanations for how those objectives square with the realities of a globalized bicycle industry in which ownership is concentrated into a corporate oligopoly and the overall commitment to workers' rights and environmental regulations is at best sketchy.

While I do not propose to have the all of the answers, it is clear that this dialogue must commence, and the sooner the better. Because while there is some truth in pitching the bicycle as an inherently "green" form of mobility, achieving any level of real sustainability—with all that the term implies—is no small matter, and it will not come from simply bracketing every major issue associated with bicycle production and capitalism writ large. Similarly, while increasing the levels of bicycle transportation worldwide—and more specifically in the United States—would be a huge step in the direction of ecological sustainability, advocates will no sooner arrive at this goal by relying on current modes of production than they will the leadership of bicycle corporations whose current vision of promoting global bicycle transportation is, regrettably, as shortsighted as the solutions offered by the automobile and oil industries. That is to say, instead of promoting non-motorized transportation through more localized, democratic modes of production and distribution, their prevailing modus operandi uncritically promotes further deregulation and consolidation of the bicycle industry—a scenario that ironically makes cheap oil a prerogative of bicycling advocates inasmuch as the low price of fuel is currently the sole factor enabling bicycle corporations to outsource, subcontract, and otherwise ship bicycles and parts across the globe.

Finale

As Langdon Winner points out in his otherwise problematic critique of the appropriate technology movement, people have always been able to build a better mousetrap in hopes of transforming society, but such technological solutions are fundamentally and perpetually constrained by the larger cultural and political contexts in which they are deployed. Understanding these contexts and daring to ask a more critical set of questions about the relationships between technologies, social change, and everyday life is a crucial task, but by no means the only task, in the broader struggle to create a better world. Indeed, the goal is not simply to interpret technologies but to change the ways in which they are used, namely, by creating the cultural and political conditions in which technologies can be put to work in service of equality, social justice, environmental sustainability, and mutual aid.

Bicycles and pedal-powered technologies can play a profound role in this process and they are intrinsic to any long-term vision of urban transportation in the twenty-first century. Perhaps most important, they are amazing tools for exploring, enjoying, rethinking, and reimagining not just cities but the possibilities for mobility itself. By taking these lessons seriously, and by using them as both a source of inspiration and a basis from which to make critiques, build coalitions, and organize political momentum, we can collectively transform the norms of transportation in ways that can profoundly impact people's lives and contribute to more sustainable, just societies. This is a far cry from merely changing the ways we get from point A to point B: it is a chance to figure out where we want to go.

Notes

CHAPTER 1

1. "Time's Up! Cycling for a Better City," *Village Voice,* July 6, 2004.

2. Chris Carlsson, "The Hidden Class Politics of Bicycling, Trains, Bikes, Cars, BART(!)," 1997, *Critical Mass Essays, Flyers, Images from San Francisco, 1992–1998,* available at http://www.processedworld.com/tfrs_web/history/classncycling.html.

3. Graham Rayman, "It's a Shameful Abuse of Power," *New York Newsday,* September 9, 2004.

4. *Hardball,* MSNBC, August 29, 2004, available at http://www.bikesagainstbush.com/blog/hardball.html.

5. Ryan Singel, "NYPD Intelligence Op Targets Dot-Matrix Graffiti Bike," *Wired,* April 10, 2007.

6. Ibid.

7. "Critical Mass Bike Rides Face Police Crackdown," *Democracy Now!* December 27, 2005; Jim Dwyer, "Police Infiltrate Protests, Videotapes Show," *New York Times,* December 23, 2005. Other bike activists (outside of New York City) were also subject to Federal Bureau of Investigation (FBI) surveillance prior to the RNC. For example, an FBI report written in December 2004 focused specifically on Sarah Bardwell, who helped to run both the Derailer Bicycle Collective and the local chapter of Food Not Bombs in Denver, Colorado. Both organizations serve the community by distributing free bikes and food that would otherwise end up in landfills. See American Civil Liberties Union (ACLU) of Colorado, "New Documents Confirm: FBIs Joint Terrorism Task Force Targets Peaceful Activists for Harassment, Political Surveillance" (press release, 2005).

8. Later in the year, the police revised their "parade" stipulations to allow up to nine people to participate in a roadway procession without a permit. See Al Baker, "Police Seek New Controls on Protesters and Bicyclists," *New York Times,* July 19, 2006.

9. Sheryl Neufeld of the New York City (NYC) Law Department, quoted in "Judge Dismisses New York's Bid to Force Bike Rally to Get Permit," *Associated Press,* December 24, 2004.

10. Charles Komanoff and Time's Up! Environmental Organization, "Cost Analysis of Government Expenditures to Suppress Critical Mass Bike Rides" (New York, 2006).

11. Geoff Tibballs, *The Mammoth Book of Zingers, Quips, and One-Liners: Over 10,000 Gems of Wit and Wisdom, One-Liners and Wisecracks* (New York: Carroll and Graf Publishers, 2004), 37.

12. Santa Barbara, California, Detective Jaycee Hunter, quoted in Nick Welsh, "Thou Shalt Have No False Dogs before Me," *Santa Barbara Independent,* April 10, 2008.

13. Kevin Krizek and Gary Barnes explain the difficulty of estimating the actual number of bike commuters in "Estimating Bicycling Demand," *Journal of the Transportation Research Board,* no. 1939 (2005): 47–48. In short, surveys often ask the wrong questions, not enough questions, or focus on too small of a sample population to make the numbers meaningful. With that being said, nearly half of the bike riders surveyed by the National Highway Traffic Safety Administration (NHTSA) in 2002 rode for recreation or health/fitness, personal errands, or visiting friends and relatives; commuting to work and/or school accounts for almost 30 percent of the trips taken by bicycle. See Bureau of Transportation Statistics and National Highway Traffic Safety Administration, "National Survey of Pedestrian and Bicyclist Attitudes and Behaviors: Highlights Report" (Washington, DC: Department of Transportation, 2003).

14. Ariel Brodsky, "Bicycling Commuters Boast Greater Numbers Queens Ledger," *Queens Ledger,* July 24, 2008; Bill Nesper, "League Names Portland a Platinum Community" (League of American Bicyclists, press release, April 29, 2008); Cascade Bicycle Club Urban Transportation Caucus (San Francisco Bicycle Coalition, Chicagoland Bicycle Federation and Transportation Alternatives), "Urban Transportation Report Card" (2007). Also see Bureau of Transportation Statistics and National Highway Traffic Safety Administration, "National Survey of Pedestrian and Bicyclist Attitudes and Behaviors."

15. Joseph A. Gambardello, "Bike Commuters Having a Two-Wheel Revolution," *Philadelphia Inquirer,* August 2, 2008; "More Ways Than Cars to Get around Town," *Shreveport Times,* June 7, 2008; Ben Arnoldy, "New Bike Commuters Hit the Classroom, Then the Road," *Christian Science Monitor,* August 25, 2008; Sue Doyle, "L.A. Transit Agency Tries to Cope with Additional Bike-Riding Commuters," *Los Angeles Daily News,* August 21, 2008; Pat Shellenbarger, "Local Bicyclists Fight for a Piece of the Road," *Grand Rapids Press,* August 5, 2008.

16. The San Francisco Municipal Transportation Authority conducted a survey of traffic on Market Street in July and found 509 bike riders versus 400 cars, 43 taxis, and 30 transit vehicles. Two months prior, bicycles outnumber cars 2:1 during morning rush hour on Bike-to-Work Day. See Michael Cabanatuan, "Bay Area Commuters Moving Beyond Cars," *San Francisco Chronicle,* August 25, 2008; San Francisco Bicycle Coalition, "Twice as Many Bikes as Cars on Market Street," press release, 2008. Also

see Anna Phillips, "High Gas Prices Cause Bike Shortages in N.Y.," *New York Sun,* May 30, 2008.

17. John Pucher and Ralph Buehler, "Making Cycling Irresistible: Lessons from the Netherlands, Denmark and Germany," *Transport Reviews* 28, no. 4 (2008): 495; U.S. Census Bureau, "2000 Decennial Census: Journey to Work" (Washington, DC: U.S. Department of Commerce, 2003); U.S. Department of Transportation, "National Household Travel Survey, 2001" (Washington, DC: Federal Highway Administration, 2003).

18. John Pucher and Ralph Buehler, "At the Frontiers of Cycling: Policy Innovations in the Netherlands, Denmark, and Germany," *World Transport Policy and Practice* 13, no. 3 (2007): 10.

19. Blaine Harden, "For Bicyclists, a Widening Patchwork World: U.S. Lags Behind Two-Wheeled Boom," *Washington Post,* August 31, 2008.

20. John Pucher and Ralph Buehler, "Why Canadians Cycle More Than Americans: A Comparative Analysis of Bicycling Trends and Policies," *Transport Policy* 13, no. 3 (2006): 265.

21. U.S. Census Bureau, "Most of Us Still Drive to Work Alone, Public Transportation Commuters Concentrated in a Handful of Large Cities" (2007).

22. In addition to a 500 percent increase in total vehicle miles traveled in the United States between 1950 and 2000 (versus an 85 percent population increase), the number of SUVs and minivans in the United States increased by 239 percent and 99 percent, respectively, between 1992 and 2002. See U.S. Department of Commerce and U.S. Census Bureau, "1997 Economic Census: Vehicle Inventory and Use Survey" (Washington, DC: 1999); U.S. Department of Commerce and U.S. Census Bureau, "2002 Economic Census: Vehicle Inventory and Use Survey" (2004). I use the phrase "almost ever-increasing" because the sales of new SUVs took an uncharacteristic dip in 2008 due to high gas and oil prices and an ongoing economic recession. It remains to be seen whether this signals a shifting sensibility about automobile size and efficiency or whether it is merely a temporary trend. On the latter note, see Chris Isidore, "Auto Sales Plunge in Face of $4 Gas," *CNNMoney.com,* June 3, 2008.

23. For example, Chicago's Mayor Daley recently agreed to an ill-conceived deal in which the city's parking meters were privatized and sold to a Morgan-Stanley-owned firm called LAZ Parking. LAZ subsequently began to replace meters with digital pay boxes, thereby eliminating roughly 36,000 spots where city residents can lock up bicycles. Aside from new problems posed by meter replacements, a lack of reliable bike parking— and by extension the fear and/or reality of bike theft—are two of the many pragmatic reasons why people do not ride bikes for transportation in U.S. cities, particularly in New York City, where only 2 percent of stolen bicycles are recovered each year. See Matthew Roth, "When Old Parking Meter Poles Go, So Often Does Bike Parking," *StreetsBlog,* July 1, 2009, available at http://sf.streetsblog.org/2009/07/01/when-old-parking-meter-poles-go-so-often-does-bike-parking; "Operation You-Lock: T.A. Investigates NYC Bike Theft," *Transportation Alternatives Magazine* (September–October 1996): 6–7; "The Bane of the Would-Be Bicyclist," *Transportation Alternatives Magazine* (Fall 2004): 4–5; Morgan O'Rourke, "Locked Out," *Risk Management* 51, no. 12 (2004): 8–9.

24. The number of independent bike shops in the United States fell from 6,195 to 4,451 between 2000 and 2007 according to the National Bicycle Dealers Association, "Industry Overview 2007," available at http://nbda.com/page.cfm?PageID=34. Also see

Jack Oortwijn, "USA Market Report 2007," *Bike Europe,* April 7, 2008. For one of many examples of online discussions focusing on the harassment of female cyclists, see "Creepy Cyclists and Women on Bikes," *Bike Portland,* May 31, 2006, available at http://bikeport-land.org/2006/05/31/creepy-cyclists-and-women-on-bikes/.

25. Ernst Poulsen, "US Motorist Sentenced to 10 Years for Assault on Cyclist," *The Bicycle News Agency,* April 16, 1999. Another incident involving Lance Armstrong and a belligerent driver is recounted in Michael Barry, *Inside the Postal Bus: My Ride with Lance Armstrong and the U.S. Postal Cycling Team* (Boulder, CO: VeloPress, 2005), 20. Also see Robert Mionske, "Assault, Battery and How to Cook a Turkey," *Velo News,* November 24, 2005.

26. Sara Stout, interview with the author, August 5, 2004.

27. John B. Rae, for example, alludes to the "love affair" in his explanation of the development of U.S. car culture in *The American Automobile Industry* (Boston: Twayne Publishers, 1984). For critical analyses of both the "love affair" narrative and its production in mass media, see (respectively) Jason Henderson, "Secessionist Automobility: Racism, Anti-urbanism, and the Politics of Automobility in Atlanta, Georgia," *International Journal of Urban and Regional Research* 30, no. 2 (2006): 295–296; Karal Ann Marling, *As Seen on TV: The Visual Culture of Everyday Life in the 1950s* (Cambridge, MA: Harvard University Press, 1994), 128–163. For examples of other work indebted to the "love affair" paradigm, see Derek Jewell, *Man and Motor: The 20th Century Love Affair* (New York: Walker, 1967); Judith Jackson and Graham Robson, *Man and the Automobile: A Twentieth-Century Love Affair* (New York: McGraw-Hill, 1979); WGBH Television and Turner Home Entertainment, *Driving Passion: America's Love Affair with the Car* (Atlanta: Turner Home Entertainment, 1995), VHS; David K. Wright, *America's 100 Year Love Affair with the Automobile: And the Snap-on Tools That Keep Them Running* (Osceola, WI: Motorbooks International, 1995); Len Frank, *Motor Trend Presents 100 Years of the Automobile in America: 10 Memorable Decades of an American Love Affair,* special collector's ed. (Los Angeles: Peterson Publishing, 1996); W. Lawson Jones, *A Love Affair with One Hundred Cars: And Ultimately with the Ultimate Woman* (Mountain View, CA: Schobert Publishing, 1997).

28. For more on race and discrimination in postwar development, see Yale Rabin, "Expulsive Zoning: The Inequitable Legacy of Euclid," in *Zoning and the American Dream: Promises Still to Keep,* ed. Charles Haar and Jerold Kayden (Washington, DC: American Planning Association Press, 1989), 101–121; Marsha Ritzdorf, "Family Values, Municipal Zoning, and African American Family Life," in *Urban Planning and the African American Community: In the Shadows,* ed. June M. Thomas and Marsha Ritzdorf (Thousand Oaks, CA: Sage Publications, 1997), 75–92; Marsha Ritzdorf, "Locked Out of Paradise: Contemporary Exclusionary Zoning, the Supreme Court, and African Americans, 1970 to the Present," in *Urban Planning and the African American Community,* 43–57. June Manning Thomas's bibliography and research agenda compiled in 1997 is also a fantastic resource for relevant literature on the subject. See "Race, Racism, and Race Relations: Linkage with Urban and Regional Planning Literature" (prepared for the American Sociological Association's Response, White House Request for Race Literature, 1997).

29. Some key works that critically address these aspects of automobility include James J. Flink, "Three Stages of American Automobile Consciousness," *American Quarterly* 24, no. 4 (1972): 451–473; James J. Flink, *The Car Culture* (Cambridge, MA: MIT Press,

1975); James J. Flink, *The Automobile Age* (Cambridge, MA: MIT Press, 1988); Clay McShane, *Down the Asphalt Path: The Automobile and the American City*, Columbia History of Urban Life (New York: Columbia University Press, 1994); Sudhir Chella Rajan, *The Enigma of Automobility: Democratic Politics and Pollution Control* (Pittsburgh, PA: University of Pittsburgh Press, 1996); Rudi Volti, "A Century of Automobility," *Technology and Culture* 37, no. 4 (1996): 663–685; Mimi Sheller and John Urry, "The City and the Car," *International Journal of Urban and Regional Research* 24, no. 4 (2000): 737–757; Nigel Taylor, "The Aesthetic Experience of Traffic in the Modern City," *Urban Studies* 40, no. 8 (2003): 1609–1625; Sarah S. Jain, "'Dangerous Instrumentality': The Bystander as Subject in Automobility," *Cultural Anthropology* 19, no. 1 (2004): 61–94; John Urry, "The 'System' of Automobility," *Theory Culture Society* 21, nos. 4–5 (2004): 25–39. Notable collections include Daniel Miller, ed., *Car Cultures* (Oxford: Berg, 2001); Peter Wollen and Joe Kerr, eds., *Autopia: Cars and Culture* (London: Reaktion Books, 2002); Mike Featherstone, ed., "Special Issue: Automobilities," *Theory, Culture and Society* 21, nos. 4–5 (2004); Steffen Böhm et al., eds., *Against Automobility* (Malden, MA: Blackwell/Sociological Review, 2006).

30. "Automobility," *New York Times*, March 3, 1922. In this same article the author similarly foreshadows the problem of auto-related energy consumption: "One of the serious problems seems now to be to find the means of continued automobility after our known stores of power have been exhausted. A day of the Mining and Metallurgical Engineers' meeting held here [New York City] last week was devoted to the discussion of this hemisphere's regional supplies of oil."

31. Steffen Böhm et al., "Introduction: Impossibilities of Automobilities," in *Against Automobility*, ed. Steffen Böhm et al. (Malden, MA: Blackwell/Sociological Review, 2006), 5.

32. For specific work on the connections between driving and the construction of nationalism and national identity, see Tim Edensor, "Automobility and National Identity: Representation, Geography and Driving Practice," *Theory Culture Society* 21, nos. 4–5 (2004): 101–120; Rudy Koshar, "Cars and Nations: Anglo-German Perspectives on Automobility between the World Wars," *Theory, Culture and Society* 21, nos. 4–5 (2004): 121–144; Sudhir Chella Rajan, "Automobility and the Liberal Disposition," in *Against Automobility*, ed. Steffen Böhm et al. (Malden, MA: Blackwell/Sociological Review, 2006), 113–129; Cotten Seiler, "'So That We as a Race Might Have Something Authentic to Travel By': African American Automobility and Cold-War Liberalism," *American Quarterly* 58, no. 4 (2006): 1091–1117; Jeremy Packer, *Mobility without Mayhem: Safety, Cars, and Citizenship* (Durham, NC: Duke University Press, 2008); Cotten Seiler, *Republic of Drivers: A Cultural History of Automobility in America* (Chicago: University of Chicago Press, 2008).

33. Benedict R. Anderson, *Imagined Communities: Reflections on the Origin and Spread of Nationalism* (London: Verso, 1991), 35.

34. Ibid.

35. U.S. Census Bureau, "American Community Survey: Means of Transportation to Work by Selected Characteristics" (Washington, DC: U.S. Department of Commerce, 2006).

36. Seiler, "So That We as a Race Might Have Something Authentic to Travel By," 1092.

37. Anderson, *Imagined Communities*, 7; U.S. Department of Transportation, "National Transportation Statistics" (Washington, DC, 2006).

38. William F. Buckley Jr., "Illegalizing Illegals," *National Review*, November 3, 2007.

39. For example, see David W. Crouse, "The Real Costs of the Automobile: A Report on Recent Research," *Bulletin of Science, Technology and Society* 20, no. 5 (2000): 366–378; Victoria Transport Policy Institute, "Transportation Cost and Benefit Analysis: Techniques, Estimates and Implications [Second Edition]," ed. Todd Litman (Vancouver, BC, 2009); Katharine T. Alvord, *Divorce Your Car! Ending the Love Affair with the Automobile* (Gabriola Island, BC: New Society Publishers, 2000); Rajesh Subramaniam, National Center for Statistics and Analysis, and National Highway Traffic Safety Administration, "Motor Vehicle Traffic Crashes as a Leading Cause of Death in the United States, 2003" (Washington, DC: Department of Transportation, 2006); National Highway Traffic Safety Administration, "Data Collection Study: Deaths and Injuries Resulting from Certain Non-traffic and Non-crash Events" (Washington, DC: Department of Transportation, 2004); Texas Transportation Institute, "Urban Mobility Report" (Texas A&M University System, 2007).

40. James A. Dunn, *Driving Forces: The Automobile, Its Enemies, and the Politics of Mobility* (Washington, DC: Brookings Institution Press, 1998), 15; John Forester, *Bicycle Transportation: A Handbook for Cycling Transportation Engineers*, 2nd ed. (Cambridge, MA: MIT Press, 1994), 154; Robert Bruegmann, *Sprawl: A Compact History* (Chicago: University of Chicago Press, 2005), 97. Timothy Davis, "Looking down the Road: J. B. Jackson and the American Highway Landscape," in *Everyday America*, ed. Chris Wilson and Paul Erling Groth (Berkeley: University of California Press, 2003), 70.

41. Rob Anderson, "Anti-car Jihad Targets Golden Gate Park," *District 5 Diary*, March 23, 2006, available at http://district5diary.blogspot.com/2006_03_23_archive.html; Rachel DiCarlo, "Hit the Road," *Weekly Standard*, January 25, 2006; Hart Seely, "On Social Highway, It's Prius against Hummer," *The Post-Standard*, August 17, 2008. See Chapter 5 for more on the construction of bicyclists' so-called elitism in the popular press.

42. Louis J. Freeh, "Threat of Terrorism to the United States" (testimony before the U.S. Senate, Committees on Appropriations, Armed Services, and Select Committee on Intelligence, May 10, 2001).

43. Alvord, *Divorce Your Car!: Ending the Love Affair with the Automobile*, 1.

44. Paul Rosen, "Up the Vélorution: Appropriating the Bicycle and the Politics of Technology," in *Appropriating Technology: Vernacular Science and Social Power*, ed. Ron Eglash (Minneapolis: University of Minnesota Press, 2002), 367.

45. Marcia D. Lowe, *The Bicycle: Vehicle for a Small Planet*, Worldwatch Paper (Washington, DC: Worldwatch Institute, 1989).

46. Tanya Einhorn, personal correspondence, January 2, 2007; Anonymous, personal correspondence, February 17, 2006.

47. Chris Bull, personal correspondence, January 21, 2007.

48. Sheldon Brown, personal correspondence, December 16, 2004.

49. Claire Stoscheck, personal correspondence, February 12, 2007.

50. Barbara Moulton, personal correspondence, January 3, 2007.

51. For more thorough explanation of *articulation*, see Stuart Hall, "On Postmodernism

and Articulation," *Journal of Communication Inquiry* 10, no. 2 (1986): 45–60; Jennifer Daryl Slack, "The Theory and Method of Articulation in Cultural Studies," in *Stuart Hall: Critical Dialogues in Cultural Studies,* ed. Stuart Hall, David Morley, and Kuan-Hsing Chen (London: Routledge, 1996), 112–127.

52. This expression is poached from Karl Marx, *The Eighteenth Brumaire of Louis Bonaparte,* translated by Daniel De Leon (New York: Labor News, 1951), 255.

53. Böhm et al., "Introduction: Impossibilities of Automobilities," 4–6.

54. Antonio Gramsci, Quintin Hoare, and Geoffrey Nowell-Smith, *Selections from the Prison Notebooks of Antonio Gramsci* (London: Lawrence and Wishart, 1971), 330–331; Tim Cresswell, *On the Move: Mobility in the Modern Western World* (New York: Routledge, 2006), 109.

55. Lance Armstrong and Sally Jenkins, *It's Not about the Bike: My Journey Back to Life* (New York: Putnam, 2000).

56. Henderson, "Secessionist Automobility: Racism, Anti-urbanism, and the Politics of Automobility in Atlanta, Georgia," 294. Notable exceptions include Kenneth R. Schneider, *Autokind vs. Mankind: An Analysis of Tyranny, a Proposal for Rebellion, a Plan for Reconstruction* (New York: Norton, 1971); George McKay, *Senseless Acts of Beauty: Cultures of Resistance since the Sixties* (London: Verso, 1996), 127–158; Aufheben, "The Politics of Anti-road Struggle and the Struggles of Anti-road Politics: The Case of the No M11 Link Road Campaign," in *DiY Culture: Party and Protest in Nineties Britain,* ed. George McKay (New York: Verso, 1998), 100–128; John Jordan, "The Art of Necessity: The Subversive Imagination of Anti-road Protest and Reclaim the Streets," in *DiY Culture: Party and Protest in Nineties Britain,* 129–151; Peter North, "'Save Our Solsbury!': The Anatomy of an Anti-roads Protest," *Environmental Politics* 7, no. 3 (1998): 1–25; Sandy McCreery, "The Claremont Road Situation," in *The Unknown City: Contesting Architecture and Social Space,* ed. Iain Borden et al. (Cambridge, MA: MIT Press, 2001), 228–245; Ferrell, *Tearing Down the Streets: Adventures in Urban Anarchy* (New York: Palgrave, 2001), 91–148; Stephen Duncombe, "Stepping Off the Sidewalk: Reclaim the Streets/NYC," in *From Act Up to the WTO: Urban Protest and Community Building in the Era of Globalization,* ed. Benjamin Heim Shepard and Ronald Hayduk (London: Verso, 2002), 215–228; Chris Carlsson, ed., *Critical Mass, Bicycling's Defiant Celebration* (Oakland, CA: AK Press, 2002); Rosen, "Up the Vélorution: Appropriating the Bicycle and the Politics of Technology"; Zack Furness, "Biketivism and Technology: Historical Reflections and Appropriations," *Social Epistemology* 19, no. 4 (2005): 401–417; Zack Furness, "'Put the Fun between Your Legs!': The Politics and Counterculture of the Bicycle" (Ph.D. diss., University of Pittsburgh, 2005); Dave Horton, "Environmentalism and the Bicycle," *Environmental Politics* 15, no. 1 (2006): 41–59; Dave Horton, "Social Movements and the Bicycle," 2006, available at http://www.bicycology.org.uk/related_articles/SocialMovementsandtheBicycle.doc; Zack Furness, "Critical Mass, Urban Space and Vélomobility," *Mobilities* 2, no. 2 (2007), 401–417.

57. See Robert D. Bullard and Glenn S. Johnson, *Just Transportation: Dismantling Race and Class Barriers to Mobility* (Gabriola Island, BC: New Society Publishers, 1997); Robert D. Bullard, Glenn S. Johnson, and Angel O. Torres, "The Routes of American Apartheid," *Forum for Applied Research and Public Policy* 15, no. 3 (2000): 66–74; Robert D. Bullard, Glenn S. Johnson, and Angel O. Torres, "Dismantling Transportation

Apartheid: The Quest for Equity," in *Sprawl City*, ed. Robert D. Bullard, Glenn S. Johnson, and Angel O. Torres (Washington, DC: Island Press, 2000), 39–68; Todd Litman, "Evaluating Transportation Equity," *World Transport Policy and Practice* 8, no. 2 (2002): 50–65; Robert D. Bullard, Glenn S. Johnson, and Angel O. Torres, *Highway Robbery: Transportation Racism and New Routes to Equity* (Cambridge, MA: South End Press, 2004). Also see Yale Rabin, "Highways as a Barrier to Equal Access," *Annals of the American Academy of Political and Social Science* 407, no. 1 (1973); Ivan Illich, *Energy and Equity* (New York: Harper and Row, 1974); Elmer W. Johnson, "Mobility, Equity, and the City," *Bulletin of the American Academy of Arts and Sciences* 47, no. 8 (1994): 51–63.

58. Andrew Feenberg, *Questioning Technology* (London: Routledge, 1999), 213; Henri Lefebvre, *The Production of Space* (Oxford, UK: Blackwell, 1991), 154; Cresswell, *On the Move*, 10. My working definitions for *space* and *place* in this book stem from the basic distinction Yi-Fu Tuan outlines in *Space and Place: The Perspective of Experience* (Minneapolis: University of Minnesota Press, 1977), 136: "Space is transformed into place as it acquires definition and meaning."

59. Iain Boal, "'Re-inventing the Wheel,'" in *Cycle History 16: Proceedings of the 16th International Cycling History Conference (Davis, Ca)*, ed. Andrew Ritchie (San Francisco: Cycle Publishing, 2006), 10.

60. Henri Lefebvre, Eleonore Kofman, and Elizabeth Lebas, *Writings on Cities* (Cambridge, MA: Blackwell Publishers, 1996), 63–184. Also see Mark Purcell, "Excavating Lefebvre: The Right to the City and Its Urban Politics of the Inhabitant," *GeoJournal* 58, nos. 2–3 (2002): 99–108; David Harvey, "The Right to the City," *International Journal of Urban and Regional Research* 27, no. 4 (2003): 939–941; Don Mitchell, *The Right to the City: Social Justice and the Fight for Public Space* (New York: Guilford Press, 2003), esp. 17–41.

CHAPTER 2

1. See "The Bicycle," *Scientific American* 75, no. 4 (1896).

2. Bicycles are of particular interest to scholars associated with the social construction of technology (SCOT) paradigm. Wiebe Bijker and Trevor Pinch spearheaded this "sub-field" of Science and Technology Studies (STS) in the 1980s and the main tenets of SCOT have since been widely applied. Key texts include Wiebe E. Bijker, Thomas Parke Hughes, and Trevor J. Pinch, *The Social Construction of Technological Systems: New Directions in the Sociology and History of Technology* (Cambridge, MA: MIT Press, 1987); Wiebe E. Bijker and John Law, *Shaping Technology/Building Society: Studies in Sociotechnical Change*, Inside Technology series (Cambridge, MA: MIT Press, 1992); Wiebe E. Bijker, *Of Bicycles, Bakelites, and Bulbs: Toward a Theory of Sociotechnical Change*, Inside Technology series (Cambridge, MA: MIT Press, 1995). Paul Rosen's innovative work on mountain bikes and the British cycling industry builds upon, and simultaneously critiques the limitations of, the SCOT model. His contributions include "The Social Construction of Mountain Bikes: Technology and Postmodernity in the Cycle Industry," *Social Studies of Science* 23, no. 3 (1993): 479–513; *Framing Production: Technology, Culture, and Change in the British Bicycle Industry*, Inside Technology series (Cambridge, MA: MIT Press, 2002). Also see Paul Shrivastava, "Toward a Socio-technological History of Bicycles," in *Cycle History 13: Proceedings of the 13th International Cycling History Conference (Münster, Germany)*, ed. Andrew Ritchie and Nicholas Clayton (San Francisco: Van der Plas/Cycle

Publishing, 2004), 9–24. Notable critiques of SCOT include Stewart Russell, "The Social Construction of Artefacts: A Response to Pinch and Bijker," *Social Studies of Science* 16, no. 2 (1986): 331–346; Langdon Winner, "Upon Opening the Black Box and Finding It Empty: Social Constructivism and the Philosophy of Technology," *Science, Technology, and Human Values* 18, no. 3 (1993): 362–378; Nick Clayton, "SCOT: Does It Answer?" *Technology and Culture* 43, no. 2 (2002): 351–360.

3. The links between the bicycle era, consumption, and consumer subjectivities are well documented in some of the following: Carla Willard, "Conspicuous Whiteness: Early Brand Advertising," in *Turning the Century: Essays in Media and Cultural Studies,* ed. C. Stabile (Boulder, CO: Westview, 2000), 193–198; Ellen Gruber Garvey, "Reframing the Bicycle: Advertising-Supported Magazines and Scorching Women," *American Quarterly* 47, no. 1 (1995): 66–101; Ross D. Petty, "Peddling the Bicycle and the Development of Mass Marketing," in *Cycle History 5: Proceedings of the 5th International Cycle History Conference (Cambridge, England),* ed. Rob Van der Plas (San Francisco: Cycle Publishing, 1995), 107–116; Glen Norcliffe, *The Ride to Modernity: The Bicycle in Canada, 1869–1900* (Toronto: University of Toronto Press, 2001), 121–148. On mass production in the bicycle industry, see Norcliffe, "Popeism and Fordism: Examining the Roots of Mass Production," *Regional Studies* 31, no. 3 (1997): 267–280; Norcliffe, *The Ride to Modernity,* 89–120; Rosen, *Framing Production;* Bruce Epperson, "Failed Colossus: Strategic Error at the Pope Manufacturing Company, 1878–1900," *Technology and Culture* 41, no. 2 (2000): 300–320.

4. For example, see Phillip Gordon Mackintosh and Glen Norcliffe, "Flâneurie on Bicycles: Acquiescence to Women in Public in the 1890s," *Canadian Geographer* 50, no. 1 (2006): 17–37; Glen Norcliffe, "Associations, Modernity and the Insider-Citizens of a Victorian Highwheel Bicycle Club," *Journal of Historical Sociology* 19, no. 2 (2006): 121–150; Phillip Gordon Mackintosh, "A Bourgeois Geography of Domestic Bicycling: Using Public Space Responsibly in Toronto and Niagara-on-the-Lake, 1890–1900," *Journal of Historical Sociology* 20 (2007): 126–157. Also see David L. Patton, "Aspects of a Historical Geography of Technology: A Study of Cycling 1919–1939," in *Cycle History 5: Proceedings of the 5th International Cycle History Conference (Cambridge, England),* ed. Rob Van der Plas (San Francisco: Cycle Publishing, 1995), 21–28.

5. Patricia Marks, *Bicycles, Bangs, and Bloomers: The New Woman in the Popular Press* (Lexington: University Press of Kentucky, 1990), 184; Steve Jones, R. D. Martin, and David R. Pilbeam, "The Cambridge Encyclopedia of Human Evolution" (Cambridge: Cambridge University Press, 1994), 443.

6. Sidney H. Aronson, "The Sociology of the Bicycle," *Social Forces* 30, no. 1 (1951): 310. Emphasis is my own.

7. Ross Petty, "The Bicycle's Role in the Development of Safety Law " in *Cycle History 4: Proceedings from the 4th International Cycling History Conference (Boston, Mass),* ed. Rob Van der Plas (San Francisco: Cycle Publishing, 1993), 125–132; Ross D. Petty, "The Bicycle as a Communications Medium: A Comparison of Bicycle Use by the U.S. Postal Service and Western Union Telegraph Company," in *Cycle History 16: Proceedings of the 16th International Cycling History Conference (Davis, Ca),* ed. Andrew Ritchie (San Francisco: Cycle Publishing, 2005), 147–159. For more on Western Union and the bicycle, see Gregory John Downey, *Telegraph Messenger Boys: Labor, Technology, and Geography, 1850–1950* (New York: Routledge, 2002).

8. See Norcliffe, "Popeism and Fordism: Examining the Roots of Mass Production"; Norcliffe, *The Ride to Modernity*, 106–108; Martha M. Trescott, "The Bicycle: A Technical Precursor of the Automobile," in *Business and Economic History*, ed. Paul Uselding (Urbana: University of Illinois Press, 1976), 51–75; David A. Hounshell, *From the American System to Mass Production, 1800-1932: The Development of Manufacturing Technology in the United States* (Baltimore: Johns Hopkins University Press, 1984), 189–216.

9. Richard Harmond, "Progress and Flight: An Interpretation of the American Cycle Craze of the 1890s," *Journal of Social History* 5, no. 2 (1971): 251.

10. Norcliffe, *The Ride to Modernity*, 3–39.

11. Ibid., 249.

12. For example, a number of bicycle history books seem to follow a standardized timeline in which the final chapters are specifically devoted to the end of the bicycle era, the rise of the automobile, and the heroic perseverance of cyclists in the twentieth century. See "The Eclipse and Restoration of the Bicycle" in Robert A. Smith, *A Social History of the Bicycle: Its Early Life and Times in America* (New York: American Heritage Press, 1972), 241–252; "Cycling in the Motor Age," in James McGurn, *On Your Bicycle: An Illustrated History of Cycling* (New York: Facts on File Publications, 1987), 162–192; and "Bicycles in the Age of the Automobile," in Pryor Dodge, *The Bicycle* (Paris: Flammarion, 1996), 174–215.

13. Notable exceptions include Ben Fincham, "Bicycle Messengers and the Road to Freedom," *Sociological Review* 54, no. 1 (2006): 208–222; Horton, "Social Movements and the Bicycle."

14. David E. Nye, *Consuming Power: A Social History of American Energies* (Cambridge, MA: MIT Press, 2001), 177.

15. McShane, *Down the Asphalt Path*, 56. Cyclists' collective role in the good roads movement is also noted by Philip P. Mason, "The League of American Wheelmen and the Good Roads Movement" (Ph.D. diss., University of Michigan, 1957); John Bell Rae, *The Road and the Car in American Life* (Cambridge, MA: MIT Press, 1971), 23–31; Peter J. Hugill, "Good Roads and the Automobile in the United States 1880–1929," *Geographical Review* 72, no. 3 (1982): 328.

16. Volti, "A Century of Automobility," 664; Flink, *The Car Culture*, 8. Also see Flink, *The Automobile Age*, 1–14.

17. Maxim quoted in McShane, *Down the Asphalt Path*, 119–120. Also see David V. Herlihy, *Bicycle: The History* (New Haven: Yale University Press, 2004), 299.

18. Flink, *The Car Culture*, 8.

19. Smith, *A Social History of the Bicycle*, 76; Norcliffe, "Associations, Modernity and the Insider-Citizens of a Victorian Highwheel Bicycle Club," 145.

20. Jonathan Sterne, *The Audible Past: Cultural Origins of Sound Reproduction* (Durham, NC: Duke University Press, 2003), 88.

21. Petty, "Peddling the Bicycle and the Development of Mass Marketing," 108.

22. Ibid.; Robert L. Steiner, "Learning from the Past-Brand Advertising and the Great Bicycle Craze of the 1890s" (paper presented at the Annual Conference of the American Academy of Advertising: Advances in Advertising Research and Marketing, 1978), 37.

23. Frank Presbrey, *The History and Development of Advertising* (Garden City, NY: Doubleday, 1929), 413. Quoted in Petty, "Peddling the Bicycle and the Development of Mass Marketing," 108.

24. Norcliffe, *The Ride to Modernity*, 108. For more on Pope's patent hording, see Bruce Epperson, "The Monopoly Machine—the Lallement Patent and the Attempted Monopolization of the American Bicycle Industry, 1880-1886," in *Cycle History 15: Proceedings from the 15th International Cycling History Conference (Vienna, Austria)*, ed. Andrew Ritchie and Nicholas Clayton (San Francisco: Cycle Publishing, 2004), 102-120.

25. Petty makes a similar point in "Peddling the Bicycle and the Development of Mass Marketing," 112.

26. These points are elaborated in Nadine Besse and André Vant, "A New View of Late 19th Century Cycle Publicity Posters," in *Cycle History 5: Proceedings of the 5th International Cycle History Conference (Cambridge, England)*, ed. Rob Van der Plas (San Francisco: Cycle Publishing, 1994), 117-121. James McGurn specifically notes that Colonel Pope's advertising sought to associate bicycle riding with "elegance and respectability," in *On Your Bicycle*, 70.

27. Thomas Frank, for example, argues that the 1960s advertising "revolution" was primarily concerned with the construction of consumer subjectivities but one could make a convincing case that bicycle manufacturers actually pioneered this approach—including some the specific tactics of market segmentation—in the 1890s. See *The Conquest of Cool: Business Culture, Counterculture, and the Rise of Hip Consumerism* (Chicago: University of Chicago Press, 1997), 24. For more on bicycle advertising and market segmentation, see Petty, "Peddling the Bicycle and the Development of Mass Marketing."

28. Norcliffe, *The Ride to Modernity*, 134. For more on the creation of male consumers in this period, see Rob Schorman, *Selling Style: Clothing and Social Change at the Turn of the Century* (Philadelphia: University of Pennsylvania Press, 2003), 18-44.

29. Norcliffe, *The Ride to Modernity*, 147.

30. Ibid., 33.

31. Garvey, "Reframing the Bicycle," 97; Ellen Gruber Garvey, *The Adman in the Parlor: Magazines and the Gendering of Consumer Culture, 1880s to 1910s* (New York: Oxford University Press, 1996), 106-134. For more on the gendered nature of bicycles, see Nicholas Oddy, "Bicycles," in *The Gendered Object*, ed. Pat Kirkham (Manchester, UK: St. Martin's Press, 1996), 60-69; Sally Helvenston Gray and Mihaela C. Peteu, "Women's Cycling Attire: The Interplay of Cycle Design and Women's Cycling Attire in the 1890s: The Inventor's Point of View," in *Cycle History 16: Proceedings of the 16th International Cycling History Conference (Davis, Ca)*, ed. Andrew Ritchie (San Francisco: Cycle Publishing, 2006), 85-97.

32. Dodge, *The Bicycle*, 72-72. Andrew Ritchie discusses women's use of tricycles in *King of the Road: An Illustrated History of Cycling* (London: Wildwood House, 1975), 151-155.

33. Frances Elizabeth Willard and Carol O'Hare, *How I Learned to Ride the Bicycle: Reflections of an Influential 19th Century Woman* (Sunnyvale, CA: Fair Oaks Publishing, 1991), 90.

34. Quoted in Smith, *A Social History of the Bicycle*, 75. Smith also details a list of such ludicrously diagnosed bike-related health conditions as "bicycle wrists," "bicycle twitch," "bicycle hands," "bicycler's heart," and my personal favorite, "bicycle face" (67-69).

35. Clay McShane notes that the "old fashioned moralists developed many of the fears that they later applied to women motorists" *Down the Asphalt Path,* 55.

36. See Patricia Marks's discussion of bicycling, clothing, and the "new woman" in Marks, *Bicycles, Bangs, and Bloomers: The New Woman in the Popular Press,* 174–203.

37. McGurn, *On Your Bicycle,* 101.

38. Frances E. Willard, "Address to Women's National Council" (paper presented at the Woman's National Council of the United States, First Triennial Meeting, February 22–25, 1891, Albaugh's Opera House, Washington, DC).

39. Lisa Strange and Robert Brown, "The Bicycle, Women's Rights, and Elizabeth Cady Stanton," *Women's Studies* 31 (2002): 616. Norcliffe and Mackintosh specifically refer to the role that women cyclists played in the "domestication of urban space" in "Flâneurie on Bicycles: Acquiescence to Women in Public in the 1890s." Elsewhere, Mackintosh argues that women in Canada advocated a feminized version of cycling that challenged the masculine norms of modernity and the public sphere. He writes: "through the bicycle, women could use their moral instincts to learn to be responsibly modern." Phillip Gordon Mackintosh, "'Wheel within a Wheel': Frances Willard and the Feminisation of the Bicycle," in *Cycle History 9: Proceedings from the 9th International Cycling History Conference (Ottawa, Canada),* ed. Glen Norcliffe and Rob Van der Plas (San Francisco: Cycle Publishing, 1999), 26. Quoted in Norcliffe, *The Ride to Modernity: The Bicycle in Canada, 1869–1900,* 193. While I disagree with Mackintosh's insinuation that women have an implicit set of moral instincts that supersede the cultural context(s) in which they live, his point is particularly interesting in that it positions the act of cycling as a pedagogical practice, which is to say that bicycling is enrolled in the project of disciplining/training people to become modern, or to literally embody modernity.

40. Willard and O'Hare, *How I Learned to Ride the Bicycle,* 32.

41. Strange and Brown, "The Bicycle, Women's Rights, and Elizabeth Cady Stanton," 621. For poignant critiques of the racism in the women's suffrage movement, and of Stanton in particular, see Angela Y. Davis, *Women, Race, and Class,* 1st ed. (New York: Random House, 1981), 70–86; Philip N. Cohen, "Nationalism and Suffrage: Gender Struggle in Nation-Building America," *Signs* 21, no. 3 (1996): 707–727.

42. According to Strange and Brown, Stanton's treatise on religion, *The Women's Bible,* ignited intense protests from the church and apparently proved so controversial that "many of [her] strongest supporters, including the National American Women Suffrage Association condemned it as heretical" "The Bicycle, Women's Rights, and Elizabeth Cady Stanton," 620. Roberta J. Park also comments on Stanton's controversial, anti-religious perspective in "'All the Freedom of the Boy': Elizabeth Cady Stanton, Nineteenth-Century Architect of Women's Rights," *International Journal of the History of Sport* 18, no. 1 (2001): 22.

43. Strange and Brown, "The Bicycle, Women's Rights, and Elizabeth Cady Stanton," 621.

44. For example, see Jacquie Phelan, "Liberation Noted from an Old Crank," *Whole Earth Review,* no. 86 (1995), 56–57; Ethan Clark and Shelley Lynn Jackson, *The Chainbreaker Bike Book* (Bloomington, IN: Microcosm Publishing, 2008); Greta Snider, *Mudflap* (San Francisco; self-published zine); Gear Up! *Dames on Frames,* nos. 1–3 (Minneapolis: self-published zine). While recent feminist support for bicycling has fortunately transcended Stanton and Anthony's racist thinking, there are virtually no feminist cyclists (women or men) who offer a critique of their views on race, much less a substan-

tive reflection on how white privilege afforded first-wave feminists the opportunity to enjoy public mobility through the bicycle. Consequently, the current circulation of pro-bicycle quotes from Anthony, Willard, and Stanton (in bike advocacy literature, bicycling Web sites, and so on) constructs an impartial narrative of bicycle liberation in which the realities of race and class that inform(ed) feminist mobility are virtually erased.

45. C. Willard, "Conspicuous Whiteness," 195.

46. Garvey, "Reframing the Bicycle," 72.

47. Ibid. On page 82, Garvey explains the shift from sales-based profit to advertising-based profit in magazine publishing. Ross Petty also discusses this issue in his analysis of bicycle marketing in "Peddling the Bicycle and the Development of Mass Marketing," 108.

48. Garvey, "Reframing the Bicycle," 66. Medical arguments for and against women's cycling are widespread in modern cycling histories as well as articles from the period. The following is one of many examples: "There is no physiological reason why women who are well and strong should not ride the bicycle. All those physicians who say otherwise are contradicted by the wisest physicians on both sides of the Atlantic. Both the *British Medical Weekly* and the *Lancet* have argued at great length, that if there be any physiological reason why either sex should not ride the bicycle, it is not the case with women." From "The Psychological and Hygienic Influence of the Bicycle," *The Chautauquan: A Weekly News Magazine* 33, no. 2 (1901).

49. Mona Domosh and Joni Seager, *Putting Women in Place: Feminist Geographers Make Sense of the World* (New York: Guilford Press, 2001), 125.

50. Garvey, "Reframing the Bicycle," 85.

51. E. Michele Ramsey, "Driven from the Public Sphere: The Conflation of Women's Liberation and Driving in Advertising from 1910 to 1920," *Women's Studies in Communication* 29, no. 1 (2006): 10.

52. George Burton Hotchkiss, *Milestones of Marketing: A Brief History of the Evolution of Market Distribution* (New York: Macmillan, 1938), 211. Quoted in Petty, "Peddling the Bicycle and the Development of Mass Marketing," 109.

53. Anne-Katrin Ebert, "Cycling towards the Nation: The Use of the Bicycle in Germany and the Netherlands, 1880–1940," *European Review of History* 11, no. 3 (2004): 349.

54. Norcliffe, *The Ride to Modernity,* 108.

55. Jeremy Packer, "Mobility without Mayhem: Disciplining Mobile America through Safety" (Ph.D. diss., Graduate College of the University of Illinois at Urbana-Champaign, 2001), 23.

56. Jennifer Bonham, "Transport: Disciplining the Body That Travels," *Sociological Review* 54, no. s1 (2006): 64. Also see Jeremy Packer, "Disciplining Mobility," in *Foucault, Cultural Studies, and Governmentality,* ed. Jack Z. Bratich, Jeremy Packer, and Cameron McCarthy (Albany: State University of New York Press, 2003), 135–164.

57. Packer, "Mobility without Mayhem," 12. Specifically, Packer argues that the governing of automobility is predicated on the capacity for drivers to be governed at a distance, through communications networks, discourses, and self-regulation. He elaborates this concept in "Mobile Communications and Governing the Mobile: CBs and Truckers," *The Communication Review* 5, no. 1 (2002): 39–57. Bonham's 2006 article follows a similar trajectory, though her focus is more broadly placed on the production/construction of mobile bodies writ large.

58. Bonham, "Transport," 57.

59. Maurice Thompson, "What We Gain in the Bicycle," *The Chautauquan* 25, no. 5 (1897): 551.

60. Oliver McKee, "The Horse or the Motor," *Lippincott's Monthly Magazine* (1896): 381.

61. Besse and Vant, "A New View of Late 19th Century Cycle Publicity Posters," 119; Arthur Penfield, "The Question of Prejudice," *Outing, a Journal of Recreation* 1, no. 3 (1882). This point is also noted by Petty ("Peddling the Bicycle and the Development of Mass Marketing," 12), who comments on an early Peugeot advertisement that depicts a horse-mounted soldier in conversation with a man on a bicycle: an indication that the two men, and by extension their forms of mobility, are of equal stature. It is also notable that the proper terminology for a bicycle seat is still a *saddle*.

62. "The Horse and the Bicycle," *Scientific American* 73, no. 3 (1895): 43.

63. "Ravages of the Bicycle Craze," *Scientific American* 74, no. 25 (1896): 391. Quoted in Smith, *A Social History of the Bicycle*, 112. Also see Foster Rhea Dulles, *A History of Recreation: America Learns to Play*, 2nd ed. (New York: Appleton-Century-Crofts, 1965), 240; McShane, *Down the Asphalt Path*, 41–56.

64. McShane, *Down the Asphalt Path*, 49, 52.

65. McKee, "The Horse or the Motor," 380. It is notable that this author actually considers the positive effects the bicycle might have on the welfare of horses, not just people. On page 381 he writes, "There is a distinct saving to humanity coincident with this displacement of the horse, which has not occurred to the men of science. They rarely look at the results of science other than as a gain for man. In the case of the horse, all men in whom the very human love of animals is not wanting will rejoice that at last a substitute for the horse has been found as a means of locomotion in cities. The horse is capable of many things, but nature never intended that he should be at the mercy of so cruel a taskmaster as the average street-cab driver."

66. Aaron Wilcher, "Velocitropics: Bodies and Machines in American Bicycling" (master's thesis, Saint Louis University, 2004), 27.

67. M. D. Bellencontre, *Hygiene du Velocipede* (Paris: L. Richard, 1869), 38. Quoted in Christopher S. Thompson, *The Tour de France: A Cultural History* (Berkeley: University of California Press, 2006), 26.

68. Louis Baudry de Saunier, *L'art de Bien Monter la Bicyclette*, 3rd ed. (Paris: 1894), 23. Quoted in Thompson, *The Tour de France: A Cultural History*, 26.

69. McGurn, *On Your Bicycle*, 122. For an astute account of the relationship between bicycle production, technological innovation, and cyborgs, see Rosen, "The Social Construction of Mountain Bikes" and "Diamonds Are Forever: The Socio-technical Shaping of Bicycle Design," in *Cycle History 5: Proceedings of the 5th International Cycle History Conference (Cambridge, England)*, ed. Rob Van der Plas (San Francisco: Cycle Publishing, 1995), 51–58.

70. Besse and Vant, "A New View of Late 19th Century Cycle Publicity Posters," 120.

71. Jim Fitzpatrick, *The Bicycle and the Bush: Man and Machine in Rural Australia* (Melbourne: Oxford University Press, 1980), 47. Quoted in Petty, "Peddling the Bicycle and the Development of Mass Marketing," 113.

72. See Aaron Wilcher, "Prisoners of the Road: American VelociPower in the 1970s,"

in *Cycle History 16: Proceedings of the 16th International Cycling History Conference (Davis, Ca)*, ed. Andrew Ritchie (San Francisco: Cycle Publishing, 2006), 15–29; Wilcher, "Velocitropics: Bodies and Machines in American Bicycling," 51–88.

73. Tim Dant, "The Driver-Car," *Theory, Culture and Society* 21, nos. 4–5 (2004): 61–79; John Urry, "Inhabiting the Car," *Sociological Review* 54, no. s1 (2006): 18.

74. "Psychology, Hygiene, and Morality of the Bicycle, Part I," *Christian Advocate* 73, no. 27 (1898): 1087.

75. Ibid., 1086.

76. H. Ansot, "A Modern Centaur," *Overland Monthly and Out West Magazine* 26, no. 152 (1895): 129.

77. "The Psychological and Hygienic Influence of the Bicycle," 207.

78. Packer, "Mobility without Mayhem," 78.

79. Thompson, "What We Gain in the Bicycle," 551.

80. For examples, see Sir Benjamin Ward Richardson, "What to Avoid in Cycling," *North American Review* 161, no. 465 (1895): 177; "Points for Bicycle Riders," *Scientific American* 74, no. 13 (1896): 202.

81. Thompson, "What We Gain in the Bicycle," 449.

82. The learning curve of bicycling is also mentioned in reference to sewing machines in Ansot, "A Modern Centaur," 128.

83. Garvey, "Reframing the Bicycle," 75.

84. Ibid.

85. Christopher S. Thompson, "Bicycling, Class, and the Politics of Leisure in Belle Epoque France," in *Histories of Leisure*, ed. Rudy Koshar (New York: Berg, 2002), 133.

86. Ebert, "Cycling towards the Nation," 352.

87. Henri Desgranges, "A Frenchman's Views on the Safety Bicycle as It Now Is and Its Probable Future," *Scientific American* 72, no. 2 (1895): 22. Emphasis is original. Sylvester Baxter also claims that a "cool, clear head and steady nerves are absolutely essential for cycling" in "Economic and Social Influences of the Bicycle," *The Arena*, no. 35 (1892): 578–584. Also see "Psychology, Hygiene, and Morality of the Bicycle, Part IV," *Christian Advocate* 73, no. 30 (1898): 1207–1209.

88. See McShane, *Down the Asphalt Path*, 53; Kathryn Grover and Margaret Woodbury, *Fitness in American Culture: Images of Health, Sport, and the Body, 1830–1940. A Symposium Held at the Margaret Woodbury Strong Museum in Spring, 1986* (Amherst: University of Massachusetts Press/Margaret Woodbury Strong Museum, 1989).

89. "The Hygiene of Cycling," *Scientific American* 55, no. 22 (1886): 341; "Psychology, Hygiene, and Morality of the Bicycle, Part I," *Christian Advocate* 73, no. 27 (1898): 1086–1087; "Psychology, Hygiene, and Morality of the Bicycle, Part II," *Christian Advocate* 73, no. 28 (1898), 1127–1130; "Psychology, Hygiene, and Morality of the Bicycle, Part IV"; H. C. Clark, *Hygienic Bicycling* (Delaware City, DE, 1897). Also see Titus Hermon Franklin, "The Clerical Wheel," *Outing, a Journal of Recreation* 1, no. 2 (1882), 101–107.

90. Quoted in Christopher S. Thompson, "The Third Republic on Wheels: A Social, Cultural, and Political History of Bicycling in France from the Nineteenth Century to World War II" (Ph.D. diss., New York University, 1997), 135; Stefano Pivato, "The Bicycle as a Political Symbol: Italy 1885–1955," *International Journal of the History of Sport* 7, no. 2 (1990): 180.

91. Brian Griffin provides a nice overview of "muscular Christianity" in "Cycling and Gender in Victorian Ireland," *Eire Ireland* 41, nos. 1–2 (2006): 220.

92. As Lewis Mumford argues in *Technics and Civilization* (New York: Harcourt Brace and World, 1963), 35–36, the church historically cultivated a hatred for the body that sought to replace the sinful flesh of humans with the extra-moral workings of the machine. This desire does not fully explain the religious and moral overtones of the cycling-as-hygiene narrative, but it speaks directly to types of purification arguments made in favor of bicycling in the 1890s.

93. Interestingly, bicycle manufacturers were the first to develop some of the mass production techniques that would later emerge in Frederick Taylor's labor experimentations. Pope's form of mass production may not have incorporated Taylorist methods per se, but it directly articulated bodily discipline to the bicycle, via production. See Wilcher's account of Taylorism, bicycle production, and bodies in "Velocitropics," 54–59. Also see Norcliffe, "Popeism and Fordism."

94. "For these reasons we may look for a notable increase in the physical and moral health of our race, together with more rational and enjoyable conditions of existence." Baxter, "Economic and Social Influences of the Bicycle," 584.

95. Garvey, "Reframing the Bicycle," 80. Also see Wilcher, "Velocitropics," 68.

96. "The Bicycle," *Scientific American* 75, no. 4 (1896): 69.

97. C. E. Hawley, "The Uses of the Bicycle," *Outing, a Journal of Recreation* 1, no. 1 (1882): 27.

98. Ironically, men in numerous countries each claimed the bicycle's unique role in expressing *their* country's national spirit, as if the bicycle was designed to implicitly enhance one's American-ness, French-ness, Italian-ness, and so on.

99. Hawley, "The Uses of the Bicycle," 25–26. Emphasis is my own.

100. Garvey, "Reframing the Bicycle," 80. Norcliffe also describes this practice among Canadian bicycle retailers, including advertisements that featured explicitly colonial themes. See Norcliffe, *The Ride to Modernity*, 115.

101. Norcliffe, *The Ride to Modernity*, 187.

102. See Norcliffe, "Associations, Modernity and the Insider-Citizens of a Victorian Highwheel Bicycle Club," 132, 136, 143.

103. Ibid., 132. Norcliffe's commentary on Pratt is part of his wider argument that cycling clubs comprised a form of "insider-citizenship." Some female cyclists started their own clubs in this period, but as Wilcher (citing Petty) argues, "the increasing number of women cyclists who formed their own clubs, sporting the new liberating bloomers of the 'New Woman,' still operated under the implicit auspices of a white, middle class 'civilized' moral normativity." See Wilcher, "Velocitropics: Bodies and Machines in American Bicycling"; Ross D. Petty, "Women and the Wheel: The Bicycle's Impact on Women," in *Cycle History 7: Proceedings of the 7th International Cycle History Conference, Buffalo, NY, USA, 4–6 September 1996,* ed. Rob Van der Plas (San Francisco: Van der Plas Publications, 1997), 125.

104. Thompson, "Bicycling, Class, and the Politics of Leisure in Belle Epoque France," 140. For more on bicycles and war, see Martin Caidin and Jay Barbree, *Bicycles in War* (New York: Hawthorn Books, 1974); George Niels Sorensen, *Iron Riders: Story of the 1890s Fort Missoula Buffalo Soldier Bicycle Corps* (Missoula, MT: Pictorial Histories Publishing, 2000).

105. A good example of the nationalism of U.S. cycling clubs is found in an article entitled "Advantages of Joining the League." The author writes: "A man should have enough patriotic pride to lend his name to increase the membership of the L.A.W., so that it will not be second in size to the C.T.C. of England. . . . Why should we take a back seat to England?" *Outing, a Journal of Recreation* 2, no. 4 (1883).

106. See Norcliffe, "Associations, Modernity and the Insider-Citizens of a Victorian Highwheel Bicycle Club." Herlihy notes the LAW's "fierce opposition" to Chinese membership in *Bicycle*, 263.

107. The complete lack of attention paid to Native Americans in cycling histories is appalling, to say the least. Norcliffe, for example, spends a good portion of his insightful book discussing the ways in which the bicycle contributed to the modernization of Canada, but the text is woefully short on any substantive analysis of the impacts of modernity on the First Nations, who unquestionably experienced much less of the subtleties than he wants to ascribe to the "locally embedded" processes associated with modernity and modernization. Indeed, any critical interrogation of the treatment of Aboriginal peoples in Canada or any other territory (formerly or presently) occupied by a colonial power reveals that, despite variations in degree (not variations in kind), the construction of modern society in North America was premised on a fairly standardized set of assumptions and practices that were/are deployed in every colonial project initiated by Euro-American colonial powers and white colonists writ large. Most explicit is the widespread use of violence, white supremacist ideology, religious zealotry, material greed, radical ethnocentrism (Orientalism is one example), and brash ignorance as a means to terrorize, subdue, and oppress indigenous populations. In short, the ethos of being "modern" is precisely that which empowers colonists and colonialists to justify their actions and to ultimately define themselves in brutal contradistinction from the ostensibly primitive "others" whose lands they invade and whose way(s) of life they utterly decimate. To date, bicycle and cycling historians writ large have yet to offer any concrete analysis (cultural, political, or otherwise) of this process, or even the most basic relationships between early cycling practices and the Indigenous peoples of the Americas. In contrast, an interesting intervention along these lines was initiated by a group of Indigenous artists (or of Aboriginal descent) who contributed their work to a Native-themed exhibition on bike culture that ran from May 3 through June 9, 2007, at the Art Gallery of Southwestern Manitoba. Presenters included America Meredith (author of the bike messenger zine *Voice of Da*), Dylan Miner, Tania Willard, Terri Saul, and Yatika Fields. As part of the exhibition, the museum published a booklet that features essays from show curator Jenny Western and artist/professor/activist Dylan Miner, whose piece entitled "Red (Pedal) Power: Natives, Bikes, and Anti-colonial Art" is perhaps the first article (albeit a short one) to specifically and critically engage with the intersections of European colonization, Native American culture, bicycles. and modernity. See Jenny Western, "Do Not Park Bicycles!" in *"Do Not Park Bicycles!"* ed. Jenny Western (Brandon, MB: Art Gallery of Southwestern Manitoba, 2007); Dylan Miner, "Red (Pedal) Power: Native, Bikes, and Anti-colonial Art," in *"Do Not Park Bicycles!"* ed. Jenny Western (Brandon, MB: Art Gallery of Southwestern Manitoba, 2007).

108. Herhily notes the way in which racist cartoons were used to admonish African American cyclists in publications like *Puck, The Judge,* and *Life*. Ritchie also offers a

critique of this practice and specifically discusses the racism against African American cyclists, and in particular cycling champion Major Taylor, in both cycling publications and the popular press. See Herlihy, *Bicycle,* 263; Andrew Ritchie, *Major Taylor: The Extraordinary Career of a Champion Bicycle Racer* (San Francisco: Bicycle Books, 1988), particularly 29–42, 85–110; Andrew Ritchie, "The League of American Wheelmen, Major Taylor and the 'Color Question' in the United States in the 1890s," *Culture, Sport, Society* 6, nos. 2–3 (2003): 12–42.

109. Ritchie, "The League of American Wheelmen, Major Taylor and the 'Color Question' in the United States in the 1890s," 24.

110. Ibid., 28.

111. Lynne Tolman, "League rights a wrong, lifting forgotten racial ban," *Telegram and Gazette,* May 30, 1999. Tolman's article and the full text to the resolution are accessible through the Major Taylor Association's Web site, available at http://www.major-taylorassociation.org.

112. Cresswell, *On the Move,* 183.

113. Harmond, "Progress and Flight: An Interpretation of the American Cycle Craze of the 1890s," 240.

114. "Ravages of the Bicycle Craze," 112. Quoted in Smith, *A Social History of the Bicycle,* 112.

115. Georges Montorgueil, *La Parisienne* (Paris: Librairie L. Conquet, 1897), 186. Quoted in Ruth E. Iskin, "The Pan-European Flâneuse in Fin-de-Siècle Posters: Advertising Modern Women in the City," *Nineteenth-Century Contexts* 25, no. 4 (2003): 349.

116. Wolfgang Schivelbusch, *The Railway Journey: The Industrialization of Time and Space in the 19th Century* (Berkeley: University of California Press, 1986), 72.

117. Ibid., 110.

118. Horton, "Social Movements and the Bicycle."

119. Baxter, "Economic and Social Influences of the Bicycle," 583. Emphasis is my own.

120. Ritchie, *King of the Road,* 113; Dodge, *The Bicycle,* 76.

121. *Boneshaker* 7, no. 66 (1972). Quoted in Dodge, *The Bicycle,* 76.

122. *Brooklyn Life,* September 14, 1895. Quoted in Herlihy, *Bicycle,* 275.

123. Bijker, *Of Bicycles, Bakelites, and Bulbs,* 40.

124. Dodge, *The Bicycle,* 164; David B. Perry, *Bike Cult: The Ultimate Guide to Human-Powered Vehicles* (New York: Four Walls Eight Windows, 1995), 296.

125. Dodge, *The Bicycle,* 164; Ebert, "Cycling towards the Nation," 360.

126. Ebert, "Cycling towards the Nation," 360.

127. Ibid.; Dodge, *The Bicycle,* 164; Perry, *Bike Cult,* 296.

128. Dodge, *The Bicycle,* 164.

129. McGurn, *On Your Bicycle,* 94.

130. Carsten Hoefer, "A Short Illustrated History of the Bicycle" (2007), available at http://www.crazyguyonabike.com/doc/1889.

131. Dennis Pye, *Fellowship Is Life: The Clarion Cycling Club 1895–1995* (Lancashire, UK: Clarion Publishing, 1995), 66.

132. David Prynn, "The Clarion Clubs, Rambling and the Holiday Associations in Britain since the 1890s," *Journal of Contemporary History* 11, nos. 2–3 (1976): 66.

133. Pye, *Fellowship Is Life,* 16–17.

134. Ibid., 27. "Merrie England" was widely read by socialists in both England and the United States. The specific influence of this work on Eugene Debs and American socialism is outlined in Jason D. Martinek, "The Workingman's Bible: Robert Blatchford Merrie England, Radical Literacy, and Making of Debsian Socialism, 1895–1900," *Journal of the Gilded Age and Progressive Era* 2, no. 3 (2003): 326–346.

135. Pye, *Fellowship Is Life*, 17.

136. Ibid., 36–41.

137. Tom Groom, quoted in ibid., 60. See Thompson, *The Tour de France*; Robert F. Wheeler, "Organized Sport and Organized Labour: The Workers' Sports Movement," *Journal of Contemporary History* 13, no. 2 (1978): 193.

138. Horton, "Social Movements and the Bicycle."

139. Pivato, "The Bicycle as a Political Symbol," 177.

140. Ibid., 179.

141. Ibid., 179–180.

142. Ibid., 180. Socialists in France shared in the Italian socialists' early skepticism over the bourgeois qualities of organized sport, but they were collectively enthusiastic about the workers' sports movement that blossomed throughout Europe in the early twentieth century. According to Christopher Thompson, they drew sharp distinctions between their sporting organization, the Socialist Fédération Sportive et Gymnique du Travail, and the capitalist aims of professional competition. They also championed the working-class racers who emerged in the early years of the Tour de France. He notes that the French Communists similarly decried the bourgeois exploitation of professional cyclists, specifically objecting to what they saw as the dehumanization of cyclists as machines, or worse yet, as beasts. See Thompson, *The Tour de France*, 185–189, 92–94, 205. Also see Wheeler, "Organized Sport and Organized Labour."

143. Horton, "Social Movements and the Bicycle."

144. Zena Steiner, for example, notes that Blatchford—the "barracks socialist"—was a "popular and passionate voice for empire, preparedness and national service." See "Views of War: Britain before the 'Great War'—and After," *International Relations* 17, no. 1 (2003): 20.

145. Eugene V. Debs, *The American Movement*, 1898 (E. V. Debs Internet Archive, available at http://www.marxists.org/archive/debs).

146. Horton, "Social Movements and the Bicycle."

147. Prynn, "The Clarion Clubs, Rambling and the Holiday Associations in Britain since the 1890s," 75.

148. Horton, "Social Movements and the Bicycle"; *Sheffield Guardian*, March 29, 1907, quoted in Prynn, "The Clarion Clubs, Rambling and the Holiday Associations in Britain since the 1890s," 69.

149. Tom Groom, quoted in Pye, *Fellowship Is Life*, 16–17. Emphasis is my own.

150. Richard Harmond comments on the availability of cheap bicycles in the United States during the late 1890s, writing: "people in the most moderate circumstances scrimped and saved to buy bicycles." See Harmond, "Progress and Flight," 249.

151. "Socialist Propaganda Awheel," *New York Times*, April 19, 1901. Another article published in 1895 also provides the address for the Socialist Wheelmen's Club: 64 East Fourth St., New York City. See "Gossip of the Cyclers," *New York Times*, December 22, 1895.

152. McShane, *Down the Asphalt Path,* 118.

153. Ibid.

154. McGurn, *On Your Bicycle,* 95. Emphasis is my own.

155. Herlihy, *Bicycle,* 205.

156. President Bates, "The Political Power of the L.A.W," *Outing, a Journal of Recreation* 2, no. 2 (1883): 98.

157. There are many examples of this language, though an article published in *The Chautauquan* outlines this premise most explicitly: "The necessity for good roads is no new thing. The necessity has grown with the civilization of the world. The primitive savage felt no need to transport more food or other material from place to place than he himself could carry, and therefore he had no need to invent vehicles for purposes of transportation nor to build roads over which vehicles could be easily drawn." Jno Gilmer Speed, "The Common Road as a Social Factor," *The Chautauquan* (February 1893): 547.

158. James W. Carey, *Communication as Culture: Essays on Media and Society* (Boston: Unwin Hyman, 1989), 16. In addition to the virtual annihilation of Native Americans, the enslavement of Africans, the pollution of the environment, and the exploitation of immigrant workers (notably the Chinese and Irish), the establishment of "God's kingdom" also required the enlistment of prison laborers who were tasked with road construction throughout the United States. Robert Smith recalls that road builders "encouraged the growth of one of the country's most infamous institutions: the convict road gang. Unhappily, cyclists stand as one of the earliest groups to advocate the widespread use of convicts as road builders" *A Social History of the Bicycle,* 213.

159. Norcliffe, *The Ride to Modernity,* 35.

160. Baxter, "Economic and Social Influences of the Bicycle," 580.

161. McShane, *Down the Asphalt Path,* 115. For an example of the elitist disposition toward the working classes in the late nineteenth century, see Gustave Le Bon, *The Crowd: A Study of the Popular Mind,* 4th impression ed. (London: T. F. Unwin, 1903).

162. Harmond, "Progress and Flight," 248, 251.

163. Herlihy, *Bicycle,* 264. This is echoed by examples in England and in Europe more broadly. See Ebert, "Cycling towards the Nation," 351; Richard Holt, "The Bicycle, the Bourgeoisie and the Discovery of Rural France, 1880–1914," *International Journal of the History of Sport* 2, no. 2 (1985): 127–139; David Rubinstein, "Cycling in the 1890s." *Victorian Studies* 21, no. 1 (1977): 47–71.

164. "Editors Open Window," *Outing and the Wheelman* 4, no. 5 (1884): 381; W. I. Lincoln Adams, "The Outing Club," *Outing, an Illustrated Monthly Magazine of Recreation* 14, no. 4 (1889): 314.

165. Ebert, "Cycling towards the Nation," 352. Garvey makes a similar point about cyclists' resistance to the "fixed routes" of the train in Garvey, "Reframing the Bicycle," 70. This point is further elaborated in Gary Allan Tobin, "The Bicycle Boom of the 1890's: The Development of Private Transportation and the Birth of the Modern Tourist," *Journal of Popular Culture* 7, no. 4 (1974): 838–849.

166. See Hugill, "Good Roads and the Automobile in the United States 1880–1929."

167. See Schivelbusch, *The Railway Journey,* 52–69.

168. Ibid., 160.

169. Neil Wynn Williams, "Some Thoughts on Landscape," *The Eclectic Magazine of Foreign Literature* 62, no. 6 (1895): 742. Emphasis is my own.

170. "A Photo-Tricycle," *Scientific American* 53, no. 12 (1885): 178. Emphasis is my own.

171. J. Pennell and E. R. Pennell, "Twenty Years of Cycling," *Fortnightly Review* (August 1897): 91. Quoted in Tobin, "The Bicycle Boom of the 1890's," 841.

172. Aaron Wilcher, "Hubs and Escape Routes," *Streetnotes,* 2004, available at http://www.xcp.bfn.org/wilcher1.html.

173. Baxter, "Economic and Social Influences of the Bicycle," 580.

174. In "The Bicycle Boom of the 1890's," Tobin writes: "they wished not only to avoid risks with the natural environment, but with the human environment as well" (843–845).

175. B. Potter Isaac, "The Bicycle Outlook," *Century Illustrated Magazine* 52, no. 5 (1896): 785.

176. See Thomas Stevens, *Around the World on a Bicycle: From San Francisco to Yokohama* (London: Century, 1988).

177. The casual nature of Stevens's disdain for Native Americans is similarly evident in his prose. Upon meeting a snake in the road, he comments, "If 'the only good Indian is a dead one,' surely the same terse remark applies with much greater force to the vicious and deadly rattler," in "Across America on a Bicycle, Part IV: From the Great Plains to the Atlantic," *Outing* 6, no. 4 (1885): 411.

178. Thomas Stevens, *Around the World on a Bicycle,* vol. 2 (Charleston, SC: BiblioBazaar, LLC, 2008), 196.

179. See Norcliffe, *The Ride to Modernity.*

180. Frederick Alderson, *Bicycling: A History* (New York: Praeger, 1972), 104. Emphasis is my own.

181. Gabrielle Barnett, "Drive-by Viewing: Visual Consciousness and Forest Preservation in the Automobile Age," *Technology and Culture* 45, no. 1 (2004): 39.

182. Ibid., 42. Also see Warren James Belasco, *Americans on the Road: From Autocamp to Motel, 1910–1945* (Cambridge, MA: MIT Press, 1979).

183. Barnett, "Drive-by Viewing," 53, 46.

184. Ibid., 41.

185. Norcliffe, *The Ride to Modernity,* 187.

CHAPTER 3

1. Winfried Wolf, *Car Mania: A Critical History of Transport,* 1st Eng. ed. (London: Pluto Press, 1996), 73.

2. Catherine Gudis, *Buyways: Billboards, Automobiles, and the American Landscape,* Cultural Spaces Series (New York: Routledge, 2004), 44. While the benefits of early automobility were unquestionably profound, this experience was obviously much different for whites than it was for African Americans. For example, see Seiler, "So That We as a Race Might Have Something Authentic to Travel By" 1091–1117. For more on the impact of automobiles on rural life in the United States, see Michael L. Berger, *The Devil Wagon in God's Country: The Automobile and Social Change in Rural America, 1893–1929* (Hamden: Archon Books, 1979).

3. Peter Norton records a number of statements to this effect from residents and officials in Chicago, Philadelphia, New York City, and St. Louis. See "Street Rivals:

Jaywalking and the Invention of the Motor Age Street," *Technology and Culture* 48, no. 2 (2007): 338.

4. Ibid., 336–339. Also see McShane, *Down the Asphalt Path,* 115.

5. "Speeder Wants All Street," *Chicago Tribune,* May 6, 1913, 5. Quoted in Norton, "Street Rivals," 337.

6. See McShane, *Down the Asphalt Path,* 134–135.

7. For example, Norton describes how two out of every three police chiefs in the nation agreed that their cities should require automobiles to have mandatory "governors"—the devices built into cars that limit their top speeds. Residents of Cincinnati supported a plan for requiring governors in 1923 and automobile clubs staged a massive media campaign to fight and ultimately defeat the ordinance. "Street Rivals," 339.

8. Ibid., 342.

9. Charles Komanoff, "Bicycling," in *Encyclopedia of Energy,* ed. Cutler J. Cleveland and Robert U. Ayres (Amsterdam: Elsevier Academic Press, 2004), 143.

10. See Bruce Epperson, "Failed Colossus."

11. Ross Petty discusses the role of bicycles as U.S. Postal Service delivery vehicles, but he says the details of this relationship are sketchy after the turn of the century. See "The Bicycle as a Communications Medium."

12. Downey, *Telegraph Messenger Boys,* 76.

13. For more on the 1939 World's Fair, see David E. Nye, *American Technological Sublime* (Cambridge, MA: MIT Press, 1994), 199–224.

14. Ibid.

15. The close timing of these events was brought to my attention in Cliff Ellis, "Lewis Mumford and Norman Bel Geddes: The Highway, the City and the Future," *Planning Perspectives* 20 (2005): 60. Also see "Toll Roads and Free Roads" (U.S. Bureau of Public Roads, 1939); "Interregional Highways" (U.S. Interregional Highway Committee, 1944).

16. Norman Bel Geddes, *Magic Motorways* (New York: Random House, 1940), 237. Also see Ellis, "Lewis Mumford and Norman Bel Geddes," 58.

17. As Kenneth T. Jackson points out in *Crabgrass Frontier,* the panel that Eisenhower assembled to take stock of the country's highway requirements was chaired by Lucius D. Clay, a board member of General Motors (249). For a classic critique of postwar urban planning, see Jane Jacobs, *The Death and Life of Great American Cities* (New York: Random House, 1961). For a detailed and critical engagement with Robert Moses's life and works, see Robert A. Caro, *The Power Broker: Robert Moses and the Fall of New York* (New York: Vintage Books, 1975).

18. The financial model for state-federal collaboration on highway projects began with the Federal-Aid Road Act in 1916 and was further solidified with the passage of the Federal Highway Act of 1921. For more on the development of the U.S. highway system, see Bruce Edsall Seely, *Building the American Highway System: Engineers as Policy Makers,* Technology and Urban Growth (Philadelphia: Temple University Press, 1987). For more on Daniel Burnham's highway plans, see Carl S. Smith, *The Plan of Chicago: Daniel Burnham and the Remaking of the American City* (Chicago: University of Chicago Press, 2006), 133–139.

19. Dwight D. Eisenhower, *At Ease: Stories I Tell to Friends,* 1st ed. (Garden City, NY: Doubleday, 1967), 166–167. Emphasis is my own.

20. Ebert, "Cycling towards the Nation," 361.

21. See William H. Rollins, "Whose Landscape? Technology, Fascism, and Environmentalism on the National Socialist Autobahn," *Annals of the Association of American Geographers* 85, no. 3 (1995): 494–520.

22. Ebert, "Cycling towards the Nation," 361. The use of forced labor (slavery) in automobile factories was extensive under the Nazi regime and facilitated by industry luminaries, including Ferdinand Porsche (Porsche and Volkswagen), Karl Benz and Gottlieb Daimler (Mercedes-Benz), Henry Ford (Ford), and the proprietors of several major automobile corporations (and/or their subsidiaries) including General Motors and Büssing. Unsurprisingly, these histories are often downplayed by apologetic automotive enthusiasts in the United States. For example, Prescott Kelly—the executive vice president of the Porsche Club of America and a Porsche historian—writes of Ferdinand Porsche: "The old Professor [he had an honorary degree, mind you] was simply politically naive; he was consumed with engineering, and it's obvious that he did not mix engineering with morality. If there was a sponsor for an engineering project, be it a race car or a tank, he wanted to design and build the best there ever was." In "The Automotive Century: Most Influential People (Ferdinand Porsche)," *Society of Automotive Historians,* available at http://www.autohistory.org/feature_6.html. For a more accurate assessment of forced auto labor under the Nazis, see Hans Mommsen and Manfred Griege, *Das Volkswagenwerk Und Seine Arbeiter Im Dritten Reich* (Düsseldorf: ECON Verlag, 1996); Neil Gregor, *Daimler-Benz in the Third Reich* (New Haven, CT: Yale University Press, 1998); Reinhold Billstein, Karola Fings, Anita Kugler, and Nicholas Levis, eds., *Working for the Enemy: Ford, General Motors, and Forced Labor in Germany during the Second World War* (New York: Berghahn Books, 2000); Ken Silverstein, "Ford and the Führer," *The Nation,* January 6, 2000; Karl Liedke, "Destruction through Work: Lodz Jews in the Büssing Truck Factory in Braunschweig, 1944–1945," *Yad Vashem Studies* 30 (2002): 153–187.

23. Norman Bel Geddes speaks directly to the role of the highway system in national defense in *Magic Motorways,* 295–297.

24. Henry Ford, *My Life and Work* (Garden City, NY: Garden City Publishing, 1922), 73.

25. It was not until the National Mass Transportation Assistance Act of 1974 that transit-operating funds were also included in federal funding. For more on the Housing Act of 1961, see Edward Weiner, *Urban Transportation Planning in the United States: An Historical Overview,* rev. and exp. ed. (Westport, CT: Praeger, 1999), 30.

26. Bill Wilkinson and Bob Chauncey, "Are We There Yet? Assessing the Performance of State Departments of Transportation on Accommodating Bicycles and Pedestrians" (National Center for Bicycling and Walking, 2003), 12. While the 1973 act authorized $40 million per year for bicycle and pedestrian projects ($2 million per state max), there were only 20 states that actually used these funds for their intended purpose between 1973 and 1991, totaling just $41 million in 18 years. See William A. Lipford and Glennon J. Harrison, "Bicycle and Pedestrian Transportation Policies," *Congressional Research Services Reports* (Washington, DC: National Council for Science and the Environment, 2000).

27. I am thinking specifically of the U.S.- and British-backed coup d'état against Iranian Prime Minister Mohammad Mosaddeq on August 19, 1953. See Mary Ann Heiss, *Empire and Nationhood: The United States, Great Britain, and Iranian Oil, 1950–1954*

(New York: Columbia University Press, 1997); Donald Wilber, "Overthrow of Premier Mossadeq of Iran, November 1952–August 1953," in *CIA Clandestine Service History* (Central Intelligence Agency, 1954); Malcolm Bryne, "Electronic Briefing Book No. 28: The Secret Cia History of the Iran Coup, 1953," *National Security Archive,* available at http://www.gwu.edu/~nsarchiv/NSAEBB/NSAEBB28; James Risen, "Secrets of History: The C.I.A. in Iran—a Special Report," *New York Times,* April 16, 2000.

28. George Gallup, "54% of Owners Don't Think Autos Vital, Gallup Finds in Survey on Tire Rationing," *New York Times,* January 23, 1942; "Bicycle Problem," *New York Times,* May 6, 1948. It is worth noting that bicycle use was already on the rise by 1935; see E. L. Yordan, "Bicycles Roll Back to Favor," *New York Times,* October 13, 1935.

29. Pucher and Buehler note that bicycling accounted for 15 percent of all trips made in the United Kingdom in 1950. See "Making Cycling Irresistible," 496. Also see McGurn, *On Your Bicycle* and Rosen, *Framing Production.*

30. Lewis Mumford's sentiments on urban planning and transportation are best put in the following texts: *The City in History: Its Origins, Its Transformations, and Its Prospects,* 1st ed. (New York: Harcourt, 1961); *The Urban Prospect* (London: Secker and Warburg, 1968); *The Highway and the City* (Westport, CT: Greenwood Press, 1981).

31. Lewis Mumford, quoted in the segment "The City: Cars or People?" from *The City—Heaven and Hell* (National Film Board of Canada, 1963), Film. Emphasis is my own.

32. Jacobs, *The Death and Life of Great American Cities,* 7.

33. Guy Debord, "Situationist Theses on Traffic," in *Situationist International Anthology,* ed. Ken Knabb (Berkeley, CA: Bureau of Public Secrets, 1981), 57 (originally published in *Internationale Situationniste,* no. 3 [December 1959]).

34. Guy Debord, *The Society of the Spectacle,* trans. Fredy Perlman and John Supak (Detroit: Black and Red, 1977).

35. Pierre Canjuers and Guy Debord, "Preliminaries toward Defining a Unitary Revolutionary Program," in *Situationist Anthology,* ed. Ken Knabb (Berkeley: Bureau of Public Secrets, 1981), 5 (originally published in July 1960).

36. Debord, "Situationist Theses on Traffic," 57.

37. Ibid., 58.

38. Sadie Plant, *The Most Radical Gesture: The Situationist International in a Postmodern Age* (London: Routledge, 1992), 91.

39. The Dutch Provos were not affiliated with the Provisional Irish Republican Army, also known as the IRA, or the Provos. Indeed, Teun Voeten notes that the term *provo* was actually coined by Dutch sociologist Buikhuizen in his description of *nozems,* the first subculture of Dutch teens not unlike the teddy boys in the United Kingdom. Voeten describes nozems as a mixture of Mods and 1950s juvenile delinquents who were notorious for *provo*king fights with the police. See "Dutch Provos." *High Times* (January 1990): 32–36, 64–66, 73.

40. Voeten describes Grootveld as the "original clown prince of popular culture" and recalls that he was an outspoken anti-capitalist who ranted about the "despicable plastic people" and the brainwashing of "addicted consumers" before large crowds of counter-cultural youth. See "Dutch Provos."

41. Richard Kempton, *Provo: Amsterdam's Anarchist Revolt* (New York: Autonomedia, 2007), 39.

42. Quoted in Rudolf De Jong, *Provos and Kabouters* (Buffalo, NY: Friends of Malatesta), 11–12. In eds. David E. Apter and James Joll, *Anarchism Today*, (London: Macmillan, 1971), 165–168.

43. Surprisingly, the Provo received 13,000 votes and one seat in the municipal elections in Amsterdam following its disruption of the royal wedding of Princess Beatrix (Netherlands) and Claus von Amsberg, (Germany). Provos infiltrated and subsequently stink bombed the wedding in protest of von Amsberg's previous membership in several Nazi youth organizations as well as the Nazi Wehrmact. See Kempton, *Provo*, 31–38.

44. Voeten, "Dutch Provos."

45. Voeten also makes note of the White Chicken Plan, organized by a Provo subcommittee called Friends of the Police: "after the police began responding to Provo demonstrations with increased violence the Provos attempted to alter the image of the police, who were known as 'blue chickens.' The new white chickens would be disarmed, ride around on white bicycles, and distribute first aid, fried chicken, and free contraceptives." Ibid.

46. Luud Schimmelpenninck, "The White Bicycle Plan," *Delta* 10, no. 3 (1967). Joep Huffener, the cycling officer for the Department of Infrastructure, Traffic, and Transport in Amsterdam, claims that the idea for a public bicycle program was first proposed by H. Brandt Corstius in the Amsterdam student publication *Propria Cures*. In 1958, Corstius wrote, "In view of people's borrowing habits and the considerable interest in bicycle ownership, I make the following suggestion. Why not nationalize bicycle ownership for the common good? This could be accomplished by a simple Act of Parliament: 'It shall be forbidden to have in one's possession a bicycle or to make said bicycle unavailable for the use of others.' Everyone who needs a bicycle simply takes one, rides it to his or her destination, and leaves it there. They need have no concerns about return, theft, parking, storage, maintenance or whatever. The State will undertake repairs and ensure that the 'fleet' is kept up to strength. The police force can be halved immediately. It will mean an end to all the world's troubles, once the bicycle is public property to the same extent as the road itself." See Joep Huffener, "Bikes on Dikes: A Dutch Plan for (Almost) Free Wheeling" (Amsterdam: Department of Infrastructure, Traffic and Transport of the City of Amsterdam, 2000), 1.

47. Provo, "Provo's Fietsenplan," in *BAMN (By Any Means Necessary): Outlaw Manifestos and Ephemera, 1965-70*, ed. Peter Stansill and David Zane Mairowitz (Harmondsworth, UK: Penguin, 1971): 26–27 (originally published in *Provokatie*, no. 5 [1965]).

48. Raul Guttierez, "The White Bicycle Plan or Why I Love the Dutch," *Mexican Pictures*, 2007, available at http://www.mexicanpictures.com/headingeast/2007/04/the-white-bicycle-plan.html.

49. Ebert, "Cycling towards the Nation," 349.

50. Ibid., 352.

51. Ibid., 356.

52. Roelof Wittink, "Planning for Cycling Supports Road Safety," in *Sustainable Transport: Planning for Walking and Cycling in Urban Environments*, ed. Rodney Tolley (Cambridge, UK: Woodhead, 2003), 175.

53. Dara Colwell, "Riding to the Rescue," *Village Voice*, August 29, 2005.

54. Kristin Ross and Henri Lefebvre, "Lefebvre on the Situationists: An Interview," *October* 79 (1997): 71.

55. Constant Nieuwenhuys, "Nieuw Urbanisme," translated as "New Urbanism," in *BAMN*, 2–6 (originally published in *Provokatie*, no. 9 [1966]).

56. Situationist International with students at the University of Strasbourg, "On the Poverty of Student Life," in *Situationist International Anthology*, ed. Ken Knabb (Berkeley, CA: Bureau of Public Secrets, 1981), 328 (originally published in Paris in 1966). Emphasis is my own. In the same essay, the SI lambasts the Provo's conceptualization of the *provotariat* as a "politico-artistic salad knocked up from the leftovers of a feast they had never known."

57. Maintenance issues and high rates of theft caused many of these programs to fail, but public-use bicycle programs have proliferated in recent years, including a number of successful models that incorporate either a refundable user fee or a cheap annual membership fee as a way to ensure the safe return of borrowed bicycles.

58. See Paul DeMaio, "Smart Bikes: Public Transportation for the 21st Century," *Transportation Quarterly* 57, no. 1 (2003): 9–11; Robert B. Noland and Muhammad M. Ishaque, "Smart Bicycles in an Urban Area: Evaluation of a Pilot Scheme in London," *Journal of Public Transportation* 9, no. 5 (2006): 71–96. Examples of coverage in the popular press include Walker Dalton, "In This Case, It's O.K. to Take a Bike That's Not Yours," *New York Times*, July 10, 2007.

59. Plant, *The Most Radical Gesture*, 93.

60. For a different take on the embodied environmental politics of cyclists, see Horton, "Environmentalism and the Bicycle," 42, 47.

61. Henri Lefebvre, *Everyday Life in the Modern World* (New York: Harper and Row, 1971), 100–101.

62. David Inglis, "Auto Couture: Thinking the Car in Post-war France," *Theory Culture Society* 21, nos. 4–5 (2004): 201.

63. David Pinder, *Visions of the City: Utopianism, Power, and Politics in Twentieth-Century Urbanism* (New York: Routledge, 2005), 137.

64. Ibid.

65. Ibid.

66. André Gorz, "The Social Ideology of the Motorcar," *Le Sauvage* (September–October 1973).

67. Several years prior, activists in the United States facilitated the passage of the Motor Vehicle Air Pollution Act of 1965. For more on the relationship(s) between air pollution and environmentalism, see Charles O. Jones, "Air Pollution and Contemporary Environmental Politics," *Growth and Change* 4, no. 3 (2006): 22–27.

68. See Frank Zahour, "Bicycle Ecology Group Denied Auto Show Spot," *Chicago Tribune*, January 31, 1971; McKay, *Senseless Acts of Beauty*, 129. Chicago's Bicycle Ecology also attempted to set up an information booth at the Chicago Auto Show in 1971, though their request was (obviously) denied.

69. David Gurin, "Ecotactic: Bicycling to Reclaim the Air," *Village Voice*, October 5, 1972.

70. "Bicyclists, in Protest, Jam Streets of Paris," *New York Times*, April 24, 1972.

71. Quoted in Gurin, "Ecotactic: Bicycling to Reclaim the Air."

72. For more on the recent political activity of Alternative Stad, see Ulf Stahre, "City in Change: Globalization, Local Politics and Urban Movements in Contemporary Stockholm," *International Journal of Urban and Regional Research* 28, no. 1 (2004): 77–80.

73. Gurin, "Ecotactic: Bicycling to Reclaim the Air."

74. In 1964, bicyclists in New York City staged a protest over their inability to cross the city's bridges, and in 1970, Barry Fishman and Harriet Green co-founded a New York City group called Bike for a Better City. See John Devlin, "150 Cycle to Fair in Rules Protest," *New York Times*, May 18, 1964; Calvin Trillin, "U.S. Journal: Manhattan Fun's Over," *The New Yorker*, October 9, 1971.

75. AAA was an obvious pun on the American Automobile Association, which prominently uses the AAA abbreviation. The "New York City Bike Advocacy Timeline," compiled for the *Why I Ride* bicycle art show, claims that Urban Underground was a part of the Movement for a Democratic Society, a "kind of post-graduate Students for a Democratic Society" Elizabeth Stuelke and Carol A. Wood, "NYC Bike Advocacy: A Preliminary Timeline," in *Why I Ride: The Art of Bicycling in New York*, ed. Elizabeth Stuelke and Carol A. Wood (published in conjunction with the "Why I Ride: The Art of Bicycling in New York" art show, New York City, May 3–June 3, 2007), 32. Available at http://www.itrnet.com/satre/whyiride/catalog_WIR_FINAL.pdf.

76. Mary Breasted, "Anti-auto Bike-In: Pied Piper on Wheels," *The Village Voice*, November 9, 1972.

77. Advocates for Highway and Auto Safety, "Motor Vehicle Traffic Fatalities and Fatality Rate: 1899–2003" (Washington, DC, 2004).

78. Paul L. Montgomery, "400 Bicyclists Pedal Demands," *New York Times*, April 8, 1973.

79. Rivvy Neshama, interview with the author, July 25, 2007.

80. Marcy Benstock founded the Clean Air Campaign and famously fought against New York City's "Westway" project—a $2 billion highway and riverfront "redevelopment" plan that sought to fill in 264 acres of the Hudson River to create a 4- to 6-lane highway through the Lower West Side of Manhattan. The Clean Air Campaign was one of the plaintiffs that successfully sued the Army Corps of Engineers in federal court, demanding that they overturn the permits issued for construction. See Albert Amateau, "Westway Vets Remember the River Battles," *Downtown Express*, June 18–24, 2004.

81. Judy Klemesrud, "At a Bike-in down Broadway, It's Ride on' Despite Motorists," *New York Times*, May 20, 1974.

82. Ibid.

83. The Manhattan Commuter Bicycle System Study, published in August 1977, found that bicycle traffic and demand had increased by a multiple of fifteen since 1971. See American Youth Hostels, Transportation Alternatives, and League of American Wheelmen, "Bicycling Programs and Facilities in New York" (New York City, 1977).

84. Perry, *Bike Cult*, 308.

85. Ibid.

86. Ibid.

87. Jeanne Iribarne, Estelle Taylor, and Michael Bloomfield, "Climate Change: A Profile for Community Action" (Victoria, BC: Harmony Foundation of Canada, 2003).

88. Perry, *Bike Cult*, 308.

89. Nate Hendley, "Bike Activism by Bob," *Eye Weekly*, September 30, 1999; Charles McCorkell, personal correspondence, January 18, 2007.

90. Robert Silverman, "Preface of *Deux Roues, Un Avenir*, by Claire Morissette (Montreal: Écosociété, 1994), available at http://www.cam.org/~rsilver/preface.htm.

91. Ibid.

92. In an interview with *Ms.* magazine in 1974, Rivvy Berkman (now Rivvy Neshama) said of bike advocacy, "It's a fight for space." See "Ecology, a Family Affair," *Ms.* (November 1974).

93. In 1973, OPEC initiated an oil embargo against the United States in retaliation for its financial, military, and political support of Israel in the Arab-Israeli War (also known as the Yom Kippur War). OPEC previously initiated an oil embargo against the United States and its allies during the Six-Day War in 1967, though its effects were negligible. For more on the embargo, see M. S. Daoudi and M. S. Dajani, *Economic Diplomacy: Embargo Leverage and World Politics,* Westview Special Studies in International Relations (Boulder, CO: Westview Press, 1985).

94. "Back to the Bike," *New York Times,* July 13, 1974.

95. Notably, these trends also changed the overall focus of bicycle production in the United States. That is to say, in addition to adults purchasing more bicycles in the early 1970s bicycle companies also began to manufacture bikes with this demographic in mind. By 1975, "adult" models accounted for roughly 65 percent of the bicycles produced in the United States, up from 12 percent in 1969. See "Coping with the Bicycle Boom," *Washington Post,* May 28, 1973; Stefan Kanfer, "The Full Circle: In Praise of the Bicycle," *Time* April 28, 1975.

96. E. F. Schumacher, *Small Is Beautiful: A Study of Economics as if People Mattered* (New York: Harper and Row, 1973). The term *appropriate* technology is often used interchangeably (though somewhat problematically) with the terms *intermediate, alternative,* or *radical* technology. See Carroll Pursell, "The Rise and Fall of the Appropriate Technology Movement in the United States, 1965–1985," *Technology and Culture* 34, no. 3 (1993): 629–637; Jordan B. Kleiman, "The Appropriate Technology Movement in American Political Culture" (Ph.D. diss., University of Rochester, 2000).

97. Illich, *Energy and Equity,* 24. Here, Illich is paraphrasing José Antonio Viera-Gallo, the longtime Chilean government official who famously stated that socialism will arrive only on a bicycle: *"El socialismo puede llegar sólo en bicicleta."*

98. Ibid., 74–75.

99. Dave Horton describes the dual importance of the bicycle as a symbol of environmentalism as well as the primary mode of everyday mobility for environmentalists in "Green Distinctions: The Performance of Identity among Environmental Activists," *Sociological Review* 51, no. 2 (2003): 63–77, and Horton, "Environmentalism and the Bicycle."

100. Arthur Asa Berger, "The Spyder (Sting-Ray, Screamer) Bike: An American Original," in *Side-Saddle on the Golden Calf: Social Structure and Popular Culture in America,* ed. George H. Lewis (Pacific Palisades, CA: Goodyear, 1972), 88.

101. John Allis, "That Was My Day: An Interview with National Road Champion John Allis," *Cyclenews* 15 (November 1974): 17–19. Quoted in Wilcher, "Prisoners of the Road," 21.

102. McCorkell, personal correspondence; Steven Faust, personal correspondence, January 17, 2007.

103. Neshama, interview.

104. Critiques of the AT movement and other proponents of "alternative technology" are most explicit in Jennifer Daryl Slack, *Communication Technologies and Society* (Norwood, NJ: Ablex Publishing Corporation, 1984), 30–39, and Langdon Winner,

The Whale and the Reactor: A Search for Limits in an Age of High Technology (Chicago: University of Chicago Press, 1986), 61–84. For contrasting perspectives on AT, see Andrew Kirk, "Appropriating Technology: The Whole Earth Catalog and Counterculture Environmental Politics," *Environmental History* 7, no. 4 (2001): 374–394; Kleiman, "The Appropriate Technology Movement in American Political Culture," esp. 296–400 (on the political economy of AT).

105. Jacobs, *The Death and Life of Great American Cities,* 370. Emphasis is my own.

106. McCorkell, personal correspondence.

107. J. B. Corgel and C.F. Floyd, "Towards a New Direction in Bicycle Transportation Policy," *Transportation Quarterly* 33, no. 2 (1979): 297–301. Quoted in Bruce Epperson, "Bicycle Planning: Growing up or Growing Old," *Race, Poverty and the Environment* 6 (Special Issue: Transportation and Social Justice), no. 1 (1995): 42. For an example of how funding was distributed in different counties and municipalities in 1974, see "11 Counties and 43 Municipalities Get $2-Million in U.S. Funds for Bikeways Along Roads," *New York Times,* December 8, 1974.

108. Epperson, "Bicycle Planning," 42.

109. For more on the history of bicycling in Davis, California, see Robert Sommer and Dale Lott, "Bikeways in Action: The Davis Experience," *Congressional Record* 117, no. 53 (1971); Bob Sommer, "Bikeway Research at the University of California, Davis in the 1960s," in *Cycle History 16: Proceedings of the 16th International Cycling History Conference (Davis, Ca),* ed. Andrew Ritchie (San Francisco: Cycle Publishing, 2006), 47–51; Theodore J. Buehler, "Fifty Years of Bicycle Policy in Davis, CA" (master's thesis, University of California, Davis, 2007).

110. Thomas R. Reid III, "A Solution to the Commuter Crisis," *Bicycling* (June 1970): 10–11, 44–45.

111. Quoted in "11 Counties and 43 Municipalities Get $2-Million in U.S. Funds for Bikeways Along Roads."

112. Epperson, "Bicycle Planning," 42.

113. John Forester, *Effective Cycling,* 6th ed. (Cambridge, MA: MIT Press, 1993).

114. Andy Clarke, personal correspondence, January 3, 2007.

115. John Franklin, the author of reputable works on cycling techniques, features an online history documenting the periods when cyclists were banned from European roads. See "A History of Cycle Paths," *Cyclecraft,* available at http://www.cyclecraft.co.uk/digest/history.html.

116. For example, the *National Bicycling and Walking Study* notes that the high rates of cycling seen in Davis, California, are almost certainly due to a "set of proactive policies and programs, many of which were inspired by the decision of UC-Davis back in the 1960's to minimize the presence of cars on campus." See S. Goldsmith, "Reasons Why Bicycling and Walking Are and Are Not Being Used More Extensively as Travel Modes," in *National Bicycling and Walking Study, Case Study #1,* ed. Federal Highway Administration (Washington, DC, 1993), 52. Quoted in David Tomlinson, "The Bicycle and Urban Sustainability," *FES Outstanding Graduate Student Paper Series* 7, no. 6 (2003): 22. For a review of studies pointing to the positive correlation between cycling infrastructure and commuter cycling, see Jennifer Dill and Theresa Carr, "Bicycle Commuting and Facilities in Major U.S. Cities: If You Build Them, Commuters Will Use Them," *Transportation Research Record,* no. 1828 (2003): 116–123.

117. Epperson, "Bicycle Planning," 42.

118. Ken Kifer, "Cycling during the Seventies: A History of US Bicycling in the 1970's," *Ken Kifer's Bike Pages,* available at http://www.kenkifer.com/bikepages/lifestyle/70s.htm. Ken Kifer was a well-known cycling advocate who was killed by a drunk driver while riding his bike on September 14, 2003. He hosted an extensive Web site of cycling-related articles and resources that are still accessible online.

119. Forester, *Bicycle Transportation,* 1. It is worth noting that Forester is not a psychologist and provides no ethnographic, qualitative, or quantitative evidence for his initial pseudo-psychological diagnosis of the "cyclist-inferiority superstition" (in *Effective Cycling*), nor his assertion that "the average person is so ignorant about cycling that he does not even understand the depths of his ignorance" (*Bicycle Transportation,* 153). Indeed, his perspective closely parallels the early rhetoric of the automobile lobby, particularly General Motors' Charles F. Kettering, who declared to the National Safety Council in 1924 that the automobile was "inherently safe," though most people did not ostensibly understand it to be so because "the general intellectual level is very low. . . . [T]hinking is something which the majority of people refuse to do" Sam Shelton, "Lack of Human Intelligence Is Cause of Most Traffic Accidents," *Automotive Industries* 51 (1924): 646. Quoted in Peter D. Norton, "Fighting Traffic: The Dawn of the Motor Age in the American City" (Ph.D. diss., University of Virginia, 2002), 333, 52.

120. One of John Forester's trademark tactics is to perpetually reference his own findings rather than engage with the wealth of studies produced since the initial publication of either of his major books (for example, see "The Place of Bicycle Transportation in Modern Industrialized Societies," delivered at the Preserving the American Dream Conference in Bloomington, Minnesota, 2005). Consequently, his readers are hard pressed to find a nuanced, much less an accurate, picture of the real benefits, desirability, and/or support for bicycle-specific facilities and infrastructure in the United States. As a case in point, John Pucher accurately notes that Forester "completely ignores the willingness, desire or need of most people to cycle at slower speeds. Thus, his analysis and policy recommendations apply mainly to the small group of high-speed, well-trained vehicular cyclists" ("Cycling Safety on Bikeways vs. Roads," *Transportation Quarterly* 55, no. 4 [2001]: 10). For examples of more objective and contextualized research on bicycle infrastructure and facilities, see David Harkey, Donald W. Reinfurt, Matthew Knuiman, J. Richard Stewart, and Alex Sorton, "Development of the Bicycle Compatibility Concept: A Level of Service Concept, Final Report" (McLean, VA: Federal Highway Administration, 1998); John Pucher and Lewis Dijkstra, "Making Walking and Cycling Safer: Lessons from Europe," *Transportation Quarterly* 54, no. 3 (2000): 25–50; Bureau of Transportation Statistics and National Highway Traffic Safety Administration, "How Bike Paths and Lanes Make a Difference" (Washington, DC, 2004); Ian Hallett, David Luskin, and Randy Machemehl, "Evaluation of On-Street Bicycle Facilities Added to Existing Roadways" (Austin, TX: Center for Transportation Research at The University of Texas–Austin, 2006); Jennifer Dill and Theresa Carr, "Bicycle Commuting and Facilities in Major U.S. Cities"; Jennifer Dill and Kim Voros, "Factors Affecting Bicycling Demand: Initial Survey Findings from the Portland Region," presented at the Transportation Research Board 86th Annual Meeting, 2007; J. D. Hunt and J. E. Abraham, "Influences on Bicycle Use," *Transportation* 34, no. 4 (2007): 453–470; Adel W.

Sadek, Alaina Skye Dickason, and Jon Kaplan, *Effectiveness of Green, High-Visibility Bike Lane and Crossing Treatment,* presented at the Transportation Research Board 86th Annual Meeting, 2007.

121. National Highway Traffic Safety Administration, "Bicyclists and Other Cyclists," in *Traffic Safety Facts, 2007 Data* (Washington, DC: Department of Transportation, 2007).

122. Forester, *Effective Cycling,* 410.

123. Forester, *Bicycle Transportation,* 154.

124. Ibid., 157, 64. Emphasis on the latter quote is my own. Elsewhere in *Bicycle Transportation,* Forester reiterates the "love it or leave it" Republican binary when talking about political bike advocates: "If they enjoyed cycling they wouldn't be so strongly motivated to change the conditions under which it is done" (154).

125. "Same roads—Same rights—Same rules" is the slogan found on Jack R. Taylor's online bicycle advocacy page called *ProBicycle: Bicycle Advocacy by Cyclists for Cyclists,* available at http://probicycle.com.

126. Thanks to Bruce Epperson for bringing the specific terms *voluntary* and *involuntary* cyclists to my attention. For more on the embedded inequalities of mobility in public (and private) spaces, see Celeste Langan, "Mobility Disability," *Public Culture* 13, no. 3 (2001): 459–484.

127. For example, one of the blurbs on Jack R. Taylor's *ProBicycle* advocacy page reads, "If American bicycle advocacy leaders had championed the civil rights movement, the 'Dream' would have been reserved seating in the back of the bus." For other examples of this pseudo-civil rights rhetoric, see North Carolina Coalition for Bicycle Driving, "The Science and Politics of Bicycle Driving," *North Carolina Coalition for Bicycle Driving,* available at http://www.humantransport.org/bicycledriving/sciencepolitics. htm; Cliff Heegel, "Bike Lane Debate," *Bike Memphis,* available at http://bikememphis. com/bike_lanes.htm; Avery Burdett, "About the OCBC," *Ontario Coalition for Better Cycling,* 2006, available at http://www.magma.ca/~ocbc/.

128. David Smith, "Re: [Cg] Digest Number 708," *Chainguard (Yahoo Group),* October 13, 2001, available at http://sports.groups.yahoo.com/group/chainguard/message/7921.

129. John Schubert, "Re: Bicycle Advisory Committees," *Chainguard (Yahoo Group),* December 4, 2001, available at http://sports.groups.yahoo.com/group/chainguard/message/8922.

130. Steven Goodridge, "Re: The Other Smart Growth," *Chainguard (Yahoo Group),* May 24, 2002, available at http://sports.groups.yahoo.com/group/chainguard/message/12542; Wayne Pein, "Re: The Other Smart Growth," *Chainguard (Yahoo Group),* May 24, 2002, available at http://sports.groups.yahoo.com/group/chainguard/message/12543.

131. For more on the so-called Universal Access paradigm, or the nuances of being a "bicycle driver," see North Carolina Coalition for Bicycle Driving, "The Science and Politics of Bicycle Driving."

132. Andy Merrifield, *Dialectical Urbanism: Social Struggles in the Capitalist City* (New York: Monthly Review Press, 2002), 156. Lefebvre further describes the right to the city as a "transformed and renewed *right to urban life*" Lefebvre, Kofman, and Lebas,

Writings on Cities, 158. For more on the "right to the city," see Purcell, "Excavating Lefebvre: The Right to the City and Its Urban Politics of the Inhabitant"; Harvey, "The Right to the City"; Mitchell, *The Right to the City.*

CHAPTER 4

1. Bicycles Bulletin, "Reclaim the Road," in *Network News,* no. 2, ed. John Dowlin (April–June 1979).

2. Robert Lamb and Friends of the Earth, *Promising the Earth* (London: Routledge, 1996), 95.

3. John Dowlin, *Network News,* no. 2 (April–June 1979).

4. Chris Carlsson, "Critical Massifesto," *Critical Mass Essays, Flyers, Images from San Francisco, 1992–1998,* 1994, available at http://www.processedworld.com/tfrs_web/history/Index.html (originally published in June 1994).

5. See Rebecca Reilly, *Nerves of Steel* (Buffalo, NY: Spoke andWord Press, 2000); Travis Hugh Culley, *The Immortal Class: Bike Messengers and the Cult of Human Power,* 1st ed. (New York: Villard, 2001). Also see "Bike Messenger Zines Worldwide," *International Federation of Bike Messenger Associations,* available at http://www.messengers.org/resources/zines.html.

6. Jym Dyer, "Flocculating in the Streets of Berkeley," *Terrain* (August 1993).

7. Susan Blickstein and Susan Hanson accurately note that most Critical Mass events consist of less than 100 people, but rides in San Francisco, New York, and Chicago have consistently drawn thousands of cyclists since the 1990s. See "Critical Mass: Forging a Politics of Sustainable Mobility in the Information Age," *Transportation* 28, no. 4 (2001): 352.

8. See Jordan, "The Art of Necessity"; Duncombe, "Stepping Off the Sidewalk."

9. The April 2008 ride in Budapest, Hungary, drew an estimated eighty thousand bicyclists, while rides in 2006 and 2007 both saw more than thirty thousand participants. See Zsolt Balla, "Critical Mass Wheels Away," *The Budapest Sun,* April 23, 2008.

10. Michael Klett, "A Uniquely Democratic Experiment," in *Critical Mass, Bicycling's Defiant Celebration,* ed. Chris Carlsson (Oakland, CA: AK Press, 2002), 90.

11. Ibid.; Steven Bodzin, "Politics Can Be Fun," in *Critical Mass, Bicycling's Defiant Celebration,* ed. Chris Carlsson (Oakland, CA: AK Press, 2002), 100–104.

12. For more on Critical Mass's encounters with police, see Michael Bluejay, "Police vs. Critical Mass," *Critical Mass Rides,* available at http://CriticalMassRides.info/police.html.

13. See Fred Nemo, "Personal History of Portland's Critical Mass," in *Critical Mass, Bicycling's Defiant Celebration,* ed. Chris Carlsson (Oakland, CA: AK Press, 2002), 204–210.

14. Matthew Arnison, "Critical Mass III (Sydney, Australia)," in *Critical Mass, Bicycling's Defiant Celebration,* ed. Chris Carlsson (Oakland, CA: AK Press, 2002), 55.

15. Ferrell, *Tearing Down the Streets,* 114–121.

16. See "October 2006 Archive," *Chicago Critical Mass,* available at http://groups.yahoo.com/group/chicago_critical_mass/messages/1677.

17. Josh Wilson, "Unleashing Public Imagination, or How 'Bout Another Shot of Existential Whup-Ass for Your Flagging Civic Libido?" in *Critical Mass, Bicycling's Defiant Celebration,* ed. Chris Carlsson (Oakland, CA: AK Press, 2002), 95.

18. Bodzin, "Politics Can Be Fun," 103.

19. The issue of representation was actively debated by Chicago Massers in the fall of 2007, following a *Chicago Tribune* review story that alluded to the "final" Chicago Critical Mass ride planned for the ten-year anniversary ride in September. Some thought it was just a prank being pulled on the reporter, while others debated the merits of actually ending the ride in the midst of its popularity. Regardless, many people were frustrated by what they perceived to be a small clique trying to determine the fate and/or direction of the ride, particularly because it allegedly involved the circulation of an official press release declaring the end of Chicago Critical Mass. See "Grand Finale Debate," *Chicago Critical Mass,* available at http://chicagocriticalmass.org/grandfinaledebate.

20. Blickstein and Hanson, "Critical Mass," 6.

21. Bernie Blaug, "Crit Mass," in *Critical Mass, Bicycling's Defiant Celebration,* ed. Chris Carlsson (Oakland, CA: AK Press, 2002), 73; Charles Higgins, "Critical to Recall Real 'Mass' Appeal," *San Francisco Guardian,* June 30, 2000; P. Krassner, "You Can't Get a Permit for the Revolution," *San Francisco Examiner,* August 24, 1997; J. Rose, "Potter Pedals with Critical Mass to Test His Political Mettle," *The Oregonian,* January 29, 2005.

22. Dyer, "Flocculating in the Streets of Berkeley."

23. Klett, "Critical Mass," 90. Alberto Melucci speaks directly to the intersections of communication, power, and politics in *Challenging Codes: Collective Action in the Information Age* (Cambridge: Cambridge University Press, 2003), esp. 176–204.

24. Stephen Duncombe describes RTS as events where "the action itself is symbolic of its demands," in "Stepping Off the Sidewalk," 222.

25. David Harvey, *Justice, Nature, and the Geography of Difference* (Cambridge, MA: Blackwell Publishers, 1996), 230.

26. For example, see David Harvey, *The Urban Experience* (Baltimore: Johns Hopkins University Press, 1989), 182; Aufheben, "The Politics of Anti-road Struggle and the Struggles of Anti-road Politics"; Benjamin Seel and Alex Plows, "Coming Live and Direct: Strategies of Earth First!" in *Direct Action in British Environmentalism,* ed. Benjamin Seel, Matthew Paterson, and Brian Doherty (London: Routledge, 2000), 112–132; McCreery, "The Claremont Road Situation"; Bullard, Johnson, and Torres, *Highway Robbery.*

27. Michael Burton, "Rugged Individualists of the Road Unite," in *Critical Mass, Bicycling's Defiant Celebration,* ed. Chris Carlsson (Oakland, CA: AK Press, 2002), 21.

28. Lefebvre specifically talks about the highway as a *dominated* space in *The Production of Space,* 164.

29. Iain Borden, *Skateboarding, Space, and the City* (New York: Berg, 2001), 211.

30. Ibid., 173. It is worth noting that Borden's analysis of skateboarding is informed by his own experiences as a skateboarder as well as his exhaustive engagement with skateboarding media published between the 1960s and 2000.

31. Borden writes: "Herein the movement of the body across urban space, and in its direct interaction with the modern architecture of the city, lies the central critique of skateboarding—a rejection both of the values and of the spatio-temporal modes of living in the contemporary capitalist city." See "A Performative Critique of the City: The Urban Practice of Skateboarding, 1958–98," in *The City Cultures Reader,* ed. M. Miles et al. (London: Routledge, 2004), 292.

32. Chris Carlsson, "Whither Bicycling?" *Critical Mass Essays, Flyers, Images from San Francisco, 1992–1998* online (1998). The quote about skateboarding not being "consciously theorized" is from Borden, *Skateboarding, Space, and the City,* 173.

33. Guy Debord, "Report on the Construction of Situations and on the International Situationist Tendency's Conditions of Organization and Action," in *Situationist International Anthology,* ed. Ken Knabb (Berkeley, CA: Bureau of Public Secrets, 1981), 18 (originally published in Paris in June 1957). COBRA is an acronym for Copenhagen, Brussels, and Amsterdam—the homes of the group's various members. For an analysis of COBRA, the Lettrist International, and the International Movement for an Imaginist Bauhaus (and other avant-garde art groups), see Stewart Home, *The Assault on Culture: Utopian Currents from Lettrisme to Class War* (London: Aporia Press/Unpopular Books, 1988).

34. See Kotanyi and Vaneigem, "Elementary Program of the Bureau of Unitary Urbanism."

35. Simon Sadler, *The Situationist City* (Cambridge, MA: MIT Press, 1998), 13.

36. Debord, "Report on the Construction of Situations," 22.

37. Sadler, *The Situationist City,* 17.

38. Plant, *The Most Radical Gesture,* 59. The phrase "Sous les pavés, la plage," or "Under the paving stones, a beach," was used by the situationists as an allusion to the beauty that is hidden by, and lies beneath, the veneer of capitalism and its material manifestations in both modern urbanism and media spectacle. During the May 1968 revolts in France, the phrase appeared as graffiti in different parts of Paris, subsequently taking on an entirely new meaning as protesting students pulled up pieces of the street and hurled them at the police.

39. For more on the *flâneur,* see Susan Buck-Morss, "The Flâneur, the Sandwichman and the Whore: The Politics of Loitering," *New German Critique* (1986); Elizabeth Wilson, "The Invisible Flâneur," *New Left Review* 191 (1992): 99–140; Mike Featherstone, "The Flâneur, the City and Virtual Public Life," *Urban Studies* 35, no. 5 (1998): 909–925; Christel Hollevoet, "The Flâneur: Genealogy of a Modernist Icon" (Ph.D. diss., City University of New York, 2001); Iskin, "The Pan-European Flâneuse in Fin-de-Siècle Posters."

40. Guy Debord, "Theory of the Dérive," in *Situationist International Anthology,* ed. Ken Knabb (Berkeley, CA: Bureau of Public Secrets, 1981), 50 (originally published in *Internationale Situationniste* [Paris], no. 2 [December 1958]).

41. McCreery, "The Claremont Road Situation," 241.

42. Plant, *The Most Radical Gesture,* 23.

43. Situationist International, "Definitions," in *Situationist International Anthology,* ed. Ken Knabb (Berkeley, CA: Bureau of Public Secrets, 1981), 45 (originally published in *Internationale Situationniste* [Paris], no. 1 [June 1958]).

44. For more on the histories, theories, prospects, and limitations of "culture jamming," see Mark Dery, *Culture Jamming: Hacking, Slashing and Sniping in the Empire of Signs* (Westfield, NJ: Open Magazine Pamphlet Series, 1993); Lisa Prothers, "Culture Jamming with Pedro Carvajal," *Bad Subjects,* no. 37 (1998); Kalle Lasn, *Culture Jamming: The Uncooling of America,* 1st ed. (New York: Eagle Brook, 1999); Naomi Klein, *No Logo: Taking Aim at the Brand Bullies* (New York: Picador, 2000), esp. 279–310; Duncombe, "Stepping Off the Sidewalk"; Andrew Boyd and Stephen Duncombe, "The Manufacture

of Dissent: What the Left Can Learn from Las Vegas," *Journal of Aesthetics and Protest* 1, no. 3 (2004): 34-47; Christine Harold, "Pranking Rhetoric: 'Culture Jamming' As Media Activism," *Critical Studies in Media Communication* 21, no. 3 (2004): 189-212; Jo Littler, "Beyond the Boycott," *Cultural Studies* 19, no. 2 (2005): 227-252; Vince Carducci, "Culture Jamming: A Sociological Perspective," *Journal of Consumer Culture* 6, no. 1 (2006): 116-138; M. E. Farrar and J. L. Warner, "Spectacular Resistance: The Billionaires for Bush and the Art of Political Culture Jamming," *Polity* 40, no. 3 (2008): 273-296. Also see Culture Jammer's Encyclopedia, available at http://www.sniggle.net.

45. Kotanyi and Vaneigem, "Elementary Program of the Bureau of Unitary Urbanism," 66.

46. Debord, "Report on the Construction of Situations," 25.

47. Guy Debord, "Introduction to a Critique of Urban Geography," in *Situationist International Anthology,* ed. Ken Knabb (Berkeley, CA: Bureau of Public Secrets, 1981), 5 (originally published in *Les Lévres Nues* [Paris], no. 6 [September 1955]).

48. The reference to breaking "topological chains" is from Debord, "Situationist Theses on Traffic," 58.

49. Sheller and Urry, "The City and the Car," 755.

50. Carlsson, "Cycling under the Radar," 81-82.

51. Jane Holtz Kay, *Asphalt Nation: How the Automobile Took over America, and How We Can Take It Back* (Berkeley: University of California Press, 1998), 14.

52. John Urry, "Automobility, Car Culture and Weightless Travel: A Discussion Paper," *On-Line Publications, Sociology at Lancaster University,* 1999, available at http://www.lancs.ac.uk/fass/sociology/papers/urry-automobility.pdf.

53. Michael Bull, "Automobility and the Power of Sound," *Theory, Culture and Society* 21, nos. 4-5 (2004): 248-249; McCreery, "The Claremont Road Situation," 311.

54. Switzky, "Critical Mass," 188.

55. Alon K. Raab, *Under the Sign of the Bicycle* (Portland: Gilgul Press, 2003), 11-12.

56. Carlsson, "Critical Massifesto."

57. Scott Larkin, interview with the author, August 7, 2004.

58. Canjuers and Debord, "Preliminaries toward Defining a Unitary Revolutionary Program," 308; Taylor, "The Aesthetic Experience of Traffic in the Modern City," 1620-1621.

59. Taylor, "The Aesthetic Experience of Traffic in the Modern City," 1620-1621. Emphasis is my own. Also see Jain, "Dangerous Instrumentality."

60. Anne Friedberg, "Urban Mobility and Cinematic Visuality: The Screens of Los Angeles—Endless Cinema or Private Telematics," *Journal of Visual Culture* 1, no. 2 (2002): 184; Don Mitchell, "The S.U.V. Model of Citizenship: Floating Bubbles, Buffer Zones, and the Rise of The "Purely Atomic" Individual," *Political Geography* 24, no. 1 (2005): 77-100.

61. See John Berger, *Ways of Seeing* (New York: Viking Press, 1973).

62. "Anti-spectacular device" from Carlsson, "Critical Massifesto"; "Capsule" from Friedberg, "Urban Mobility and Cinematic Visuality," 184.

63. Lee Williams, "Community," *Cranked,* no. 4 (2006): 46.

64. This is precisely what Gorz alludes to in his 1973 article "The Ideology of the Motorcar." He writes, "The way our space is arranged carries on the disintegration of

people that begins with the division of labour in the factory. It cuts a person into slices, it cuts our time, our life, into separate slices so that in each one you are a passive consumer at the mercy of the merchants, so that it never occurs to you that work, culture, communication, pleasure, satisfaction of needs, and personal life can and should be one and the same thing: a unified life, sustained by the social fabric of the community." Murray Bookchin, whose work is also heavily influenced by Karl Marx, makes a similar point: "City planning is an expression of mistrust in the spontaneity of contemporary social relations, and for good reason. Bourgeois society divides virtually all spheres of life against each other; it universalizes competition, profit, and the primacy of exchange value over mutual aid, art, and utility." *The Limits of the City* (New York: Harper and Row, 1974), 100.

65. Louis Mendoza, "A Few Reflections in Response to Prompts from Readers," *A Journey across Our America: Observations and Reflections on the Latinoization of the U.S.*, August 12, 2007, available at http://journeyacrossouramerica.blogspot.com/2007/08/few-reflections-in-response-to-prompts.html.

66. Louis Mendoza, personal correspondence, January 25, 2008.

67. The terms *cage* (a car) and *cager* (a driver) were appropriated from the lingo of motorcycle riders and are used by some Critical Mass participants in online forums and e-mail listservs.

68. Jen Petersen, "Pedaling Hope," *Monu: Magazine on Urbanism,* no. 6 (2007): 37.

69. Shelly Lynn Jackson, ed., *Chainbreaker* (New Orleans), no. 4, 1 (self-published zine).

70. Jeff Ferrell, "Maybe You Should Check the Statute," in *Critical Mass: Bicycling's Defiant Celebration,* ed. Chris Carlsson (Oakland, CA: AK Press, 2002), 124.

71. Hakim Bey, *T.A.Z.: The Temporary Autonomous Zone, Ontological Anarchy, Poetic Terrorism* (Brooklyn, NY: Autonomedia, 1991), 12–13. For other articles that draw a connection between Critical Mass and the TAZ, see "Critical Mass: Reclaiming Space and Combating the Car," *Do or Die,* no. 5 (1996); Michael I. Niman, "Critical Mass!" *ArtVoice,* June 20, 2002; Ben Shepard and Kelly Moore, "Reclaiming the Streets of New York," in *Critical Mass: Bicycling's Defiant Celebration,* ed. Chris Carlsson (Oakland, CA: AK Press, 2002): 195–203; Furness, "Critical Mass, Urban Space and Vélomobility," 308–309.

72. Mikhail Bakhtin, *Rabelais and His World,* 1st Midland book ed. (Bloomington: Indiana University Press, 1984), 10.

73. Murray Bookchin, *Social Anarchism or Lifestyle Anarchism: The Unbridgeable Chasm* (San Francisco: AK Press, 1995), 24.

74. For good examples, see the collection of essays featured in McKay, *DiY Culture;* Stephen Duncombe, *Cultural Resistance Reader* (London: Verso, 2002); Benjamin Heim Shepard and Ronald Hayduk, *From Act Up to the WTO: Urban Protest and Community Building in the Era of Globalization* (London: Verso, 2002).

75. Ferrell, *Tearing Down the Streets,* 115; Higgins, "Critical to Recall Real 'Mass' Appeal."

76. Mindy Bond, "Matthew Roth, Bicycle Enthusiast, Time's Up," *Gothamist,* April 29, 2005, available at http://gothamist.com/2005/04/29/matthew_roth_bicycle_enthusiast_times_up.php; Isral DeBruin, "Critical Mass: A Personal Perspective," *The University of Wisconsin–Milwaukee Post,* September 5, 2006.

77. Stephen Duncombe, *Dream: Re-imagining Progressive Politics in an Age of Fantasy* (New York: New Press, 2007), 138.

78. Elliot Mallen, "Don't You Wish You Were Riding One?" *Michigan Daily,* October 10, 2005.

79. For a different semiotic analysis of cities, see Roland Barthes's essay "Semiotics and Urbanism" in *The Semiotic Challenge* (Berkeley: University of California Press, 1994), 191–201.

80. Sarah Boothroyd, "Spraypaint Slingers, Celebration, and a Tidal Wave of Outrage," in *Critical Mass, Bicycling's Defiant Celebration,* ed. Chris Carlsson (Oakland, CA: AK Press, 2002), 23.

81. John W. Delicath and Kevin Michael DeLuca define *image events* as "staged acts of protest designed for media dissemination," in "Image Events, the Public Sphere, and Argumentative Practice: The Case of Radical Environmental Groups," *Argumentation* 17, no. 3 (2003): 315.

82. Kevin Michael DeLuca, "Unruly Arguments: The Body Rhetoric of Earth First! Act Up and Queer Nation," *Argumentation and Advocacy,* no. 36 (1999): 10.

83. Since the 1890s, a number of companies produced ads that prominently feature cyclists—or in the case of Huffy, a bicycle salesman—with bikes raised high above their heads. Notable examples include ads from Deesse Bicycles (1898), Rambler Bicycles (1901), Peugeot (1922), Huffy (1957), and Browning (1974).

84. See Pamela Walker Laird, "'The Car without a Single Weakness': Early Automobile Advertising," *Technology and Culture* 37, no. 4 (1996): 796–812.

85. Rebar, "The Parkcycle," available at http://www.rebargroup.org/projects/parkcycle/index.html.

86. Robyn Doolittle, "Bike Activists Going Guerrilla," *Toronto Star,* June 18, 2007.

87. "4th Street Bicycle Boulevard," available at http://www.4sbb.com/.

88. "Clowns Serious about Parking in Bike Lanes," *The Villager,* August 31–September 6, 2005.

89. Pictures of Right of Way's stencils, as well as their essays and research, were accessed on the group's (now defunct) Web site at http://www.cars-suck.org.

90. The most comprehensive collection of news articles, links, and essays pertaining to ghost bikes is available at http://www.ghostbikes.org. Also see "Ghost Bikes," *Urban Velo,* no. 11 (2008): 56–68.

91. Ryan Nuckel, personal correspondence, January 17, 2007.

92. "Critical Mass Flame War," *Monkey Chicken,* available at http://www.monkey-chicken.com/fwar.htm.

93. Ibid. See posts 14 and 84.

94. Ibid. See post 25

95. For examples, see Alex Storozynski, "End the Anarchy: Critical Mass Deserves a Police Escort to Keep It Safe," *A.M. New York,* November 5, 2004; "Critical Mass Bike Rides Face Police Crackdown"; Elizabeth Press, Andrew Lynn, and Chris Ryan, *Still We Ride* (In Tandem Production, 2005).

96. Coverage of the 1997 incident in San Francisco (particularly the police violence) is available at http://www.brasscheck.com/cm.

97. Quoted in Howard Besser, "Victorious Critical Mass Lawsuit," in *Critical Mass, Bicycling's Defiant Celebration,* ed. Chris Carlsson (Oakland, CA: AK Press, 2002), 219–222.

98. Dave Snyder, "Good for the Bicycling Cause," in *Critical Mass, Bicycling's Defiant Celebration,* ed. Chris Carlsson (Oakland, CA: AK Press, 2002), 112.

99. Blickstein and Hanson, "Critical Mass," 360.

100. Martin Wachs, "Creating Political Pressure for Cycling," *Transportation Quarterly* 52, no. 1 (1998): 6.

101. For more on the "radical flank effect," see William A. Gamson, *The Strategy of Social Protest* (Homewood, IL: Dorsey Press, 1975); H. H. Haines, "Black Radicalization and the Funding of Civil Rights: 1957–1970," *Social Problems* 32, no. 1 (1984): 31–43; Larry Isaac, Steve McDonald, and Greg Lukasik, "Takin' It from the Streets: How the Sixties Mass Movement Revitalized Unionization," *American Journal of Sociology* 112, no. 1 (2006): 46–96.

102. Amy Stork, interview with the author, August 6, 2004.

103. For examples, see Zamora Jim Herron, "'Critical Mess' at Year One Calm Predicted as Thousands of Cyclists Are Expected Friday," *San Francisco Examiner,* July 30, 1998; Erik Baard, "Critical Mess," *Village Voice,* August 31, 2004; Patricia Calhoun, "Critical Mess," *Denver Westword News,* May 4, 2006; Anita Quigley, "Disturbing Cycle a Critical Mess," *The Daily Telegraph,* November 25, 2006; Todd Balf, "Critical Mess," *Bicycling Magazine* (December 2007): 41–61.

104. Martha Moore, "Transportation Alternatives," *USA Today,* November 15, 2004.

105. Scott Spitz, *Leapfrog* (Indianapolis), no. 7, 14 (self-published zine).

106. Quoted in Dave Newbart, "Has 'Mass' Ride Run Its Course? Some Urge End to 10-Year Spectacle," *Chicago Sun-Times,* August 5, 2007.

107. Christopher Wallace, personal correspondence, January 16, 2007.

108. Dan Herbeck and Holly Auer, "Charges Fly as Bicyclists and Police Clash," *Buffalo News,* June 1, 2003.

109. In 2006 the American Civil Liberties Union (ACLU) finally settled a case filed in 1998 against the Eastpointe Police Department (Eastpointe, Michigan) for a systematic campaign of racial profiling against African American kids harassed for "Biking While Black" in the mid-1990s. Fred DeWeese, the former Eastpointe police chief, specifically instructed his officers to investigate any black youths riding through the predominantly white suburb of Detroit, and according to the ACLU, police logs identified more than one hundred incidents in a three-year span in which African American youths between the ages of eleven and eighteen were detained. The twenty-two men represented in the lawsuit were each pulled over, questioned and/or searched, and in some cases had their bikes confiscated and sold. See Elizabeth Rusch, "Biking While Black," *Mother Jones* (September–October 2002): 25; American Civil Liberties Union, "Federal Appeals Court Revives Michigan "Bicycling-While-Black" Lawsuit," June 8, 2005.

110. Nathan Brubaker, "Welcome to the Police State," *Pittsburgh Critical Mass Arrests Blog,* 2006, available at http://criticalmassarrests.blogspot.com/2006/03/welcome-to-police-state-in-my.html.

111. See John Pucher and John Renne, "Socioeconomics of Urban Travel: Evidence from the 2001 NHTS," *Transportation Quarterly* 57, no. 3 (2003); Dan Koeppel and Ben Maddox, "Invisible Riders," *Bicycling* (December 2005): 46–55.

112. For instance, see Adam Kessel, "Response to Boston CM Critics," *Chicago Critical Mass,* April 9, 2000, available at http://chicagocriticalmass.org/about/faq/adamkessel; Adam Kessel, "Why They're Wrong about Critical Mass!" in *Critical Mass: Bicycling's Defiant Celebration,* ed. Chris Carlsson (Oakland, CA: AK Press, 2002), 107.

113. Dyer, "Flocculating in the Streets of Berkeley."

114. Debord, "Report on the Construction of Situations," 25. Block quote from Dave Horton, "Lancaster Critical Mass: Does It Still Exist?" in *Critical Mass, Bicycling's Defiant Celebration,* ed. Chris Carlsson (Oakland, CA: AK Press, 2002), 63–64.

115. On this point, Dave Horton writes: "Locally dense spatialities promote locally dense socialities; carlessness produces compact lives. Thus, in the search for sustainability, it might well be the spatial impacts of car free life which ultimately prove more important than the direct ecological impacts of 'one less car.'" See "Computers, Cars and Televisions: The Role of Objects in Cultivating Sustainable Lifestyles," a paper presented at the *Manchester Environmental Forum Postgraduate Conference,* University of Manchester, 2003. Available through *Shifting Ground* at http://www.shiftingground.freeuk.com/compcars.htm, 2003).

116. Carlsson, "Cycling under the Radar: Assertive Desertion," 78.

117. John Arquilla, David F. Ronfeldt, and U.S. Department of Defense (Office of the Secretary of Defense), *Networks and Netwars: The Future of Terror, Crime, and Militancy* (Santa Monica, CA: Rand, 2001), 336–337.

118. Time's Up! "Time's Up! Opens a Bike Convergence Center for Rnc," *Interactivist Info Exchange,* July 21, 2004.

119. Joshua Robin, "Bike National Convention," *New York Newsday,* June 23, 2004.

120. See Conrad Schmidt, *Indecent Exposure to Cars: The Story of the World Naked Bike Ride* (Ragtag Productions, 2007). Also see the *World Naked Bike Ride* Web site, available at http://www.worldnakedbikeride.org.

121. Charles Komanoff, "Avenues for Activism," a paper presented at the First Annual Bike Summer, San Francisco, August 1, 1999.

122. Blickstein and Hanson, "Critical Mass," 360.

123. Bihui Li, personal correspondence, January 1, 2007.

124. Ayleen Crotty, personal correspondence, January 3, 2007.

125. Higgins, "Critical to Recall Real 'Mass' Appeal."

126. For examples of academic literature on collective identity in social movements see William A. Gamson, *Talking Politics* (Cambridge: Cambridge University Press, 1992), 84–109; V. Taylor and N. E. Whittier, "Collective Identity in Social Movement Communities: Lesbian Feminist Mobilization," *Frontiers in Social Movement Theory* (1992): 104–129; Alberto Melucci, "The Process of Collective Identity," *Social Movements and Culture* 4 (1995): 41–63; Alberto Melucci, *Challenging Codes;* John Drury, Steve Reicher, and Clifford Stott, "Transforming the Boundaries of Collective Identity: From the 'Local' Anti-road Campaign to 'Global' Resistance?" *Social Movement Studies* 2, no. 2 (2003): 191–212; Ross Haenfler, "Collective Identity in the Straight Edge Movement: How Diffuse Movements Foster Commitment, Encourage Individualized Participation, and Promote Cultural Change," *Sociological Quarterly* 45, no. 4 (2004): 785–805.

127. Bijker, *Of Bicycles, Bakelites, and Bulbs: Toward a Theory of Sociotechnical Change,* 273–275.

128. For an interesting political assessment of pie throwing, see the Biotic Baking Brigade (BBB)—a group of activists who are "Speaking Pie to Power!" In particular, the BBB notes "pie-slinging is just one tool in a large toolbox of resistance to the dominant paradigm." See *Pie Any Means Necessary: The Biotic Baking Brigade Cookbook* (Oakland, CA: AK Press/Rebel Folk Press, 2004).

129. David Pinder, "Commentary-Writing Cities against the Grain," *Urban Geography* 25, no. 8 (2004): 794.

130. David Harvey, *Spaces of Hope* (Berkeley: University of California Press, 2000), 237–238.

131. Pinder, "Commentary-Writing Cities against the Grain," 792. Also see David Pinder, "In Defence of Utopian Urbanism: Imagining Cities after the 'End of Utopia,'" *Geografiska Annaler. Series B. Human Geography* (2002): 229–241.

132. Guy Debord, "For a Revolutionary Judgment of Art," in *Situationist International Anthology,* ed. Ken Knabb (Berkeley, CA: Bureau of Public Secrets, 1981), 312 (originally published in Paris, February 1961).

CHAPTER 5

1. "Legal Developments in Marketing," *Journal of Marketing* 44, no. 1 (1980): 86.

2. Ross Petty, "Regulation vs. the Market: The Case of Bicycle Safety (Parts 1 and 2)" *Risk: Issues in Health, Safety and Environment* 77, no. 92 (1991): 77–88, 93–120.

3. Bill Wilkinson, "Nonmotorized Transportation: The Forgotten Modes," *Annals of the American Academy of Political and Social Science* 553 (1997): 87.

4. P. J. O'Rourke, *Republican Party Reptile: Essays and Outrages* (New York: Atlantic Monthly Press, 1987), 122–127.

5. Ibid., 126.

6. Tim Burton, *Pee-wee's Big Adventure* (Warner Bros, 1985); Vittorio De Sica, *The Bicycle Thief* (Produzioni De Sica, 1948).

7. Gary Gardner, "When Cities Take Bicycle Seriously," *Worldwatch Institute* 11, no. 5 (1998): 16–23.

8. R. Anthony Slagle, "Queer Criticism and Sexual Normativity: The Case of Pee-wee Herman," *Journal of Homosexuality* 45, nos. 2–4 (2003): 138.

9. Notably, this scene also transforms Pee-wee's friend Dotty, a modest-looking woman bicycle mechanic, into a leather-clad blonde "bombshell" (played by Morgan Fairchild).

10. Frank Oz, *In and Out* (Paramount Pictures, 1997).

11. With respect to the image of cyclists as sexually bizarre, it is worth mentioning that a two-part episode of the 1980s hit TV show *Diff'rent Strokes* focused on a bike shop owner who sexually molests children. See Gerren Keith, "The Bicycle Man, Part 1," and "The Bicycle Man, Part 2," *Diff'rent Strokes* (NBC-TV, 1983).

12. Judd Apatow, *40-Year-Old Virgin* (Universal Pictures, 2005).

13. David O'Russell, *I Heart Huckabees* (Fox Searchlight Pictures, 2004).

14. Thomas Michael Donnelly, *Quicksilver* (Columbia Pictures Corporation, 1986).

15. For more on the articulation of the yuppie through mass media in the 1980s, see Jane Feuer, *Seeing through the Eighties: Television and Reaganism* (Durham, NC: Duke University Press, 1995).

16. Another cult classic involving bicycles is *Breaking Away* (20th Century Fox, 1979), a story about four friends struggling to get out of their hometown of Bloomington, Indiana. Though the plot revolves around a bike-riding protagonist, his interest in cycling is explicitly tied to racing and I am trying to focus here on representations of bicycling as a mode of everyday transportation.

NOTES TO PAGES 112-115 · 259

17. Michael Lembeck, *Double Rush* (CBS Television, 1995).

18. Despite his short stint on MTV and his questionable history as an actual bike messenger, "Puck" brought substantial (and international) negative attention to bike messengers. In reference to Puck's appearance on the *Real World,* veteran San Francisco bike messenger Yini Yohans wrote in 2000: "I could explain my job anywhere on the globe now, from Los Angeles to Lisbon, and expect the same response: 'Oh, like Puck?' Puck's contribution to the image of messengers as smelly, drug-addled, psychotic socio-paths made good old Crud [a SF messenger in the late 1970s and 1980s] seem like Martha Stewart" Yini Yohans, "Spokes Person," *San Francisco Call,* September 11, 2000.

19. Mitchell Hurwitz, *Arrested Development* (20th Century Fox Home Entertainment, 2003); Anthony Russo and Joe Russo, *You, Me and Dupree* (Universal Pictures, 2006).

20. J. Pucher, Charles Komanoff, and Paul Schimek, "Bicycling Renaissance in North America? Recent Trends and Alternative Policies to Promote Bicycling," *Transportation Research Part A* 33, no. 7 (1999): 22.

21. Ibid.

22. Ibid.

23. These lovely devices are also sold under the names Bumper Nuts, Bulls Balls, Big Boy Balls, and Big Boy Nuts (alternatively spelled as Nutz). For one of the most surreal Web pages ever posted on the Internet, see the comparison chart and accompanying prose that the Bulls Balls manufacturers—who are, incidentally, trademark holders for the phrase "Made to Swing"—created as a way to demonstrate the ostensibly superior quality of their products. It is entitled: "Truck Nuts—A Quest for the Truth." See *Bulls Balls,* available at http://www.bullsballs.com/compare/truck/nuts.html.

24. For a few notable examples of scholarship on the construction and/or performance of gender through mobility, see Merritt Polk, "Gender Mobility: A Study of Women's and Men's Relations to Automobility in Sweden" (Ph.D. diss., Göteborg University, 1998); Robin Law, "Beyond 'Women and Transport': Towards New Geographies of Gender and Daily Mobility," *Progress in Human Geography* 23, no. 4 (1999): 567–588; Domosh and Seager, *Putting Women in Place,* 123–128; Sarah S. Jain, "Violent Submission: Gendered Automobility," *Cultural Critique,* no. 61 (2005): 186–214; Clive Kenneth Williams, "Stealing a Car to Be a Man: The Importance of Cars and Driving in the Gender Identity of Adolescent Males" (Ph.D. diss., Queensland University of Technology, 2005); Catharina Landström, "A Gendered Economy of Pleasure: Representations of Cars and Humans in Motoring Magazines," *Science Studies* 19, no. 2 (2006): 31–53.

25. James Curran, Michael Gurevitch, and Janet Woollacott, *Mass Communication and Society* (Beverly Hills, CA: Sage Publications, 1982), 27.

26. Steven Spielberg's *E.T.* (1982) was one of the first feature films to introduce many U.S. children to BMX bicycles despite their popularity on the West Coast since the mid-1970s. In addition to *BMX Bandits* (Brian Trenchard-Smith, 1983) and *Rad* (Hal Needham, 1986), BMX bikes make notable appearances in *The Karate Kid* (John G. Avildsen, 1984) and *Better Off Dead* (Savage Steve Hollan, 1985). Special thanks to Matt Lisowski for bring the film *Rad* to my attention some years ago.

27. Ruth Schwartz Cowan, *More Work for Mother: The Ironies of Household Technology from the Open Hearth to the Microwave* (New York: Basic Books, 1983); Lynn Spigel, *Make Room for TV: Television and the Family Ideal in Postwar America* (Chicago: University of Chicago Press, 1992).

28. It is notable that men are predominantly shown as the drivers—hence authority figures—in films and television shows of the 1950s and 1960s, despite the increasing role that women actually played as automotive chauffeurs and errand runners in the United States. On this latter point, see Cowan, *More Work for Mother*, 79–84.

29. Other details include the production of mock gas tanks on bicycle frames as well as the early appearance of hubcaps on certain models. Leon Dixon is the foremost authority on *classic bicycles,* having literally coined the term and amassed what is probably the largest collection in the world. He is the curator of the National Bicycle History Archive of America and has written widely about classic bicycles. See Leon Dixon, *National Bicycle History Archive,* available at http://nbhaa.com/.

30. Schwinn nearly doubled its bicycles sales from 1950 to 1959 (2 million to 3.6 million) and the Murray Bicycle Company was also widely successful in this period, in some cases besting Schwinn's sales. See Lou Dzierzak, *Schwinn* (St. Paul, MN: MBI Publishing, 2002), 29.

31. For more on road trip films, see Edward Dimendberg, "The Will to Motorization: Cinema, Highways, and Modernity," *October,* no. 73 (1995): 90–137; Ron Eyerman and Orvar Lofgren, "Romancing the Road: Road Movies and Images of Mobility," *Theory, Culture and Society* 12, no. 1 (1995): 53–79; Steven Cohan and Ina Rae Hark, *The Road Movie Book* (London: Routledge, 1997); David Laderman, *Driving Visions: Exploring the Road Movie* (Austin: University of Texas Press, 2002); Katie Mills, *The Road Story and the Rebel: Moving through Film, Fiction, and Television* (Carbondale: Southern Illinois University Press, 2006). Also see Gary Handman, "Road Movies: A Bibliography of Materials in the University of California Berkeley Library," available at http://www.lib.berkeley.edu/MRC/roadmoviesbib.html.

32. *Drive Your Bicycle* (Sullivan, 1955); *Bicycle Today—Automobile Tomorrow* (Sid Davis Productions, 1969); *I Like Bikes* (Centron Films with General Motors, 1978).

33. *Tomorrow's Drivers* (Handy Jam Organization with Chevrolet Division, General Motors Corporation, 1954). Chevrolet included a segment that is similar to *Tomorrow's Drivers* in a promotional film from 1936, in which tricycle-riding children were directed through an outdoor driving course by a police officer. The narrator says, "'Get 'em young and teach 'em everything' is the motto of Inspector of Traffic Fred J. Manning." This film was one of the many propaganda pieces put out by Chevrolet in the 1930s alone, including 1935's *The Safest Place* (which is, of course, in your car). See *The Safest Place* (Handy Jam Organization with Chevrolet Division, General Motors Corporation, 1935); *Chevrolet Leader News* 2, no. 1 (Handy Jam Organization with Chevrolet Division, General Motors Corporation, 1936).

34. *I Like Bikes.* One could easily interpret this film as part of an effort to assuage anxieties brought about from the oil embargo, the energy crisis, and "bicycle boom" that preceded this film's production by only a few years. My sincere thanks to Matt Sharp for bringing *I Like Bikes* to my attention.

35. See *You and Your Bicycle* (Progressive Pictures, 1948); *Bicycle Safety* (Centron Productions/Young America Films, 1950); *A Monkey Tale* (Encyclopedia Britannica Films, 1954); *Bicycle Clown* (Sid Davis Productions, 1958); *One Got Fat* (Interlude Films, 1963).

36. Jacquie Phelan has been a longtime critic of the blatantly sexist imagery used in bicycle advertising. For example, see her designation of the "Golden Testicle" award

online at *Women's Mountain Bike and Tea Society (WOMBATS)*, October 26, 1994, available at http://www.wombats.org/jacquie5.html.

37. Walter Lippmann, *Public Opinion* (New York: Harcourt, Brace, 1922), 3–34.

38. See Jennings Bryant and Dolf Zillmann, *Media Effects: Advances in Theory and Research*, 2nd ed., Lea's Communication Series (Mahwah, NJ: L. Erlbaum Associates, 2002). For a critique of media effects research and the role of causality in traditional communication research, see Fred Fejes, "Critical Mass Communications Research and Media Effects: The Problem of the Disappearing Audience," *Media Culture Society* 6, no. 3 (1984): 219–232; Carey, *Communication as Culture*, 37–88; Stuart Hall, "Ideology and Communication Theory," in *Rethinking Communication*, vol. 1, ed. B. Dervin et al. (London: Sage, 1989): 40–52; Sonia Livingstone, "On the Continuing Problems of Media Effects Research," in *Mass Media and Society*, ed. James Curran and Michael Gurevitch (London: Edward Arnold, 1996), 305–324.

39. This mode of analysis can best be described as a "cultural studies" approach to media that, broadly speaking, is used to critically interrogate the ideological, social, and fundamentally political processes and practices associated with the production of meaning, knowledge, and power at a given historical conjuncture. Two classic examples of (media-focused) research along these lines include Stuart Hall et al., *Culture, Media, Language: Working Papers in Cultural Studies, 1972–1979* (London: Routledge in Association with the Centre for Contemporary Cultural Studies, University of Birmingham, 1980), and Carey, *Communication as Culture*. For introductions to the field of cultural studies, see Lawrence Grossberg, Cary Nelson, and Paula A. Treichler, *Cultural Studies* (New York: Routledge, 1992); Meenakshi Gigi Durham and Douglas Kellner, *Media and Cultural Studies: Keyworks*, rev. ed., Keyworks in Cultural Studies (Malden, MA: Blackwell, 2006); Simon During, *The Cultural Studies Reader*, 3rd ed. (London: Routledge, 2007).

40. Donald Lewis Shaw and Maxwell E. McCombs, *The Emergence of American Political Issues: The Agenda-Setting Function of the Press* (St. Paul: West Publishing, 1977); Robert McChesney, *The Problem of the Media: U.S. Communication Politics in the Twenty-first Century* (New York: Monthly Review Press, 2004), 70.

41. Michael Schudson, *The Power of News* (Cambridge, MA: Harvard University Press, 1995), 18.

42. A 2003 household survey conducted by the Bureau of Transportation Services found that of the 20.9 million people who reported riding bicycles, the majority did so for exercise/health (41 percent) and recreation (37 percent). Only 5 percent reported commuting to work by bicycle as the primary way in which they used their bicycle during the previous thirty days. Bureau of Transportation Statistics and National Highway Traffic Safety Administration, "National Survey of Pedestrian and Bicyclist Attitudes and Behaviors: Highlights Report."

43. James Mayer, "Portland Ranks First in Nation for Biking to Work," *The Oregonian*, June 14, 2007.

44. It is worth mentioning that the *Chicago Tribune* is one of the only U.S. newspapers that featured a column devoted specifically to bicycling in recent decades. "Ask Dr. Bicycle" ran from spring 1973 through the end of November 1974.

45. "War Brings Desired Bicycling," *New York Times*, January 6, 1942; "War Increases Bicycle's Popularity among Women," *New York Times*, January 13, 1942; "Road to Park

Commuters' Bikes," *New York Times,* January 20, 1942; "Bishop Takes to a Bicycle," *New York Times,* January 25, 1942; "Messenger Field Reopens to Women," *New York Times,* January 30, 1942; "Motor Age, Reversed," *New York Times,* March 8, 1942; "Bicycles Get Parking Racks," *New York Times,* March 9, 1942; Arthur Liebers, "More Bicycles to Keep Nation on Wheels," *New York Times,* March 22, 1942; "Cycling Days Are Here Again," *New York Times,* March 22, 1942; "Trolley Lines Will Aid Cyclists," *New York Times,* April 2, 1942; "Bicycle Parking for $2 a Month," *New York Times,* April 5, 1942; "Bicycle Parade Takes on Dignity," *New York Times,* April 27, 1942.

46. For example, see "Cycle to Work," *Chicago Daily Tribune,* January 25, 1942. A fact sheet published by the Wisconsin Motor Vehicle Department in 1942 similarly alludes to the benefits and rewards of using bicycle transportation in wartime, whether for work, business, or allowing housewives to "cut down on the use of the family car" Wisconsin Department of Transportation, "History of Bicycling in Wisconsin," available at http://www.dot.wisconsin.gov/travel/bike-foot/docs/history.pdf. Advertising also played a notable role in this process and bicycle companies were quick to play up the theme of patriotism during World War II. Columbia Bicycles led the charge, as one of their print ads clearly illustrates: "America's defense workers and civilians, too, find another important use for Columbias as an ever-ready means of transportation to and from the job day after day—saving gasoline and oil, and time and trouble in parking and traffic. Once again the experience, skill and workmanship that have made Columbia 'America's FIRST Bicycle' are meeting the demands of these times of conservation and emergency." Columbia also ran an entire ad campaign that (separately) featured personnel from the U.S. Navy, U.S. Marines, the French Armed Forces, and the Chinese Armed Forces. Despite variations in the copy, the ads in the latter series uniformly highlight the ways in which *Bicycles Serve the Services.* By the end of the war, one finds Columbia returning to a marketing strategy that explicitly targets children ("Be out in front on a new Columbia"), women, and potential leisure cyclists ("It's enjoyable exercise"), rather than making specific appeals to masculinity, nationalism, or the ethics of conservation.

47. "Henderson Tries Out New 'Victory' Bike," *The Evening Independent,* January 14, 1942; "Henderson Rides New 'Victory' Bicycle: 750,000 Planned for '42 and for Adults Only," *New York Times,* January 14, 1942; "Mr. Henderson Awheel," *New York Times,* January 17, 1942. The plants that built Victory bicycles during the war were the Westfield Manufacturing Company in Westfield, Massachusetts (then home of Columbia Bicycles), and the Huffman Manufacturing Company in Dayton, Ohio (which became Huffy Bicycles in 1953). See Downey, *Telegraph Messenger Boys,* 74; Charles A. Myers, "Wartime Concentration of Production," *Journal of Political Economy* 51, no. 3 (1942): 222–234.

48. A follow-up article from the *Los Angeles Times* begins by asking readers, "Are you making the most of your Victory bikes?" Margaret Carrick, "Cycle for Health and Fun," *Los Angeles Times,* June 20, 1943.

49. Charles Komanoff, interview with the author, January 22, 2007.

50. For example, see "Our Programs," *League of American Bicyclists,* available at http://www.bikeleague.org/programs.

51. Notable examples of the bicycle versus car "war" theme include Lance Morrow, "The Great Bicycle Wars," *Time,* November 24, 1980; Melvin Maddocks, "Bicycle

Wars: The Newest Arms Race," *Christian Science Monitor*, November 19, 1986; Indira Lakshmanan, "When Paths Cross: Bikers, Skaters, Pedestrians Clash Along Charles," *Boston Globe*, August 23, 1993; Johnny Diaz, "War of the Wheels: As Bicyclists and in-Line Skaters Fight for Space, Who Rules the Road?" *Boston Globe*, August 7, 1995; Larry Fish, "Taking Back the Streets on Two Wheels: It's Bicycling en Masse and with Attitude," *Philadelphia Inquirer*, October 26, 1996; Richard Price, "Road Wars: Urban Bicyclists Try to Establish Right to Ride, Bike Riders Becoming Major Political Force," *USA Today*, August 1, 1997; Mac Daniel, "Cycle of Antagonism Resentment Rolls on City Streets When Bikes, Cars Clash," *Boston Globe*, January 28, 2002; Christopher West Davis, "Tug of War on the Roads: Bikes against Cars," *New York Times*, August 10, 2003; Kyra Kyles, "Wheel Wars: Cyclists, Drivers Get Fired Up over Who Rules the Road in Chicago," *Chicago Redeye*, March 24, 2006; Jaxon Van Derbeken Michael Cabanatuan, Cecilia M. Vega, "Clash Reignites Road Wars," *San Francisco Chronicle*, Thursday, April 5, 2007.

52. Storozynski, "End the Anarchy."

53. See Baard, "Critical Mess"; Calhoun, "Critical Mess"; Todd and Mattheis, "Critical Mess."

54. Herbeck and Auer, "Charges Fly as Bicyclists and Police Clash"; "The Chain Gang: Bicyclists Face Off with Police, and the Ride Goes to Court," *Buffalo News*, June 11, 2003; Michael Beebe and Vanessa Thomas, "Riding at Their Own Risk," *Buffalo News*, June 5, 2003.

55. Joy Powell, "19 Bicyclists Arrested after Rally Turns into Melee," *Star Tribune*, September 1, 2007.

56. Ros Davidson, "Power to the Pedal: Bicycle Anarchists Fight for US Roads," *Scotland on Sunday*, August 17, 1997. For a more productive assessment of the relationships between Critical Mass and anarchism, see Ferrell, *Tearing Down the Streets*, 91–148.

57. John McDonnell, personal correspondence, January 3, 2007.

58. Steve Lopez, "The Scariest Biker Gang of All," *Time*, August 11, 1997, 4. Also see Michael Blanding and Travis Lea, "How Mild-Mannered Bicyclists Were Turned into 'Wolves,'" *Salon.com*, July 30, 1997, available at http://dir.salon.com/story/news/feature/1997/07/30/news/.

59. Phillip Matier and Andrew Ross, "Minivan's Rude Introduction to Critical Smash," *San Francisco Chronicle*, April 4, 2007. Josh Wilson provides a poignant analysis of this initial story and the massive response it triggered on the *San Francisco Chronicle*'s Web forum. See "The Critical Press," *Grade the News*, April 16, 2007, available at http://www.gradethenews.org/commentaries/criticalmass.htm.

60. *Massholes* is not my term, but rather one used egregiously on the Internet.

61. Morrow, "The Great Bicycle Wars." Contrary to John Forester's nearly fact-free analysis of Transportation Alternatives and New York City bike activism in *Bicycle Transportation* (162), the pedestrian deaths in 1980 were caused by errant bicyclists, not the bike paths he so passionately opposed/opposes.

62. "Gridlock" Sam Schwartz (former transportation engineer for the City of New York), interview by the author, August 16, 2007; Laurie Johnston, "As Their Legs Tire, Some Are Beginning to Kick a Little," *New York Times*, April 8, 1980.

63. Charles Komanoff, interview with the author, October 15, 2004. Komanoff also notes the reassertion of automobility after oil prices fell in 1982–1983 and then crashed in 1986.

64. Ibid. Examples of references to "kamikaze" New York City cyclists and messengers in this period are found in William E. Geist, "Fastest Is Best as Messengers Pedal in Pursuit of a $100 Day," *New York Times,* December 2, 1983; Myra Alperson, "Other Cyclists Resent Daredevils on Wheels," *New York Times,* March 26, 1986; Peter Forstenzer, "Undone by the Attack of the Kamikaze Cyclists," *New York Times,* November 14, 1988; Evelyn Williams, "License Bicycles," *New York Times,* November 26, 1988; Frank Trippett, "Scaring the Public to Death': On City Streets and Country Roads, the War Rages against Cyclists," *Time,* October 5, 1987, 29.

65. "Lax Pursuit of Reckless Bikers," *New York Times,* June 5, 1986. This was one of several anti-cycling articles featured in the *New York Times'* "Worm and the Apple" column between 1983 and 1986. A printed response to "Lax Pursuit," from Police Commissioner Benjamin Ward, contextualizes the lunacy of the initial piece: "You suggest diverting police officers to issue summonses to kids on bicycles who violate traffic regulations—and this at a time of rising drug use and crime in New York City. With a fiscal year 1987 no-growth budget, a crime rate that is going up and an epidemic of crack—a potent form of cocaine—the Police Department is using all the police officers it can spare to chase bike riders in midtown Manhattan." See Benjamin Ward, "After That Bike," *New York Times,* June 20, 1986.

66. Charlie McCorkell puts the bicycle-pedestrian accidents of 1986 into context: "If these accidents involved only the 35,000 commuter and commercial cyclists—an extreme assumption—then the average rider will hit a pedestrian only once in 55 years. . . . [I]f only messengers were involved in these accidents—an even more extreme assumption— the average messenger would collide with a pedestrian once in 8 years." See "The Truth about the Bike Ban," *City Cyclist* (October–November 1987): 9.

67. For example, cyclists faced 19,148 traffic-violations summonses in 1986 alone. See Elizabeth Neuffer, "Bicycling to the Job Is on Rise," *New York Times* 1987.

68. "Bike Messengers: Life in Tight Lane," *New York Times,* September 4, 1987; Reilly, *Nerves of Steel,* 301.

69. Reilly, *Nerves of Steel,* 301.

70. Ibid.

71. McCorkell, "The Truth about the Bike Ban," 9–10.

72. Trippett, "Scaring the Public to Death."

73. For example, bike messengering is widely considered to be the most dangerous job in the United States, with an injury rate that is roughly three times higher than that of the second most dangerous job (meat packing). See Jack Tigh Dennerlein and John D. Meeker, "Occupational Injuries among Boston Bicycle Messengers," *American Journal of Industrial Medicine* 42, no. 6 (2002): 519–525.

74. "Red Light for Reckless Bikes," *New York Times,* December 9, 1983.

75. Trippett, "Scaring the Public to Death."

76. Bike messengers in 2000 made about $21,600 a year, and Rebecca Reilly quotes a ten-year veteran messenger who claims that a good messenger makes between $500 and $550 a week: "If a messenger makes $600–700 a week, it means he is working from 7 am to 8 pm." Reilly, *Nerves of Steel,* 18.

77. Ibid., 29.

78. Kevin Wehr, "Bicycle Messengers and Fast Capitalism: An Old-School Solution

to the Needs of Technocapitalism," *Fast Capitalism* 2, no. 1 (2006), available at http://www.uta.edu/huma/agger/fastcapitalism/2_1/wehr.html.

79. Bob Levey, "Hope Amid the Spokes and Wheels," *Washington Post,* February 17, 1989. Joe Hendry has catalogued excerpts from Bob Levey's inflammatory, anti-cycling columns from 1987 to 1992, including some of the following gems: "Do the Messengers Own Their Bikes?" *Washington Post,* September 4, 1987; "Bike Messenger Watch: More Horrors," *Washington Post,* October 27, 1987; "Bike Messenger Watch: Yes, More," *Washington Post,* December 15, 1987; "His Fault, but She Rhymes with Witch," *Washington Post,* December 27, 1988; "Bike Messenger Reports Progress (!)," *Washington Post,* August 5, 1988; "Antibicyclist? Not Guilty, Your Honor," *Washington Post,* September 22, 1988; "The Squirrel That Got Biked to Death," *Washington Post,* November 21, 1991; "Bike Messengers up to Their Old Tricks," *Washington Post,* November 15, 1995; "Another Nasty, Wrong Bike Messenger," *Washington Post,* May 11, 1995; "Bike Messengers Still Just Don't Get It," *Washington Post,* November 30, 1995. Also see Joe Hendry, "The Bigots' Views," *Messenger Institute for Media Accuracy,* available at http://www.messmedia.org/messville/QUOTE.HTM.

80. Charles Komanoff and Members of Right of Way, "Killed by Automobile: Death in the Streets in New York City 1994–1997" (New York: Right of Way, 1999), 38. Emphasis is my own.

81. Ibid. Also see Michael Smith and Charles Komanoff, "Spin City: Or, Some Deaths Are More Equal Than Others," *Bike Reader: A Reader's Digest,* 1998, available at http://www.bikereader.com/contributors/carssuck/post.html.

82. For example, Eva S. Moskowitz, the Upper East Side councilwoman, defended a bill against sidewalk cycling in 2002 by saying "the bicycle menace is worse than all other menaces." On a related note, see "Forbidden Words for Newspaper Articles about Messengers," *Voice of Da,* no. 8 (1999). The humorous list includes such over-used journalistic descriptors as *Generation X, Gen-X, kamikaze, Lycra-clad, menace (car~, taxi~, or bike~), miscreants, nose-ringed, outlaw (urban ~, ~ culture), pierced.*

83. Fincham, "Bicycle Messengers and the Road to Freedom," 212.

84. Harold Gluck, "A Call for Regulating Use of Bicycles on Our Roads," *New York Times,* June 26, 1983.

85. Ibid.

86. Gluck, "A Call for Regulating Use of Bicycles on Our Roads." Emphasis is my own.

87. Fincham, "Bicycle Messengers and the Road to Freedom," 212.

88. "Cycle Wars" *The Evening Standard* (London), March 30, 2006; Michael Hodges, "Two-Wheeled Fascism: The Trouble with London's Cyclists," *Time Out London,* May 9, 2007. Also see Tom Bogdanowicz, "Cycling and the Media," *Intermedia* 32, no. 3 (2004): 21–22.

89. Tom Coghlan, "We're Not Lycra Louts, We're the Future," *The Evening Standard* (London), June 29, 2001; Bryan Appleyard, "One Day, I'll Kill a Lycra Lout," *The Sunday Times* (United Kingdom), July 28, 2002; David Bamber, "'Lycra Louts' Face Curbs in New Cycle Crackdown," *Sunday Telegraph* (London), June 30, 2002; Kate Hoey, "Lycra Louts: The Real Menace on Britain's Roads Are Selfish, Aggressive, Lawbreaking and Infuriatingly Smug," *Mail on Sunday,* October 19, 2003; Andrew Martin, "Out of Control: Confessions of a Lycra Lout," *The Independent on Sunday* 2003; Sam Halstead,

"Breaking the Cycle of City's Lycra Louts," *Evening News* (Edinburgh), September 18, 2004; "Lycra Louts Are a Road Menace," *The Evening Chronicle* (New Castle), November 5, 2005; "Will Number Plates on Bikes Halt Lycra Louts?" *Daily Mail,* July 28, 2006.

90. David Rowan, "Two Wheeled Terrors," *The Evening Standard* (London), August 8, 2002.

91. Fincham, "Bicycle Messengers and the Road to Freedom," 221.

92. See The Car Party, available at http://www.thecarparty.org.uk (defunct link as of spring 2009).

93. Kirsten Dizonk, "Behind the Wheel: Drivers Sound Off about Reckless Cyclists," *Seattle Post-Intelligencer,* August 29, 2005. Emphasis is my own.

94. Quigley, "Disturbing Cycle a Critical Mess."

95. Stuart Hall speaks to the discursive role of silences in "The Narrative Construction of Reality," *Context,* no. 10 (1983), available at http://www.centerforbookculture.org/context/no10/hall.html.

96. L. Basford et al., "Drivers' Perceptions of Cyclists" (Berkshire: Transport Research Laboratory, 2002), 4. See the Right of Way Web site for more on "Thugarchy."

97. Ibid., 11. Emphasis is my own. The TRL study continually references the way drivers position themselves as "in groups" and "out groups," in accordance with their 'theory of planned behavior' framework. The problem with this approach is that behavior is not simply an "endpoint of cognitive decisions," but rather, an expression and embodiment of cultural norms—from the way people walk (i.e., their "strut") to the ideological and communicative frameworks that organize people's morality, ethics, and beliefs. In short, people do not make all of their individual choices throughout a given day by perpetually asking themselves the question: "what would society think?" Rather, human behavior is much more intuitive and not always pragmatically weighed in terms of a cost/benefit analysis. This is particularly true when it comes to the type of emotionally grounded responses that TRL researchers are rightfully invested in documenting. I raise this issue not to discount an otherwise excellent study but to re-emphasize the importance of analyzing cultural norms, ideology, and context when discussing social trends, rather than examining atomized behavioral tendencies through a somewhat rigid, and thus limited, theoretical framework.

98. Ibid., 9.

99. Thanks to the eminent John Baynard Woods Jr. for the translation.

100. Packer, "Mobility without Mayhem," 87.

101. For example, a 2005 poll conducted by *ABC News, Time Magazine,* and the *Washington Post* found that 82 percent of drivers said they often see other drivers speeding, 71 percent see inattentive driving, 64 percent witness aggressive driving, 40 percent witness people running red lights and stop signs, 34 percent see "impolite gestures," and 27 percent see other drivers exhibiting road rage. A different study conducted by Nationwide Insurance found that most U.S. drivers believe they are safe drivers (more than 83 percent) and more than 50 percent do not consider themselves distracted drivers despite the fact that 73 percent talk on cell phones, only 16 percent drive at or below the speed limit, and 38 percent admit to driving a certain distance without any recollection of doing so. Roughly one-third of younger drivers also admit to text messaging while driving, and 57 percent of drivers admit to not using their turn signals, including 7 percent

who do so because "it makes driving more exciting." See Gary Langer, "Poll: Traffic in the United States: A Look under the Hood of a Nation on Wheels," *ABC News,* February 13, 2005; Ryan Holeywell, "Busted for DWD: Driving While Distracted," *USA Today,* January 23, 2007; "Study: 32 Percent of Young Drivers Text Message Behind the Wheel," *WKMG Orlando News,* October 24, 2006.

102. Jorge Casuso, "Bike Dislike," *LA Weekly,* October 24, 2007.

103. Walt Seifert, "Scofflaw Cyclists," *Sacramento Area Bicycle Advocates,* available at http://saba.phpwebhosting.com/articles/article.php?mode=display&lognum=20.

104. It is worth noting that there are also very different laws regarding "fault" for auto accidents outside of the United States and the United Kingdom, namely, in countries with long-standing utilitarian cycling traditions.

105. Peter D. Norton, "Fighting Traffic: The Dawn of the Motor Age in the American City" (Ph.D. diss., University of Virginia, 2002), 255.

106. Ibid., 249. Elsewhere, Norton describes transition from when pedestrians and children first became complicit in "recklessness" on city streets. See "Street Rivals," 335.

107. Norton, "Fighting Traffic," 253, 258.

108. Ibid., 249. It is notable that the goal of making pedestrians ultimately responsible for their on-the-street safety was emphasized well beyond the 1930s. For example, see *When You Are a Pedestrian* (Progressive Pictures, 1948).

109. See *You and Your Bicycle; Bicycle Safety; Bicycle Clown;* and *One Got Fat.*

110. As a case in point, when a New York City teacher and activist named Eric Ng was killed while riding his bicycle in 2006, the *New York Times* reported the story as follows (here excerpted): "The police said that Mr. Ng's new bike had been equipped with reflectors, but that they could not tell if it had bike lights. Both are required by city law. Mr. Ng's father said he had installed the reflectors on his son's new bike personally, and had urged him to wear a helmet—optional for riders 14 and over—when riding. The police said that *Mr. Ng was not wearing a helmet when he was hit*" Nicholas Confessore and Kate Hammer, "Drunken Driver Kills Rider on Bicycle Path, Police Say," *New York Times,* December 3, 2006 (emphasis is my own). Like so many other stories about cycling fatalities and injuries, the insinuation that Ng was potentially irresponsible, neglectful, or even acting in an unlawful manner unquestionably muddies one of clearest examples of automotive manslaughter in recent decades. That is to say, Eric Ng was killed by a man (Eugenio Cidron) who was speeding down the Hudson River bike path—a swath of road specifically restricted to all cars except for New York City department vehicles. To add insult to injury, the reporters claimed that Cidron's wrong turn "appeared to be accidental," despite the fact that he was driving down a bike path, at night, while drunk. Moreover, the *New York Daily News* (whose account paints a rather different picture of the incident) reported that Cidron drove for a full mile along the path before hitting Ng with "such force that the victim's bicycle and one of his black Converse All Stars flew onto the adjacent West Side Highway." Indeed, Ng's body was thrown fifty feet from the initial point of impact. See Kerry Burke and Carrie Melago, "DWI Kills NYU Grad on Bike, Cops Say," *New York Daily News,* December 2, 2006.

111. Statistics on the culpability of cyclists in auto-bicycle accidents vary widely and are highly questionable for several reasons including, but certainly not limited to, the accuracy of the police report (if/when one is filed), the high number of accidents not

reported to police, the production of statistics based solely on accident report checklists as opposed to police testimony (if one is even available), and, most important, the gray areas often surrounding what constitutes "right of way." Charles Komanoff and Michael J. Smith are two of the only researchers to actually re-examine police reports on automobile crashes in order to assess culpability, and their findings are significant. In "Killed By Automobile," they expose the over-inflated numbers of pedestrians and cyclists found to be "at fault" or partially "at fault" in auto accidents, and their bike-specific study, "The Only Good Cyclist: NYC Bicycle Fatalities—Who's Responsible?" finds that "although police blame cyclist error for three fourths (75%) of cyclist fatalities, in fact, driver error was the principal cause in 57–66% of recent fatal bicycle crashes and at least a contributing cause in 78–85%."

112. Matt Seaton, "A Licence to Stop at Red," *The Guardian*, December 21, 2005.

113. Cyclists have similarly brandished the *elitist* moniker against other bike riders and cycling advocates since the 1980s. For example, James A. Smith, the head of Bicycle Commuters of New York—a group that called for more police regulation of cyclists in the early 1980s—pushed for the creation of laws that would have required all New York City cyclists to register their bikes and carry IDs (or face mandatory fines). The city debated registration, but Mayor Koch ultimately found the measures too costly and impossible to enforce. Smith responded by saying that Mayor Koch gave into the "*elitism* of those who see the bicycle as the last bastion of freedom of movement." See Glenn Fowler, "City Working on Plan to Register Bikes," *New York Times*, July 21, 1980; Ronald Smothers, "City Vetoes Registering of Bicycles," *New York Times*, August 26, 1980.

114. Ben McGrath, "Holy Rollers: The City's Bicycle Zealots," *New Yorker*, November 13, 2006.

115. Philip Nolan, "On Yer Bikes!" *Daily Mail* (London), November 16, 2007.

116. Dunn, *Driving Forces*, 15. For an example of a bicyclist using this same tactic, see Forester, *Bicycle Transportation*, 165–166.

117. Komanoff and Smith's study "Killed by Automobile" shows that in New York City alone, only *16 percent* of drivers who killed pedestrians or cyclists between 1994 and 1997 (1,020 killed) were issued moving violations and just *9 percent* were issued non-moving violations pertaining to inspection, insurance, registration, and so on ("Killed by Automobile," 9). A study published in 2003 by the Silicon Valley Bicycle Coalition similarly found that most "at fault" drivers who kill pedestrians and cyclists are rarely even cited— roughly 1 out of 4—let alone jailed (Silicon Valley Bicycle Coalition and Peninsula Bicycle and Pedestrian Coalition, *Spinning Crank* 17, no. 6 [2003]: 2). Jake Voelcker acknowledges this same problem in the United Kingdom, where "drivers are less harshly punished, and that this is due to a bias in the criminal justice system because of a lack of representation of vulnerable road users amongst judiciary, policy makers and legal officials . . . unequal class and power relations allow the interests of drivers to be over-represented whilst the rights of pedestrians and cyclists are eroded." See "A Critical Review of the Legal Penalties for Drivers Who Kill Cyclists or Pedestrians" (master's thesis, University of Bristol, 2007), 1. The Bicycle Austin project, based out of Austin, Texas, features various online resources about the lack of justice for cyclists hit or killed by automobiles. See "No Justice for Cyclists," *Bicycle Austin*, available at http://bicycleaustin.info/justice.

118. Angela Galloway, "Should Bicyclists Be Licensed to Ride?" *Seattle Post-Intelligencer*, December 25, 2007.

119. Hoey, "Lycra Louts."

120. One of the few studies to actually document the rate of car ownership among bike commuters (though not all bike users) finds that 70 percent of bike commuters also own at least one car, and 32 percent own two or three cars. See Pnina Plaut, "Non-motorized Commuting in the US," *Transportation Research Part D: Transport and Environment* 10, no. 5 (2005): 351.

121. The TRL perception study suggests that drivers raise this issue without provocation or justification: "interestingly, there was no mention even among those who cycled that cyclists pay taxes indirectly, such as through council tax and other general taxation; or that many cyclists are also car owners and therefore do pay road tax; or that some cyclists do choose to carry third party liability insurance" Basford et al., "Drivers' Perceptions of Cyclists," 9. For a more realistic analysis of who actually "pays their share" on the road, see Crouse, "The Real Costs of the Automobile"; Mark A. Delucchi, "Do Motor-Vehicle Users in the U.S. Pay Their Way?" *Transportation Research Part A: Policy and Practice* 41, no. 10 (2007): 982–1003; Victoria Transport Policy Institute, "Transportation Cost and Benefit Analysis: Techniques, Estimates and Implications [Second Edition]."

122. "Bicycle Menace," *Orlando Sentinel,* June 22, 2006, emphasis is my own. Incidentally, the Surface Transportation Policy Partnership ranks Orlando as one of the most dangerous metropolitan areas for pedestrians in the entire United States (number 1 in 2004). In addition, Florida is consistently one of the most lethal states in the country for bicyclists (often ranked number 1 for cyclist fatalities). See Michelle Ernst and Surface Transportation Policy Project, "Mean Streets 2004" (Washington, DC: Surface Transportation Policy Project, 2004); National Highway Traffic Safety Administration, "Data Collection Study: Deaths and Injuries Resulting from Certain Non-traffic and Non-crash Events."

123. John Ritter, "Narrowed Roads Gain Acceptance in Colo., Elsewhere," *USA Today,* July 30, 2007.

124. Brian Doherty, *Radicals for Capitalism: A Freewheeling History of the Modern American Libertarian Movement* (New York: Public Affairs Books, 2007).

125. An updated list of the Reason Foundation's news features and individual contributors is available at http://www.reason.org/press/.

126. Source Watch (a project of the Center for Media and Democracy) and Media Transparency both feature extensive coverage on right wing and/or Libertarian think tanks, as well as their financial/political connections. See: "Think Tanks," *Source Watch,* available at http://www.sourcewatch.org/index.php?title=Think_tanks; "Conservative Philanthropies," *Media Transparency,* available at http://mediatransparency.org/funders. php.

127. Gorz, "The Social Ideology of the Motorcar."

128. Transportation Alternatives, "T.A. Bulletin," *Transportation Alternatives,* April 25, 2003, available at http://www.transalt.org/files/newsroom/streetbeat/askta/030425. html.

129. For more on mass media coverage of political dissidents, see Todd Gitlin, *The Whole World Is Watching: Mass Media in the Making and Unmaking of the New Left* (Berkeley: University of California Press, 1980); Kevin Michael DeLuca, *Image Politics: The New Rhetoric of Environmental Activism,* Revisioning Rhetoric (New York: Guilford Press, 1999); Jules Boykoff, *The Suppression of Dissent: How the State and Mass*

Media Squelch Usamerican Social Movements, New Approaches in Sociology (New York: Routledge, 2006).

130. O'Toole is highly critical of "smart growth" urbanism, environmental regulations, and light-rail transit systems, particularly in Portland, Oregon. While Portland is widely viewed as the model for emergent sustainable transportation initiatives and also has the highest bike commuter rate in the United States, he calls it the "city that doesn't work." For a prime example of O'Toole's brand of corporate propaganda, see "Is Urban Planning 'Creeping Socialism'?" *The Independent Review* 4, no. 4 (2000): 501–516; *The Best-Laid Plans: How Government Planning Harms Your Quality of Life, Your Pocketbook, and Your Future* (Washington, DC: Cato Institute, 2007). For a thorough critique of O'Toole's Portland data, see Michael Lewyn, "Debunking Cato: Why Portland Works Better Than the Analysis of Its Chief Neo-Libertarian Critic," *Congress for New Urbanism,* 2007, available at http://www.cnu.org/node/1532.

131. Randal O'Toole, "Mobility Counted Most in Fleeing New Orleans," *Seattle Times,* September 14, 2005.

CHAPTER 6

1. See Michael Green, "Bike Culture for Sale (?)," *Bike Blog,* February 28, 2006, available at http://bikeblog.blogspot.com/2006/02/bike-culture-for-sale.html; Tod Seelie, "Brooklyn vs. Brokelyn," *Suckapants,* February 23, 2006, available at http://suckapants.com/2006/02/brooklyn-vs-brokelyn.html; Jake Dobkin, "Bikers to Brooklyn Industries: F-U!" *Gothamist,* February 24, 2006, available at http://gothamist.com/2006/02/24/bikers_to_brook.php; Karen Iris Tucker, "Mutant Bike Gangs of New York: Tall-Bike Clubs Live Free, Ride High, and Don't Want Your Stinking Logo," *Village Voice,* March 14, 2006. Also see Kerrie Mitchell, "Hip Store, on the Hot Seat," *New York Times,* March 19, 2006.

2. Karl Anderson (aka Megulon 5), interview with the author, August 8, 2004.

3. Rosen, "Up the Vélorution," 366.

4. Chris Atton, *Alternative Media* (London: Sage, 2002), 16.

5. Stuart Hall, "The Problem of Ideology: Marxism without Guarantees," in *Stuart Hall: Critical Dialogues in Cultural Studies,* ed. Stuart Hall, David Morley, and Kuan-Hsing Chen (London: Routledge, 1996), 41.

6. Articles and/or photo essays on bike tinkering were regularly published in magazines like *Popular Science, Mechanix Illustrated,* and *Modern Mechanix* throughout the 1930s and 1940s. For example, see "New Bicycle Gearshift and Man with Telephoto Eyes," *Modern Mechanix* (May 1934); "Eccentric Cycles," *Mechanix Illustrated* (September 1949). Recently, someone took the liberty of posting images and articles from *Modern Mechanix* online, including a range of bicycle-themed content (available at the Modern Mechanix Blog, http://blog.modernmechanix.com).

7. Duncombe, "Stepping Off the Sidewalk," 219.

8. Nolan, "Debut Column," 13.

9. Any terms used to label specific assemblages of punks and/or punk practices are necessarily inadequate and bound to raise more issues than they resolve. Consequently, I use the terms *punk culture, DIY punk culture, DIY culture, the punk underground, underground culture,* and *the punk community* interchangeably not out of laziness but

because they are simply different ways of talking about the same people and practices, however resistant to classification some of them might be. Longtime zine writer and punk drummer Aaron Cometbus spoke to the latter point in 2000: "I like that about punk and fanzines—that it's a community that's very ill-defined. As much as 90% of what we talk about is defining it, and still it's very ill-defined" (*Maximumrocknroll*, no. 200). For more on defining and naming punk practices, see Alan O'Connor "Local Scenes and Dangerous Crossroads: Punk and Theories of Cultural Hybridity," *Popular Music* 21, no. 2 (2002): 226; Alan O'Connor, *Punk Record Labels and the Struggle for Autonomy: The Emergence of DIY* (Lanham, MD: Lexington Books, 2008), 3.

10. "Appeal to the International Provotariat," *Provo*, no. 11. Emphasis is my own.

11. There are obvious and severe limitations to anyone's ability to gain "independence" from the oil industry, particularly because the global market is saturated with petroleum byproducts and additives that are found in any number of non-automotive goods. Ironically, two examples are bicycle tires and vinyl records.

12. See Jim Phillips, "Oops . . . This Bike Wasn't a Pipe Bomb," *Columbus Dispatch*, March 3, 2006; Allie Zendrian, "Bellarmine Bomb Scare a Big Bust," *The Hawk* (St. Josephs University), March 17, 2006.

13. Pink Floyd, "Bike," in *The Piper at the Gates of Dawn* (Capitol Records, 1967), LP.

14. Divide and Conquer, "Bike Punx," *Sanjam Split International Compilation* (Sanjam Records, 1996), LP. The band also has a song called "Bike Militia" on their EP entitled *The Need to Amputate* (Ginger Liberation/Maloka Records, 1999).

15. Atton, *Alternative Media*, 67–68. Interestingly, the first uses of the term *bike punks* in popular culture were references to gay motorcycle gangs in Michael Scott's racy pulp novels. See *Threeway Team* (Santee, CA: Surrey House, 1977), 53; *Biker in Bondage* (Santee, CA: Surree Limited, 1979), 16. To my knowledge, the first time that *bike punks* is used in reference to bicycle riding punk rockers is in *Maximumrocknroll*, no. 16 (1984), where columnist Vic Notorious mentions the new phenomena of "bike punks" in Toronto, Canada. See "Toronto Scene Report."

16. Manuel Castells, *The Power of Identity* (Malden, MA: Blackwell, 1997), 8. Quoted in Atton, *Alternative Media*, 67–68.

17. Rambo, *Wall of Death the System* (625 Records, 2000), LP.

18. Pinhead Gunpowder, *West Side Highway* (Recess Records, 2008), seven-inch record.

19. Switzky, "Critical Mass," 186.

20. Petersen, "Pedaling Hope," 37.

21. Stephen Duncombe, *Notes from Underground: Zines and the Politics of Alternative Culture* (London: Verso, 1997), 59.

22. Erik Ruin, "Real Time Detroit," in *Trouble in Mind* (Detroit).

23. Mike Scenery and Travis Fristoe, "Biking," in *The Zine Yearbook*, vol. 5, ed. Jen Angel and Jason Kucsma (Bowling Green: Become the Media, 2001), 82 (originally published in *Drinking Sweat in the Ash Age*, self-published zine).

24. Defiance, Ohio, *Share What Ya Got* (Friends and Relatives Records, 2004), LP.

25. Jimmy Baker, personal correspondence, July 6, 2008. Nate Powell, a comic artist, zine writer, and former member of the band Soophie Nun Squad, reiterates this perspective and frames it in terms of personal responsibility and empowerment: "It's easy to ignore or put aside the passive support we lend a violent and heartless group of men and

272 NOTES TO PAGES 147-148

their interests by the way we spend our money, the kind of transportation we use, where we give our time and efforts at our jobs. . . . It is empowering to be in control of one's body and decisions about where to put energy, to choose very carefully on what to support." Evi, "Interview with Soophie Nun Squad," *Enough Fanzine,* February 9, 2003.

26. Jeff Lockwood, "Interview with Mike Watt," *Dirt Rag,* no. 95 (August 2002), available at http://www.dirtragmag.com/print/article.php?ID=418. In the same interview, Watt reflects further on his love of biking: "You don't have to be part of, or held hostage by, this fucking nightmare of traffic. It's very much a personal expression. The physicalness of it too . . . punk music for me has always been very physical like that. You know I just don't stand there and play the riffs, it's sort of like I whip myself into a state . . . sort of like a dervish thing."

27. Eric Boerer, personal correspondence, January 15, 2007.

28. Joel Schalit, "Just Say No to Rock and Roll," *Bad Subjects,* no 27 (1996), available at http://bad.eserver.org/issues/1996/27/joel.html.

29. Jim Carey, "Fresh Flavour in the Media Soup: The Story of Squall Magazine," in *DiY Culture: Party and Protest in Nineties Britain,* ed. George McKay (London: Verso, 1998), 58–78. Quoted in Chris Atton, "The Infoshop: The Alternative Information Centre of the 1990s," *New Library World* 100 (1999): 26.

30. Of the fifty or so interviews I conducted with self-identified "punks" about bicycling between 2003 and 2008, roughly one dozen were formal, sit-down interviews in which I asked people a range of questions about bicycling, bike advocacy, or some specific activity or practice that made me seek out the interviewee in the first place (e.g., the person makes bikes for a living, volunteers at a community bicycle organization, or plays in a band with other bicyclists). Another dozen of these interviews consisted of open-ended e-mail exchanges as well as responses I received from punks who either completed a lengthy survey I circulated online, or used the survey as an opportunity to initiate a more substantive conversation. The remaining interviews were informal conversations about bicycling, punk, and DIY ethics that took place at punk shows, coffee shops, bike shops, bars, food co-ops, and parking lots in more than a dozen cities throughout the United States.

31. Zack Furness, "Microcosm Publishing," *Punk Planet* (January–February 2005): 46–47.

32. Just a few examples of van references in punk music, include The Descendents, "Van," *Somery* (SST Records, 1991), LP; Screeching Weasel, "Punk Rock Explained," *Four on the Floor* (Lookout! Records, 1999), EP; Mr. T Experience, "Dumb Little Band," *Love Is Dead* (Lookout! Records, 1996), LP; The Ramones, "Touring," *Mondo Bizarro* (Radioactive Records, 1992), LP; Avail, "South Bound 95," *Dixie* (Lookout! Records, 1994), LP; Against Me! "We Laugh at Danger (and Break All the Rules)," *Reinventing Axl Rose* (No Idea Records, 2002), LP; The Broadways, *Broken Van* (Asian Man Records, 2000), LP; Ghost Mice, "Austin to El Paso," *Split with Defiance, Ohio* (Plan-it-X Records, 2004), CD; Shelter, "In the Van Again," in *When 20 Summers Pass* (Victory Records, 2000), CD. Also see Henry Rollins, *Get in the Van* (Los Angeles: 2.13.61, 1994).

33. Jason Trashville and Braxie Hicks, "Because Some Times You Just Want to Ride Your Bike to the Show . . . All of Them: Tales from the 2002 Dead Things Punk Rock Bike Tour of N.C." (unpublished).

34. Dead Things, "Bike Tour Press Release" (2002).

35. See Paul Rosen, "'It Was Easy, It Was Cheap, Go and Do It!': Technology and Anarchy in the UK Music Industry," in *Twenty-first Century Anarchism: Unorthodox Ideas for a New Millennium,* ed. Jonathan Purkis and James Bowen (London: Cassell, 1997), 99–116.

36. Ibid.

37. Desperate Bicycles, "Cars," *New Cross, New Cross* (Refill Records, 1978), LP.

38. Buzzcocks, "Fast Cars," *Another Music in a Different Kitchen* (United Artists, 1978), LP; The Jam, "Bricks and Mortar," in *In the City* (Polydor Records, 1977), LP; The Jam, "London Traffic," in *This Is the Modern World* (Polydor Records, 1977), LP.

39. For more on anarcho-punk, see Tim Gosling, "'Not for Sale': The Underground Network of Anarcho-Punk," in *Music Scenes: Local, Translocal and Virtual,* ed. Andy Bennett and Richard A. Peterson (Nashville: Vanderbilt University Press, 2004), 168–186; Ian Glasper, *The Day the Country Died: A History of Anarcho Punk 1980 to 1984* (London: Cherry Red Books, 2006).

40. Gee Vaucher, as performed by Crass, "Contaminational Power," *Stations of the Crass* (Crass Records, 1979), LP.

41. Gee Vaucher, as performed by Crass, "Big Man, Big M.A.N.," *Stations of the Crass* (Crass Records, 1979), LP. Also see/hear Crass, "Deadhead," *Christ the Album* (Crass Records, 1982), LP.

42. Amebix, "Largactyl," *Arise!* (Alternative Tentacles, 1985), LP.

43. In addition to the relevant essays featured in *DiY Culture* and *The Unknown City,* see Derek Wall, *Earth First! and the Anti-roads Movement* (London: Routledge, 1999).

44. George McKay, "DiY Culture: Notes towards an Intro," in *DiY Culture,* 4 (emphasis is original); Iris Marion Young, *Justice and the Politics of Difference* (Princeton, NJ: Princeton University Press, 1990), 86. As a case in point, former Crass member Penny Rimbaud—who is not one to shy away from self-criticism or a scathing critique of punk—specifically alludes to the role that Crass played in the rejuvenating the Campaign for Nuclear Disarmament in the late 1970s, namely, by introducing anti-nuclear politics to "thousands of people who would later become the backbone of its revival." See *Shibboleth: My Revolting Life* (Oakland, CA: AK Press, 1998), 109.

45. For examples, see Oi Polloi, "No More Roads," *Fuaim Catha* (Skuld Records, 1999), LP; Nausea, "Tech.No.Logic.Kill," *Extinction* (Profane Existance, 1990), LP; Antischism, "Factory," *End of Time* (Stereonucleosis Records, 1990), seven-inch record; Anti-product, *The Deafening Silence of Grinding Gears* (Tribal War Records, 1999), LP; His Hero is Gone, *Monuments to Thieves* (Prank Records, 1997), LP; Aus Rotten, *The System Works for Them* (Tribal War Records, 1996), LP.

46. See Atton, *Alternative Media;* Maxwell Dervin Schnurer, "Conscious Rebellion: A Rhetorical Analysis of Political Cross-fertilization in the Animal Rights Movement" (Ph.D. diss., University of Pittsburgh, 2002), 46–54. For more on primitivism, see John Zerzan's *Elements of Refusal* (Columbia, MO: CAL Press, 1999) and *Running on Emptiness: The Pathology of Civilization* (Los Angeles: Feral House, 2002).

47. Fifteen, "Petroleum Distillation," *Choice of a New Generation* (Lookout! Records, 1989), LP.

48. Mumford, *Technics and Civilization,* 21.

49. This view is well put in Murray Bookchin, *Post-scarcity Anarchism* (Berkeley, CA: Ramparts Press, 1971). With respect to "technoskepticism," I concur with Andrew Ross

when he describes this disposition as a necessary condition for social change in "Hacking Away at the Counterculture," *Postmodern Culture* 1, no. 1 (1990): 39. For one of the best analyses of the political prospects and limitations of technoskepticism, see Carol Stabile, *Feminism and the Technological Fix* (Manchester, UK: Manchester University Press, 1994).

50. "Interview with Creation Is Crucifixion," *Infinite Monkey*, no. 2, available at http://www.geocities.com/snufffan/interviews/cic.html.

51. For example, see *Evasion* (Atlanta: CrimethInc., 2001).

52. San Francisco Bike Messengers Association, "Bike Messengering," *Shaping San Francisco,* 1996, available at http://foundsf.org/index.php?title=BIKE_MESSENGERING (originally published in a pamphlet by the San Francisco Bike Messengers Association, 1996).

53. See "Cars, I Hate the Fucking Things," in *Voice of Da,* no. 4, ed. America Meredith (San Francisco: Self-published, 1997).

54. Dick Hebdige, "Travelling Light: One Route into Material Culture," *RAIN,* no. 59 (1983): 13; Deborah A. Chambers, "Symbolic Equipment and the Objects of Leisure Images," *Leisure Studies* 2, no. 3 (1983): 305.

55. C. Ondine Chavoya, "Customized Hybrids: The Art of Ruben Ortiz Torres and Lowriding in Southern California," *CR: The New Centennial Review* 4, no. 2 (2005): 173.

56. Sheldon Brown also sees the interest in single-speed mountain bikes as a "rebellion against the excessive complication, fragility and weight of current mountain bikes," in "Single Speed Conversions," *Sheldon Brown's Bicycle Technical Information,* July 3, 1999, available at http://www.sheldonbrown.com/singlespeed.html.

57. Rosen, "Up the Vélorution," 374.

58. Ibid., 368–370. Rosen specifically refers to the work of Lewis Mumford, Langdon Winner, and Richard Sclove in his discussion of "democratic technics." For the seminal piece by Lewis Mumford, see "Authoritarian and Democratic Technics," *Technology and Culture* 5, no. 1 (1964): 1–8.

59. Chris Carlsson, "'Outlaw' Bicycling," *Affinities: A Journal of Radical Theory, Culture, and Action* 1, no. 1 (2007): 90.

60. Ross Evans, interview with the author, August 7, 2007; Aaron Weiler, *Namibian Bicycle Ambulance Project,* available at http://bikecart.pedalpeople.com/namibia.

61. See Megulon 5, "I Meet the Hard Times Bike Club and Live to Tell the Tale," *Chunk 666,* October 10, 1997, available at http://www.dclxvi.org/chunk/outside/htbc/meet.html; C. Bales, "The Rat Patrol," in *Reglar Wiglar,* no. 19 (Chicago: Self-published, 2003). For more on Circus Redickuless and the Hard Times Bike Club, see Brian Doherty, *This Is Burning Man: The Rise of a New American Underground* (New York: Little and Brown, 2004), 140–146.

62. Mykle Hansen, "Hell on Wheels," *The Portland Mercury,* June 8, 2000.

63. Johnny Payphone, "Mutant Bike Culture Past and Present," *Ghostride Magazine,* no. 4 (2006): 23–26; Chris Carlsson, *Nowtopia: How Pirate Programmers, Outlaw Bicyclists, and Vacant-Lot Gardeners Are Inventing the Future Today* (Oakland, CA: AK Press, 2008), 117.

64. Payphone, "Mutant Bike Culture Past and Present."

65. For example, see "New Bicycle Gearshift and Man with Telephoto Eyes"; "Eccentric Cycles"; "Bike Side Car for Baby Passenger," *Modern Mechanix* (January

1932). Kristen Haring offers an analysis of "technical" culture in *Ham Radio's Technical Culture* (Cambridge, MA: MIT Press, 2007), 1–18.

66. Fernando Ruelas, one of the founding members of Duke's Car Club—the longest running and arguably most influential lowrider car club in the United States—helped to pioneer the lowrider bicycle craze while teaching his son Jay how to refurbish and modify old bikes in the 1960s. By the mid-1960s, Chicano youth in Los Angeles (predominantly East Los Angeles) were building lowrider bicycles with the help of their dads and brothers, though the popularity of lowrider bicycles really took off in the 1970s following the availability of surplus Sting-Ray bikes and parts throughout Southern California. See Duke's Car Club, "History," available at http://www.dukescarclub.com/history/history.html; Paige R. Penland, *Lowrider: History, Pride, Culture* (St. Paul, MN: Motorbooks International, 2003), 1957–1958. Also see Denise Michelle Sandoval, "Bajito y Suavecito/Low and Slow: Cruising through Lowrider Culture" (Ph.D. diss., Claremont Graduate University, 2003); Ben Chappell, "'Take a Little Trip with Me': Lowriding and the Poetics of Scale," in *Technicolor: Race, Technology, and Everyday Life*, ed. Alondra Nelson, Thuy Linh N. Tu, and Alicia Headlam Hines (New York: New York University Press, 2001), 100–120. For more on BMX, see Jeffrey E. Nash, "Expensive Dirt: Bicycle Motocross and Everyday Life," *Journal of Popular Culture* 20, no. 2 (1986): 97–122.

67. Dink Bridgers offers one of the best, if not the most entertaining, assessments of early mountain biking: "I'm writing this to remind a new generation of two-wheeled enthusiasts that the sport of mountainbiking was born in *America*, the child of a downhill race called Repack that emerged in a time of growing *spiritual awareness*, when those who rode into the mountains and raced a mountainbike on weekends didn't give a damn if it was 'cool.' Pot smoking peacenik misfits in flannel and denim, somewhat distracted by the destruction of the rainforests and the assassinations of George Moscone and Harvey Milk, duked it out for nothing more than bragging rights, on rattling, cobbled-together contraptions weighing 40 pounds with ever-fading and smoking brakes, and *they actually had more fun doing it this way*. And yes, they were really stoned." In "Wheels of Fortune." Also see Charles Kelly, "Clunkers among the Hills," *Bicycling* (January 1979): 40–42; Billy Savage, *Klunkerz* (Pumelo Pictures, 2007).

68. See Gene Balsley, "The Hot-Rod Culture," *American Quarterly* 2, no. 4 (1950): 353–358.

69. For more examples along these lines, see Ron Eglash, ed., *Appropriating Technology: Vernacular Science and Social Power* (Minneapolis: University of Minnesota Press, 2004).

70. The cover of Chunk 666, no. 1 reads "Preparing for the Carmageddon" and there are a number of punk songs about biking that also toy with this theme, including Rambo's "Apocalyse Riders" (from their split seven-inch record with Crucial Unit on Ed Walters Records, 2002) and The Awakening's "Front Wheel," and "Back Wheel" (from their split seven-inch record with Virginia Black Lung on Ed Walters Records, 2003).

71. Karl (aka Megulon 5) Anderson, "Why?" *Chunk 666*, October 4, 2008, available at http://www.dclxvi.org/chunk/why.

72. Ibid.

73. Chambers, "Symbolic Equipment and the Objects of Leisure Images," 306.

74. On this point, Megulon-5 notes: "You don't have to spend a lot of money to have

fun. You don't have to work for a car. You can make your own fun. The Man wants to find out what's fun so he can buy it all and sell it to you, but you have to pay him to have that fun. But it doesn't have to be that way." Quoted in Hansen, "Hell on Wheels."

75. The cover of Chunk 666, no. 3 features the line "To Heed the Moronic Dictum." In the documentary film *B.I.K.E.*, Johnny Payphone alludes to how bikes are in some ways secondary to the purpose and meaning of community in Rat Patrol: "The Rat Patrol is really just an equation, or a system for connection people who are into other interesting things: microcasting . . . dumpster dining or guerilla puppetry, circuit bending. . . . [I]t's just a way to connect to all these people who have other skills, who can feed upon each others creativity and create wonderful things, and worlds." Elsewhere he states, "Can you see how this all really has nothing to do with bikes?" See Jacob Septimus and Anthony Howard, *B.I.K.E.* (Fountainhead Films, 2007); "Interview with Johnny Payphone," *Relational Aesthetics,* June 8, 2007, available at http://relationalcate.blogspot.com/2007/06/johnny-payphone-of-rat-patrol.html. Also see Dan Weissmann, "Johnny Joins the Freak-Bike Gang," *Chicago Reader,* April 9, 2004.

76. Tony Lack, "Consumer Society and Authenticity: The (Il)Logic of Punk Practices," *Undercurrent,* no. 3 (1995).

77. "The Cycling Market," *Bicycling Magazine Media Kit,* available at http://www.bicycling.com/mediakit/audience_cyclingmarket.html; Andy Clarke, personal correspondence, January 3, 2007.

78. Randy Komisar, Silicon Valley venture capitalist, quoted in Alex Williams, "Wheels and Deals in Silicon Valley," *New York Times,* December 4, 2005.

79. Former Goldman Sachs investment banker, David Wagener, and hedge fund trader Dave "Tiger" Williams, quoted in Lisa Kassenaar, "Lance's Bankers Bring Bike Tour to Central Park: It's about the Bike," *Bloomberg.com,* October 7, 2005. SugarCRM CEO, John Roberts, quoted in "Pedal Power," *CNBC European Business* (July 2007), available at http://cnbceb.com/sports-sports-marketing/pedal-power/199.

80. Williams, "Wheels and Deals in Silicon Valley."

81. Douglas Belkin, "Would You Spend $14,000 for This Bike?" *Boston Globe,* April 23, 2006. Also see the $23,225 "dream bike" featured in *Bicycling,* December 2006, 72–75.

82. L. Jacque, "Bike Culture Always for Sale," *The Diary of the Ultimate Bromancer,* June 6, 2007, available at http://totalbromance.blogspot.com/2007/06/bike-culture-always-for-sale.html.

83. Jefferson Siegel, "Cyclists: DKNY Knocked Off Our 'Ghost Bike' Idea," *The Villager,* February 13–19, 2008.

84. Yokota Fritz, "DKNY Orange Bicycles in London," *Cycleicious Blog,* May 19, 2008, available at http://www.cyclelicio.us/2008/05/dkny-orange-bicycles-in-london.html.

85. Brad Aaron, "Macy's: Leave the Car at Home," *Streetsblog.com,* April 23, 2008, available at http://www.streetsblog.org/2008/04/23/macys-leave-the-car-at-home.

86. Hilary Howard, "W Celebrates Earth Day," *New York Times,* April 13, 2008.

87. Lesser Chris, "Puma Aligns Itself with Bike Messengers, Street Image," *Bicycle Retailer and Industry News* 14, no. 13 (2005).

88. Charles Kernaghan, "Child Labor Is Back: Children Are Again Sewing Clothing for Major U.S. Companies" (Washington, DC: National Labor Committee, 2006);

Charles Kernaghan, "Puma's Workers in China Facing an Olympian Struggle to Survive" (Washington, DC: National Labor Committee and China Labor Watch, 2004).

89. The retailer to most effectively "commodify the dissent" of urban bicyclists is arguably the New York City bike shop King Kog, which has previously sold "Outlaw" cycling sweatshirts (they feature detachable, pseudo-anarchist black bandana facemasks), as well as T-shirts that co-opted the logo of seminal anarcho-punk band, Crass. Shortly after receiving an e-mail from a friend who spotted the Crass shirt in Brooklyn (in 2008), I had the pleasure of running across a work of genius that the NYC Bike Snob penned on the subject (it is highly recommended). See "Product Review: King Kog Crass T-Shirt," *Bike Snob NYC*, July 24, 2008, available at http://bikesnobnyc.blogspot.com/2008/07/bsnyc-product-review-king-kog-crass-t.html.

90. The slogan "Give Hipsters a Brake" (with an image of a bike brake) comes from a U.S. T-shirt design circa 2006–2007.

91. For one of the many articles that offer an overview of fixed-gear bikes and biking, see Jeff Guerrero, "The Next Page: The Limberness of the Fixed Gear Mind," *Pittsburgh Post-Gazette*, September 9, 2007.

92. For more on fixed-gear terminology, see Buffalo Bill, "Guardian Style Journalist 'Discovers' Fixies," *Moving Target Zine*, September 3, 2008, available at http://www.movingtargetzine.com/article/guardian-style-journalist-discovers-fixies.

93. Sheldon Brown, "Fixed Gear Bicycles for the Road," *Sheldon Brown's Bicycle Technical Information*, available at http://www.sheldonbrown.com/fixed.html; Guerrero, "The Next Page: The Limberness of the Fixed Gear Mind"; Greg Goode, "No Brakes . . . Or, Zen on Wheels," *Nonduality Salon Magazine*, no. 1, September 1, 2000, available at http://www.nonduality.com/900gg.htm; William Blaze, "Visceral Aesthetics (Fixed Gear)," *Abstract Dynamics*, May 27, 2005, available at http://www.abstractdynamics.org/archives/2005/05/27/visceral_aesthetics_fixed_gear.html.

94. Erin Feher and Sonia Beauchamp, "Fixie or Forget It," *[X]press* (October 2005), available at http://xpress.sfsu.edu/archives/magazine/004697.html. For a more even handed assessment of fixed gears, see Gabe Meline, "Pedal to the Mettle," *North Bay Bohemian*, September 15–21, 2004.

95. Theodor W. Adorno, "Veblen's Attack on Culture," in *Prisms* (Cambridge, MA: MIT Press, 1983), 75–76 (originally published in *Studies in Philosophy and Social Science* 9, no. 3 [1941]: 389–413). John Cunningham Wood offers a slightly different translation of Adorno's phrase, calling it "indirect utility" instead of "mediated utility" in *Thorstein Veblen: Critical Assessments* (London: Routledge, 1993), 4. Chambers raises a similar point about the cachet of (sub)cultural practices in "Symbolic Equipment and the Objects of Leisure Images."

96. For example, see Michael Martin and Gabe Morford, *Mash SF* (Mash Transit Productions, 2007); David Rowe, *Fast Friday* (Infinite Quest Productions, 2008).

97. Dick Hebdige gives an analogous reading of Italian scooters in "Travelling Light," 13.

98. In particular, see "The Genuine Article: Reporting on the Fixed Gear Phenomenon," *Bike Snob NYC*, December 4, 2007, available at http://bikesnobnyc.blogspot.com/2007/12/genuine-article-reporting-on-fixed-gear.html.

99. Chambers, "Symbolic Equipment and the Objects of Leisure Images," 306.

100. This is not to be confused with the *Pornography of the Bicycle* film festival that Reverend Phil Sano curated in 2007 (currently in its third year running).

101. Feher and Beauchamp, "Fixie or Forget It"; Vanessa Hua, "One Gear, Will Travel," *San Francisco Chronicle,* September 11, 2006. Also see "Firing Off at Fixed Gears," *San Francisco Bay Guardian,* September 26, 2006.

102. The "fake ass messenger" quote is from Dan Charles, *Cyclists Switch to Single-Speed Bikes* (National Public Radio, 2007). Also see Buffalo Bill, "Fakenger," *Moving Target Zine,* March 2, 2007, available at http://www.movingtargetzine.com/article/fakenger.

103. Benjamin Stewart discusses alleycat races in "Bicycle Messengers and the Dialectics of Speed," in *Fighting for Time,* ed. Cynthia Fuchs Epstein and Arne L. Kalleberg (New York: Russell Sage, 2004), 172. Joe Hendry has a page devoted to alley-cats that is available through the *Messenger Institute for Media Accuracy* at http://www.messmedia.org/alleycats.html.

104. Joe Hendry, personal correspondence, January 21, 2007.

105. Elżbieta Drążkiewicz, "On the Bicycle towards Freedom: Bicycle Messengers' Answer for Identity Crisis" (master's thesis, Lund University, 2003), 40.

106. For an overview of bike messenger organizations, labor issues, and unioniza-tion efforts, see Carlsson, *Nowtopia,* 135–139; Joe Hendry, "Labour Issues," *Messenger Institute for Media Accuracy,* available at http://www.messmedia.org/labour.html; San Francisco Bike Messenger Association and International Longshore and Warehouse Union, "Partnership for Justice for the Bay Area Courier Industry," *San Francisco Bike Messenger Association,* 1997, available at http://www.ahalenia.com/sfbma/whitepaper.html.

107. Jeffrey L. Kidder discusses the lifestyle aspects of being a messenger in "Bike Messengers and the Really Real: Effervescence, Reflexivity, and Postmodern Identity," *Symbolic Interaction* 29, no. 3 (2006): 356–357. On page 368, he notes that out of the roughly two thousand messengers in New York City, only a few hundred actually participate in the rituals and events associated with messenger culture. Also see Jeffrey L. Kidder, "Style and Action: A Decoding of Bike Messenger Symbols," *Journal of Contemporary Ethnography* 34, no. 3 (2005): 344–367.

108. Rebecca Reilly, personal correspondence, July 29, 2007.

109. David Varno, "Bike Messengers: Beta Still Rules on the Street," *The Brooklyn Rail,* November 5, 2005, available at http://www.thebrooklynrail.org/archives/nov05/STREETS/bikemessengers.html.

110. Kidder speaks to the issue of seniority in "Bike Messengers and the Really Real: Effervescence, Reflexivity, and Postmodern Identity," 353.

111. Quoted in John Greenfield, "Shoot the Messenger," *Chicago Reader,* March 29, 2001.

112. Hendry, personal correspondence, January 21, 2007.

113. For an example of a well-intentioned but otherwise unproductive critique of hipsters (and their bikes), see Douglas Haddow, "Hipster: The Dead End of Western Civilization," *Adbusters,* no 79 (2008), available at https://www.adbusters.org/maga-zine/79/hipster.html.

114. Bull, personal correspondence, January 21, 2007.

115. Boerer, personal correspondence January 15, 2007. Tony Fast quoted in Brad Quartuccio, "Fixed Freestyle," *Urban Velo,* no. 7 (2008): 38. Famed bike builder Dave Moulton similarly writes, "It doesn't matter that people are getting into this trend for

all the wrong reasons. For a few, cycling will get into their blood and they will continue in some form or other long after this trend has passed." In "Fixing Fixed Wheel Terminology," *Dave Moulton's Bike Blog,* March 10, 2008, available at http://davesbikeblog.blogspot.com/2008/03/fixing-fixed-wheel-terminology.html.

116. Bill Chappell, "Love That City Bike," *National Public Radio Blog,* February 14, 2008, available at http://www.npr.org/blogs/bryantpark/2008/02/love_that_city_bike. html; Eli Milchman, "'City Bike' Hot New Category at Bicycle Industry Show," *Wired,* September 27, 2007.

117. Rubén Ortiz Torres quoted in Chavoya, "Customized Hybrids," 145. Minister Brian Dale, a blogger and avid cyclist, provides a different perspective on the ways in which style can be a "function of politics" as he underscores the need for bike manufacturers to better address the needs and desires of both African American youth and a wider "urban audience." See Minister Brian Dale, "Bicycle Design for the Urban Audience," *Marshall Taylor Blog,* May 28, 2007, available at http://marshalltaylor.blogspot.com/2007/05/bicycle-design-for-urban-audience.html.

118. North American Handmade Bicycle Show, available at http://www.handmadebicycleshow.com.

119. Portland began to showcase the city's own bike builders and artists in 2006 through the development of the Made in Portland: Bicycle Show and Art Exhibition. A list of Portland builders is accessible through the Bike Portland Web site and a (partial) list of independent bike builders in the United States is available via Spoken Wheel Blog at http://www.thespokenwheel.com/2008/07/30/custom-bicycle-builders-usa. Also see Ben Jacklet, "Geared Up," *Oregon Business Magazine* (January 2009); United Bicycle Institute, available at http://bikeschool.com; Oregon Bicycle Constructors Association, available at http://www.oregonframebuilders.org.

120. Bull, personal correspondence; Aaron Cometbus, "Interview with Eric Zo," *Cometbus,* no. 49. Kipchoge Spencer, the ex-president of Xtracycle, also speaks to the influence of small bike companies on the larger bike industry in "Spencer for Tire," *Grist Magazine,* January 9, 2006, available at http://www.grist.org/comments/interactivist/2006/01/09/spencer/.

121. Just a few of these businesses include R. E. Load Baggage (Philadelphia, Pennsylvania), BaileyWorks (Portsmouth, New Hampshire), Haley Tricycles (Philadelphia, Pennsylvania), and Resource Revival (Portland, Oregon).

122. Noah Adams and Madeleine Brand, "U.S. Firm Keeps Toehold in Bike Basket Business," National Public Radio, July 28, 2005.

123. Human Powered Machines and Haley Tricycles both maintain Web sites online. For more on cargo bicycles, tricycles, and other pedal-powered work vehicles, see Bikes at Work, available at http://www.bikesatwork.com.

124. Warren McLaren, "Worksman Cycles (USA's Oldest) Get a Touch of Sun," *TreeHugger.com,* March 10, 2008, available at http://www.treehugger.com/files/2008/03/worksman_cycles.php. Among their other environmental initiatives, The United Bicycle Institute similarly converted part of its facilities to run on solar power in 2005. See "United Bicycle Institute," available at http://www.ashland.or.us/Page.asp?NavID=12024.

125. Lawrence Grossberg, "Another Boring Day in Paradise: Rock and Roll and the Empowerment of Everyday Life," *Popular Music* 4 (1984): 227.

126. For more on subcultural capital, see Sarah Thornton, *Club Cultures: Music, Media, and Subcultural Capital* (Hanover, NH: University Press of New England, 1996), 1–13, 98–104.

127. Barnes and Krizek acknowledge the potential role of "subcultural attitudes" in the perception of bicycling as "an appealing or even normal thing for an adult to do," in "Estimating Bicycling Demand," *Journal of the Transportation Research Board*, no. 1939 (2005): 51.

128. Duncombe, *Notes from Underground*, 177, 90; Phil Cohen, "Subcultural Conflict and Working-Class Community," in *Culture, Media, Language: Working Papers in Cultural Studies, 1972–1979*, ed. Stuart Hall, et al. (London: Routledge in Association with the Centre for Contemporary Cultural Studies, University of Birmingham, 1980), 71. For further critiques of the "subculture-as-style-as-resistance" narrative, see Thomas Frank and Matt Weiland, eds., *Commodify Your Dissent: Salvos from the Baffler* (New York: Norton, 1997).

CHAPTER 7

1. Youth Bicycle Education Network, "Trends in Bicycle Education," available at http://www.yben.org/newsletter/four-key-program-models.

2. Myrla Raymundo, "The Teen Workshop," *Union City Historical Museum Newsletter* 6, no. 5 (2005); Delphine Taylor, "Tools for Life," *Transportation Alternatives Magazine* (1996): 12–13.

3. Catherine Duising and John Calhoun, "History: 1965–2000," *Central Indiana Bicycling Association*, available at http://www.cibaride.org/history/history.html.

4. Ibid.

5. "The Bicycle Action Project (Factsheet)," *Youth Employment Summit: YES Campaign*, available at http://www.yesweb.org/gkr/project_factsheet.html?pid=317; Youth Bicycle Education Network, "Trends in Bicycle Education."

6. Carl Kurz, personal correspondence, February 2, 2008.

7. The International Bicycle Fund maintains several updated lists of community bicycle organizations and community cycling projects/programs in the United States and abroad. See David Mozer, "Youth and Young People, Bicycle Recycle, Earn-a-Bike Programs," *International Bicycle Fund*, available at http://www.ibike.org/encouragement/youth.htm.

8. "Interview with Rick Jarvis," in *Leapfrog* (Indianapolis), no. 8, ed. Scott Spitz (self-published zine).

9. Ian Fritz, Troy Neiman, and John Gerken, eds., *Bicycle Organization Project* (Tucson, AZ: BICAS, 2006), 3.

10. For example, the Community Cycling Center in Portland, Oregon recycled 31,840 pounds of material and reused a total of 70,228 pounds (more than 15 school buses in volume) in 2002. "Reusing and Recycling Bikes and Parts Locally," *Recycling Advocates* (October 2003).

11. In particular, see Bullard, Johnson, and Torres, "Dismantling Transportation Apartheid"; Bullard, Johnson, and Torres, *Highway Robbery*.

12. Leann M. Tigges, Irene Browne, and Gary P. Green, "Social Isolation of the Urban Poor: Race, Class, and Neighborhood Effects on Social Resources," *Sociological*

Quarterly (1998): 53–77; Shannon N. Zenk et al., "Neighborhood Racial Composition, Neighborhood Poverty, and the Spatial Accessibility of Supermarkets in Metropolitan Detroit," *American Journal of Public Health* 95, no. 4 (2005): 660–667; K. Morland et al., "Neighborhood Characteristics Associated with the Location of Food Stores and Food Service Places," *American Journal of Preventive Medicine* 22, no. 1 (2002): 23–29; Rogelio Saenz, "The Social and Economic Isolation of Urban African Americans," *Population Reference Bureau* (October 2005), available at http://www.prb.org/Articles/2005/ TheSocialandEconomicIsolationofUrbanAfricanAmericans.aspx.

13. Mary Blue and Andrew Lynn, *Velorution: The Unofficial Documents of a Bicycle Underground* 1 (2004): 19.

14. Ibid., 15–17, 37–38.

15. Robert Galdins, personal correspondence, January 25, 2005.

16. "Create a Commuter Program," *Community Cycling Center,* available at http:// www.communitycyclingcenter.org/index.php/programs/create-a-commuter.

17. See S. C. Kinnevy et al., "Bicycleworks: Task-Centered Group Work with High-Risk Youth," *Social Work with Groups* 22, no. 1 (1999): 33–48; Charles Higgins, *Bike Traffic: Building Opportunity and Community in San Francisco* (San Francisco: Bicycle Community Project, 1999).

18. Taylor, "Tools for Life."

19. Lisa M. Bouillion and Louis M. Gomez, "Connecting School and Community with Science Learning: Real World Problems and School-Community Partnerships as Contextual Scaffolds," *Journal of Research in Science Teaching* 38, no. 8 (2001): 878–898; L. Carlson and J. Sullivan, "Hands-on Engineering: Learning by Doing in the Integrated Teaching and Learning Program," *International Journal of Engineering Education* 15, no. 1 (1999): 20–31; Gary Robert Muschla and Judith A. Muschla, *Hands-on Math Projects with Real-Life Applications: Ready to Use Lessons and Materials for Grades 6–12* (West Nyack, NY: Center for Applied Research in Education, 1996).

20. Neighborhood Bike Works (Philadelphia) has hosted an annual Bike Part Art Show since 2003; BICAS (Bicycle Inter-Community Art and Salvage) similarly provides free access spare materials for art projects in Tucson, Arizona.

21. Karen Overton, quoted in Taylor, "Tools for Life."

22. Young, *Justice and the Politics of Difference,* 85.

23. Carlsson, "'Outlaw' Bicycling," 97.

24. The Mr. Roboto project was modeled after the 924 Gilman St. project in Berkeley, California. Shows at Roboto are open to the public, but people buy yearly memberships that are used to pay for the venue's rent, bills, and maintenance. Any member can reserve an open day on the calendar on which they can host their own event; they also receive a discount on any event they attend at the space. Shows rarely cost more than $5 or $6 and bands keep almost all the money collected at the door. Finally, an elected board keeps the day-to-day affairs running smoothing and board meetings are open to the public.

25. Elizabeth DiNovella, "Bikes for the World," *Progressive* (April 2004).

26. Chris Atton, "A Reassessment of the Alternative Press," *Media, Culture and Society* 21, no. 1 (1999): 69.

27. "Interview with Rick Jarvis."

28. McCorkell, personal correspondence, January 18, 2007.

29. "The History," *Bicycle Habitat.* available at http://bicyclehabitat.com/page.cfm?pageID=540.

30. Brad Quartuccio, "A Rider's Refuge: Kraynick's Bike Shop," *Dirt Rag,* July 1, 2002.

31. Law, "Beyond 'Women and Transport'"; Jain, "Violent Submission"; Tanu Priya Uteng and Tim Cresswell, *Gendered Mobilities* (Hampshire, UK: Ashgate Publishing, 2008).

32. James E. Gruber and Lars Bjorn, "Blue-Collar Blues: The Sexual Harassment of Women Autoworkers," *Work and Occupations* 9, no. 3 (1982): 271–298; Ian Ayres, "Fair Driving: Gender and Race Discrimination in Retail Car Negotiations," *Harvard Law Review* 104 (1990): 817–872; Alexander Styhre, Maria Backman, and Sofia Borjesson, "The Gendered Machine: Concept Car Development at Volvo Car Corporation," *Gender, Work and Organization* 12, no. 6 (2005): 551–571; "Women in the Automotive Industry," *Catalyst* (March 2009), available at http://www.catalyst.org/publication/235/women-in-the-automotive-industry.

33. Dwight A. Hennessy and David L. Wiesenthal, "Aggression, Violence, and Vengeance among Male and Female Drivers," *Transportation Quarterly* 56, no. 4 (2002): 62–75; Barbara Krahé and Ilka Fenske, "Predicting Aggressive Driving Behavior: The Role of Macho Personality, Age, and Power of Car," *Aggressive Behavior* 28, no. 1 (2002): 21–29; Ivonne Audirac, "Sharing Fast-Speed and Slow-Speed Roads with Bicyclists and Pedestrians: A Source of Female and Male Driver Frustration?" *Transportation Research Record: Journal of the Transportation Research Board* 2067, no. 1 (2008): 65–74.

34. It is worth noting that while social and cultural norms undoubtedly impact the number of women who use bikes for daily transportation and/or utilitarian purposes in the United States, there is far more evidence that points to a general lack of safe bicycling infrastructure. For example, see Pucher and Renne, "Socioeconomics of Urban Travel: Evidence from the 2001 NHTS," 67–68; Kevin Krizek, Pamela Jo Johnson, and Nebiyou Tilahun, "Gender Differences in Bicycling Behavior and Facility Preferences" (paper presented at the Conference on Research on Women's Issues in Transportation, 2005); Plaut, "Non-motorized Commuting in the US"; Dill and Carr, "Bicycle Commuting and Facilities in Major U.S. Cities"; Dill and Voros, "Factors Affecting Bicycling Demand"; J. Garrard, G. Rose, and S. K. Lo, "Promoting Transportation Cycling for Women: The Role of Bicycle Infrastructure," *Preventive Medicine* 46, no. 1 (2008): 55–59.

35. Alex McFarland, interview with the author, August 5, 2004.

36. Ibid.

37. Shelley Lynn Jackson, ed., *Chainbreaker* (New Orleans), no. 2 (self-published zine).

38. Victoria Bortman, interview with the author, August 5, 2004.

39. Elicia Cardenas, interview with the author, August 5, 2004.

40. "Derailing Sexism: The Evolution of a Female Bike Mechanic," in Andalusia Knoll, ed., *Clitical Mass* (Pittsburgh): 33 (self-published zine).

41. Adrian, "Bike Girl Blues," in ibid., 46.

42. Linda Stout, "Bicycle Shop Brings Community Together," *Ithaca Journal,* December 7, 2007; John Gerken, "Plan B," in *Chainbreaker* (New Orleans), no. 1, ed. Shelly Jackson (self-published zine).

43. Phelan, "Liberation Noted from an Old Crank."

44. Kim Fey, interview with the author, August 6, 2004. In addition to her work with N. Portland Bike Works, Fey hosts a radical bike history tour of Portland and has authored an audio version of the tour and an accompanying booklet entitled *Portland Radical History Tour* (available through Microcosm Publishing, http://microcosmpublishing.com).

45. Claire Stoscheck, personal correspondence, February 12, 2007. Stoscheck taught the course through Macalester's Experimental College (EXCO) in 2007.

46. Carl Kurz, personal correspondence, February 4, 2008.

47. Howard LaFranchi, "Aid to Nicaragua: People to People While Governments Look On," *Christian Science Monitor*, December 24, 1985; Tom Carter, "Bikes Being Sent to Needy Nations," *Washington Times*, September 6, 1990.

48. Carl Kurz, personal correspondence, February 4, 2008.

49. Filmmakers Eric Matthies and Tricia Todd document the Village Bicycle Project in their feature-length film *Ayamye,* which premiered in the 2007 Bicycle Film Festival (Project Lab/EMP, 2007).

50. Village Bicycle Project, "2006: The Year in Review" (Moscow, ID: Village Bicycle Project, 2007).

51. Suzanne Van Dam, "Pedaling out of Poverty: How One Guatemalan NGO Is Helping Rural Communities Help Themselves," *Bikes Not Bombs,* 2002, available at http://www.bikesnotbombs.org/maya-pedal.htm.

52. Bikes for Chiapas was a joint project of the Committee on U.S.-Latin American Relations (CUSLAR), Recycle Ithaca's Bicycles (RIBs), and Schools for Chiapas (San Diego). Bikes Across Borders, based in Austin, Texas, organizes caravans to deliver bicycles to Cuba, Mexico, and Central America. See Bikes Across Borders, available at http://www.bikesacrossborders.org.

53. Arjun Appadurai, "Grassroots Globalization and the Research Imagination," *Public Culture* 12, no. 1 (2000): 17–18.

54. Jürgen Heyen-Perschon, "Non-motorised Transport and Its Socio-economic Impact on Poor Households in Africa: Cost-Benefit Analysis of Bicycle Ownership in Rural Uganda" (Hamburg: FABIO/BSPW (Jinja, Uganda), 2001), 3.

55. Michael Replogle, "Sustainable Transportation Strategies for Third-World Development," *Transportation Research Record,* no. 1294 (1991): 1–8.

56. United Nations Conference on Trade and Development and Global Agreement on Tariffs and Trade, "Bicycles and Components: A Pilot Survey of Opportunities for Trade among Developing Countries" (Geneva: United Nations, 1985).

57. World Bank, "China Transport Sector Study" (Washington, DC: 1985); Jun-Meng Yang, "Bicycle Traffic in China," *Transportation Quarterly* 39, no. 1 (1985): 93–107; Zhang Xunhai, "Enterprise Response to Market Reforms: The Case of the Chinese Bicycle Industry," *Australian Journal of Chinese Affairs,* no. 28 (1992): 111–139.

58. World Bank, "A Decade of Action in Transport: An Evaluation of World Bank Assistance to the Transport Sector, 1995–2005" (Washington, DC: The International Bank for Reconstruction and Development/World Bank, 2007), xvii.

59. Ibid., 63.

60. Walter Hook, "Wheels out of Balance: Suggested Guidelines for Intermodal Transport Sector Lending at the World Bank—a Case Study of Hungary" (New York: Institute for Transportation and Development Policy, 1996).

61. G. H. Pirie, "The Decivilizing Rails: Railways and Underdevelopment in Southern Africa," *Tijdschrift voor Economische en Sociale Geografie* 73, no. 4 (1982): 221–228; H. W. Dick and P. J. Rimmer, "Urban Public Transport in Southeast Asia: A Case Study of Technological Imperialism?" *International Journal of Transport Economics* 13, no. 2 (1986): 177–196; John Stubbs and Rodney Pearson, "Moroccan Rail Transport Investment: Accumulation versus Legitimation," *Tijdschrift voor Economische en Sociale Geografie* 85, no. 2 (1994): 141–152.

62. Akin L. Mabogunje, "Urban Planning and the Post-colonial State in Africa: A Research Overview," *African Studies Review* 33, no. 2 (1990): 151.

63. From a speech given by Roger S. Smith (former executive vice president and chairman-elect of General Motors) to the National Foreign Trade convention, New York, October 20, 1980. Smith referred to the "untapped markets" in developing countries as potential locations for up to 60 to 70 percent of future sales. Quoted in George Work and Laurence Malone, "Bicycles, Development, and the Third World," *Environment* 25, no. 1 (1983): 41.

64. Clarisse Cunha, "Understanding the Community Impact: Bicycles in Sub-Saharan Africa," *Sustainable Transport,* no. 18 (2006): 24–25.

65. For example, see Heyen-Perschon, "Non-motorised Transport and Its Socio-economic Impact on Poor Households in Africa." Page 22 has further statistics on women's labor, including the transport of heavy goods.

66. Cunha, "Understanding the Community Impact."

67. M. Grieco, J. Turner, and E. A. Kwakye, "A Tale of Two Cultures: Ethnicity and Cycling Behavior in Urban Ghana," *Transportation Research Record,* no. 1441 (1994): 101–107; Nitya Rao, "Cycling into the Future: A Report on Women's Participation in a Literacy Campaign in Tamil Nadu, India," *Gender, Technology and Development* 3, no. 3 (1999): 457–474; Deike Peters, "Gender and Transport in Less Developed Countries: A Background Paper in Preparation for CSD-9," paper presented at the "Gender Perspectives for Earth Summit 2002: Energy, Transport, Information for Decision-Making" conference, Berlin, Germany, January 10–12, 2001; Sylvia Welke and Jennifer Allen, "Cycling Freedom for Women," *Women and Environments International Magazine,* nos. 62–63 (2004): 34–37.

68. Karen Overton, "Women Take Back the Streets. Overcoming Gender Obstacles to Women's Mobility in Africa," *Sustainable Transport* 3 (1994), 6, 7, 17; Karen Overton, "Using the Bicycle for Women's Empowerment in Africa," *Sustainable Transport* 6 (1996): 6–10; Julia Philpott, "Women and Nonmotorized Transport: Connection in Africa between Transportation and Economic Development," *Transportation Research Record,* no. 1441 (1994): 39–43. Also see Deborah Fahy Bryceson and John Howe, "Rural Household Transport in Africa: Reducing the Burden on Women?" *World Development* 21, no. 11 (1993): 725–739; Deborah Fahy Bryceson, "The Scramble in Africa: Reorienting Rural Livelihoods," *World Development* 30, no. 5 (2002): 725–739; Deborah Fahy Bryceson, T. C. Mbara, and D. Maunder, "Livelihoods, Daily Mobility and Poverty in Sub-Saharan Africa," *Transport Reviews* 23, no. 2 (2003): 177–196.

69. Village Bicycle Project, "2006: The Year in Review."

70. A. O. Urebvu, "Culture and Technology: A Study of the 1997 Theme World Decade for Cultural Development 1988–1997" (UNESCO, 1997), 19. Also see N. Jequier, "Appropriate Technology: Some Criteria," in *Towards Global Action for Appropriate*

Technology: Discussion Papers and Proposals of an Expert Meeting on International Action for Appropriate Technology, Geneva, Dec 1977, ed. A. S. Bhalla (Oxford: Pergamon Press, 1979), 1–22.

71. Caroll Pursell notes that shortly after Ronald Reagan's inauguration in 1981 he terminated the federal Community Services Administration, and by extension, the funding and support for the National Center for Appropriate Technology (NCAT). Incidentally, Reagan took the extra and wholly unnecessary step of having solar panels removed from the roof of the White House during routine repairs in 1982—a fitting end to the energy policies at least partly supported by President Jimmy Carter, who had the panels installed just three years prior. After a decade in storage, the panels were shipped to a liberal arts college in Maine. Pursell, "The Rise and Fall of the Appropriate Technology Movement in the United States, 1965–1985," 600, 33.

72. Sarah Van Gelder, "Finding a Balance: An Interview with Ricardo Navarro," *In Context,* no. 36 (Fall 1993): 36.

73. Ricardo Navarro, Urs Heierli, and Victor Beck, *Alternativas de Transporte en America Latina: La Bicicleta y los Triciclos* (SKAT Centro Suizo De Technologia Apropiada, 1985). Also see Ricardo Navarro, Urs Heierli, and Victor Beck, "Bicycles, Intelligent Transport in Latin America," *Development: Seeds of Change,* no. 4 (1986): 45–48.

74. Kleiman, "The Appropriate Technology Movement in American Political Culture," 21.

75. Winner, *The Whale and the Reactor,* 62, 97. For Winner's full assessment/critique of the AT movement, see the chapter entitled "Building the Better Mousetrap" (61–84).

76. Ivan Illich, *Celebration of Awareness: A Call for Institutional Revolution* (Garden City, NY: Doubleday, 1970), 181.

77. On the latter point, see Michael Evans, "'Para-Politics' Goes Bananas," *The Nation,* April 4, 2007.

78. For more on theorizing and/or contesting globalization, see Suzanne Bergeron, "Political Economy Discourses of Globalization and Feminist Politics," *Signs* 26, no. 4 (2001): 983–1006; Arturo Escobar, "Culture Sits in Places: Reflections on Globalism and Subaltern Strategies of Localization," *Political Geography* 20, no. 2 (2001): 139–174; Cindi Katz, "On the Grounds of Globalization: A Topography for Feminist Political Engagement," *Signs* 26, no. 4 (2001): 1213–1234; Douglas Kellner, "Theorizing Globalization," *Sociological Theory* 20, no. 3 (2002): 285–305; Richa Nagar et al., "Locating Globalization: Feminist (Re)Readings of the Subjects and Spaces of Globalization," *Economic Geography* 78, no. 3 (2002): 257–284; David Harvey, *Spaces of Global Capitalism: A Theory of Uneven Geographical Development* (New York: Verso, 2006).

79. Nagar et al., "Locating Globalization," 262.

80. Ivan Illich lays out a number of these issues in a speech he delivered to aspiring American volunteer workers attending the Conference on InterAmerican Student Projects (CIASP) in Cuernavaca, Mexico, on April 20, 1968. See "To Hell with Good Intentions," April 20, 1968, available at http://www.swaraj.org/illich_hell.htm.

81. Honor Ford-Smith, "Ring Ding in a Tight Corner: Sistren, Collective Democracy, and the Organization of Cultural Production," in *Feminist Genealogies, Colonial Legacies, Democratic Futures,* ed. M. Jacqui Alexander and Chandra Talpade Mohanty (New York: Routledge, 1997), 229.

82. David Peckham, "2004 Annual Report," *Village Bicycle Project,* April 15, 2005, available at http://www.ghanabikes.org/ar04.htm.

83. David Peckham, "2002 Annual Report," *Village Bicycle Project,* November 29, 2002, available at http://www.ghanabikes.org/ar02.htm.

84. Jon Snyder, "How Did That Bike Get to Africa?" *Out There Monthly* (September 2007), available at http://www.outtheremonthly.com/otm.php?art=archives/sept07/africa.

85. David Peckham, "Annual Report," *Village Bicycle Project,* 1999, available at http://www.ghanabikes.org/ar99.htm.

86. Robert Lovinger, "David Schweidenback Recyles Cycles for the World," *UMass Dartmouth Alumni Magazine* (2005): 10–11; Francesco Raeli, "Pedal Power," 2007, available at http://rolexawards.com/en/the-laureates/davidschweidenback-the-project.jsp.

87. Stacy A. Anderson, "Westchester Cycle Club Collects Used Bikes for the Less Fortunate," *Journal News,* May 25, 2008.

88. See Nava Ashraf, James Berry, and Jesse Shapiro, "Can Higher Prices Stimulate Product Use? Evidence from a Field Experiment in Zambia," *National Bureau of Economic Research Working Paper,* no. 13247 (2007); William Russell Easterly, *The White Man's Burden: Why the West's Efforts to Aid the Rest Have Done So Much Ill and So Little Good* (New York: Penguin Press, 2006), 13.

89. Jessica Cohen and Pascaline Dupas, "Free Distribution or Cost-Sharing? Evidence from a Malaria Prevention Experiment," *Brookings Global Economy and Development Working Paper,* no. 11 (2007); Michael Kremer and Edward Miguel, "The Illusion of Sustainability," *Quarterly Journal of Economics* 122, no. 3 (2007): 1007–1065; Christopher Shea, "A Handout, Not a Hand Up: A Popular Approach to 'Sustainable Development' Doesn't Work, Critics Say," *Boston Globe,* November 11, 2007.

90. Martin Fisher, of Kickstart, says, "The disadvantage to giving things away is that it's not really fair. How do you decide who is going to get one of these things and who isn't going to get one of these things. . . . You really don't appreciate it in the same way as something that you buy. . . . [W]hen you give things away you're really just creating dependency and people are hanging out waiting for more handouts." "African Farmers Try Kickstarting Their Farms," National Public Radio, July 22, 2006.

91. Nancy Rose Hunt, *A Colonial Lexicon of Birth Ritual, Medicalization, and Mobility in the Congo* (Durham, NC: Duke University Press, 1999), 176.

92. Ibid. Ute Luig recalls that Zambians sometimes named spirits after the machines of colonization, including the bicycle. See "Constructing Local Worlds," in *Spirit Possession, Modernity and Power in Africa,* ed. Heike Behrend and Ute Luig (Madison: University of Wisconsin Press, 1999), 131.

93. Rubber was also extracted from parts of Central and South America and in several African countries, most notably Liberia. See Marc Edelman, "A Central American Genocide: Rubber, Slavery, Nationalism, and the Destruction of the Guatusos-Malekus," *Comparative Studies in Society and History* 40, no. 2 (2004): 356–390; Emily Lynn Osborn, "'Rubber Fever' Commerce and French Colonial Rule in Upper Guinée 1890–.1913," *Journal of African History* 45, no. 3 (2004): 445–465; Robtel Pailey, "Slavery Ain't Dead, It's Manufactured in Liberia's Rubber," in *From the Slave Trade to "Free" Trade: How Trade Undermines Democracy and Justice in Africa,* ed. Patrick Burnett and Firoze Manji (Nairobi: Fahamu, 2007), 77–83.

94. Osumaka Likaka, *Rural Society and Cotton in Colonial Zaire* (Madison: University of Wisconsin Press, 1997), 60.

95. Ibid., 67.

96. David Peckham, "Sustaining Bicycles as Desirable Rural Transport," *The International Forum for Rural Transport and Development,* available at http://ifrtd. gn.apc.org/new/issues/op_bicycles4.php.

97. Firoze Manji and Carl O'Coill, "The Missionary Position: NGOs and Development in Africa," *International Affairs (Royal Institute of International Affairs 1944–)* 78, no. 3 (2002): 574.

98. Peckham, "Annual Report." On a related note, Craig Calfee, a renowned professional bike builder, traveled to Ghana to conduct a bamboo bicycle making workshop only to find that "it has been difficult breaking through the mentality that the rich American is obligated to pay for everything—even when bringing free training for a new skill." His frustration stemmed from being expected to pay for the crew's transportation both to and from the workshop (a whopping 20 cents per ride), even though Calfee bikes (i.e., the frame, front fork, and paint job) retail for no less than $2,000, with most hovering around the $3,000–$6,000 range. See "Ghana Bamboo Bike Journal, February 2008 Trip," *Calfee Design,* available at http://www.calfeedesign.com/Ghana2008.htm.

99. Thomas L. Friedman, *The World Is Flat: A Brief History of the Twenty-first Century* (New York: Farrar, Straus and Giroux, 2007), 537. The literal dogma of free market capitalism is perhaps best articulated by an executive at Opportunity International (the company formerly run by Eric Thurman, coauthor of *A Billion Bootstraps*): "Serving the poor is an act of worship. Every time you serve the poor, you express your love for Jesus. *If Jesus came today, he would be a microfinance banker*" Isaac Phiri, "From Hand Out to Hand Up," *Christianity Today* (October 2007). Emphasis is my own.

100. David Mozer offers an expansive and substantive analysis of bicycling and sustainable tourism in the studies he publishes through the International Bicycle Fund, available at http://www.ibike.org. For more on the problematics of tourism, see John Urry, *The Tourist Gaze* (London: Sage Publications, 2002).

101. "Pedals for Progress to Hit Milestone," *Pedals for Progress,* available at http://www.p4p.org/PDF/100kcourier.pdf (originally published in *Courier News Online,* June 23, 2006); "Impact," *World Bicycle Relief,* available at http://www.worldbicyclerelief.org/impact/index.php. Emphasis in the latter is my own.

102. For an extreme example of this ideology, see Michael Strong, *Be the Solution: How Entrepreneurs and Conscious Capitalists Can Solve All the Worlds Problems* (Hoboken, NJ: Wiley, 2009).

103. "Interview with David Schweidenback," *Social Edge,* March 13, 2007, available at http://www.socialedge.org/blogs/peace-corps-entrepreneurs/david-schweidenback/.

104. Muhammad Yunus and Alan Jolis, *Banker to the Poor: Micro-Lending and the Battle against World Poverty* (New York: Public Affairs, 2003), 204 and 206. Emphasis is my own.

105. Michael Strong, "The Opportunity: The Creative Powers of a Free Civilization," in *Working for Good Curriculum,* ed. Michael Strong (FLOW, 2003), 20. Available at http://www.flowidealism.org/Downloads/Working-for-Good.pdf.

106. See Appadurai, "Grassroots Globalization and the Research Imagination," 17–18.

CHAPTER 8

1. H.R.2776, or the Renewable Energy and Energy Conservation Tax Act of 2007, passed in the House and was eventually transformed into part of the Bailout Bill of 2008 (HR 1424, which later became Public Law 110–343). Section 211 specifically addresses "Transportation Fringe Benefit to Bicycle Commuters."

2. Republican politicians like Colorado House Representative Frank McNulty and Colorado Senator Josh Penry are at the forefront of this trend, going so far as to publicly condemn their state's participation in Bike to Work Day, 2008. In response to the event, McNulty stated: "You've got to be kidding. . . . Colorado families are struggling at the pump and the answer we are getting from Colorado Democrats is shut down oil and gas production in Colorado and ride your bike—unbelievable. I'd like to see how they expect a mother of three in my district to get her kids to school and to buy groceries for her family using a bicycle." A similarly grumpy Senator Penry described Bike to Work Day—which, incidentally, featured the participation of 940 companies, 20,000 riders, and the support of the Denver Regional Council of Governments—as the "most absurd, ridiculous and totally convincing explanation of why Colorado Democrats are clueless when it comes to addressing our energy crisis." See Peter Marcus, "GOP Bashes Bike to Work," *Denver Daily News,* June 25, 2008.

3. Tami Toroyan and Margie Peden, "Youth and Road Safety" (Geneva: World Health Organization, 2007), 3.

4. Zerzan, *Elements of Refusal,* 10.

5. Ernest Istook, "Frittering Away Road Money," *Washington Times,* September 30, 2007.

6. See Al Gore, *An Inconvenient Truth: The Crisis of Global Warming,* rev. ed. (New York: Viking, 2007); Kenneth S. Deffeyes, *Hubbert's Peak: The Impending World Oil Shortage* (Princeton, NJ: Princeton University Press, 2001); Kenneth S. Deffeyes, *Beyond Oil: The View from Hubbert's Peak,* 1st ed. (New York: Hill and Wang, 2005).

7. Deffeyes, *Hubbert's Peak,* 11. For a critique of Al Gore's film *An Inconvenient Truth,* see Zack Furness, "An Inconvenient Truth," *Bad Subjects* (2006), available at http://bad.eserver.org/reviews/2006/gore.html.

8. For more on Firestone/Bridgestone, see the "Stop Firestone" campaign at http://www.stopfirestone.org.

9. Michael Bell, *An Invitation to Environmental Sociology,* 2nd ed. (Thousand Oaks, CA: Pine Forge Press, 2004), 226.

10. Nearly half of the hybrid model SUVs scheduled for production in 2009 boasted roughly the same maximum fuel efficiency rating as the Model T (up to twenty-one miles per gallon). See Holly Reich, "Eco-friendly Interiors," *New York Daily News,* March 21, 2008; Ford Motor Company, "Model T Facts," available at http://media.ford.com/article_display.cfm?article_id=858; U.S. Department of Energy, "2009 Hybrid Vehicles," in *Fuel Economy Guide* (2008); Mazda, "Mazda Develops World's First Biofabric Made with 100 Percent Plant-Derived Fiber for Vehicle Interiors," Mazda Press Release no. 26889, 2007.

11. Daniel J. Weiss et al., "The Clean Coal Smoke Screen," Center for American Progress, 2008.

12. See George V. Davis, "Where Once There Were Mountains: The Grassroots Struggle against Mountaintop Removal Coal Mining in Central Appalachia," *Environmen-*

tal Politics 18, no. 1 (2009): 135–140; Silas House and Jason Howard, *Something's Rising: Appalachians Fighting Mountaintop Removal* (Lexington: University of Kentucky Press, 2009).

13. Zack Furness, "Blackout," *Bad Subjects* no. 64 (2003), available at http://bad. eserver.org/issues/2003/64/furness.html.

14. The ASCE estimates that $1.6 trillion is needed over a five-year period in order to raise the nation's infrastructure to "good" condition from its current "D" grade. The author of the study specifically notes that this figure does not take population increases into consideration, nor does it account for infrastructure growth. In short, much more money would be required to accommodate the country's ever-increasing travel miles (automobile and aviation) or rates of energy use (due to computers, handheld devices, air conditioners, and so on). See American Society of Civil Engineers, *Infrastructure Report Card,* available at http://www.infrastructurereportcard.org.

15. U.S. Census Bureau, "An Older and More Diverse Nation by Midcentury" (Washington, DC: Department of Commerce, 2008); United Nations Department of Economic and Social Affairs, "World Urbanization Prospects—the 2007 Revision: Highlights," (New York: United Nations, 2008).

16. Geddes, *Magic Motorways,* 238.

17. Texas Transportation Institute, "Urban Mobility Report."

18. "MIT Worldwide Mobility Study Warns of Chronic Gridlock, Pollution; Outlines 'Grand Challenges,'" *MIT News Office,* October 30, 2001; Will Sullivan, "Road Warriors Tie-Ups. Backups. Gridlock. The American Commute Has Never Been So Painful. Is There Any Solution?" *U.S. News and World Report,* April 29, 2007.

19. Sullivan, "Road Warriors"

20. World Bank, "A Decade of Action in Transport: An Evaluation of World Bank Assistance to the Transport Sector, 1995–2005," xiii–xiv.

21. See David T. Hartgen and M. Gregory Fields, "Building Roads to Reduce Traffic Congestion in America's Cities: How Much and at What Cost?" (Reason Foundation, 2006); Theodore Balaker and Sam Staley, *The Road More Traveled: Why the Congestion Crisis Matters More Than You Think, and What We Can Do about It* (Lanham, MD: Rowman and Littlefield, 2006).

22. Hartgen and Fields, "Building Roads to Reduce Traffic Congestion in America's Cities" 36. My calculations are based on the following equation: 228,073 (miles) × 5280 (feet per mile) = 1,204,225,440 feet. 1,204,225,440 feet × 11 feet (average lane width) = 13,246,479,840 (square feet) = 475.15 square miles (total). Lane widths range between 10 feet on rural roads and at least 12 feet on highways. By using the 11-foot urban road standard, I am most likely underestimating the total square mileage of the Reason Foundation's proposal.

23. Janet Larsen, "Land Area Devoted to Roads in the United States" (Washington, DC: Earth Policy Institute, 2001). The total area of paved parking spaces and roads, as of 2001, was roughly 61,466 square miles.

24. Mumford, *Technics and Civilization,* 429.

25. On this point, see Mike Featherstone, "Automobilities: An Introduction," *Theory Culture Society* 21, nos. 4–5 (2004): 17.

26. Quoted in Terry Slavin, "The Motown Missionary," *The Observer,* November 12, 2000, 5.

27. Maurie J. Cohen, "A Social Problems Framework for the Critical Appraisal of Automobility and Sustainable Systems Innovation," *Mobilities* 1, no. 1 (2006): 34.

28. Ritchie, *King of the Road,* 179.

29. Pucher and Buehler, "Making Cycling Irresistible."

30. Gorz, "The Social Ideology of the Motorcar."

31. Quoted in Evan George, "Lessons from Colombia," *L.A. Downtown News,* February 21, 2007.

32. Ibid.

33. Petersen, "Pedaling Hope," 37.

34. Bruce Epperson, interview with the author, July 28, 2007.

35. The location and availability of food stores, food production, schools, hospitals, and retail establishments are all factors that are intricately connected to transportation. For example, independent grocery wholesalers saw a rapid decline from 1990 to 2007 (from more than 350 to less than 100) while 5 corporations now account for roughly half of national grocery sales in the United States. In addition to the scarcity of grocery stores and fresh produce in many cities (areas known as *food deserts*), the number of farms nationwide plummeted from 6.8 million in 1935 to 2.1 million in 2002 (black-owned farms decreased from 14 percent of all farms in 1925 to less than 1 percent in 2003). Consequently, food travels 50 percent farther than it did two decades ago. Corporate consolidation and the subsequent geographic dispersal of basic amenities is similarly evident with hospitals (the total number in the United States declined from 7,156 in 1975 to 5,764 in 2003), local retail (50 percent of independent bookstores went out of business between 1990 and 2002; 33 percent of independent music stores closed since 1998; more than 4,000 independent video stores closed since 2000; and about 5,000 independent hardware stores closed since 1990), and schools. With respect to the latter, the number of U.S. children who walk or bike to school decreased from approximately 41 percent in 1969 to 15 percent in 2001 and 75 percent of all trips to school by students age 16 to 18 are by private vehicle (most with no passengers). Moreover, distance and traffic dangers are the two most frequently cited reasons for children and teens not biking or walking to school. For more on these issues, see Brian Halweil and Thomas Prugh, *Home Grown: The Case for Local Food in a Global Market* (Washington, DC: Worldwatch Institute, 2002); Anuradha Mittal, "Giving Away the Farm: The 2002 Farm Bill," *Food First Backgrounder* 8, no. 3 (2002): 1–5; Stacy Mitchell, *Big-Box Swindle: The True Cost of Mega-retailers and the Fight for America's Independent Businesses* (Boston: Beacon Press, 2006), 10–11; Hillary J. Shaw, "Food Deserts: Towards the Development of a Classification," *Geografiska Annaler: Series B, Human Geography* 88, no. 2 (2006): 231–247; United American Nurses, "The Hospital Industry (Figures from the National Center for Health Statistics and American Hospital Association)," *United American Nurses* (March 2005), available at http://www.uannurse.org/research/trends.html; S. Martin and S. Carlson, "Barriers to Children Walking to or from School—United States, 2004," *Morbidity and Mortality Weekly Report* 54, no. 38 (2005): 949–952.

36. I say that questions of *how* are "easily solvable" with respect to urban and/or transportation planning because there are clearly enough talented engineers and federal dollars in the United States to take up any transportation and/or public works project(s). Any U.S. city could be redesigned to privilege bicycle transportation (or mass transit), and there are numerous successful models from which to choose. The limitations, in

other words, are not technological, nor are they financial: the United States currently spends trillions of (deficit-accruing) dollars on war and corporate bailouts, among other things. Rather, these limitations are political and cultural. Consequently, unless people in the United States collectively rethink transportation along the latter lines—rather than needlessly rehashing the same debates about the value of bicycle facilities or the merits of becoming effective "bicycle drivers"—the core issues will remain on the back burner.

37. Horton, "Computers, Cars and Televisions."

38. Rosen, "Up the Vélorution," 375.

39. Navarro, Heierli, and Beck, "Bicycles, Intelligent Transport in Latin America." More specifically, Navarro states: "Decentralised production and assembly is only feasible if a regular supply of all parts is provided, and this requires an efficient organisation. Creating a new bicycle industry in a small country should start in any case with assembling, based on imported parts; in a later stage, the frame could be produced locally and step by step some part factories could be created. In order to provide the central management for the importation of raw materials and parts, a 'Bicycle Promotion Agency or Association' should be created, which delivers parts and accessories to small workshops."

40. The specific breakdown of sales figures is from Bicycle Industry and Retailer News, "Bike Stats 2008," available at http://www.bicycleretailer.com/downloads/BIKE STATS.pdf.

41. National Bicycle Dealers Association, "Industry Overview 2007."

42. Ibid.; Griff Witte, "A Rough Ride for Schwinn Bicycle," *Washington Post*, December 3, 2004.

43. See Andrew Tanzer, "Bury Thy Teacher," *Forbes*, December 21, 1992; Judith Crown and Glenn Coleman, *No Hands: The Rise and Fall of the Schwinn Bicycle Company: An American Institution*, 1st ed. (New York: H. Holt, 1996).

44. Tanzer, "Bury Thy Teacher."

45. Michael White, *A Short Course in International Marketing Blunders: Mistakes Made by Companies That Should Have Known Better*, The Short Course in International Trade Series (Novato, CA: World Trade Press, 2002), 11.

46. Witte, "A Rough Ride for Schwinn Bicycle."

47. See Huffy's profile in Thomas Derdak, Tina Grant, and Jay P. Pederson, *International Directory of Company Histories*, vol. 86 (Farmington Hills, MI: Gale, 2006), 7, 30.

48. Sherrod Brown, "Brown Joins Senate Hearing to Examine Whether 'Free Trade' Policies Are Working [press release]," *Senator Sherrod Brown*, April 18, 2007; Byron L. Dorgan, *Take This Job and Ship It: How Corporate Greed and Brain-Dead Politics Are Selling out America*, 1st ed. (New York: Thomas Dunne Books/St. Martin's Press, 2006), 27.

49. Stanley Aronowitz, *Just around the Corner: The Paradox of the Jobless Recovery* (Philadelphia: Temple University Press, 2005), 7. "Huffy Closes Last Manufacturing Plant in Mexico," *Bicycle Retailer*, December 21, 2001.

50. Charles Kernaghan and National Labor Committee Education Fund in Support of Worker and Human Rights in Central America, "Made in China: The Role of U.S. Companies in Denying Human and Worker Rights" (Washington, DC: National Labor Committee, 2000); Senate Democratic Policy Committee Hearing, *Are We Exporting American Jobs?* 108th Cong., 1st Sess., November 14, 2003.

51. According to the 10-Q SEC document filed by Huffy on August 13, 1998, the company was also designated as a potentially responsible party (PRP) by the U.S. Environmental Protection Agency for discharging "hazardous substances" into the San Gabriel Valley Superfund site. For details on Huffy's financial matters at the time of the plant closing, see Betsy Leondar-Wright, "Shareholders Press Huffy on Wage Gap, CEO Raise after Plant Closing and 1,000 Layoffs [press release]," *Responsible Wealth,* April 20, 1999.

52. Kernaghan and National Labor Committee Education Fund, "Made in China."

53. Kerry Roberts, "Where Was My Bike Made? Or, Who Actually Made My Bike?" March 18, 2008, available at http://allanti.com/page.cfm?PageID=328.

54. Carlton Reid, "Interbike Survey Results Released at Ibd Conference," *BikeBiz. Com,* February 15, 2007, available at http://www.bikebiz.com/news/25726/Interbike-survey-results-released-at-IBD-conference. Emphasis is my own.

55. Interbike participants and visitors routinely upload hundreds of pictures of these women, who are usually decked out in skin-tight T-shirts bearing the names of bike companies (SRAM upped the ante at Interbike 2007 by hiring four buxom "Little Red Riding Hoods" to stand by their display area). For example, see "2007 Interbike Hotties and People," *Mountain Bike Product Reviews,* available at http://gallery.mtbr. com/showgallery.php/cat/1186. Hiring display models is certainly not a practice unique to Interbike. At the Taipei Bike Show, an event where bike industry representatives are positioned as the buyers rather than the sellers of Taiwanese goods, scantily clad models were hired to parade their "parts" (literally and figuratively) around the conference room in the attempt to entice bike industry representatives. Todd "Wildman" Lyons, a former professional BMX racer and current brand manager for SE Bikes, draws not-so-subtle attention to the latter in "Spicy Girls in Taiwan!" *Toddlyons.com,* March 23, 2007, available at http://www.toddlyons.com/2007/03/spicy-girls-in-taiwan.html.

56. Chris King, "Thoughts on Manufacturing Overseas," *Chris King Precision Components,* available at http://www.chrisking.com/asiamfg. Commuter Bicycles—a Santa Barbara, California, bike shop—called for a ban on Chinese bicycles in 2003 as a response to China's persistent human rights violations. See Ben Delaney, "Human Rights, Not Cheap Bikes Retailer Advocates Industry-Wide Boycott of China," *Commuter Bicycles,* available at http://www.commuterbicycles.com/news.php (originally published in *Bicycle Retailer and Industry News,* 2003).

57. See "Made in China/Taiwan," *Bike Forums,* thread started on August 15, 2008, available at http://www.bikeforums.net/showthread.php?t=454443; "Rock Shox Forks Are Made in China??!!" *Bike Forums,* Thread started on October 3, 2006, available at http://www.bikeforums.net/showthread.php?t=233986; "Are All Bikes under $1000 (New) Made in China or Taiwan?" *Bike Forums,* thread started on May 24, 2008, available at http://www.bikeforums.net/showthread.php?t=421843.

58. Glenn Smith, "Lo and Behold, Giant's President Talks Trade," *Bikebiz.com,* June 4, 2002, available at http://www.bikebiz.com/news/21808/Lo-and-behold-Giants-president-talks-trade.

59. Ibid.

60. Jack Oortwijn, "Taiwan Bike Makers Cashing in on Europe," *Bike Europe,* September 2, 2008, available at http://www.bike-eu.com/news/2677/taiwan-bike-mak-ers-cashing-in-on-europe.html.

61. Wheel Giant, "Recent Developments in China's Bike Industry," *Bike Market Update E-Newsletter,* no. 22, June 11, 2007, available at http://www.biketaiwan.com/New/script/Newsletter/news_main.asp?issue=22&language=E; Matt Wiebe, "Increase in Sales Dollars Reflects Higher Cost of Manufacturing," *Bicycle Retailer and Industry News,* April 1, 2008.

62. Wheel Giant, "Recent Developments in China's Bike Industry"; Carlton Reid, "Taiwan and Vietnam Look to India and Africa for Bike Plants," *BikeBiz. Com,* October 20, 2006, available at http://www.bikebiz.com/news/24582/Taiwan-and-Vietnam-look-to-India-and-Africa-for-bike-plants; "Ten Taiwanese Bike Part Makers Invest in Philippines," *BikeBiz.Com,* January 5, 2006, available at http://www.bikebiz.com/news/23412/Ten-Taiwanese-bike-part-makers-invest-in-Philippines; "Taiwanese Bicycle-Makers Eye Indian Alliance," *The Times of India,* October 20, 2006.

63. It is worth noting recent efforts to design bicycle frames out of strong, renewable materials such as bamboo. Famed bicycle designer Craig Calfee is at the forefront of this trend, though bamboo bicycles were actually made in the United States more than a century ago. Huesby and Company in Milwaukee, Wisconsin, was one of the companies who made bikes with bamboo wheels and frames (with steel forks) in 1897. See Leander Kahney, "Bamboo Bike Maker Grows His Frames, Bonsai Style," *Wired,* September 25, 2008, available at http://www.wired.com/gadgetlab/2008/09/growing-bamboo; "Fishing Pole Bike," *Wisconsin Historical Society,* available at http://www.wisconsinhistory.org/turningpoints/search.asp?id=1130 (originally published in *Milwaukee Sentinel,* November 24, 1942). Also see Walter Ulreich, "The Bamboo Bicycles of Grundner and Lemisch," in *Cycle History 5: Proceedings of the 5th International Cycle History Conference (Cambridge, England),* ed. Rob Van der Plas (San Francisco: Cycle Publishing, 1995), 61–70.

64. Rosen, *Framing Production,* 64.

Bibliography

Aaron, Brad. "Macy's: Leave the Car at Home." *Streetsblog.com*, April 23, 2008. Available at http://www.streetsblog.org/2008/04/23/macys-leave-the-car-at-home.

Adams, W. I. Lincoln. "The Outing Club." *Outing, an Illustrated Monthly Magazine of Recreation* 14, no. 4 (1889): 314.

Adorno, Theodor W. "Veblen's Attack on Culture." In *Prisms*, 73–94. Cambridge, MA: MIT Press, 1983. Originally published in *Studies in Philosophy and Social Science* 9, no. 3 (1941): 389–413.

"Advantages of Joining the League." *Outing, a Journal of Recreation* 2, no. 4 (1883): 310–311.

Advocates for Highway and Auto Safety. "Motor Vehicle Traffic Fatalities and Fatality Rate: 1899–2003." Washington, DC, 2004.

Against Me! *Reinventing Axl Rose*. No Idea Records, 2002. LP.

Alderson, Frederick. *Bicycling: A History*. New York: Praeger, 1972.

Alvord, Katharine T. *Divorce Your Car!: Ending the Love Affair with the Automobile*. Gabriola Island, BC: New Society Publishers, 2000.

Amateau, Albert. "Westway Vets Remember the River Battles." *Downtown Express*, June 18–24, 2004.

Amebix. *Arise!* Alternative Tentacles, 1985. LP.

American Civil Liberties Union. "Federal Appeals Court Revives Michigan 'Bicycling-While-Black' Lawsuit." Press release, June 8, 2005.

American Civil Liberties Union of Colorado. "New Documents Confirm: Fbis Joint Terrorism Task Force Targets Peaceful Activists for Harassment, Political Surveillance." Press release, 2005.

American Society of Civil Engineers. *Infrastructure Report Card* Available at http://www.infrastructurereportcard.org.

American Youth Hostels, Transportation Alternatives, and League of American Wheelmen. "Bicycling Programs and Facilities in New York." New York, 1977.

Anderson, Benedict R. *Imagined Communities: Reflections on the Origin and Spread of Nationalism.* London: Verso, 1991.

Anderson, Karl (aka Megulon 5). "Why?" *Chunk 666*, October 4, 2008. Available at http://www.dclxvi.org/chunk/why.

Anderson, Rob. "Anti-car Jihad Targets Golden Gate Park." *District 5 Diary*, March 23, 2006. Available at http://district5diary.blogspot.com/2006_03_23_archive.html.

Anderson, Stacy A. "Westchester Cycle Club Collects Used Bikes for the Less Fortunate." *Journal News*, May 25, 2008.

Ansot, H. "A Modern Centaur." *Overland Monthly and Out West Magazine* 26, no. 152 (1895): 121–130.

Anti-product. *The Deafening Silence of Grinding Gears.* Tribal War Records, 1999. LP.

Antischism. *End of Time.* Stereonucleosis Records, 1990. Seven-inch record.

Apatow, Judd. *40-Year-Old Virgin.* Universal Pictures, 2005. Film.

Appadurai, Arjun. "Grassroots Globalization and the Research Imagination." *Public Culture* 12, no. 1 (2000): 1–19.

"Appeal to the International Provotariat." *Provo*, no. 11.

"Are All Bikes under $1000 (New) Made in China or Taiwan?" *Bike Forums*, thread started on May 24, 2008. Available at http://www.bikeforums.net/showthread.php?t=421843.

Armstrong, Lance, and Sally Jenkins. *It's Not about the Bike: My Journey Back to Life.* New York: Putnam, 2000.

Arnison, Matthew. "Critical Mass III (Sydney, Australia)." In *Critical Mass: Bicycling's Defiant Celebration*, edited by Chris Carlsson, 55–56. Oakland, CA: AK Press, 2002.

Arnoldy, Ben. "New Bike Commuters Hit the Classroom, Then the Road." *Christian Science Monitor*, August 25, 2008.

Aronowitz, Stanley. *Just around the Corner: The Paradox of the Jobless Recovery.* Philadelphia: Temple University Press, 2005.

Aronson, Sidney H. "The Sociology of the Bicycle." *Social Forces* 30, no. 1 (1951): 305–312.

Arquilla, John, David F. Ronfeldt, and U.S. Department of Defense (Office of the Secretary of Defense). *Networks and Netwars: The Future of Terror, Crime, and Militancy.* Santa Monica, CA: Rand, 2001.

Ashraf, Nava, James Berry, and Jesse Shapiro. "Can Higher Prices Stimulate Product Use? Evidence from a Field Experiment in Zambia." *National Bureau of Economic Research Working Paper*, no. 13247 (2007).

Atton, Chris. *Alternative Media.* London: Sage, 2002.

———. "The Infoshop: The Alternative Information Centre of the 1990s." *New Library World* 100 (1999): 24–29.

———. "A Reassessment of the Alternative Press." *Media, Culture and Society* 21, no. 1 (1999): 51–76.

Audirac, Ivonne. "Sharing Fast-Speed and Slow-Speed Roads with Bicyclists and Pedestrians: A Source of Female and Male Driver Frustration?" *Transportation Research Record: Journal of the Transportation Research Board* 2067, no. 1 (2008): 65–74.

Aufheben. "The Politics of Anti-road Struggle and the Struggles of Anti-road Politics: The Case of the No M11 Link Road Campaign." In *DiY Culture: Party and Protest in Nineties Britain*, edited by George McKay, 100–128. New York: Verso, 1998.

Aus Rotten. *The System Works for Them*. Tribal War Records, 1996. LP.

Avail. *Dixie*. Lookout! Records, 1994. LP.

Ayres, Ian. "Fair Driving: Gender and Race Discrimination in Retail Car Negotiations." *Harvard Law Review* 104 (1990): 817–872.

Bakhtin, Mikhail. *Rabelais and His World*. 1st Midland book ed. Bloomington: Indiana University Press, 1984.

Balaker, Theodore, and Sam Staley. *The Road More Traveled: Why the Congestion Crisis Matters More Than You Think, and What We Can Do about It*. Lanham, MD: Rowman and Littlefield, 2006.

Bales, C. "The Rat Patrol." In *Reglar Wiglar #19*. Chicago: Self-published, 2003.

Balf, Todd. "Critical Mess." *Bicycling* (December 2007): 41–61.

Balsley, Gene. "The Hot-Rod Culture." *American Quarterly* 2, no. 4 (1950): 353–358.

"The Bane of the Would-Be Bicyclist," *Transportation Alternatives Magazine* (2004): 4–5.

Barnes, Gary, and Kevin J. Krizek. "Estimating Bicycling Demand." *Journal of the Transportation Research Board*, no. 1939 (2005): 45–51.

Barnett, Gabrielle. "Drive-by Viewing: Visual Consciousness and Forest Preservation in the Automobile Age." *Technology and Culture* 45, no. 1 (2004): 30–54.

Barry, Michael. *Inside the Postal Bus: My Ride with Lance Armstrong and the U.S. Postal Cycling Team*. Boulder, CO: VeloPress, 2005.

Barthes, Roland. *The Semiotic Challenge*. Berkeley: University of California Press, 1994.

Basford, L., S. Reid, T. Lester (TRL Ltd.), J. Thomson, and A. Tolmie. "Drivers' Perceptions of Cyclists." Berkshire: Transport Research Laboratory, 2002.

Baudry de Saunier, Louis. *L'art de Bien Monter la Bicyclette*. 3rd ed. Paris, 1894.

Baxter, Sylvester. "Economic and Social Influences of the Bicycle." *The Arena*, no. 35 (1892): 578–584.

Belasco, Warren James. *Americans on the Road: From Autocamp to Motel, 1910–1945*. Cambridge, MA: MIT Press, 1979.

Bell, Michael. *An Invitation to Environmental Sociology*. 2nd ed. Thousand Oaks, CA: Pine Forge Press, 2004.

Bellencontre, M. D. *Hygiene Du Velocipede*. Paris: L. Richard, 1869.

Berger, Arthur Asa. "The Spyder (Sting-Ray, Screamer) Bike: An American Original." In *Side-Saddle on the Golden Calf: Social Structure and Popular Culture in America*, edited by George H. Lewis, 154–156. Pacific Palisades, CA: Goodyear, 1972.

Berger, John. *Ways of Seeing*. New York: Viking Press, 1973.

Berger, Michael L. *The Devil Wagon in God's Country: The Automobile and Social Change in Rural America, 1893–1929*. Hamden: Archon Books, 1979.

Bergeron, Suzanne. "Political Economy Discourses of Globalization and Feminist Politics." *Signs* 26, no. 4 (2001): 983–1006.

Besse, Nadine, and André Vant. "A New View of Late 19th Century Cycle Publicity Posters." In *Cycle History 5: Proceedings of the 5th International Cycle History Conference (Cambridge, England)*, edited by Rob Van der Plas, 117–122. San Francisco: Cycle Publishing, 1994.

Besser, Howard. "Victorious Critical Mass Lawsuit." In *Critical Mass: Bicycling's Defiant Celebration*, edited by Chris Carlsson, 219–222. Oakland, CA: AK Press, 2002.

Bey, Hakim *T.A.Z.: The Temporary Autonomous Zone, Ontological Anarchy, Poetic Terrorism*. Brooklyn, NY: Autonomedia, 1991.

"The Bicycle." *Scientific American* 75, no. 4 (1896): 68–69.

"The Bicycle Action Project (Factsheet)." *Youth Employment Summit: YES Campaign*. Available at http://www.yesweb.org/gkr/project_factsheet.html?pid=317.

Bicycle Clown. Sid Davis Productions, 1958. Film.

Bicycle Industry and Retailer News. "Bike Stats 2008." Available at http://www.bicycleretailer.com/downloads/BIKE STATS.pdf.

Bicycle Safety. Centron Productions/Young America Films, 1950. Film.

Bicycle Today-Automobile Tomorrow. Sid Davis Productions, 1969. Film.

Bijker, Wiebe E. *Of Bicycles, Bakelites, and Bulbs: Toward a Theory of Sociotechnical Change*. Inside Technology series. Cambridge, MA: MIT Press, 1995.

Bijker, Wiebe E., Thomas Parke Hughes, and Trevor J. Pinch. *The Social Construction of Technological Systems: New Directions in the Sociology and History of Technology*. Cambridge, MA: MIT Press, 1987.

Bijker, Wiebe E., and John Law. *Shaping Technology/Building Society: Studies in Sociotechnical Change*. Inside Technology series. Cambridge, MA: MIT Press, 1992.

"Bike Messenger Zines Worldwide." *International Federation of Bike Messenger Associations*. Available at http://www.messengers.org/resources/zines.html.

Bikes Across Borders. Available at http://www.bikesacrossborders.org.

Bikes at Work. Available at http://www.bikesatwork.com.

"Bike Side Car for Baby Passenger." *Modern Mechanix*, January 1932.

Billstein, Reinhold, Karola Fings, Anita Kugler, and Nicholas Levis, eds. *Working for the Enemy: Ford, General Motors, and Forced Labor in Germany during the Second World War*. New York: Berghahn Books, 2000.

Biotic Baking Brigade. *Pie Any Means Necessary: The Biotic Baking Brigade Cookbook*. Oakland, CA: AK Press/Rebel Folk Press, 2004.

Blanding, Michael, and Travis Lea. "How Mild-Mannered Bicyclists Were Turned into 'Wolves.'" *Salon.com*, July 30, 1997. Available at http://dir.salon.com/story/news/feature/1997/07/30/news/.

Blaug, Bernie. "Crit Mass." In *Critical Mass: Bicycling's Defiant Celebration*, edited by Chris Carlsson, 73. Oakland, CA: AK Press, 2002.

Blaze, William. "Visceral Aesthetics (Fixed Gear)." *Abstract Dynamics*, May 27, 2005. Available at http://www.abstractdynamics.org/archives/2005/05/27/visceral_aesthetics_fixed_gear.html.

Blickstein, Susan, and Susan Hanson. "Critical Mass: Forging a Politics of Sustainable Mobility in the Information Age." *Transportation* 28, no. 4 (2001): 347–362.

Blue, Mary, and Andrew Lynn. *Velorution: The Unofficial Documents of a Bicycle Underground* 1 (2004).

Bluejay, Michael. "Police vs. Critical Mass." *Critical-Mass.info*. Available at http://CriticalMassRides.info/police.html.

Boal, Iain. "'Re-inventing the Wheel.'" In *Cycle History 16: Proceedings of the 16th International Cycling History Conference (Davis, Ca)*, edited by Andrew Ritchie, 8–10. San Francisco: Cycle Publishing, 2006.

Bodzin, Steven. "Politics Can Be Fun." In *Critical Mass: Bicycling's Defiant Celebration*, edited by Chris Carlsson, 100–104. Oakland, CA: AK Press, 2002.

Bogdanowicz, Tom. "Cycling and the Media." *Intermedia* 32, no. 3 (2004): 21–22.

Böhm, Steffen, Campbell Jones, Chris Land, and Matthew Paterson, eds. *Against Automobility*. Malden, MA: Blackwell/Sociological Review, 2006.

———. "Introduction: Impossibilities of Automobilities." In *Against Automobility*, edited by Steffen Böhm, Campbell Jones, Chris Land, and Matthew Paterson, 3–16. Malden, MA: Blackwell/Sociological Review, 2006.

Bonham, Jennifer. "Transport: Disciplining the Body That Travels." *Sociological Review* 54, no. s1 (2006): 55–74.

Bookchin, Murray. *The Limits of the City*. New York: Harper and Row, 1974.

———. *Post-scarcity Anarchism*. Berkeley, CA: Ramparts Press, 1971.

———. *Social Anarchism or Lifestyle Anarchism: The Unbridgeable Chasm*. San Francisco: AK Press, 1995.

Boothroyd, Sarah. "Spraypaint Slingers, Celebration, and a Tidal Wave of Outrage." In *Critical Mass: Bicycling's Defiant Celebration*, edited by Chris Carlsson, 23–29. Oakland, CA: AK Press, 2002.

Borden, Iain. "A Performative Critique of the City: The Urban Practice of Skateboarding, 1958–98." In *The City Cultures Reader*, edited by Malcolm Miles, Tim Hall, and Iain Borden, 291–297. London: Routledge, 2004.

———. *Skateboarding, Space, and the City*. New York: Berg, 2001.

Bouillion, Lisa M., and Louis M. Gomez. "Connecting School and Community with Science Learning: Real World Problems and School-Community Partnerships as Contextual Scaffolds." *Journal of Research in Science Teaching* 38, no. 8 (2001): 878–898.

Boyd, Andrew, and Stephen Duncombe. "The Manufacture of Dissent: What the Left Can Learn from Las Vegas." *Journal of Aesthetics and Protest* 1, no. 3 (2004): 34–47.

Boykoff, Jules. *The Suppression of Dissent: How the State and Mass Media Squelch Usamerican Social Movements*. New Approaches in Sociology. New York: Routledge, 2006.

Bridgers, Dink. "Wheels of Fortune." *Dreamride*, 1997. Available at http://www.dreamride.com/wheels2.html.

The Broadways. *Broken Van*. Asian Man Records, 2000. CD.

Brown, Sheldon. "Fixed Gear Bicycles for the Road." *Sheldon Brown's Bicycle Technical Information*. Available at http://www.sheldonbrown.com/fixed.html.

———. "Single Speed Conversions." *Sheldon Brown's Bicycle Technical Information*, July 3, 1999. Available at http://www.sheldonbrown.com/singlespeed.html.

Brown, Sherrod. "Brown Joins Senate Hearing to Examine Whether 'Free Trade' Policies Are Working." Press release, April 18, 2007. Available at http://brown.senate.gov/newsroom/press_releases/release/?id=58363a0f-3228-4433-a70d-d18a98b2ace0.

Brubaker, Nathan. "Welcome to the Police State." *Pittsburgh Critical Mass Arrests Blog*, 2006. Available at http://criticalmassarrests.blogspot.com/2006/03/welcome-to-police-state-in-my.html.

Bruegmann, Robert. *Sprawl: A Compact History*. Chicago: University of Chicago Press, 2005.

Bryant, Jennings, and Dolf Zillmann. *Media Effects: Advances in Theory and Research*. 2nd ed. Lea's Communication series. Mahwah, NJ: L. Erlbaum Associates, 2002.

Bryceson, Deborah Fahy. "The Scramble in Africa: Reorienting Rural Livelihoods." *World Development* 30, no. 5 (2002): 725–739.

Bryceson, Deborah Fahy, and John Howe. "Rural Household Transport in Africa: Reducing the Burden on Women?" *World Development* 21, no. 11 (1993): 1715–1728.

Bryceson, Deborah Fahy, T. C. Mbara, and D. Maunder. "Livelihoods, Daily Mobility and Poverty in Sub-Saharan Africa." *Transport Reviews* 23, no. 2 (2003): 177–196.

Bryne, Malcolm "Electronic Briefing Book No. 28: The Secret CIA History of the Iran Coup, 1953." *National Security Archive*. Available at http://www.gwu.edu/~nsarchiv/NSAEBB/NSAEBB28.

Buck-Morss, Susan. "The Flâneur, the Sandwichman and the Whore: The Politics of Loitering." *New German Critique* (1986): 99–140.

Buehler, Theodore J. "Fifty Years of Bicycle Policy in Davis, CA." Master's thesis, University of California, Davis, 2007.

Buffalo Bill. "Fakenger." *Moving Target Zine*, March 2, 2007. Available at http://www.movingtargetzine.com/article/fakenger.

———. "Guardian Style Journalist 'Discovers' Fixies." *Moving Target Zine*, September 3, 2008. Available at http://www.movingtargetzine.com/article/guardian-style-journalist-discovers-fixies.

Bull, Michael. "Automobility and the Power of Sound." *Theory, Culture and Society* 21, nos. 4–5 (2004): 243–260.

Bullard, Robert D., and Glenn S. Johnson. *Just Transportation: Dismantling Race and Class Barriers to Mobility*. Gabriola Island, BC: New Society Publishers, 1997.

Bullard, Robert D., Glenn S. Johnson, and Angel O. Torres. "Dismantling Transportation Apartheid: The Quest for Equity." In *Sprawl City*, edited by Robert D. Bullard, Glenn S. Johnson, and Angel O. Torres, 39–68. Washington, DC: Island Press, 2000.

———. *Highway Robbery: Transportation Racism and New Routes to Equity*. Cambridge, MA: South End Press, 2004.

———. "The Routes of American Apartheid." *Forum for Applied Research and Public Policy* 15, no. 3 (2000): 66–74.

Burdett, Avery. "About the OCBC." *Ontario Coalition for Better Cycling*, 2006. Available at http://www.magma.ca/~ocbc/.

Burton, Michael. "Rugged Individualists of the Road Unite." In *Critical Mass: Bicycling's Defiant Celebration*, edited by Chris Carlsson, 18–22. Oakland, CA: AK Press, 2002.

Burton, Tim. *Pee-wee's Big Adventure*. Warner Bros, 1985. Film.

Buzzcocks. *Another Music in a Different Kitchen*: United Artists, 1978. LP.

Caidin, Martin, and Jay Barbree. *Bicycles in War*. New York: Hawthorn Books, 1974.

Calfee, Craig. "Ghana Bamboo Bike Journal, February 2008 Trip." *Calfee Design.* Available at http://www.calfeedesign.com/Ghana2008.htm.

Canjuers, Pierre, and Guy Debord. "Preliminaries toward Defining a Unitary Revolutionary Program." In *Situationist Anthology*, edited by Ken Knabb, 305–310. Berkeley: Bureau of Public Secrets, 1981. Originally published in July 1960.

Carducci, Vince. "Culture Jamming: A Sociological Perspective." *Journal of Consumer Culture* 6, no. 1 (2006): 116–138.

Carey, James W. *Communication as Culture: Essays on Media and Society.* Boston: Unwin Hyman, 1989.

Carey, Jim. "Fresh Flavour in the Media Soup: The Story of Squall Magazine." In *DiY Culture: Party and Protest in Nineties Britain*, edited by George McKay, 58–78. London: Verso, 1998.

Carlson, L., and J. Sullivan. "Hands-on Engineering: Learning by Doing in the Integrated Teaching and Learning Program." *International Journal of Engineering Education* 15, no. 1 (1999): 20–31.

Carlsson, Chris. "Critical Massifesto." June 7, 1994. *Critical Mass Essays, Flyers, Images from San Francisco, 1992–1998.* Available at http://www.processedworld.com/tfrs_web/history/cmassifesto.html.

———. "Cycling under the Radar: Assertive Desertion." In *Critical Mass: Bicycling's Defiant Celebration*, edited by Chris Carlsson, 75–82. Oakland, CA: AK Press, 2002.

———. "The Hidden Class Politics of Bicycling, Trains, Bikes, Cars, BART(!)" 1997. *Critical Mass Essays, Flyers, Images from San Francisco, 1992–1998.* Available at http://www.processedworld.com/tfrs_web/history/classncycling.html.

———. *Nowtopia: How Pirate Programmers, Outlaw Bicyclists, and Vacant-Lot Gardeners Are Inventing the Future Today.* Oakland, CA: AK Press, 2008.

———. "'Outlaw' Bicycling." *Affinities: A Journal of Radical Theory, Culture, and Action* 1, no. 1 (2007): 86–106.

———. "Whither Bicycling?" *Critical Mass Essays, Flyers, Images from San Francisco, 1992–1998*, September 25, 1998. Available at http://www.processedworld.com/tfrs_web/history/whither.html.

———, ed. *Critical Mass: Bicycling's Defiant Celebration.* Oakland, CA: AK Press, 2002.

Caro, Robert A. *The Power Broker: Robert Moses and the Fall of New York.* New York: Vintage Books, 1975.

The Car Party. Accessed at http://www.thecarparty.org.uk (dead link as of spring 2009).

Castells, Manuel. *The Power of Identity.* Malden, MA: Blackwell, 1997.

Chambers, Deborah A. "Symbolic Equipment and the Objects of Leisure Images." *Leisure Studies* 2, no. 3 (1983): 301–315.

Chappell, Ben. "'Take a Little Trip with Me': Lowriding and the Poetics of Scale." In *Technicolor: Race, Technology, and Everyday Life*, edited by Alondra Nelson, Thuy Linh N. Tu, and Alicia Headlam Hines, 100–120. New York: New York University Press, 2001.

Chavoya, C. Ondine. "Customized Hybrids: The Art of Ruben Ortiz Torres and Lowriding in Southern California." *CR: The New Centennial Review* 4, no. 2 (2005): 141–184.

Chevrolet Leader News 2, no. 1. Handy (Jam) Organization with Chevrolet Division, General Motors Corporation, 1936. Film.

The City—Heaven and Hell. National Film Board of Canada, 1963. Film.

Clark, Ethan, and Shelley Lynn Jackson. *The Chainbreaker Bike Book*. Bloomington, IN: Microcosm Publishing, 2008.

Clark, H. C. *Hygienic Bicycling*. Delaware City, DE, 1897.

Clayton, Nick. "SCOT: Does It Answer?" *Technology and Culture* 43, no. 2 (2002): 351–360.

Cohan, Steven, and Ina Rae Hark. *The Road Movie Book*. London: Routledge, 1997.

Cohen, Jessica, and Pascaline Dupas. "Free Distribution or Cost-Sharing? Evidence from a Malaria Prevention Experiment." *Brookings Global Economy and Development Working Paper*, no. 11 (2007).

Cohen, Maurie J. "A Social Problems Framework for the Critical Appraisal of Auto-mobility and Sustainable Systems Innovation." *Mobilities* 1, no. 1 (2006): 23–38.

Cohen, Phil. "Subcultural Conflict and Working-Class Community." In *Culture, Media, Language: Working Papers in Cultural Studies, 1972–1979*, edited by Stuart Hall, Dorothy Hobson, Andrew Lowe, and Paul Willis, 66–75. London: Routledge in Association with the Centre for Contemporary Cultural Studies, University of Birmingham, 1980.

Cohen, Philip N. "Nationalism and Suffrage: Gender Struggle in Nation-Building America." *Signs* 21, no. 3 (1996): 707–727.

Cometbus, Aaron. "Interview with Eric Zo." *Cometbus*, no. 49. Self-published zine.

"Conservative Philanthropies." *Media Transparency*. Available at http://mediatranspar-ency.org/funders.php.

Corgel, J. B., and C. F. Floyd. "Towards a New Direction in Bicycle Transportation Policy." *Transportation Quarterly* 33, no. 2 (1979): 297–301.

Cowan, Ruth Schwartz. *More Work for Mother: The Ironies of Household Technology from the Open Hearth to the Microwave*. New York: Basic Books, 1983.

Crass. *Christ the Album*. Crass Records, 1982.

———. *Stations of the Crass*. Crass Records, 1979.

"Create a Commuter Program." *Community Cycling Center*. Available at http://www.communitycyclingcenter.org/index.php/programs/create-a-commuter/.

"Creepy Cyclists and Women on Bikes." *Bike Portland*, May 31, 2006. Available at http://bikeportland.org/2006/05/31/creepy-cyclists-and-women-on-bikes/.

Cresswell, Tim. *On the Move: Mobility in the Modern Western World*. New York: Routledge, 2006.

"Critical Mass Flame War." *Monkey Chicken*. Available at http://www.monkeychicken.com/fwar.htm.

"Critical Mass: Reclaiming Space and Combating the Car." *Do or Die*, no. 5 (1996): 65–67. Zine.

Crouse, David W. "The Real Costs of the Automobile: A Report on Recent Research." *Bulletin of Science, Technology and Society* 20, no. 5 (2000): 366–378.

Crown, Judith, and Glenn Coleman. *No Hands: The Rise and Fall of the Schwinn Bicycle Company: An American Institution*. New York: H. Holt, 1996.

Culley, Travis Hugh. *The Immortal Class: Bike Messengers and the Cult of Human Power*. New York: Villard, 2001.

Culture Jammer's Encyclopedia. Available at http://www.sniggle.net.

Cunha, Clarisse. "Understanding the Community Impact: Bicycles in Sub-Saharan Africa." *Sustainable Transport*, no. 18 (2006): 24–25.

Curran, James, Michael Gurevitch, and Janet Woollacott. *Mass Communication and Society*. Beverly Hills, CA: Sage Publications, 1982.

"The Cycling Market." *Bicycling Magazine Media Kit*. Available at http://www.bicycling.com/mediakit/audience_cyclingmarket.html.

Dale, Minister Brian. "Bicycle Design for the Urban Audience." *Marshall Taylor Blog*, May 28, 2007. Available at http://marshalltaylor.blogspot.com/2007/05/bicycle-design-for-urban-audience.html.

Dant, Tim. "The Driver-Car," *Theory, Culture and Society* 21, no. 4/5 (2004): 61–79.

Daoudi, M. S., and M. S. Dajani. *Economic Diplomacy: Embargo Leverage and World Politics*. Westview Special Studies in International Relations series. Boulder, CO: Westview Press, 1985.

Davis, Angela Y. *Women, Race, and Class*. New York: Random House, 1981.

Davis, George V. "Where Once There Were Mountains: The Grassroots Struggle against Mountaintop Removal Coal Mining in Central Appalachia." *Environmental Politics* 18, no. 1 (2009): 135–140.

Davis, Timothy. "Looking down the Road: J.B. Jackson and the American Highway Landscape." In *Everyday America*, edited by Chris Wilson and Paul Erling Groth, 62–80. Berkeley: University of California Press, 2003.

Dead Things. *Because Sometimes You Just Want to Ride Your Bike to the Show*. Slave Records, 2002. CD.

———. "Bike Tour Press Release." 2002.

Debord, Guy. "For a Revolutionary Judgment of Art." In *Situationist International Anthology*, edited by Ken Knabb, 310–311. Berkeley, CA: Bureau of Public Secrets, 1981. Originally published in February 1961.

———. "Introduction to a Critique of Urban Geography." In *Situationist International Anthology*, edited by Ken Knabb, 5–8. Berkeley, CA: Bureau of Public Secrets, 1981. Originally published in *Les Lévres Nues*, no. 6 (September 1955).

———. "Report on the Construction of Situations and on the International Situationist Tendency's Conditions of Organization and Action." In *Situationist International Anthology*, edited by Ken Knabb, 17–25. Berkeley, CA: Bureau of Public Secrets, 1981. Originally published in June 1957.

———. "Situationist Theses on Traffic." In *Situationist International Anthology*, edited by Ken Knabb, 55–58. Berkeley, CA: Bureau of Public Secrets, 1981. Originally published in *Internationale Situationniste*, no. 3 (December 1959).

———. *The Society of the Spectacle*, translated by Fredy Perlman and John Supak. Detroit: Black and Red, 1977.

———. "Theory of the Dérive." In *Situationist International Anthology*, edited by Ken Knabb, 50–54. Berkeley, CA: Bureau of Public Secrets, 1981. Originally published in *Internationale Situationniste*, no. 2 (December 1958).

Debs, Eugene V. *The American Movement*. 1998. Available at the E. V. Debs Internet Archive, http://www.marxists.org/archive/debs.

Deffeyes, Kenneth S. *Beyond Oil: The View from Hubbert's Peak*. New York: Hill and Wang, 2005.

———. *Hubbert's Peak: The Impending World Oil Shortage*. Princeton, NJ: Princeton University Press, 2001.

Defiance, Ohio. *Share What Ya Got*. Friends and Relatives Records, 2004. LP.

De Jong, Rudolf. *Provos and Kabouters*. Buffalo, NY: Friends of Malatesta. In *Anarchism Today*, edited by David E. Apter and James Joll, 165–168. London: Macmillan, 1971.

Delaney, Ben. "Human Rights, Not Cheap Bikes Retailer Advocates Industry-Wide Boycott of China." *Commuter Bicycles*. Available at http://www.commuterbicycles. com/news.php. Originally published in *Bicycle Retailer and Industry News*, 2003.

Delicath, John W., and Kevin Michael DeLuca. "Image Events, the Public Sphere, and Argumentative Practice: The Case of Radical Environmental Groups." *Argumentation* 17, no. 3 (2003): 315–333.

DeLuca, Kevin Michael. *Image Politics: The New Rhetoric of Environmental Activism*. Revisioning Rhetoric. New York: Guilford Press, 1999.

——. "Unruly Arguments: The Body Rhetoric of Earth First! Act Up and Queer Nation." *Argumentation and Advocacy*, no. 36 (1999): 9–21.

Delucchi, Mark A. "Do Motor-Vehicle Users in the U.S. Pay Their Way?" *Transportation Research Part A: Policy and Practice* 41, no. 10 (2007): 982–1003.

DeMaio, Paul. "Smart Bikes: Public Transportation for the 21st Century." *Transportation Quarterly* 57, no. 1 (2003): 9–11.

Dennerlein, Jack Tigh, and John D. Meeker. "Occupational Injuries among Boston Bicycle Messengers." *American Journal of Industrial Medicine* 42, no. 6 (2002): 519–525.

Department of Transportation Statistics, and National Highway Traffic Safety Administration. "How Bike Paths and Lanes Make a Difference." Washington, DC, 2004.

——. "National Survey of Pedestrian and Bicyclist Attitudes and Behaviors: Highlights Report." Washington, DC: Department of Transportation, 2003.

Derdak, Thomas, Tina Grant, and Jay P. Pederson. *International Directory of Company Histories*. Vol. 86. Farmington Hills, MI: Gale, 2006.

Dery, Mark. *Culture Jamming: Hacking, Slashing and Sniping in the Empire of Signs*. Westfield, NJ: Open Magazine Pamphlet Series, 1993.

The Descendents. *Somery*. SST Records, 1991. LP.

Desgranges, Henri. "A Frenchman's Views on the Safety Bicycle as It Now Is and Its Probable Future." *Scientific American* 72, no. 2 (1895): 22.

De Sica, Vittorio. *The Bicycle Thief (Ladri Di Biciclette)*. Produzioni De Sica, 1948. Film.

Desperate Bicycles. *New Cross, New Cross*. Refill Records #3, 1978. Seven-inch record.

DiCarlo, Rachel. "Hit the Road." *Weekly Standard*, January 25, 2006.

Dick, H. W., and P. J. Rimmer. "Urban Public Transport in Southeast Asia: A Case Study of Technological Imperialism?" *International Journal of Transport Economics* 13, no. 2 (1986): 177–196.

Dill, Jennifer, and Theresa Carr. "Bicycle Commuting and Facilities in Major U.S. Cities: If You Build Them, Commuters Will Use Them." *Transportation Research Record*, no. 1828 (2003): 116–123.

Dill, Jennifer, and Kim Voros. "Factors Affecting Bicycling Demand: Initial Survey Findings from the Portland Region." Paper presented at the Transportation Research Board 86th Annual Meeting, 2007.

Dimendberg, Edward. "The Will to Motorization: Cinema, Highways, and Modernity." *October*, no. 73 (1995): 90–137.

DiNovella, Elizabeth. "Bikes for the World." *Progressive* (April 2004): 16.

Divide and Conquer. *The Need to Amputate*. Ginger Liberation/Maloka Records, 1999. LP.

——. *Sanjam Split International Compilation*. Sanjam Records, 1996. LP.

Dix, W. F. "Motoring for People of Moderate Means." *The Independent* 70 (April 13, 1911): 775–777.

Dixon, Leon. *National Bicycle History Archive.* Available at http://nbhaa.com/.

Dodge, Pryor. *The Bicycle.* Paris: Flammarion, 1996.

Doherty, Brian. *Radicals for Capitalism: A Freewheeling History of the Modern American Libertarian Movement.* New York: Public Affairs Books, 2007.

———. *This Is Burning Man: The Rise of a New American Underground.* New York: Little and Brown, 2004.

Domosh, Mona, and Joni Seager. *Putting Women in Place: Feminist Geographers Make Sense of the World.* New York: Guilford Press, 2001.

Donnelly, Thomas Michael. *Quicksilver.* Columbia Pictures Corporation, 1986. Film.

Dorgan, Byron L. *Take This Job and Ship It: How Corporate Greed and Brain-Dead Politics Are Selling Out America.* New York: Thomas Dunne Books/St. Martin's Press, 2006.

Dowlin, John. *Network News,* no. 2 (April–June 1979).

Downey, Gregory John. *Telegraph Messenger Boys: Labor, Technology, and Geography, 1850–1950.* New York: Routledge, 2002.

Drążkiewicz, Elżbieta. "On the Bicycle towards Freedom: Bicycle Messengers' Answer for Identity Crisis." Master's thesis, Lund University, 2003.

Drive Your Bicycle. Sullivan, 1955. Film.

Drury, John, Steve Reicher, and Clifford Stott. "Transforming the Boundaries of Collective Identity: From the 'Local' Anti-road Campaign to 'Global' Resistance?" *Social Movement Studies* 2, no. 2 (2003): 191–212.

Duising, Catherine, and John Calhoun. "History: 1965–2000." *Central Indiana Bicycling Association.* Available at http://www.cibaride.org/history/history.html.

Duke's Car Club. "History." Available at http://www.dukescarclub.com/history/history.html.

Dulles, Foster Rhea. *A History of Recreation: America Learns to Play.* New York: Appleton-Century-Crofts, 1965.

Duncombe, Stephen. *Dream: Re-imagining Progressive Politics in an Age of Fantasy.* New York: New Press, 2007.

———. *Notes from Underground: Zines and the Politics of Alternative Culture.* London: Verso, 1997.

———. "Stepping off the Sidewalk: Reclaim the Streets/NYC." In *From Act Up to the WTO: Urban Protest and Community Building in the Era of Globalization,* edited by Benjamin Heim Shepard, and Ronald Hayduk, 215–228. London: Verso, 2002.

———, ed. *Cultural Resistance Reader.* London: Verso, 2002.

Dunn, James A. *Driving Forces: The Automobile, Its Enemies, and the Politics of Mobility.* Washington, DC: Brookings Institution Press, 1998.

Durham, Meenakshi Gigi, and Douglas Kellner. *Media and Cultural Studies: Keyworks.* Malden, MA: Blackwell, 2006.

During, Simon. *The Cultural Studies Reader.* 3rd ed. London: Routledge, 2007.

Dyer, Jym. "Flocculating in the Streets of Berkeley." *Terrain* (August 1993).

Dzierzak, Lou. *Schwinn.* St. Paul, MN: MBI Publishing, 2002.

Easterly, William Russell. *The White Man's Burden: Why the West's Efforts to Aid the Rest Have Done So Much Ill and So Little Good.* New York: Penguin Press, 2006.

Ebert, Anne-Katrin. "Cycling towards the Nation: The Use of the Bicycle in Germany and the Netherlands, 1880–1940." *European Review of History* 11, no. 3 (2004): 347.

"Eccentric Cycles." *Mechanix Illustrated* (September 1949): 70–71.

"Ecology, a Family Affair." *Ms.* (November 1974): 119.

Edelman, Marc. "A Central American Genocide: Rubber, Slavery, Nationalism, and the Destruction of the Guatusos-Malekus." *Comparative Studies in Society and History* 40, no. 2 (2004): 356–390.

Edensor, Tim. "Automobility and National Identity: Representation, Geography and Driving Practice." *Theory Culture Society* 21, nos. 4–5 (2004): 101–120.

"Editors Open Window." *Outing and the Wheelman* 4, no. 5 (1884): 381.

Eglash, Ron, ed. *Appropriating Technology: Vernacular Science and Social Power.* Minneapolis: University of Minnesota Press, 2004.

Eisenhower, Dwight D. *At Ease: Stories I Tell to Friends.* Garden City, NY: Doubleday, 1967.

Ellis, Cliff. "Lewis Mumford and Norman Bel Geddes: The Highway, the City and the Future." *Planning Perspectives* 20 (2005): 51–68.

Epperson, Bruce. "Bicycle Planning: Growing Up or Growing Old." *Race, Poverty and the Environment* 6 (Special Issue: Transportation and Social Justice), no. 1 (1995): 42–44.

———. "Failed Colossus: Strategic Error at the Pope Manufacturing Company, 1878–1900." *Technology and Culture* 41, no. 2 (2000): 300–320.

———. "The Monopoly Machine—the Lallement Patent and the Attempted Monopolization of the American Bicycle Industry, 1880–1886." In *Cycle History 15: Proceedings from the 15th International Cycling History Conference (Vienna, Austria)*, edited by Andrew Ritchie and Nicholas Clayton, 102–120. San Francisco: Cycle Publishing, 2004.

Ernst, Michelle, and Surface Transportation Policy Project. "Mean Streets 2004." Washington, DC: Surface Transportation Policy Project, 2004.

Escobar, Arturo. "Culture Sits in Places: Reflections on Globalism and Subaltern Strategies of Localization." *Political Geography* 20, no. 2 (2001): 139–174.

Evans, Michael. "'Para-Politics' Goes Bananas." *The Nation*, April 4, 2007.

Evasion. Atlanta: CrimethInc., 2001.

Evi. "Interview with Soophie Nun Squad." *Enough Fanzine*, February 9, 2003.

Eyerman, Ron, and Orvar Lofgren. "Romancing the Road: Road Movies and Images of Mobility." *Theory, Culture and Society* 12, no. 1 (1995): 53–79.

Farrar, M. E., and J. L. Warner. "Spectacular Resistance: The Billionaires for Bush and the Art of Political Culture Jamming." *Polity* 40, no. 3 (2008): 273–296.

Featherstone, Mike. "Automobilities: An Introduction." *Theory Culture Society* 21, nos. 4–5 (2004): 1–24.

———. "The Flâneur, the City and Virtual Public Life." *Urban Studies* 35, no. 5 (1998): 909–925.

———, ed. "Special Issue: Automobilities." *Theory, Culture and Society* 21, nos. 4–5 (2004).

Feenberg, Andrew. *Questioning Technology.* London: Routledge, 1999.

Feher, Erin, and Sonia Beauchamp. "Fixie or Forget It." *[X]press* (October 2005). Available at http://xpress.sfsu.edu/archives/magazine/004697.html.

Fejes, Fred. "Critical Mass Communications Research and Media Effects: The Problem of the Disappearing Audience." *Media Culture Society* 6, no. 3 (1984): 219–232.

Ferrell, Jeff. "Maybe You Should Check the Statute." In *Critical Mass: Bicycling's Defiant Celebration*, edited by Chris Carlsson, 122–128. Oakland, CA: AK Press, 2002.

———. *Tearing Down the Streets: Adventures in Urban Anarchy*. New York: Palgrave, 2001.

Feuer, Jane. *Seeing through the Eighties: Television and Reaganism*. Console-Ing Passions. Durham, NC: Duke University Press, 1995.

Fifteen. *Choice of a New Generation*. Lookout! Records, 1989. LP.

Fincham, Ben. "Bicycle Messengers and the Road to Freedom." *Sociological Review* 54, no. 1 (2006): 208–222.

Fitzpatrick, Jim. *The Bicycle and the Bush: Man and Machine in Rural Australia*. Melbourne: Oxford University Press, 1980.

Flink, James J. *The Automobile Age*. Cambridge, MA: MIT Press, 1988.

———. *The Car Culture*. Cambridge, MA: MIT Press, 1975.

———. "Three Stages of American Automobile Consciousness." *American Quarterly* 24, no. 4 (1972): 451–473.

"Forbidden Words for Newspaper Articles about Messengers." *Voice of Da*, edited by America Meredith, no. 8 (1999). Zine.

Ford, Henry. *My Life and Work*. Garden City, NY: Garden City Publishing, 1922.

Ford Motor. "Model T Facts." Available at http://media.ford.com/article_display.cfm?article_id=858.

Ford-Smith, Honor. "Ring Ding in a Tight Corner: Sistren, Collective Democracy, and the Organization of Cultural Production." In *Feminist Genealogies, Colonial Legacies, Democratic Futures*, edited by M. Jacqui Alexander and Chandra Talpade Mohanty, 213–258. New York: Routledge, 1997.

Forester, John. *Bicycle Transportation: A Handbook for Cycling Transportation Engineers*. 2nd ed. Cambridge, MA: MIT Press, 1994.

———. *Effective Cycling*. 6th ed. Cambridge, MA: MIT Press, 1993.

———. "The Place of Bicycle Transportation in Modern Industrialized Societies." Paper presented at the Preserving the American Dream Conference, Bloomington, MN, 2005.

4th Street Bicycle Boulevard. Available at http://www.4sbb.com/.

Frank, Len. *Motor Trend Presents 100 Years of the Automobile in America: 10 Memorable Decades of an American Love Affair*. Special collector's ed. Los Angeles: Peterson Publishing, 1996.

Frank, Thomas. *The Conquest of Cool: Business Culture, Counterculture, and the Rise of Hip Consumerism*. Chicago: University of Chicago Press, 1997.

Frank, Thomas, and Matt Weiland, eds. *Commodify Your Dissent: Salvos from the Baffler*. New York: Norton, 1997.

Franklin, John. "A History of Cycle Paths." *Cyclecraft*. Available at http://www.cyclecraft.co.uk/digest/history.html.

Franklin, Titus Hermon. "The Clerical Wheel." *Outing, a Journal of Recreation* 1, no. 2 (1882): 101–107.

Freeh, Louis J. "Threat of Terrorism to the United States." Testimony before the United States Senate, Committees on Appropriations, Armed Services, and Select Committee on Intelligence, May 10, 2001.

Friedberg, Anne. "Urban Mobility and Cinematic Visuality: The Screens of Los Angeles—Endless Cinema or Private Telematics." *Journal of Visual Culture* 1, no. 2 (2002): 183–204.

Friedman, Thomas L. *The World Is Flat: A Brief History of the Twenty-first Century.* New York: Farrar, Straus and Giroux, 2007.

Fritz, Ian, Troy Neiman, and John Gerken, eds. *Bicycle Organization Project (BOOP).* Tucson, AZ: BICAS, 2006. Zine.

Fritz, Yokota. "DKNY Orange Bicycles in London." *Cycleicious Blog,* May 19, 2008. Available at http://www.cyclelicio.us/2008/05/dkny-orange-bicycles-in-london.html.

Furness, Zack. "Biketivism and Technology: Historical Reflections and Appropriations." *Social Epistemology* 19, no. 4 (2005): 401–417.

———. "Blackout." *Bad Subjects* 64 (2003).

———. "Critical Mass, Urban Space and Vélomobility." *Mobilities* 2, no. 2 (2007): 299–319.

———. "An Inconvenient Truth." *Bad Subjects,* 2006. Available at http://bad.eserver.org/reviews/2006/gore.html.

———. "Microcosm Publishing." *Punk Planet* (January–February 2005): 46–47.

———. "'Put the Fun between Your Legs!': The Politics and Counterculture of the Bicycle." Ph.D. diss., University of Pittsburgh, 2005.

Gamson, W. A. *Talking Politics.* Cambridge: Cambridge University Press, 1992.

Gamson, William A. *The Strategy of Social Protest.* Homewood, IL: Dorsey Press, 1975.

Gardner, Gary. "When Cities Take Bicycle Seriously." *Worldwatch Institute* 11, no. 5 (1998): 16–23.

Garrard, J., G. Rose, and S. K. Lo. "Promoting Transportation Cycling for Women: The Role of Bicycle Infrastructure." *Preventive Medicine* 46, no. 1 (2008): 55–59.

Garvey, Ellen Gruber. *The Adman in the Parlor: Magazines and the Gendering of Consumer Culture, 1880s to 1910s.* New York: Oxford University Press, 1996.

———. "Reframing the Bicycle: Advertising-Supported Magazines and Scorching Women." *American Quarterly* 47, no. 1 (1995): 66–101.

Gear Up! *Dames on Frames* (Minneapolis), nos. 1–3. Self-published zine.

Geddes, Norman Bel. *Magic Motorways.* New York: Random House, 1940.

Gelder, Sarah Van. "Finding a Balance: An Interview with Ricardo Navarro." *In Context,* no. 36 (Fall 1993): 36.

"The Genuine Article: Reporting on the Fixed Gear Phenomenon." *Bike Snob NYC,* December 4, 2007. Available at http://bikesnobnyc.blogspot.com/2007/12/genuine-article-reporting-on-fixed-gear.html.

Gerken, John. "Plan B." *Chainbreaker* (New Orleans), no. 1, edited by Shelly Jackson. Self-published zine.

Ghost Bikes. Available at www.ghostbikes.org.

"Ghost Bikes." *Urban Velo,* no. 11 (2008): 56–68.

Ghost Mice. *Ghost Mice/Defiance, Ohio.* Plan-It-X Records, 2004. CD.

Gitlin, Todd. *The Whole World Is Watching: Mass Media in the Making and Unmaking of the New Left.* Berkeley: University of California Press, 1980.

Glasper, Ian. *The Day the Country Died: A History of Anarcho Punk 1980 to 1984.* London: Cherry Red Books, 2006.

Goldsmith, S. "Reasons Why Bicycling and Walking Are and Are Not Being Used More Extensively as Travel Modes." In *National Bicycling and Walking Study, Case Study #1*, edited by Federal Highway Administration. Washington, DC, 1993.

Goode, Greg. "No Brakes . . . Or, Zen on Wheels." *Nonduality Salon Magazine* 1 (September 2000). Available at http://www.nonduality.com/900gg.htm.

Goodridge, Steven. "Re: The Other Smart Growth." *Chainguard (Yahoo Group)*, May 24, 2002. Available at http://sports.groups.yahoo.com/group/chainguard/message/12542.

Gore, Albert. *An Inconvenient Truth: The Crisis of Global Warming*. Rev. ed. New York: Viking, 2007.

Gorz, André. "The Social Ideology of the Motorcar." *Le Sauvage* (September–October 1973). Available at http://www.worldcarfree.net/resources/freesources/TheSocialIdeology.rtf.

Gosling, Tim. "'Not for Sale': The Underground Network of Anarcho-Punk." In *Music Scenes: Local, Translocal and Virtual*, edited by Andy Bennett and Richard A. Peterson, 168–186. Nashville: Vanderbilt University Press, 2004.

Gramsci, Antonio, Quintin Hoare, and Geoffrey Nowell-Smith. *Selections from the Prison Notebooks of Antonio Gramsci*. London: Lawrence and Wishart, 1971.

"Grand Finale Debate." *Chicago Critical Mass*. Available at http://chicagocriticalmass.org/grandfinaledebate.

Gray, Sally Helvenston, and Mihaela C. Peteu. "Women's Cycling Attire: The Interplay of Cycle Design and Women's Cycling Attire in the 1890s: The Inventor's Point of View." In *Cycle History 16: Proceedings of the 16th International Cycling History Conference (Davis, Ca)*, edited by Andrew Ritchie, 85–97. San Francisco: Cycle Publishing, 2006.

Green, Michael. "Bike Culture for Sale (?)." *Bike Blog*, February 28, 2006. Available at http://bikeblog.blogspot.com/2006/02/bike-culture-for-sale.html.

Gregor, Neil. *Daimler-Benz in the Third Reich*. New Haven, CT: Yale University Press, 1998.

Grieco, M., J. Turner, and E. A. Kwakye. "A Tale of Two Cultures: Ethnicity and Cycling Behavior in Urban Ghana." *Transportation Research Record*, no. 1441 (1994): 101–107.

Griffin, Brian. "Cycling and Gender in Victorian Ireland." *Eire Ireland* 41, nos. 1–2 (2006): 213–241.

Grossberg, Lawrence. "Another Boring Day in Paradise: Rock and Roll and the Empowerment of Everyday Life." *Popular Music* 4 (1984): 225–258.

Grossberg, Lawrence, Cary Nelson, and Paula A. Treichler. *Cultural Studies*. New York: Routledge, 1992.

Grover, Kathryn, and Margaret Woodbury. *Fitness in American Culture: Images of Health, Sport, and the Body, 1830-1940. A Symposium Held at the Margaret Woodbury Strong Museum in Spring, 1986*. Amherst, MA: University of Massachusetts Press/Margaret Woodbury Strong Museum, 1989.

Gruber, James E., and Lars Bjorn. "Blue-Collar Blues: The Sexual Harassment of Women Autoworkers." *Work and Occupations* 9, no. 3 (1982): 271–298.

Gudis, Catherine. *Buyways: Billboards, Automobiles, and the American Landscape*. Cultural Spaces series. New York: Routledge, 2004.

Guttierez, Raul. "The White Bicycle Plan or Why I Love the Dutch." *Mexican Pictures,* 2007. Available at http://www.mexicanpictures.com/headingeast/2007/04/the-white-bicycle-plan.html.

Haddow, Douglas. "Hipster: The Dead End of Western Civilization." *Adbusters* 79 (2008). Available at https://www.adbusters.org/magazine/79/hipster.html.

Haenfler, Ross. "Collective Identity in the Straight Edge Movement: How Diffuse Movements Foster Commitment, Encourage Individualized Participation, and Promote Cultural Change." *Sociological Quarterly* 45, no. 4 (2004): 785–805.

Haines, H. H. "Black Radicalization and the Funding of Civil Rights: 1957–1970." *Social Problems* 32, no. 1 (1984): 31–43.

Hall, Stuart. "Ideology and Communication Theory." In *Rethinking Communication,* vol. 1, edited by B. Dervin, L. Grossberg, B. O'Keefe, and E. Wartella, 40–52. London: Sage, 1989.

——. "The Narrative Construction of Reality." *Context,* no. 10 (1983). Available at http://www.centerforbookculture.org/context/no10/hall.html.

——. "On Postmodernism and Articulation." *Journal of Communication Inquiry* 10, no. 2 (1986): 45–60.

——. "The Problem of Ideology: Marxism without Guarantees." In *Stuart Hall: Critical Dialogues in Cultural Studies,* edited by Stuart Hall, David Morley, and Kuan-Hsing Chen, 25–46. London: Routledge, 1996.

Hall, Stuart, Dorothy Hobson, Andrew Lowe, and Paul Willis. *Culture, Media, Language: Working Papers in Cultural Studies, 1972–1979.* London: Routledge in Association with the Centre for Contemporary Cultural Studies, University of Birmingham, 1980.

Hallett, Ian, David Luskin, and Randy Machemehl. "Evaluation of On-Street Bicycle Facilities Added to Existing Roadways." Austin: Center for Transportation Research at the University of Texas at Austin, 2006.

Halweil, Brian, and Thomas Prugh. *Home Grown: The Case for Local Food in a Global Market.* Washington, DC: Worldwatch Institute, 2002.

Handman, Gary. "Road Movies: A Bibliography of Materials in the University of California Berkeley Library." Available at http://www.lib.berkeley.edu/MRC/road-moviesbib.html.

Haring, Kristen. *Ham Radio's Technical Culture.* Cambridge, MA: MIT Press, 2007.

Harkey, David, Donald W. Reinfurt, Matthew Knuiman, J. Richard Stewart, and Alex Sorton. "Development of the Bicycle Compatibility Concept: A Level of Service Concept: Final Report." McLean, VA: Federal Highway Administration, 1998.

Harmond, Richard. "Progress and Flight: An Interpretation of the American Cycle Craze of the 1890s." *Journal of Social History* 5, no. 2 (1971): 235–257.

Harold, Christine. "Pranking Rhetoric: "Culture Jamming" As Media Activism." *Critical Studies in Media Communication* 21, no. 3 (2004): 189–212.

Hartgen, David T., and M. Gregory Fields. "Building Roads to Reduce Traffic Congestion in America's Cities: How Much and at What Cost?" Reason Foundation, July 2006.

Harvey, David. *Justice, Nature, and the Geography of Difference.* Cambridge, MA: Blackwell Publishers, 1996.

——. "The Right to the City." *International Journal of Urban and Regional Research* 27, no. 4 (2003): 939–941.

———. *Spaces of Global Capitalism: A Theory of Uneven Geographical Development.* New York: Verso, 2006.

———. *Spaces of Hope.* Berkeley: University of California Press, 2000.

———. *The Urban Experience.* Baltimore: Johns Hopkins University Press, 1989.

Hawley, C. E. "The Uses of the Bicycle." *Outing, a Journal of Recreation* 1, no. 1 (1882): 22–30.

Hebdige, Dick. "Travelling Light: One Route into Material Culture." *RAIN*, no. 59 (1983): 11–13.

Heegel, Cliff. "Bike Lane Debate." *Bike Memphis.* Available at http://bikememphis.com/bike_lanes.htm.

Heiss, Mary Ann. *Empire and Nationhood: The United States, Great Britain, and Iranian Oil, 1950–1954.* New York: Columbia University Press, 1997.

Henderson, Jason. "Secessionist Automobility: Racism, Anti-urbanism, and the Politics of Automobility in Atlanta, Georgia." *International Journal of Urban and Regional Research* 30, no. 2 (2006): 293.

Hendry, Joe. "Alleycat Races." *Messenger Institute for Media Accuracy.* Available at http://www.messmedia.org/alleycats.html.

———. "The Bigots' Views." *Messenger Institute for Media Accuracy.* Available at www.messmedia.org/messville/QUOTE.HTM.

———. "Labour Issues." *Messenger Institute for Media Accuracy.* Available at http://www.messmedia.org/labour.html.

Hennessy, Dwight A., and David L. Wiesenthal. "Aggression, Violence, and Vengeance among Male and Female Drivers." *Transportation Quarterly* 56, no. 4 (2002): 62–75.

Henry, Thomas P. "Address to the Annual Meeting of the Councillors of the American Automobile Association." Presented at the 34th Annual Meeting of the Councillors of the American Automobile Association, Detroit, 1936.

Herlihy, David V. *Bicycle: The History.* New Haven, CT: Yale University Press, 2004.

Heyen-Perschon, Jürgen. "Non-motorised Transport and Its Socio-economic Impact on Poor Households in Africa: Cost-Benefit Analysis of Bicycle Ownership in Rural Uganda." Hamburg: FABIO/BSPW (Jinja, Uganda), 2001.

Higgins, Charles. *Bike Traffic: Building Opportunity and Community in San Francisco.* San Francisco: Bicycle Community Project, 1999.

His Hero is Gone. *Monuments to Thieves.* Prank Records, 1997. LP.

"The History." *Bicycle Habitat.* Available at http://bicyclehabitat.com/page.cfm?pageID=540.

Hodges, Michael. "Two-Wheeled Fascism: The Trouble with London's Cyclists." *Time Out London*, May 9, 2007. Available at www.timeout.com/london/big-smoke/features/2897/Two-wheeled_fascism-the_trouble_with_London-s_cyclists.html.

Hoefer, Carsten. "A Short Illustrated History of the Bicycle." 2007. Available at http://www.crazyguyonabike.com/doc/1889.

Hollevoet, Christel. "The Flâneur: Genealogy of a Modernist Icon." Ph.D. diss., City University of New York, 2001.

Holt, Richard. "The Bicycle, the Bourgeoisie and the Discovery of Rural France, 1880–1914." *International Journal of the History of Sport* 2, no. 2 (1985): 127–139.

Home, Stewart. *The Assault on Culture: Utopian Currents from Lettrisme to Class War.* London: Aporia Press/Unpopular Books, 1988.

Hook, Walter. "Wheels out of Balance: Suggested Guidelines for Intermodal Transport Sector Lending at the World Bank—a Case Study of Hungary." New York: Institute for Transportation and Development Policy, 1996.

"The Horse and the Bicycle." *Scientific American* 73, no. 3 (1895): 43.

Horton, Dave. "Computers, Cars and Televisions: The Role of Objects in Cultivating Sustainable Lifestyles." Paper presented at the Manchester Environmental Forum Postgraduate Conference, University of Manchester, 2003. Available at www.shifting ground.freeuk.com/compcars.htm, 2003.

———. "Environmentalism and the Bicycle." *Environmental Politics* 15, no. 1 (2006): 41–59.

———. "Green Distinctions: The Performance of Identity among Environmental Activists." *Sociological Review* 51, no. 2 (2003): 63–77.

———. "Lancaster Critical Mass: Does It Still Exist?" In *Critical Mass: Bicycling's Defiant Celebration*, edited by Chris Carlsson, 60–67. Oakland, CA: AK Press, 2002.

———. "Social Movements and the Bicycle." 2006. Available at http://www.bicycology. org.uk/related_articles/SocialMovementsandtheBicycle.doc.

Hotchkiss, George Burton. *Milestones of Marketing: A Brief History of the Evolution of Market Distribution*. New York: Macmillan, 1938.

Hounshell, David A. *From the American System to Mass Production, 1800–1932: The Development of Manufacturing Technology in the United States*. Baltimore: Johns Hopkins University Press, 1984.

House, Silas, and Jason Howard. *Something's Rising: Appalachians Fighting Mountaintop Removal*. Lexington: University of Kentucky Press, 2009.

Huffener, Joep. "Bikes on Dikes: A Dutch Plan for (Almost) Free Wheeling." Amsterdam: Department of Infrastructure, Traffic and Transport of the City of Amsterdam, 2000.

"Huffy Closes Last Manufacturing Plant in Mexico." *Bicycle Retailer and Industry News*, December 21, 2001.

Hugill, Peter, J. "Good Roads and the Automobile in the United States 1880–1929." *Geographical Review* 72, no. 3 (1982): 327–349.

Hunt, J. D., and J. E. Abraham. "Influences on Bicycle Use." *Transportation* 34, no. 4 (2007): 453–470.

Hunt, Nancy Rose. *A Colonial Lexicon of Birth Ritual, Medicalization, and Mobility in the Congo*. Durham, NC: Duke University Press, 1999.

Hurwitz, Mitchell. *Arrested Development*. 20th Century Fox Home Entertainment, 2003. TV series.

"The Hygiene of Cycling." *Scientific American* 55, no. 22 (1886): 341.

I Like Bikes. Centron Films (with General Motors), 1978. Film.

Illich, Ivan. *Celebration of Awareness: A Call for Institutional Revolution*. Garden City, NY: Doubleday, 1970.

———. *Energy and Equity*. New York: Harper and Row, 1974.

———. "To Hell with Good Intentions." *Swaraj Foundation*, April 20, 1968. Available at http://www.swaraj.org/illich_hell.htm.

———. *Tools for Conviviality*. New York: Harper and Row, 1973.

"Impact." *World Bicycle Relief*. Available at www.worldbicyclerelief.org/impact/index. php.

Inglis, David. "Auto Couture: Thinking the Car in Post-war France." *Theory Culture Society* 21, nos. 4–5 (2004): 197–219.

International Bicycle Fund. Available at http://www.ibike.org.

"Interregional Highways." U.S. Interregional Highway Committee, 78th U.S. Congress, House, Committee on Roads, Session 2. H Doc 379, 1944.

"Interview with Aaron Cometbus." *Maximumrocknroll*, no. 200 (2000). Zine.

"Interview with Creation Is Crucifixion." *Infinite Monkey*, no. 2. Zine. Available at http://www.geocities.com/snufffan/interviews/cic.html.

"Interview with David Schweidenback." *Social Edge*, March 13, 2007. Available at http://www.socialedge.org/blogs/peace-corps-entrepreneurs/david-schweidenback/.

"Interview with Johnny Payphone." *Relational Aesthetics*, June 8, 2007. Available at http://relationalcate.blogspot.com/2007/06/johnny-payphone-of-rat-patrol.html.

"Interview with Rick Jarvis." *Leapfrog* (Indianapolis), no. 8, edited by Scott Spitz. Self-published zine.

Iribarne, Jeanne, Estelle Taylor, and Michael Bloomfield. "Climate Change: A Profile for Community Action." Victoria, BC: Harmony Foundation of Canada, 2003.

Isaac, B. Potter. "The Bicycle Outlook." *Century Illustrated Magazine* 52, no. 5 (1896): 785.

Isaac, Larry, Steve McDonald, and Greg Lukasik. "Takin' It from the Streets: How the Sixties Mass Movement Revitalized Unionization." *American Journal of Sociology* 112, no. 1 (2006): 46–96.

Iskin, Ruth E. "The Pan-European Flâneuse in Fin-de-Siècle Posters: Advertising Modern Women in the City." *Nineteenth-Century Contexts* 25, no. 4 (2003): 333–356.

Jackson, Judith, and Graham Robson. *Man and the Automobile: A Twentieth-Century Love Affair.* New York: McGraw-Hill, 1979.

Jackson, Shelly Lynn, ed. *Chainbreaker* (New Orleans), nos. 1–4. Self-published zine.

Jacobs, Jane. *The Death and Life of Great American Cities.* New York: Random House, 1961.

Jacque, L. "Bike Culture Always for Sale." *The Diary of the Ultimate Bromancer*, June 6, 2007. Available at http://totalbromance.blogspot.com/2007/06/bike-culture-always-for-sale.html.

Jain, Sarah S. "'Dangerous Instrumentality': The Bystander as Subject in Automobility." *Cultural Anthropology* 19, no. 1 (2004): 61–94.

Jain, Sarah S. "Violent Submission: Gendered Automobility." *Cultural Critique*, no. 61 (2005): 186–214.

The Jam. *In the City.* Polydor Records, 1977. LP.

———. *This Is the Modern World.* Polydor Records, 1977. LP.

Jequier, N. "Appropriate Technology: Some Criteria." In *Towards Global Action for Appropriate Technology: Discussion Papers and Proposals of an Expert Meeting on International Action for Appropriate Technology, Geneva, Dec 1977*, edited by A. S. Bhalla, 1–22. Oxford: Pergamon Press, 1979.

Jewell, Derek. *Man and Motor: The 20th Century Love Affair.* New York: Walker, 1967.

Johnson, Elmer W. "Mobility, Equity, and the City." *Bulletin of the American Academy of Arts and Sciences* 47, no. 8 (1994): 51–63.

Jones, Charles O. "Air Pollution and Contemporary Environmental Politics." *Growth and Change* 4, no. 3 (2006): 22–27.

Jones, Steve, R. D. Martin, and David R. Pilbeam. "The Cambridge Encyclopedia of Human Evolution." 520. Cambridge; New York: Cambridge University Press, 1994.

Jones, W. Lawson. *A Love Affair with One Hundred Cars: And Ultimately with the Ultimate Woman.* Mountain View, CA: Schobert Publishing, 1997.

Jordan, John. "The Art of Necessity: The Subversive Imagination of Anti-road Protest and Reclaim the Streets." In *DiY Culture: Party and Protest in Nineties Britain*, edited by George McKay, 129–151. London: Verso, 1998.

Kahney, Leander. "Bamboo Bike Maker Grows His Frames, Bonsai Style." *Wired*, September 25, 2008. Available at http://www.wired.com/gadgetlab/2008/09/growing-bamboo.

Kanfer, Stefan. "The Full Circle: In Praise of the Bicycle." *Time*, April 28, 1975, p. 70.

Katz, Cindi. "On the Grounds of Globalization: A Topography for Feminist Political Engagement." *Signs* 26, no. 4 (2001): 1213–1234.

Kay, Jane Holtz. *Asphalt Nation: How the Automobile Took over America, and How We Can Take It Back.* Berkeley: University of California Press, 1998.

Keith, Gerren. "The Bicycle Man, Parts 1 and 2." *Diff'rent Strokes*: NBC-TV, 1983. TV series.

Kellner, Douglas. "Theorizing Globalization." *Sociological Theory* 20, no. 3 (2002): 285–305.

Kelly, Charles. "Clunkers among the Hills." *Bicycling* (January 1979): 40–42.

Kelly, Prescott. "The Automotive Century: Most Influential People (Ferdinand Porsche)." *Society of Automotive Historians.* Available at http://www.autohistory.org/feature_6.html.

Kempton, Richard. *Provo: Amsterdam's Anarchist Revolt.* New York: Autonomedia, 2007.

Kernaghan, Charles. "Child Labor Is Back: Children Are Again Sewing Clothing for Major U.S. Companies." Washington, DC: National Labor Committee, 2006.

———. "Puma's Workers in China Facing an Olympian Struggle to Survive." Washington, DC: National Labor Committee and China Labor Watch, 2004.

Kernaghan, Charles, and National Labor Committee Education Fund in Support of Worker and Human Rights in Central America. "Made in China: The Role of U.S. Companies in Denying Human and Worker Rights." Washington, DC: National Labor Committee, 2000.

Kessel, Adam. "Response to Boston CM Critics." *Chicago Critical Mass*, April 9, 2000. Available at http://chicagocriticalmass.org/about/faq/adamkessel.

———. "Why They're Wrong about Critical Mass!" In *Critical Mass: Bicycling's Defiant Celebration*, edited by Chris Carlsson, 105–111. Oakland, CA: AK Press, 2002.

Kidder, Jeffrey L. "Bike Messengers and the Really Real: Effervescence, Reflexivity, and Postmodern Identity." *Symbolic Interaction* 29, no. 3 (2006): 349–371.

———. "Style and Action: A Decoding of Bike Messenger Symbols." *Journal of Contemporary Ethnography* 34, no. 3 (2005): 344–367.

Kifer, Ken. "Cycling during the Seventies: A History of US Bicycling in the 1970's." *Ken Kifer's Bike Pages.* Available at http://www.kenkifer.com/bikepages/lifestyle/70s.htm.

King, Chris. "Thoughts on Manufacturing Overseas." *Chris King Precision Components.* Available at http://www.chrisking.com/asiamfg.

Kinnevy, S. C., B. P. Healey, D. E. Pollio, and C. S. North. "Bicycleworks: Task-Centered Group Work with High-Risk Youth." *Social Work with Groups* 22, no. 1 (1999): 33–48.

Kirk, Andrew. "Appropriating Technology: The Whole Earth Catalog and Counterculture Environmental Politics." *Environmental History* 7, no. 4 (2001): 374–394.

Kleiman, Jordan B. "The Appropriate Technology Movement in American Political Culture." Ph.D. diss., University of Rochester, 2000.

Klein, Naomi. *No Logo: Taking Aim at the Brand Bullies.* New York: Picador, 2000.

Klett, Michael "A Uniquely Democratic Experiment." In *Critical Mass: Bicycling's Defiant Celebration*, edited by Chris Carlsson, 90–93. Oakland, CA: AK Press, 2002.

Knoll, Andalusia, ed. *Clitical Mass* (Pittsburgh). Self-published zine.

Koeppel, Dan, and Ben Maddox. "Invisible Riders." *Bicycling* (December 2005): 46–55.

Komanoff, Charles. "Avenues for Activism: A Talk at the Start of Bikesummer." Delivered at the First Annual "Bike Summer," San Francisco, August 1, 1999.

———. "Bicycling." In *Encyclopedia of Energy*, edited by Cutler J. Cleveland and Robert U. Ayres, 141–150. Amsterdam: Elsevier Academic Press, 2004.

Komanoff, Charles, and Members of Right of Way. "Killed by Automobile: Death in the Streets in New York City 1994–1997." New York: Right of Way, 1999.

Komanoff, Charles, and Michael J. Smith. "The Only Good Cyclist: NYC Bicycle Fatalities—Who's Responsible?" New York: Right of Way, 2000.

Komanoff, Charles, and Time's Up! Environmental Organization. "Cost Analysis of Government Expenditures to Suppress Critical Mass Bike Rides." New York City, 2006.

Koshar, Rudy. "Cars and Nations: Anglo-German Perspectives on Automobility between the World Wars." *Theory, Culture and Society* 21, nos. 4–5 (2004): 121–144.

Kotanyi, Attila, and Raoul Vaneigem. "Elementary Program of the Bureau of Unitary Urbanism." In *Situationist International Anthology*, edited by Ken Knabb, 65–67. Berkeley, CA: Bureau of Public Secrets, 1981. Originally published in *Internationale Situationniste*, no. 6 (1961).

Krahé, Barbara, and Ilka Fenske. "Predicting Aggressive Driving Behavior: The Role of Macho Personality, Age, and Power of Car." *Aggressive Behavior* 28, no. 1 (2002): 21–29.

Kremer, Michael, and Edward Miguel. "The Illusion of Sustainability." *Quarterly Journal of Economics* 122, no. 3 (2007): 1007–1065.

Krizek, Kevin, Pamela Jo Johnson, and Nebiyou Tilahun. "Gender Differences in Bicycling Behavior and Facility Preferences." Paper presented at the Conference on Research on Women's Issues in Transportation, 2005.

Lack, Tony. "Consumer Society and Authenticity: The (Il)Logic of Punk Practices." *Undercurrent*, no. 3 (1995).

Laderman, David. *Driving Visions: Exploring the Road Movie.* Austin: University of Texas Press, 2002.

Laird, Pamela Walker. "'The Car without a Single Weakness': Early Automobile Advertising." *Technology and Culture* 37, no. 4 (1996): 796–812.

Lamb, Robert, and Friends of the Earth. *Promising the Earth.* London: Routledge, 1996.

Landström, Catharina. "A Gendered Economy of Pleasure: Representations of Cars and Humans in Motoring Magazines." *Science Studies* 19, no. 2 (2006): 31–53.

Langan, Celeste. "Mobility Disability." *Public Culture* 13, no. 3 (2001): 459–484.

Larsen, Janet. "Land Area Devoted to Roads in the United States." Washington, DC: Earth Policy Institute, 2001.

Lasn, Kalle. *Culture Jamming: The Uncooling of America.* New York: Eagle Brook, 1999.

Law, Robin. "Beyond 'Women and Transport': Towards New Geographies of Gender and Daily Mobility." *Progress in Human Geography* 23, no. 4 (1999): 567–588.

Le Bon, Gustave. *The Crowd: A Study of the Popular Mind.* 4th impression ed. London: T. F. Unwin, 1903.

Lefebvre, Henri. *Everyday Life in the Modern World.* New York: Harper and Row, 1971.

———. *The Production of Space.* Oxford: Blackwell, 1991.

Lefebvre, Henri, Eleonore Kofman, and Elizabeth Lebas. *Writings on Cities.* Cambridge, MA: Blackwell Publishers, 1996.

"Legal Developments in Marketing." *Journal of Marketing* 44, no. 1 (1980): 81–88.

Lembeck, Michael. *Double Rush.* CBS Television, 1995. TV series.

Leondar-Wright, Betsy. "Shareholders Press Huffy on Wage Gap, CEO Raise after Plant Closing and 1,000 Layoffs." *Responsible Wealth* press release, April 20, 1999. Available at http://www.responsiblewealth.org/press/1999/huffy_pr.html.

Lewyn, Michael. "Debunking Cato: Why Portland Works Better Than the Analysis of Its Chief Neo-Libertarian Critic." *Congress for New Urbanism,* 2007. Available at http://www.cnu.org/node/1532.

Liedke, Karl. "Destruction through Work: Lodz Jews in the Büssing Truck Factory in Braunschweig, 1944–1945." *Yad Vashem Studies* 30 (2002): 153–187.

Likaka, Osumaka. *Rural Society and Cotton in Colonial Zaire.* Madison: University of Wisconsin Press, 1997.

Lipford, William A., and Glennon J. Harrison. "Bicycle and Pedestrian Transportation Policies." *Congressional Research Services Reports.* Washington, DC: National Council for Science and the Environment, February 14, 2000. Document #RS20469.

Lippmann, Walter. *Public Opinion.* New York: Harcourt, Brace, 1922.

Litman, Todd. "Economic Value of Walkability." *Transportation Research Record: Journal of the Transportation Research Board* 1828, no. 1 (2003): 3–11.

———. "Evaluating Transportation Equity." *World Transport Policy and Practice* (2002).

———. "Land Use Impact Costs of Transportation." *World Transport Policy and Practice* 1 (1995): 9–16.

———. "Whose Roads? Defining Bicyclists' and Pedestrians' Right to Use Public Roadways." Victoria, Canada, Victoria Transport Policy Institute, February 9, 2001.

Littler, Jo. "Beyond the Boycott." *Cultural Studies* 19, no. 2 (2005): 227–252.

Livingstone, Sonia. "On the Continuing Problems of Media Effects Research." In *Mass Media and Society,* edited by James Curran and Michael Gurevitch, 305–324. London: Edward Arnold, 1996.

Lockwood, Jeff. "Interview with Mike Watt." *Dirt Rag,* no. 95 (August 2002). Available at http://www.dirtragmag.com/print/article.php?ID=418.

Lopez, Steve. "The Scariest Biker Gang of All." *Time,* August 11, 1997, p. 4.

Lovinger, Robert. "David Schweidenback Recyles Cycles for the World." *UMass Dartmouth Alumni Magazine* (2005): 10–11.

Lowe, Marcia D. *The Bicycle: Vehicle for a Small Planet.* Worldwatch Paper. Washington, DC: Worldwatch Institute, 1989.

Luig, Ute. "Constructing Local Worlds." In *Spirit Possession, Modernity and Power in Africa*, edited by Heike Behrend and Ute Luig, 124–141. Madison: University of Wisconsin Press, 1999.

Lyons, Todd. "Spicy Girls in Taiwan!" *Toddlyons.com*, March 23, 2007. Available at www.toddlyons.com/2007/03/spicy-girls-in-taiwan.html.

Mabogunje, Akin L. "Urban Planning and the Post-colonial State in Africa: A Research Overview." *African Studies Review* 33, no. 2 (1990): 121–203.

Mackintosh, Phillip Gordon. "A Bourgeois Geography of Domestic Bicycling: Using Public Space Responsibly in Toronto and Niagara-on-the-Lake, 1890–1900." *Journal of Historical Sociology* 20 (2007): 126–157.

———. "'Wheel within a Wheel': Frances Willard and the Feminisation of the Bicycle." In *Cycle History 9: Proceedings from the 9th International Cycling History Conference (Ottawa, Canada)*, edited by Glen Norcliffe and Rob Van der Plas, 21–28. San Francisco: Cycle Publishing, 1999.

Mackintosh, Phillip Gordon, and Glen Norcliffe. "Flâneurie on Bicycles: Acquiescence to Women in Public in the 1890s." *Canadian Geographer* 50, no. 1 (2006): 17–37.

Maddocks, Melvin. "Bicycle Wars: The Newest Arms Race." *Christian Science Monitor*, November 19, 1986, p. 29.

"Made in China/Taiwan." *Bike Forums*, thread started on August 15, 2008. Available at http://www.bikeforums.net/showthread.php?t=454443.

Manji, Firoze, and Carl O'Coill. "The Missionary Position: Ngos and Development in Africa." *International Affairs (Royal Institute of International Affairs 1944–)* 78, no. 3 (2002): 567–583.

Marillier, Harry C. "The Automobile: A Forecast." *The Eclectic Magazine of Foreign Literature* 62, no. 6 (1895): 774–781.

Marks, Patricia. *Bicycles, Bangs, and Bloomers: The New Woman in the Popular Press.* Lexington: University Press of Kentucky, 1990.

Marling, Karal Ann. *As Seen on TV: The Visual Culture of Everyday Life in the 1950s.* Cambridge, MA: Harvard University Press, 1994.

Martin, Michael, and Gabe Morford. *Mash SF.* Mash Transit Productions, 2007. Film.

Martin, S., and S. Carlson. "Barriers to Children Walking to or from School—United States, 2004." *Morbidity and Mortality Weekly Report* 54, no. 38 (2005): 949–952.

Martinek, Jason D. "The Workingman's Bible: Robert Blatchford Merrie England, Radical Literacy, and Making of Debsian Socialism, 1895–1900." *Journal of the Gilded Age and Progressive Era* 2, no. 3 (2003): 326–346.

Marx, Karl. *The Eighteenth Brumaire of Louis Bonaparte*, translated by Daniel De Leon. New York: Labor News, 1951.

Mason, Philip P. "The League of American Wheelmen and the Good Roads Movement." Ph.D. diss., University of Michigan, 1957.

Matthies, Eric, and Tricia Todd. *Ayamye.* Project Lab/EMP, 2007. Film.

Mazda. "Mazda Develops World's First Biofabric Made with 100 Percent Plant-Derived Fiber for Vehicle Interiors." Mazda press release #26889, 2007.

McChesney, Robert. *The Problem of the Media: U.S. Communication Politics in the Twenty-first Century.* New York: Monthly Review Press, 2004.

McCorkell, Charlie. "The Truth about the Bike Ban." *City Cyclist* (October–November 1987): 8–11.

McCreery, Sandy. "The Claremont Road Situation." In *The Unknown City: Contesting Architecture and Social Space*, edited by Iain Borden, Joe Kerr, Jane Rendell, and Alicia Pivaro, 228–45. Cambridge, MA: MIT Press, 2001.

McGurn, James. *On Your Bicycle: An Illustrated History of Cycling*. New York: Facts on File Publications, 1987.

McKay, George. *DiY Culture: Party and Protest in Nineties Britain*. London: Verso, 1998.

———. "DiY Culture: Notes towards an Intro." In *DiY Culture: Party and Protest in Nineties Britain*, edited by George McKay, 1–53. London: Verso, 1998.

———. *Senseless Acts of Beauty: Cultures of Resistance since the Sixties*. London: Verso, 1996.

McKee, Oliver. "The Horse or the Motor." *Lippincott's Monthly Magazine* (1896): 379–385.

McLaren, Warren. "Worksman Cycles (USA's Oldest) Get a Touch of Sun." *TreeHugger.com*, March 10, 2008. Available at http://www.treehugger.com/files/2008/03/worksman_cycles.php.

McShane, Clay. *Down the Asphalt Path: The Automobile and the American City*. Columbia History of Urban Life. New York: Columbia University Press, 1994.

Megulon 5. "I Meet the Hard Times Bike Club and Live to Tell the Tale." *Chunk 666*, October 10, 1997. Available at http://www.dclxvi.org/chunk/outside/htbc/meet.html.

Meline, Gabe. "Pedal to the Mettle." *North Bay Bohemian*, September 15–21, 2004.

Melucci, Alberto. *Challenging Codes: Collective Action in the Information Age*. Cambridge Cultural Social Studies. Cambridge: Cambridge University Press, 1996.

———. "The Process of Collective Identity." *Social Movements and Culture* 4 (1995): 41–63.

Mendoza, Louis. "A Few Reflections in Response to Prompts from Readers." *A Journey across Our America: Observations and Reflections on the Latinoization of the U.S.*, August 12, 2007. Available at http://journeyacrossouramerica.blogspot.com/2007/08/few-reflections-in-response-to-prompts.html.

Meredith, America ed. *Voice of Da* (San Francisco), no. 4. Self-published zine, 1997.

Merrifield, Andy. *Dialectical Urbanism: Social Struggles in the Capitalist City*. New York: Monthly Review Press, 2002.

Milchman, Eli. "'City Bike' Hot New Category at Bicycle Industry Show." *Wired*, September 27, 2007.

Miller, Daniel, ed. *Car Cultures*. Oxford: Berg, 2001.

Mills, Katie. *The Road Story and the Rebel: Moving through Film, Fiction, and Television*. Carbondale: Southern Illinois University Press, 2006.

Miner, Dylan. "Red (Pedal) Power: Native, Bikes, and Anti-colonial Art." In *"Do Not Park Bicycles!"* edited by Jenny Western, 9–12. Brandon, Canada: Art Gallery of Southwestern Manitoba, 2007.

Mionske, Robert. "Assault, Battery and How to Cook a Turkey." *Velo News*, November 24, 2005.

"Mit Worldwide Mobility Study Warns of Chronic Gridlock, Pollution; Outlines 'Grand Challenges.'" *MIT News Office*, October 30, 2001.

Mitchell, Don. *The Right to the City: Social Justice and the Fight for Public Space*. New York: Guilford Press, 2003.

———. "The S.U.V. Model of Citizenship: Floating Bubbles, Buffer Zones, and the Rise of The 'Purely Atomic' Individual." *Political Geography* 24, no. 1 (2005): 77–100.

Mitchell, Stacy. *Big-Box Swindle: The True Cost of Mega-retailers and the Fight for America's Independent Businesses*. Boston: Beacon Press, 2006.

Mittal, Anuradha. "Giving Away the Farm: The 2002 Farm Bill." *Food First Backgrounder* 8, no. 3 (2002): 1–5.

Modern Mechanix Blog. Available at http://blog.modernmechanix.com/.

Mommsen, Hans, and Manfred Griege. *Das Volkswagenwerk Und Seine Arbeiter Im Dritten Reich*. Düsseldorf: ECON Verlag, 1996.

A Monkey Tale. Encyclopedia Britannica Films, 1954. Film.

Montorgueil, Georges. *La Parisienne*. Paris: Librairie L. Conquet, 1897.

Morland, K., S. Wing, A. Diez Roux, and C. Poole. "Neighborhood Characteristics Associated with the Location of Food Stores and Food Service Places." *American Journal of Preventive Medicine* 22, no. 1 (2002): 23–29.

Morrow, Lance. "The Great Bicycle Wars." *Time*, November 24, 1980, p. 110.

Moulton, Dave. "Fixing Fixed Wheel Terminology." *Dave Moulton's Bike Blog*, March 10, 2008. Available at http://davesbikeblog.blogspot.com/2008/03/fixing-fixed-wheel-terminology.html.

Mozer, David. "Youth and Young People, Bicycle Recycle, Earn-a-Bike Programs." *International Bicycle Fund*. Available at http://www.ibike.org/encouragement/youth.htm.

Mr. T Experience. *Love Is Dead*. Lookout! Records, 1996. LP.

Mumford, Lewis. "Authoritarian and Democratic Technics." *Technology and Culture* 5, no. 1 (1964): 1–8.

———. *The City in History: Its Origins, Its Transformations, and Its Prospects*. New York: Harcourt, 1961.

———. *The Highway and the City*. Westport, CT: Greenwood Press, 1981.

———. *Technics and Civilization*. New York: Harcourt, 1963.

———. *The Urban Prospect*. London: Secker and Warburg, 1968.

Muschla, Gary Robert, and Judith A. Muschla. *Hands-on Math Projects with Real-Life Applications : Ready to Use Lessons and Materials for Grades 6–12*. West Nyack, NY: Center for Applied Research in Education, 1996.

Myers, Charles A. "Wartime Concentration of Production." *Journal of Political Economy* 51, no. 3 (1942): 222–234.

Nagar, Richa, Victoria Lawson, Linda McDowell, and Susan Hanson. "Locating Globalization: Feminist (Re)Readings of the Subjects and Spaces of Globalization." *Economic Geography* 78, no. 3 (2002): 257–284.

Nash, Jeffrey E. "Expensive Dirt: Bicycle Motocross and Everyday Life." *Journal of Popular Culture* 20, no. 2 (1986): 97–122.

National Bicycle Dealers Association. "Industry Overview 2007." Available at http://nbda.com/page.cfm?PageID=34.

National Highway Traffic Safety Administration. "Bicyclists and Other Cyclists." In *Traffic Safety Facts, 2007 Data*. Washington, DC: Department of Transportation, 2007.

———. "Data Collection Study: Deaths and Injuries Resulting from Certain Non-traffic and Non-crash Events." Washington, DC: Department of Transportation, 2004.

Nausea. *Extinction*. Profane Existance, 1990. LP

Navarro, Ricardo, Urs Heierli, and Victor Beck. *Alternativas de Transporte en America Latina: La Bicicleta y los Triciclos*: SKAT Centro Suizo de Technologia Apropiada, 1985.

———. "Bicycles, Intelligent Transport in Latin America." *Development: Seeds of Change*, no. 4 (1986): 45–48.

Nemo, Fred. "Personal History of Portland's Critical Mass." In *Critical Mass: Bicycling's Defiant Celebration*, edited by Chris Carlsson, 204–210. Oakland, CA: AK Press, 2002.

Nesper, Bill. "League Names Portland a Platinum Community." League of American Bicyclists press release, April 29, 2008.

"New Bicycle Gearshift and Man with Telephoto Eyes." *Modern Mechanix* (May 1934): 59.

Nieuwenhuys, Constant. "Nieuw Urbanisme," trans. as "New Urbanism," *Provo*, no. 9 (1966). In *BAMN (By Any Means Necessary): Outlaw Manifestos and Ephemera, 1965–70*, edited by Peter Stansill and David Zane Mairowitz, 2–6. Buffalo, NY: Friends of Malatesta, 1970.

Niman, Michael I. "Critical Mass!" *ArtVoice*, June 20, 2002.

"No Justice for Cyclists." *Bicycle Austin*. Available at http://bicycleaustin.info/justice.

Nolan, Kim. "Debut Column." *Punk Planet*, no. 1 (1994): 12–13.

Noland, Robert B., and Muhammad M. Ishaque. "Smart Bicycles in an Urban Area: Evaluation of a Pilot Scheme in London." *Journal of Public Transportation* 9, no. 5 (2006): 71–96.

Norcliffe, Glen. "Associations, Modernity and the Insider-Citizens of a Victorian Highwheel Bicycle Club." *Journal of Historical Sociology* 19, no. 2 (2006): 121–150.

———. "Popeism and Fordism: Examining the Roots of Mass Production." *Regional Studies* 31, no. 3 (1997): 267–280.

———. *The Ride to Modernity: The Bicycle in Canada, 1869–1900*. Toronto: University of Toronto Press, 2001.

North, Peter. "'Save Our Solsbury!': The Anatomy of an Anti-roads Protest." *Environmental Politics* 7, no. 3 (1998): 1–25.

North American Handmade Bicycle Show. Available at http://www.handmadebicycle-show.com.

North Carolina Coalition for Bicycle Driving. "The Science and Politics of Bicycle Driving." *North Carolina Coalition for Bicycle Driving*. Available at http://www.humantransport.org/bicycledriving/sciencepolitics.htm.

Norton, Peter D. "Fighting Traffic: The Dawn of the Motor Age in the American City." Ph.D. diss., University of Virginia, 2002.

———. "Street Rivals: Jaywalking and the Invention of the Motor Age Street." *Technology and Culture* 48, no. 2 (2007): 331–359.

Notorious, Vic. "Toronto Scene Report." *Maximumrocknroll*, no. 16 (1984).

Nye, David E. *American Technological Sublime*. Cambridge, MA: MIT Press, 1994.

———. *Consuming Power: A Social History of American Energies*. Cambridge, MA: MIT Press, 2001.

———. *Narratives and Spaces: Technology and the Construction of American Culture*. New York: Columbia University Press, 1997.

O'Connor, Alan. "Local Scenes and Dangerous Crossroads: Punk and Theories of Cultural Hybridity." *Popular Music* 21, no. 2 (2002): 225–236.

———. *Punk Record Labels and the Struggle for Autonomy: The Emergence of DIY.* Critical Media Studies. Lanham, MD: Lexington Books, 2008.

"October 2006 Archive." *Chicago Critical Mass.* Available at http://groups.yahoo.com/group/chicago_critical_mass/messages/1677.

Oddy, Nicholas. "Bicycles." In *The Gendered Object*, edited by Pat Kirkham, 60–69. Manchester, UK: St. Martin's Press, 1996.

O'Grady, Patrick. "Two Things You Don't Need for a Good Ride in Colorado: Critical Mass and Boulder." *Bicycle Retailer and Industry News*, June 15, 2001, p. 27.

Oi Polloi. *Fuaim Catha.* Skuld Records, 1999. LP.

One Got Fat. Interlude Films, 1963. Film.

Oortwijn, Jack. "Taiwan Bike Makers Cashing in on Europe." *Bike Europe*, September 2, 2008. Available at http://www.bike-eu.com/news/2677/taiwan-bike-makers-cashing-in-on-europe.html.

———. "USA Market Report 2007." *Bike Europe*, April 7, 2008, 2007.

"Operation You-Lock: T.A. Investigates NYC Bike Theft." *Transportation Alternatives Magazine* (1996): 6–7.

Oregon Bicycle Constructors Association. Available at http://www.oregonframebuilders.org.

O'Rourke, Morgan. "Locked Out." *Risk Management* 51, no. 12 (2004): 8–9.

O'Rourke, P. J. *Republican Party Reptile: Essays and Outrages.* New York: Atlantic Monthly Press, 1987.

O'Russell, David. *I Heart Huckabees.* Fox Searchlight Pictures, 2004. Film.

Osborn, Emily Lynn. "'Rubber Fever' Commerce and French Colonial Rule in Upper Guinée 1890–1913." *Journal of African History* 45, no. 3 (2004): 445–465.

O'Toole, Randal. *The Best-Laid Plans: How Government Planning Harms Your Quality of Life, Your Pocketbook, and Your Future.* Washington, DC: Cato Institute, 2007.

———. "Is Urban Planning 'Creeping Socialism'?" *The Independent Review* 4, no. 4 (2000): 501–516.

"Our Programs." *League of American Bicyclists.* Available at http://www.bikeleague.org/programs/index.php.

Overton, K. "Using the Bicycle for Women's Empowerment in Africa." *Sustainable Transport* (1996): 6–10.

Overton, Karen. "Women Take Back the Streets: Overcoming Gender Obstacles to Women's Mobility in Africa." *Sustainable Transport* (1994): 6, 7, 17.

Oz, Frank. *In and Out.* Paramount Pictures, 1997. Film.

Packer, Jeremy. "Disciplining Mobility." In *Foucault, Cultural Studies, and Governmentality*, edited by Jack Z. Bratich, Jeremy Packer, and Cameron McCarthy, 135–164. Albany: State University of New York Press, 2003.

———. "Mobile Communications and Governing the Mobile: CBs and Truckers." *Communication Review* 5, no. 1 (2002): 39–57.

———. "Mobility without Mayhem: Disciplining Mobile America through Safety." Ph.D. diss., Graduate College of the University of Illinois–Urbana-Champaign, 2001.

———. *Mobility without Mayhem: Safety, Cars, and Citizenship.* Durham, NC: Duke University Press, 2008.

Packer, Jeremy, and Mary K. Coffey. "Hogging the Road: Cultural Governance and the Citizen Cyclist." *Cultural Studies* 18, no. 5 (2004): 641–674.

Packer, Jeremy, and Craig Robertson, eds. *Thinking with James Carey: Essays on Communications, Transportation, History.* New York: Peter Lang, 2006.

Pailey, Robtel. "Slavery Ain't Dead, It's Manufactured in Liberia's Rubber." In *From the Slave Trade to "Free" Trade: How Trade Undermines Democracy and Justice in Africa,* edited by Patrick Burnett and Firoze Manji, 77–83. Nairobi: Fahamu, 2007.

Park, Roberta J. "'All the Freedom of the Boy': Elizabeth Cady Stanton, Nineteenth-Century Architect of Women's Rights." *International Journal of the History of Sport* 18, no. 1 (2001): 7–26.

Patton, David L. "Aspects of a Historical Geography of Technology: A Study of Cycling 1919–1939." In *Cycle History 5: Proceedings of the 5th International Cycle History Conference (Cambridge, England),* edited by Rob Van der Plas, 21–28. San Francisco: Cycle Publishing, 1995.

Payphone, Johnny. "Mutant Bike Culture Past and Present." *Ghostride Magazine,* no. 4 (2006): 23–26.

Peckham, David. "Sustaining Bicycles as Desirable Rural Transport." *International Forum for Rural Transport and Development.* Available at http://ifrtd.gn.apc.org/new/issues/op_bicycles4.php.

———. "1999 Annual Report." *Village Bicycle Project.* Available at http://www.ghana-bikes.org/ar99.htm.

———. "2002 Annual Report." *Village Bicycle Project,* November 29, 2002. Available at http://www.ghanabikes.org/ar02.htm.

———. "2004 Annual Report." *Village Bicycle Project,* April 15, 2005. Available at http://www.ghanabikes.org/ar04.htm.

———. "2006: The Year in Review." Moscow, ID: Village Bicycle Project, 2007.

Pein, Wayne. "Re: The Other Smart Growth." *Chainguard (Yahoo Group),* May 24, 2002. Available at http://sports.groups.yahoo.com/group/chainguard/message/12543.

Penfield, Arthur. "The Question of Prejudice." *Outing, a Journal of Recreation* 1, no. 3 (1882): 183.

Penland, Paige R. *Lowrider: History, Pride, Culture.* St. Paul, MN: Motorbooks International, 2003.

Pennell, J. and E. R. Pennell. "Twenty Years of Cycling." *Fortnightly Review* 68 (1897): 191.

Perry, David B. *Bike Cult: The Ultimate Guide to Human-Powered Vehicles.* New York: Four Walls Eight Windows, 1995.

Peters, Deike. "Gender and Transport in Less Developed Countries: A Background Paper in Preparation for CSD-9." Presented at the "Gender Perspectives for Earth Summit 2002: Energy, Transport, Information for Decision-Making" conference, Berlin, Germany, January 10–12, 2001.

Petersen, Jen. "Pedaling Hope." *Monu: Magazine on Urbanism,* no. 6 (2007): 36–39.

Petty, Ross D. "The Bicycle as a Communications Medium: A Comparison of Bicycle Use by the U.S. Postal Service and Western Union Telegraph Company." In *Cycle History 16: Proceedings of the 16th International Cycling History Conference (Davis, Ca),* edited by Andrew Ritchie, 147–159. San Francisco: Cycle Publishing, 2005.

———. "The Bicycle's Role in the Development of Safety Law " In *Cycle History 4: Proceedings from the 4th International Cycling History Conference (Boston, Mass),* edited by Rob Van der Plas, 125–132. San Francisco: Cycle Publishing, 1993.

———. "Peddling the Bicycle and the Development of Mass Marketing." In *Cycle History 5: Proceedings of the 5th International Cycle History Conference (Cambridge, England)*, edited by Rob Van der Plas, 107–116. San Francisco: Cycle Publishing, 1995.

———. "Regulation vs. the Market: The Case of Bicycle Safety (Parts 1 and 2)." *Risk: Issues in Health, Safety and Environment* 77, no. 92 (1991): 77–88, 93–120.

———. "Women and the Wheel: The Bicycle's Impact on Women." In *Cycle History 7: Proceedings of the 7th International Cycle History Conference, Buffalo, NY, USA, 4–6 September 1996*, edited by Rob Van der Plas, 112–133. San Francisco: Van der Plas Publications, 1997.

Phelan, Jacquie. "Golden Testicle Award." *Women's Mountain Bike and Tea Society (WOMBATS)*, October 26, 1994. Available at www.wombats.org/jacquie5.html.

———. "Liberation Noted from an Old Crank." *Whole Earth Review*, no. 86 (1995): 56–57.

Philpott, Julia. "Women and Nonmotorized Transport: Connection in Africa between Transportation and Economic Development." *Transportation Research Record*, no. 1441 (1994): 39–43.

"A Photo-Tricycle." *Scientific American* 53, no. 12 (1885): 178.

Pinder, David. "Commentary-Writing Cities against the Grain." 25, no. 8 (2004): 792–795.

———."In Defence of Utopian Urbanism: Imagining Cities after the 'End of Utopia.'" *Geografiska Annaler: Series B, Human Geography* (2002): 229–241.

———. *Visions of the City: Utopianism, Power, and Politics in Twentieth-Century Urbanism*. New York: Routledge, 2005.

Pinhead Gunpowder. *West Side Highway*. Recess Records, 2008. Seven-inch record.

Pink Floyd. *The Piper at the Gates of Dawn*. Capitol Records, 1967. LP.

Pirie, G. H. "The Decivilizing Rails: Railways and Underdevelopment in Southern Africa." *Tijdschrift voor Economische en Sociale Geografie* 73, no. 4 (1982): 221–228.

Pivato, Stefano. "The Bicycle as a Political Symbol: Italy 1885–1955." *International Journal of the History of Sport* 7, no. 2 (1990): 173–187.

Plant, Sadie. *The Most Radical Gesture: The Situationist International in a Postmodern Age*. London: Routledge, 1992.

Plaut, Pnina. "Non-motorized Commuting in the US." *Transportation Research Part D: Transport and Environment* 10, no. 5 (2005): 347–356.

"Points for Bicycle Riders." *Scientific American* 74, no. 13 (1896): 202.

Polk, Merritt "Gender Mobility: A Study of Women's and Men's Relations to Automobility in Sweden." Ph.D. diss., Göteborg University, 1998.

Presbrey, Frank. *The History and Development of Advertising*. Garden City, NY: Doubleday, 1929.

President Bates. "The Political Power of the L.A.W." *Outing, a Journal of Recreation* 2, no. 2 (1883): 98.

Press, Elizabeth, Andrew Lynn, and Chris Ryan. *Still We Ride*. In Tandem Production, 2005. Film.

"Press Room." *Reason Foundation*. Available at http://www.reason.org/press/.

"Product Review: King Kog Crass T-Shirt." *Bike Snob NYC*, July 24, 2008. Available at http://bikesnobnyc.blogspot.com/2008/07/bsnyc-product-review-king-kog-crass-t.html.

Prothers, Lisa. "Culture Jamming with Pedro Carvajal." *Bad Subjects*, no. 37 (1998). Available at http://eserver.org/bs/37/prothers.html.

Provo. "Provo's Fietsenplan (from *Provokatie*, no. 5 [1965])." In *BAMN (By Any Means Necessary): Outlaw Manifestos and Ephemera, 1965–70*, edited by Peter Stansill and David Zane Mairowitz, 26–27. Harmondsworth, UK: Penguin, 1971.

Prynn, David. "The Clarion Clubs, Rambling and the Holiday Associations in Britain since the 1890s." *Journal of Contemporary History* 11, nos. 2–3 (1976): 65–77.

"The Psychological and Hygienic Influence of the Bicycle." *The Chautauquan: A Weekly Newsmagazine* 33, no. 2 (1901): 207–208.

"Psychology, Hygiene, and Morality of the Bicycle, Part I." *Christian Advocate* 73, no. 27 (1898): 1086–1087.

"Psychology, Hygiene, and Morality of the Bicycle, Part II." *Christian Advocate* 73, no. 28 (1898): 1127–1130.

"Psychology, Hygiene, and Morality of the Bicycle, Part IV." *Christian Advocate* 73, no. 30 (1898): 1207–1209.

Pucher, John. "Cycling Safety on Bikeways vs. Roads." *Transportation Quarterly* 55, no. 4 (2001): 9–11.

Pucher, John, and Ralph Buehler. "At the Frontiers of Cycling: Policy Innovations in the Netherlands, Denmark, and Germany." *World Transport Policy and Practice* 13, no. 3 (2007): 8–57.

———. "Making Cycling Irresistible: Lessons from the Netherlands, Denmark and Germany." *Transport Reviews* 28, no. 4 (2008): 495–528.

———. "Why Canadians Cycle More Than Americans: A Comparative Analysis of Bicycling Trends and Policies." *Transport Policy* 13, no. 3 (2006): 265–279.

Pucher, John, and Lewis Dijkstra. "Making Walking and Cycling Safer: Lessons from Europe." *Transportation Quarterly* 54, no. 3 (2000): 25–50.

Pucher, John, Charles Komanoff, and Paul Schimek. "Bicycling Renaissance in North America? Recent Trends and Alternative Policies to Promote Bicycling." *Transportation Research Part A* 33, nos. 7–8 (1999): 625–654.

Pucher, John, and John Renne. "Socioeconomics of Urban Travel: Evidence from the 2001 NHTS." *Transportation Quarterly* 57, no. 3 (2003): 49–77.

Purcell, Mark. "Excavating Lefebvre: The Right to the City and Its Urban Politics of the Inhabitant." *GeoJournal* 58, nos. 2–3 (2002): 99–108.

Pursell, Carroll. "The Rise and Fall of the Appropriate Technology Movement in the United States, 1965–1985." *Technology and Culture* 34, no. 3 (1993): 629–637.

Pye, Dennis. *Fellowship Is Life: The Clarion Cycling Club 1895–1995*. Lancashire, UK: Clarion Publishing, 1995.

Quartuccio, Brad. "Fixed Freestyle." *Urban Velo*, no. 7 (2008): 26–39.

———. "A Rider's Refuge: Kraynick's Bike Shop." *Dirt Rag*, no. 94 (2002). Available at http://www.dirtrag.com/print/article.php?ID=391.

Raab, Alon K. *Under the Sign of the Bicycle*. Portland: Gilgul Press, 2003. Zine.

Rabin, Yale. "Expulsive Zoning: The Inequitable Legacy of Euclid." In *Zoning and the American Dream: Promises Still to Keep*, edited by Charles Haar and Jerold Kayden, 101–121. Washington, DC: American Planning Association Press, 1989.

———. "Highways as a Barrier to Equal Access." *Annals of the American Academy of Political and Social Science* 407, no. 1 (1973): 63–77.

Rae, John Bell. *The American Automobile Industry*. Boston: Twayne Publishers, 1984.

———. *The Road and the Car in American Life*. Cambridge, MA: MIT Press, 1971.

Raeli, Francesco. "Pedal Power." *Rolex Awards*, 2007. Available at http://rolexawards. com/en/the-laureates/davidschweidenback-the-project.jsp.

Rajan, Sudhir Chella. "Automobility and the Liberal Disposition." In *Against Automobility*, edited by Steffen Böhm, Campbell Jones, Chris Land, and Matthew Paterson, 113–129. Malden, MA: Blackwell/Sociological Review, 2006.

———. *The Enigma of Automobility: Democratic Politics and Pollution Control*. Pittsburgh, PA: University of Pittsburgh Press, 1996.

Rambo. *Wall of Death the System*. 625 Records, 2000. LP.

The Ramones. *Mondo Bizarro*. Radioactive Records, 1992. LP.

Ramsey, E. Michele. "Driven from the Public Sphere: The Conflation of Women's Liberation and Driving in Advertising from 1910 to 1920." *Women's Studies in Communication* 29, no. 1 (2006): 88.

Rao, Nitya. "Cycling into the Future: A Report on Women's Participation in a Literacy Campaign in Tamil Nadu, India." *Gender, Technology and Development* 3, no. 3 (1999): 457–474.

"Ravages of the Bicycle Craze." *Scientific American* 74, no. 25 (1896): 391.

Raymundo, Myrla. "The Teen Workshop." *Union City Historical Museum Newsletter* 6, no. 5 (2005).

Rebar. "The Parkcycle." Available at http://www.rebargroup.org/projects/parkcycle/index.html.

Reid, Carlton. "Interbike Survey Results Released at Ibd Conference." *BikeBiz.Com*, February 15, 2007. Available at http://www.bikebiz.com/news/25726/Interbike-survey-results-released-at-IBD-conference.

———. "Taiwan and Vietnam Look to India and Africa for Bike Plants." *BikeBiz.Com*, October 20, 2006. Available at http://www.bikebiz.com/news/24582/Taiwan-and-Vietnam-look-to-India-and-Africa-for-bike-plants.

Reid, Thomas R., III. "A Solution to the Commuter Crisis." *Bicycling* (June 1970): 10–11, 44–45.

Reilly, Rebecca. *Nerves of Steel*. Buffalo, NY: Spoke and Word Press, 2000.

Replogle, Michael. "Sustainable Transportation Strategies for Third-World Development." *Transportation Research Record*, no. 1294 (1991): 1–8.

"Reusing and Recycling Bikes and Parts Locally." *Recycling Advocates* (October 2003): 1–2.

Richardson, Sir Benjamin Ward. "What to Avoid in Cycling." *North American Review* 161, no. 465 (1895): 177.

Right of Way. Available at http://www.cars-suck.org/.

Rimbaud, Penny. *Shibboleth: My Revolting Life*. Oakland, CA: AK Press, 1998.

Ritchie, Andrew. *King of the Road: An Illustrated History of Cycling*. London: Wildwood House, 1975.

———. "The League of American Wheelmen, Major Taylor and the 'Color Question' in the United States in the 1890s." *Culture, Sport, Society* 6, nos. 2–3 (2003): 12–42.

———. *Major Taylor: The Extraordinary Career of a Champion Bicycle Racer*. San Francisco: Bicycle Books, 1988.

Ritter, John. "Narrowed Roads Gain Acceptance in Colo., Elsewhere." *USA Today*, July 30, 2007.

Ritzdorf, Marsha. "Family Values, Municipal Zoning, and African American Family Life." In *Urban Planning and the African American Community: In the Shadows*, edited by June M. Thomas and Marsha Ritzdorf, 75–92. Thousand Oaks, CA: Sage Publications, 1997.

———. "Locked Out of Paradise: Contemporary Exclusionary Zoning, the Supreme Court, and African Americans, 1970 to the Present." In *Urban Planning and the African American Community: In the Shadows*, edited by June M. Thomas and Marsha Ritzdorf, 43–57. Thousand Oaks, CA: Sage Publications, 1997.

Roberts, Kerry. "Where Was My Bike Made? Or, Who Actually Made My Bike?" March 18, 2008. Available at http://allanti.com/page.cfm?PageID=328.

"Rock Shox Forks Are Made in China??!!" *Bike Forums*, thread started on October 3, 2006. Available at http://www.bikeforums.net/showthread.php?t=233986.

Rollins, Henry. *Get in the Van*. Los Angeles: 2.13.61, 1994.

Rollins, William H. "Whose Landscape? Technology, Fascism, and Environmentalism on the National Socialist Autobahn." *Annals of the Association of American Geographers* 85, no. 3 (1995): 494–520.

Rosen, Paul. "Diamonds Are Forever: The Socio-technical Shaping of Bicycle Design." In *Cycle History 5: Proceedings of the 5th International Cycle History Conference (Cambridge, England)*, edited by Rob Van der Plas, 51–58. San Francisco: Cycle Publishing, 1995.

———. *Framing Production: Technology, Culture, and Change in the British Bicycle Industry*. Inside Technology series. Cambridge, MA: MIT Press, 2002.

———. "'It Was Easy, It Was Cheap, Go and Do It!': Technology and Anarchy in the UK Music Industry." In *Twenty-First Century Anarchism: Unorthodox Ideas for a New Millennium*, edited by Jonathan Purkis and James Bowen, 99–116. London: Cassell, 1997.

———. "The Social Construction of Mountain Bikes: Technology and Postmodernity in the Cycle Industry." *Social Studies of Science* 23, no. 3 (1993): 479–513.

———. "Up the Vélorution: Appropriating the Bicycle and the Politics of Technology." In *Appropriating Technology: Vernacular Science and Social Power*, edited by Ron Eglash, 365–390. Minneapolis: University of Minnesota Press, 2002.

Ross, Andrew. "Hacking Away at the Counterculture." *Postmodern Culture* 1, no. 1 (1990): 1–43.

Ross, Kristin, and Henri Lefebvre. "Lefebvre on the Situationists: An Interview." *October* 79 (1997): 69–83.

Roth, Matthew. "When Old Parking Meter Poles Go, So Often Does Bike Parking." *StreetsBlog*, July 1, 2009. Available at http://sf.streetsblog.org/2009/07/01/when-old-parking-meter-poles-go-so-often-does-bike-parking/.

Rowe, David. *Fast Friday*. Infinite Quest Productions, 2008. Film.

Rubinstein, David. "Cycling in the 1890s." *Victorian Studies* 21, no. 1 (1977): 47–71.

Ruin, Erik. "Real Time Detroit." In *Trouble in Mind* (Detroit). Self-published zine.

Rusch, Elizabeth. "Biking While Black." *Mother Jones* (September–October 2002): 25.

Russell, Stewart. "The Social Construction of Artefacts: A Response to Pinch and Bijker." *Social Studies of Science* 16, no. 2 (1986): 331–346.

Russo, Anthony, and Joe Russo. *You, Me and Dupree*. Universal Pictures, 2006. Film.

Sadek, Adel W., Alaina Skye Dickason, and Jon Kaplan. *Effectiveness of Green, High-*

Visibility Bike Lane and Crossing Treatment, Transportation Research Board 86th Annual Meeting: Transportation Research Board, 2007.

Sadler, Simon. *The Situationist City.* Cambridge MA: MIT Press, 1998.

Saenz, Rogelio. "The Social and Economic Isolation of Urban African Americans." *Population Reference Bureau* (October 2005).

The Safest Place. Handy (Jam) Organization with Chevrolet Division, General Motors Corporation, 1935. Film.

Sandoval, Denise Michelle. "Bajito y Suavecito/Low and Slow: Cruising through Low-rider Culture." Ph.D. diss., Claremont Graduate University, 2003.

San Francisco Bicycle Coalition. "Twice as Many Bikes as Cars on Market Street." Press release, 2008.

San Francisco Bike Messenger Association. "Bike Messengering." *Shaping San Francisco,* 1996. Available at http://foundsf.org/index.php?title=BIKE_MESSENGERING. (Originally published in a pamphlet by the San Francisco Bike Messenger Association, 1996).

San Francisco Bike Messenger Association, and International Longshore and Warehouse Union. "Partnership for Justice for the Bay Area Courier Industry." *San Francisco Bike Messenger Association,* 1997. Available at http://www.ahalenia.com/sfbma/whitepaper.html.

Savage, Billy. *Klunkerz.* Pumelo Pictures, 2007. Film.

Scenery, Mike, and Travis Fristoe. "Biking." In *The Zine Yearbook,* vol. 5, edited by Jen Angel and Jason Kucsma, 81–83. Bowling Green: Become the Media, 2001. Originally published in *Drinking Sweat in the Ash Age* (Gainesville). Self-published zine.

Schalit, Joel. "Just Say No to Rock and Roll." *Bad Subjects* no. 27 (1996). Available at http://bad.eserver.org/issues/1996/27/joel.html.

Schimmelpenninck, Luud. "The White Bicycle Plan." *Delta* 10, no. 3 (1967): 39–40.

Schivelbusch, Wolfgang. *The Railway Journey: The Industrialization of Time and Space in the 19th Century.* Berkeley: University of California Press, 1986.

Schmidt, Conrad. *Indecent Exposure to Cars: The Story of the World Naked Bike Ride.* Ragtag Productions, 2007. Film

Schneider, Kenneth R. *Autokind vs. Mankind: An Analysis of Tyranny, a Proposal for Rebellion, a Plan for Reconstruction.* New York: Norton, 1971.

Schnurer, Maxwell Dervin. "Conscious Rebellion: A Rhetorical Analysis of Political Cross-fertilization in the Animal Rights Movement." Ph.D. diss., University of Pittsburgh, 2002.

Schorman, Rob. *Selling Style: Clothing and Social Change at the Turn of the Century.* Philadelphia: University of Pennsylvania Press, 2003.

Schubert, John. "Re: Bicycle Advisory Committees." *Chainguard (Yahoo Group),* December 4, 2001. Available at http://sports.groups.yahoo.com/group/chainguard/message/8922.

Schudson, Michael. *The Power of News.* Cambridge, MA: Harvard University Press, 1995.

Schumacher, E. F. *Small Is Beautiful: A Study of Economics as if People Mattered.* New York: Harper and Row, 1973.

Scott, Michael. *Biker in Bondage.* Santee, CA: Surree Limited, 1979.

——. *Threeway Team.* Santee, CA: Surrey House, 1977.

Screeching Weasel. *Four on the Floor*. Lookout! Records, 1999. EP.

Seel, Benjamin, and Alex Plows. "Coming Live and Direct: Strategies of Earth First!" In *Direct Action in British Environmentalism*, edited by Benjamin Seel, Matthew Paterson, and Brian Doherty, 112–132. London: Routledge, 2000.

Seelie, Tod. "Brooklyn vs. Brokelyn." *Suckapants*, February 23, 2006. Available at http://suckapants.com/2006/02/brooklyn-vs-brokelyn.html.

Seely, Bruce Edsall. *Building the American Highway System: Engineers as Policy Makers*. Technology and Urban Growth series. Philadelphia: Temple University Press, 1987.

Seifert, Walt. "Scofflaw Cyclists." *Sacramento Area Bicycle Advocates*. Available at http://saba.phpwebhosting.com/articles/article.php?mode=display&lognum=20.

Seiler, Cotten. *Republic of Drivers: A Cultural History of Automobility in America*. Chicago: University of Chicago Press, 2008.

———. "'So That We as a Race Might Have Something Authentic to Travel By': African American Automobility and Cold-War Liberalism." *American Quarterly* 58, no. 4 (2006): 1091–1117.

Senate Democratic Policy Committee Hearing. *Are We Exporting American Jobs?* 108th Cong., 1st Sess., November 14, 2003.

Septimus, Jacob, and Anthony Howard. *B.I.K.E.* Fountainhead Films, 2007. Film.

Shaw, Donald Lewis, and Maxwell E. McCombs. *The Emergence of American Political Issues: The Agenda-Setting Function of the Press*. St. Paul: West Publishing, 1977.

Shaw, Hillary J. "Food Deserts: Towards the Development of a Classification." *Geografiska Annaler: Series B, Human Geography* 88, no. 2 (2006): 231–247.

Sheller, Mimi, and John Urry. "The City and the Car." *International Journal of Urban and Regional Research* 24, no. 4 (2000): 737–757.

Shelter. *When 20 Summers Pass*. Victory Records, 2000. LP.

Shelton, Sam. "Lack of Human Intelligence Is Cause of Most Traffic Accidents." *Automotive Industries* 51 (1924): 646–647.

Shepard, Ben, and Kelly Moore. "Reclaiming the Streets of New York." In *Critical Mass: Bicycling's Defiant Celebration*, edited by Chris Carlsson, 195–203. Oakland, CA: AK Press, 2002.

Shepard, Benjamin Heim, and Ronald Hayduk. *From Act Up to the WTO: Urban Protest and Community Building in the Era of Globalization*. London: Verso, 2002.

Shrivastava, Paul. "Toward a Socio-technological History of Bicycles." In *Cycle History 13: Proceedings of the 13th International Cycling History Conference (Münster, Germany)*, edited by Andrew Ritchie and Nicholas Clayton, 9–24. San Francisco: Van der Plas/Cycle Publishing, 2004.

Silicon Valley Bicycle Coalition, and Peninsula Bicycle and Pedestrian Coalition. *Spinning Crank* 17, no. 6 (2003).

Silverman, Robert. "Preface of *Deux Roues, Un Avenir*, by Claire Morissette (Montreal: Écosociété, 1994)." *Robert Silverman Homepage*, April 1994. Available at http://www.cam.org/~rsilver/preface.htm.

Singel, Ryan. "NYPD Intelligence Op Targets Dot-Matrix Graffiti Bike." *Wired*, April 10, 2007.

Situationist International. "Definitions." In *Situationist International Anthology*, edited by Ken Knabb, 45–46. Berkeley: Bureau of Public Secrets, 1981. Originally published in Internationale Situationniste (Paris), no. 1 (June 1958).

Situationist International with students at the University of Strasbourg. "On the Poverty of Student Life." In *Situationist International Anthology*, edited by Ken Knabb, 319–337. Berkeley, CA: Bureau of Public Secrets, 1981. Originally published in Paris, 1966.

Slack, Jennifer Daryl. "The Theory and Method of Articulation in Cultural Studies." In *Stuart Hall: Critical Dialogues in Cultural Studies*, edited by Stuart Hall, David Morley, and Kuan-Hsing Chen, 112–127. London: Routledge, 1996.

Slagle, R. Anthony. "Queer Criticism and Sexual Normativity: The Case of Pee-Wee Herman." *Journal of Homosexuality* 45, nos. 2–4 (2003): 129–146.

Smith, Carl S. *The Plan of Chicago: Daniel Burnham and the Remaking of the American City*. Chicago: University of Chicago Press, 2006.

Smith, David. "Re: [Cg] Digest Number 708." *Chainguard (Yahoo Group)*, October 13, 2001. Available at http://sports.groups.yahoo.com/group/chainguard/message/7921.

Smith, Glenn. "Lo and Behold, Giant's President Talks Trade." *Bikebiz.com*, June 4, 2002. Available at http://www.bikebiz.com/news/21808/Lo-and-behold-Giants-president-talks-trade.

Smith, Michael, and Charles Komanoff. "Spin City: Or, Some Deaths Are More Equal Than Others." *Bike Reader: A Reader's Digest*, 1998. Available at http://www.bike-reader.com/contributors/carssuck/post.html.

Smith, Robert A. *A Social History of the Bicycle: Its Early Life and Times in America*. New York: American Heritage Press, 1972.

Snider, Greta. *Mudflap* (San Francisco). Self-published zine.

Snyder, Dave. "Good for the Bicycling Cause." In *Critical Mass: Bicycling's Defiant Celebration*, edited by Chris Carlsson, 112–115. Oakland, CA: AK Press, 2002.

Snyder, Jon. "How Did That Bike Get to Africa?" *Out There Monthly* (September 2007). Available at http://www.outtheremonthly.com/otm.php?art=archives/sept07/africa.

Sommer, Bob. "Bikeway Research at the University of California, Davis in the 1960s." In *Cycle History 16: Proceedings of the 16th International Cycling History Conference (Davis, Ca)*, edited by Andrew Ritchie, 47–51. San Francisco: Cycle Publishing, 2006.

Sommer, Robert, and Dale Lott. "Bikeways in Action: The Davis Experience." *Congressional Record* 117, no. 53 (1971).

Sorensen, George Niels. *Iron Riders: Story of the 1890s Fort Missoula Buffalo Soldier Bicycle Corps*. Missoula, MT: Pictorial Histories Publishing, 2000.

Speed, Jno Gilmer. "The Common Road as a Social Factor." *The Chautauquan* (February 1893): 547–552.

"Spencer for Tire." *Grist Magazine*, January 9, 2006. Available at http://www.grist.org/comments/interactivist/2006/01/09/spencer/.

Spigel, Lynn. *Make Room for TV: Television and the Family Ideal in Postwar America*. Chicago: University of Chicago Press, 1992.

Spitz, Scott. *Leapfrog* (Indianapolis), no. 7. Self-published zine.

Spoken Wheel Blog. Available at http://www.thespokenwheel.com/2008/07/30/custom-bicycle-builders-usa.

Stabile, Carol. *Feminism and the Technological Fix*. Manchester, UK: Manchester University Press, 1994.

Stahre, Ulf. "City in Change: Globalization, Local Politics and Urban Movements in Contemporary Stockholm." *International Journal of Urban and Regional Research* 28, no. 1 (2004): 68–85.

Steiner, Robert L. "Learning from the Past-Brand Advertising and the Great Bicycle Craze of the 1890s." Paper presented at the Annual Conference of the American Academy of Advertising: Advances in Advertising Research and Marketing, 1978.

Steiner, Zara. "Views of War: Britain before the 'Great War'—and After." *International Relations* 17, no. 1 (2003): 7–33.

Sterne, Jonathan. *The Audible Past: Cultural Origins of Sound Reproduction*. Durham, NC: Duke University Press, 2003.

Stevens, Thomas. "Across America on a Bicycle, Part IV: From the Great Plains to the Atlantic." *Outing* 6, no. 4 (1885): 410–423.

———. *Around the World on a Bicycle: From San Francisco to Yokohama*. London: Century, 1988.

———. *Around the World on a Bicycle*. Vol. 2. Charleston, SC: BiblioBazaar, LLC, 2008.

Stewart, Benjamin. "Bicycle Messengers and the Dialectics of Speed." In *Fighting for Time*, edited by Cynthia Fuchs Epstein and Arne L. Kalleberg, 150–190. New York: Russell Sage, 2004.

Strange, Lisa, and Robert Brown. "The Bicycle, Women's Rights, and Elizabeth Cady Stanton." *Women's Studies* 31 (2002): 609–626.

Strong, Michael. *Be the Solution: How Entrepreneurs and Conscious Capitalists Can Solve All the Worlds Problems*. Hoboken, NJ: Wiley, 2009.

———. "The Opportunity: The Creative Powers of a Free Civilization." In *Working for Good*, edited by Michael Strong, 18–29. FLOW, 2003. Available at http://www.flow-idealism.org/Downloads/Working-for-Good.pdf

Stubbs, John, and Rodney Pearson. "Moroccan Rail Transport Investment: Accumulation versus Legitimation." *Tijdschrift voor Economische en Sociale Geografie* 85, no. 2 (1994): 141–152.

Stuelke, Elizabeth, and Carol A. Wood. "NYC Bike Advocacy: A Preliminary Timeline." In *Why I Ride: The Art of Bicycling in New York*, edited by Elizabeth Stuelke and Carol A. Wood, 32–35. Published in conjunction with the "Why I Ride: The Art of Bicycling in New York" art show, New York, May 3–June 3, 2007. Available at http://www.itrnet.com/satre/whyiride/catalog_WIR_FINAL.pdf.

Styhre, Alexander, Maria Backman, and Sofia Borjesson. "The Gendered Machine: Concept Car Development at Volvo Car Corporation." *Gender, Work and Organization* 12, no. 6 (2005): 551–571.

Subramaniam, Rajesh, National Center for Statistics and Analysis, and National Highway Traffic Safety Administration. "Motor Vehicle Traffic Crashes as a Leading Cause of Death in the United States, 2003." Washington, DC: Department of Transportation, 2006.

Sullivan, Will. "Road Warriors Tie-ups. Backups. Gridlock. The American Commute Has Never Been So Painful. Is There Any Solution?" *U.S. News and World Report*, April 29, 2007.

Switzky, Joshua. "Riding to See." In *Critical Mass: Bicycling's Defiant Celebration*, edited by Chris Carlsson, 186–192. Oakland, CA: AK Press, 2002.

Tanzer, Andrew. "Bury Thy Teacher." *Forbes*, December 21, 1992, p. 90.

Taylor, Delphine. "Tools for Life." *Transportation Alternatives Magazine* (1996): 12–13.

Taylor, Jack R. *ProBicycle: Bicycle Advocacy by Cyclists for Cyclists*. Available at http://probicycle.com.

Taylor, Nigel. "The Aesthetic Experience of Traffic in the Modern City." *Urban Studies* 40, no. 8 (2003): 1609–1625.

Taylor, V., and N. E. Whittier. "Collective Identity in Social Movement Communities: Lesbian Feminist Mobilization." *Frontiers in Social Movement Theory* (1992): 104–129.

"Ten Taiwanese Bike Part Makers Invest in Philippines." *BikeBiz.Com*, January 5, 2006. Available at http://www.bikebiz.com/news/23412/Ten-Taiwanese-bike-part-makers-invest-in-Philippines.

Texas Transportation Institute. "Urban Mobility Report." Texas A&M University System, 2007.

"That Was My Day: An Interview with National Road Champion John Allis." *Cyclenews* (1974): 17–19.

"Think Tanks." *Source Watch*. Available at http://www.sourcewatch.org/index.php?title=Think_tanks.

Thomas, June Manning. "Race, Racism, and Race Relations: Linkage with Urban and Regional Planning Literature." Prepared for the American Sociological Association's Response, White House Request for Race Literature, 1997.

Thompson, Christopher S. "Bicycling, Class, and the Politics of Leisure in Belle Epoque France." In *Histories of Leisure*, edited by Rudy Koshar, 131–146. New York: Berg, 2002.

———. "The Third Republic on Wheels: A Social, Cultural, and Political History of Bicycling in France from the Nineteenth Century to World War II." Ph.D. diss., New York University, 1997.

———. *The Tour de France: A Cultural History*. Berkeley: University of California Press, 2006.

Thompson, Maurice. "What We Gain in the Bicycle." *The Chautauquan* 25, no. 5 (1897): 549–551.

Thornton, Sarah. *Club Cultures: Music, Media, and Subcultural Capital*. Hanover, NH: University Press of New England, 1996.

Tibballs, Geoff. *The Mammoth Book of Zingers, Quips, and One-Liners: Over 10,000 Gems of Wit and Wisdom, One-Liners and Wisecracks*. New York: Carroll and Graf Publishers, 2004.

Tigges, Leann M., Irene Browne, and Gary P. Green. "Social Isolation of the Urban Poor: Race, Class, and Neighborhood Effects on Social Resources." *Sociological Quarterly* (1998): 53–77.

Time's Up! "Time's Up! Opens a Bike Convergence Center for RNC." *Interactivist Info Exchange*, July 21, 2004.

Tobin, Gary Allan. "The Bicycle Boom of the 1890's: The Development of Private Transportation and the Birth of the Modern Tourist." *Journal of Popular Culture* 7, no. 4 (1974): 838–849.

"Toll Roads and Free Roads." U.S. Bureau of Public Roads, 1939.

Tomlinson, David. "The Bicycle and Urban Sustainability." *FES Outstanding Graduate Student Paper Series* 7, no. 6 (2003).

Tomorrow's Drivers. Handy (Jam) Organization with Chevrolet Division, General Motors Corporation, 1954. Film.

Toroyan, Tami, and Margie Peden. "Youth and Road Safety." Geneva: World Health Organization, 2007.

Transportation Alternatives. "T.A. Bulletin." *Transportation Alternatives*, April 25, 2003. Available at http://www.transalt.org/files/newsroom/streetbeat/askta/030425.html

Trashville, Jason, and Braxie Hicks. "Because Some Times You Just Want to Ride Your Bike to the Show . . . All of Them: Tales from the 2002 Dead Things Punk Rock Bike Tour of N.C." Unpublished.

Trescott, Martha M. "The Bicycle: A Technical Precursor of the Automobile." In *Business and Economic History*, edited by Paul Uselding, 51–75. Urbana: University of Illinois Press, 1976.

Trillin, Calvin. "U.S. Journal: Manhattan Fun's Over." *New Yorker*, October 9, 1971.

Trippett, Frank. "'Scaring the Public to Death': On City Streets and Country Roads, the War Rages against Cyclists." *Time*, October 5, 1987, p. 29.

"Truck Nuts—a Quest for the Truth." *Bulls Balls.* Available at http://www.bullsballs.com/compare/truck/nuts.html.

Tuan, Yi-fu. *Space and Place: The Perspective of Experience.* Minneapolis: University of Minnesota Press, 1977.

Tucker, Karen Iris. "Mutant Bike Gangs of New York: Tall-Bike Clubs Live Free, Ride High, and Don't Want Your Stinking Logo." *Village Voice*, March 14, 2006.

"2007 Interbike Hotties and People." *Mountain Bike Product Reviews (Mtbr.com).* Available at http://gallery.mtbr.com/showgallery.php/cat/1186.

Ulreich, Walter. "The Bamboo Bicycles of Grundner and Lemisch." In *Cycle History 5: Proceedings of the 5th International Cycle History Conference (Cambridge, England)*, edited by Rob Van der Plas, 61–70. San Francisco: Cycle Publishing, 1995.

United American Nurses. "The Hospital Industry (Figures from the National Center for Health Statistics and American Hospital Association)." *United American Nurses* (March 2005). Available at http://www.uannurse.org/research/trends.html.

United Bicycle Institute. Available at http://bikeschool.com.

"United Bicycle Institute." *City of Ashland, Oregon.* Available at http://www.ashland.or.us/Page.asp?NavID=12024.

United Nations Conference on Trade and Development, and Global Agreement on Tariffs and Trade. "Bicycles and Components: A Pilot Survey of Opportunities for Trade among Developing Countries." Geneva: United Nations, 1985.

United Nations Department of Economic and Social Affairs. "World Urbanization Prospects—the 2007 Revision: Highlights." New York: United Nations, 2008.

Urban Transportation Caucus (San Francisco Bicycle Coalition, Cascade Bicycle Club, Chicagoland Bicycle Federation and Transportation Alternatives). "Urban Transportation Report Card," 2007.

Urebvu, A. O. "Culture and Technology: A Study of the 1997 Theme World Decade for Cultural Development 1988–1997." UNESCO, 1997.

Urry, John. "Automobility, Car Culture and Weightless Travel: A Discussion Paper." *On-Line Publications, Sociology at Lancaster University*, 1999. Available at http://www.lancs.ac.uk/fass/sociology/papers/urry-automobility.pdf.

———. "Inhabiting the Car." *Sociological Review* 54, no. s1 (2006): 17–31.

———. "The 'System' of Automobility." *Theory Culture Society* 21, nos. 4–5 (2004): 25–39.

———. *The Tourist Gaze*. London: Sage Publications, 2002.

U.S. Census Bureau. "American Community Survey: Means of Transportation to Work by Selected Characteristics." Washington, DC: U.S. Department of Commerce, 2006.

———. "Most of Us Still Drive to Work Alone, Public Transportation Commuters Concentrated in a Handful of Large Cities ." Washington, DC: U.S. Department of Commerce, 2007.

———. "An Older and More Diverse Nation by Midcentury." Washington, DC: Department of Commerce, 2008.

———. "1997 Economic Census: Vehicle Inventory and Use Survey." Washington, DC: Department of Commerce, 1999.

———. "2000 Decennial Census: Journey to Work." Washington, DC: U.S. Department of Commerce, 2003.

———. "2002 Economic Census: Vehicle Inventory and Use Survey." Washington, DC: Department of Commerce, 2004.

U.S. Department of Energy. "2009 Hybrid Vehicles." *Fuel Economy Guide*, Washington, DC, 2008.

U.S. Department of Transportation. "National Household Travel Survey, 2001." Washington, DC: Federal Highway Administration, 2003.

———. "National Transportation Statistics." Table VM-1. Washington, DC, 2006.

Uteng, Tanu Priya, and Tim Cresswell. *Gendered Mobilities*. Hampshire, UK: Ashgate Publishing, 2008.

Van Dam, Suzanne. "Pedaling out of Poverty: How One Guatemalan NGO Is Helping Rural Communities Help Themselves." *Bikes Not Bombs*, 2002. Available at http://www.bikesnotbombs.org/maya-pedal.htm.

Varno, David. "Bike Messengers: Beta Still Rules on the Street." *The Brooklyn Rail*, November 5, 2005. Available at http://www.thebrooklynrail.org/archives/nov05/STREETS/bikemessengers.html.

Victoria Transport Policy Institute. "Transportation Cost and Benefit Analysis: Techniques, Estimates and Implications [Second Edition]," edited by Todd Litman. Vancouver, BC, 2009.

Voelcker, Jake. "A Critical Review of the Legal Penalties for Drivers Who Kill Cyclists or Pedestrians." Master's thesis, University of Bristol, 2007.

Voeten, Teun. "Dutch Provos." *High Times* (January 1990): 32–36, 64–66, 73.

Volti, Rudi. "A Century of Automobility." *Technology and Culture* 37, no. 4 (1996): 663–685.

Wachs, Martin. "Creating Political Pressure for Cycling." *Transportation Quarterly* 52, no. 1 (1998): 6–8.

Wall, Derek. *Earth First! and the Anti-roads Movement*. London: Routledge, 1999.

Wehr, Kevin. "Bicycle Messengers and Fast Capitalism: An Old-School Solution to the Needs of Technocapitalism." *Fast Capitalism* 2, no. 1 (2006). Available at http://www.uta.edu/huma/agger/fastcapitalism/2_1/wehr.html.

Weiler, Aaron. *Namibian Bicycle Ambulance Project*. Available at http://bikecart.pedal-people.com/namibia.

Weiner, Edward. *Urban Transportation Planning in the United States: An Historical Overview*. Rev. and expanded ed. Westport, CT: Praeger, 1999.

Weiss, Daniel J., Nick Kong, Sam Schiller, and Alexandra Kougentakis. "The Clean Coal Smoke Screen." Center for American Progress, December 16, 2008.

Welke, Sylvia, and Jennifer Allen. "Cycling Freedom for Women." *Women and Environments International Magazine*, nos. 62–63 (2004): 34–37.

Western, Jenny. "'Do Not Park Bicycles!'" In *"Do Not Park Bicycles!"* edited by Jenny Western, 1–6. Brandon, MB: Art Gallery of Southwestern Manitoba, 2007.

WGBH Television and Turner Home Entertainment. *Driving Passion: America's Love Affair with the Car*. Atlanta, GA: Turner Home Entertainment, 1995. VHS.

Wheeler, Robert F. "Organized Sport and Organized Labour: The Workers' Sports Movement." *Journal of Contemporary History* 13, no. 2 (1978): 191–210.

Wheel Giant. "Recent Developments in China's Bike Industry." *Bike Market Update E-Newsletter Issue*, no. 22, June 11, 2007. Available at http://www.biketaiwan.com/New/script/Newsletter/news_main.asp?issue=22&language=E.

When You Are a Pedestrian. Progressive Pictures, 1948. Film.

White, Michael. *A Short Course in International Marketing Blunders: Mistakes Made by Companies That Should Have Known Better*. Short Course in International Trade series. Novato, CA: World Trade Press, 2002.

Wilber, Donald. "Overthrow of Premier Mossadeq of Iran, November 1952–August 1953." In *CIA Clandestine Service History*. Central Intelligence Agency, 1954.

Wilcher, Aaron. "Hubs and Escape Routes." *Streetnotes*, 2004. Available at http://www.xcp.bfn.org/wilcher1.html.

———. "Prisoners of the Road: American VelociPower in the 1970s." In *Cycle History 16: Proceedings of the 16th International Cycling History Conference (Davis, Ca)*, edited by Andrew Ritchie, 15–29. San Francisco: Cycle Publishing, 2006.

———. "Velocitropics: Bodies and Machines in American Bicycling." Master's thesis, Saint Louis University, 2004.

Wilkinson, Bill. "Nonmotorized Transportation: The Forgotten Modes." *Annals of the American Academy of Political and Social Science* 553 (1997): 87.

Wilkinson, Bill, and Bob Chauncey. "Are We There Yet? Assessing the Performance of State Departments of Transportation on Accommodating Bicycles and Pedestrians." National Center for Bicycling and Walking, 2003.

Willard, Carla. "Conspicuous Whiteness: Early Brand Advertising." In *Turning the Century: Essays in Media and Cultural Studies*, edited by C. Stabile, 187–216. Boulder, CO: Westview, 2000.

Willard, Frances E. "Address to Women's National Council." Paper presented at the Woman's National Council of the United States, First Triennial Meeting, Albaugh's Opera House, Washington, DC, February 22–25, 1891.

Willard, Frances Elizabeth, and Carol O'Hare. *How I Learned to Ride the Bicycle: Reflections of an Influential 19th Century Woman*. Sunnyvale, CA: Fair Oaks Publishing, 1991.

Williams, Clive Kenneth. "Stealing a Car to Be a Man: The Importance of Cars and Driving in the Gender Identity of Adolescent Males." Ph.D. diss., Queensland University of Technology, 2005.

Williams, Lee. "Community." *Cranked*, no. 4 (2006): 46–47.

Williams, Neil Wynn. "Some Thoughts on Landscape." *The Eclectic Magazine of Foreign Literature* 62, no. 6 (1895): 742.

"Willie Brown Responds to Critics of His Transit Policy." *Brass Check.* Available at http://www.brasscheck.com/cm.

Wilson, Elizabeth. "The Invisible Flâneur." *New Left Review* 191 (1992): 90–110.

Wilson, Josh. "The Critical Press." *Grade the News,* April 16, 2007. Available at http://www.gradethenews.org/commentaries/criticalmass.htm.

———. "Unleashing Public Imagination, or How 'bout Another Shot of Existential Whup-Ass for Your Flagging Civic Libido?" In *Critical Mass: Bicycling's Defiant Celebration,* edited by Chris Carlsson, 94–99. Oakland, CA: AK Press, 2002.

Winner, Langdon. "Upon Opening the Black Box and Finding It Empty: Social Constructivism and the Philosophy of Technology." *Science, Technology, and Human Values* 18, no. 3 (1993): 362–378.

———. *The Whale and the Reactor: A Search for Limits in an Age of High Technology.* Chicago: University of Chicago Press, 1986.

Wisconsin Department of Transportation. "History of Bicycling in Wisconsin." Available at http://www.dot.wisconsin.gov/travel/bike-foot/docs/history.pdf.

Wittink, Roelof. "Planning for Cycling Supports Road Safety." In *Sustainable Transport: Planning for Walking and Cycling in Urban Environments,* edited by Rodney Tolley, 172–188. Cambridge: Woodhead, 2003.

Wolf, Winfried. *Car Mania: A Critical History of Transport.* 1st English ed. London: Pluto Press, 1996.

Wollen, Peter, and Joe Kerr, eds. *Autopia: Cars and Culture.* London: Reaktion Books, 2002.

"Women in the Automotive Industry." *Catalyst* (March 2009). Available at http://www.catalyst.org/publication/235/women-in-the-automotive-industry.

Wood, John Cunningham. *Thorstein Veblen: Critical Assessments.* London: Routledge, 1993.

Work, George, and Laurence Malone. "Bicycles, Development, and the Third World." *Environment* 25, no. 1 (1983): 41.

World Bank. "China Transport Sector Study." Washington, DC, 1985.

———. "A Decade of Action in Transport: An Evaluation of World Bank Assistance to the Transport Sector, 1995–2005." Washington DC: The International Bank for Reconstruction and Development/World Bank, 2007.

World Naked Bike Ride. Available at http://www.worldnakedbikeride.org.

Wright, David K. *America's 100 Year Love Affair with the Automobile: And the Snap-on Tools That Keep Them Running.* Osceola, WI: Motorbooks International, 1995.

Xunhai, Zhang. "Enterprise Response to Market Reforms: The Case of the Chinese Bicycle Industry." *Australian Journal of Chinese Affairs,* no. 28 (1992): 111–139.

Yang, Jun-Meng. "Bicycle Traffic in China." *Transportation Quarterly* 39, no. 1 (1985): 93–107.

Yates, Peter. *Breaking Away.* 20th Century Fox, 1979. Film.

You and Your Bicycle. Progressive Pictures, 1948. Film.

Young, Iris Marion. *Justice and the Politics of Difference.* Princeton, NJ: Princeton University Press, 1990.

Youth Bicycle Education Network. "Trends in Bicycle Education." *Youth Bicycle*

Education Network. Available at http://www.yben.org/newsletter/four-key-program-models/.

Yunus, Muhammad, and Alan Jolis. *Banker to the Poor: Micro-Lending and the Battle against World Poverty*. New York: Public Affairs, 2003.

Zenk, Shannon N., Amy J. Schulz, Barbara A. Israel, Sherman A. James, Shuming Bao, and Mark L. Wilson. "Neighborhood Racial Composition, Neighborhood Poverty, and the Spatial Accessibility of Supermarkets in Metropolitan Detroit." *American Journal of Public Health* 95, no. 4 (2005): 660–667.

Zerzan, John. *Elements of Refusal*. Columbia, MO: CAL Press, 1999.

———. *Running on Emptiness: The Pathology of Civilization*. Los Angeles: Feral House, 2002.

Index